The German Experience of Japan's Treaty Port System

The German Experience of Japan's Treaty Port System

A Case Study of C. Nickel & Co. Ltd., 1860–1923

Prue S. Holstein

ROUTLEDGE
Routledge
Taylor & Francis Group
LONDON AND NEW YORK

The publication of this book is made possible by grants from Monash University and a Japan Studies Grant from the Harold S. Williams Trust Fund at the National Library of Australia.

First published in 2025 by Amsterdam University Press Ltd.

Published 2025 by Routledge
4 Park Square, Milton Park, Abingdon, Oxon OX14 4RN
605 Third Avenue, New York, NY 10158

Routledge is an imprint of the Taylor & Francis Group, an informa business

ISBN: 9789048560554 (hbk)
ISBN: 9781041187981 (pbk)
ISBN: 9781003706274 (ebk)

Cover illustration: Ships in Kobe Harbour in the 1880s with stately houses in the background along the Bund. Courtesy: Meiji Showa Photo Agency.

Cover design: Coördesign, Leiden

DOI: 10.4324/9781003706274

For Product Safety Concerns and Information please contact our EU representative:
GPSR@taylorandfrancis.com
Taylor & Francis Verlag GmbH, Kaufingerstraße 24, 80331 München, Germany

Table of Contents

Part IV World War One

Editor's Preface

Although the Nickel/Holstein family had long been involved in the Hamburg world of shipping and commerce, what took Carl Nickel to the East remains obscure. According to Prue Holstein, having arrived in Shanghai in 1859, he subsequently made his way to Japan and set himself up in business in the treaty ports of Nagasaki and, fifteen years later, Yokohama. But seeing new opportunities in Kobe, he moved to the treaty port in 1879. It was there that, through a combination of skill, hard work and good fortune, he built up what she aptly calls "a waterfront empire." Although benefitting from extraterritorial privileges, as a German merchant, Nickel and other foreign merchants faced many challenges, given the restrictions imposed on foreigners by the Japanese government. Holding himself aloof from the European community, he chose to live in the Native Town, operating in a Conradian world of "mechanics and blacksmiths ... ship's chandlers and ... sailor's hostels and grog shops."

Over time, he was able to straddle both worlds, bridging the social divide and his transnational skills and his long-established connections within the Foreign Settlement to source his clients, and to access the local Japanese government and British power structures. Having invited his cousin and godson, Christian Holstein, to join him in 1897, the two merchants prepared to face the new challenges which arose with the abolition of extraterritoriality two years later. At home on the waterfront, Nickel also had a canny commercial sense. Realizing he needed to obtain British cooperation; he incorporated the principal trading company in Hong Kong and brought in British merchants as his business partners to their mutual benefit. Assuming control in 1906, Holstein built on this success, ensuring that the busy and congested Kobe harbour was modernized, a fit-for-purpose infrastructure devised for loading and unloading vessels and the company's predominantly Japanese and unskilled workforce brought into line.

This coincided with the massive expansion of global shipping which, as recent scholarship has shown, opened China and Japan to multinational trade, and provided imperial Germany with the opportunity to extend her influence into East Asia. Locating her study within that scholarship, Holstein uses the individual stories of these two German merchants to explore how, as part of that process, and against stiff competition and antiforeign sentiment, C. Nickel & Co. made a major contribution to the development of Kobe so that by 1914, it had become a significant trading centre and transport network.

However, with the outbreak of war and the outlawing of trading with the enemy, Holstein faced an uncertain future. With the British insisting that all commercial links with Germany and its nationals were severed, he and the German staff were inevitably ousted. Not only did he lose control of the company he had done so much to build up, but he was then subjected to a lengthy prosecution on what the author suggests were trumped-up charges. Although ultimately acquitted, this ended any chance of Holstein renewing his involvement with the company when the war ended. But the legacy of what he and Carl Nickel had achieved was there for all to see, a thriving stevedoring business and commercial port.

Both Nickel and Holstein were men of their time. Twice married—Nickel's first wife and business partner died without having children and he became estranged from his second wife upon the death of his only son—Nickel remains elusive as an individual, his brief obituary saying almost nothing about his private life. Devoted to his work, although well-connected, he confined himself to a close circle of friends. By contrast, Holstein became a part of the establishment. While socializing mainly through work, he forged good relationships across the British, German, American and Japanese communities. Continuing to live and promote a range of commercial ventures in Japan, "he was," as Holstein concludes, "well integrated into the fabric of the Port of Kobe and remained so for the rest of his life."

Two skilled entrepreneurs and two contrasting characters, through this account, we are able to obtain an excellent understanding of how, not least thanks to their efforts, by the early years of the twentieth century, Kobe had become a bustling, successful and cosmopolitan port city.

Andrew Hillier
University of Bristol
March 2025

Acknowledgements

I wish to thank Associate Professor Beatrice Trefalt, Monash University for her encouragement for this project without which it would not have come into existence. Her own dedication to giving voice to actors from the past that would otherwise have been lost to history has provided me with the inspiration needed to complete this work. Her knowledge of Japanese history has also helped me place the actions of my protagonists into the proper context.

I also wish to acknowledge and thank Associate Professor Franz-Josef Deiters and Associate Professor Christiane Weller for their guidance and input in placing my two protagonists into the context of their German cultural heritage.

My grateful thanks go to Mr Ryōhei (Rick) Taniguchi, member of the Kobe Gaikokujin Kyōryūchi Kenkyūkai (Kobe Foreign Settlement Research Society). For eight years Rick has been most generous with his time and knowledge in assisting me find a wide range of Japanese material held in archives, libraries, and other collections in Kobe. He has arranged appointments with the Kobe Public Archives, the Kobe and Suma Land Registration offices, the Kobe Museum and other bodies. Together we enjoyed exploring the locations and sites relevant to the lives of my two protagonists in Kobe, Nagasaki and Nagato.

My grateful thanks also go to the former Master of the Kobe Public Archives, Mr Matsumoto Shōzō for his generosity and support for my project.

Thank you also to Mrs Miyoko Ouchi Cleland who, with her knowledge of old Japanese characters, assisted me translate Japanese newspaper articles from 1914.

My sincere gratitude goes also to Mr Bernd Lepach who, based in Leipzig, Germany, recorded a wealth of information in his Meiji Portraits Website about foreign residents in Japan from 1856–1911. I want to also thank Brian Burke-Gaffney of Nagasaki Institute of Applied Science and Lane Earns, Emeritus Provost and Vice Chancellor at University of Wisconsin–Oshkosh for access to their website on the Nagasaki Foreign Settlement. This website has just been taken down temporarily until a new home is found.

Grateful thanks for expertise, advice, interest, encouragement and support also go to: in Japan, Sven Saaler, Bettina Gramlich-Oka, Maike Roeder, Susan Menadue-Chun, Yu Serizawa, Roslyn Hayman and Shuji Sakuma and Patricia Bader Johnston and Brad Johnston; in Germany, Holmer Stahncke, Katja Schmidtpott, Peter Panzer, Herbert Karbach, Christian Schwarzbach, Ralf

Engel, Helga Mugge, Christine Heitmann, Karin and Peter Ahrens, Inger Schliemann, Anneli and Bernd Wegner, Astrid Cohrs-Dreessen, Gabriele Weber and the late Fred Flakowski; in the UK, Stefan Manz, Sir Christopher Clark, David Hinds and Kate Cleeland; in Australia, Darren Swanson, Mayumi Shinozaki, Rika Wright, Sue Larkin, Anita Forsyth, Gaye Cleeland and John and Helga Rose; and in the United States, Daniel Botsman and the late Tom Jordan.

I have been very grateful to Monash for their financial support for this project. Thank you also to the National Library of Australia for their generous support through awarding me a Japan Study Grant, funded by Harold S. Williams Trust Fund in 2014.

Special thanks must also go to Series Editor Andrew Hillier who was wonderfully supportive in helping me improve the final version of this book and in the process, adding to my understanding of the historical context in which this narrative takes place. My thanks also go to James Hoare OBE for his enduring interest, guidance and support.

Finally, thank you to my late husband, Jens Holstein for leaving me with the legacy of his wonderful stories of his family's history in Japan and to my daughter Christiane Holstein for her loving support.

Editorial Notes

The following are clarifications to explain the basis on which certain decisions were taken in writing this document.

Japanese names:	All Japanese names are presented in the traditional format of surnames followed by first names.
Japanese currency:	All Japanese Sen or Yen values have been calculated to provide an equivalent Yen value as at 2019 using the Yaruzou-net website at https://yaruzou.net/hprice/hprice-calc.html I have calculated the English pound equivalent value converting the 2019 Yen value using the exchange rate converter Yen to Pounds website available on Google: ¥1 = ¥.0052 as of 14 April 2024.
Variations in Spelling:	Just as English spelling in the nineteenth and early twentieth centuries varied, so did Japanese spelling in Roman lettering and German spelling. I have endeavored to be consistent in the spelling of particular words. For example, I have used the place name Hyogo in referring to this town but have adopted the alternate spelling Hiogo when it was thus used in names. Macrons are used to indicate long vowels except in well-known place names such as Tokyo or Kyoto.

Prologue

This book grew out of my experience working with Australian companies on the challenges they faced marketing products and services in Japan whilst living in Japan for a total of fourteen years over a thirty-year period. It also grew out of a desire to understand what led to the success of one German merchant family with a 140-year history of conducting business in Japan. By the early 1970s, Japan had become Australia's largest trading partner and Australians including myself were encouraged to study Japanese language and culture. Upon graduating, I was employed by the Tokyo liaison office of an international mining company. Returning to Australia, I expanded my business experience and completed a Master of Business Administration, intending to return to Japan. In the early 1980s, I joined the Australian Trade Commissioner Service, and after serving in Chicago, USA, as Consul and Trade Commissioner, I returned to Osaka, Japan, in a similar role and remained until the late 1990s. In the 2000s, I returned to Tokyo to represent the Victorian State Government responsible for Japan and Korea.

My interest in the German way of conducting business in Japan commenced when, during my term in Osaka, I met and married Jens Holstein. Jens, a German national, was the third generation of his family living in Kobe, running a company importing chemicals and handling licence agreements between European and Japanese pharmaceutical companies. Living in Kobe, I experienced the pride this city took in its international origins and its role as host to an international community since 1868. By the 1990s, Kobe was still the base for the German consulate and the residence of many of the CEOs of European pharmaceutical companies. Jens was a part of a small community of descendants of German families remaining in Japan since the early treaty port days. His narrative around the family's origins in Japan became a source of fascination. In the tradition of being a good storyteller, his narrative was somewhat incomplete.

Initially, I intended to write a family history but, in conducting archival research across Japan, Germany, the United Kingdom and Australia, I found a story that would go beyond being a chronicle of the family's life in Japan. I have reconstructed the history of the company, C. Nickel & Co. Ltd. founded and run by Carl Nickel until 1906, and then until 1914, by his successor—his relative, Christian Holstein, father of my late husband. This story allows us to understand how some German merchants conducted business in Japan during the Meiji Era (1868–1911) until the First World War in a time of great change, in what became a long-standing practice of collaboration with their

Anglophone counterparts. The company founded by Carl Nickel, and which became Nickel & Lyons in 1913, remains today in Kobe in Japanese hands.

Working with Australian companies developing markets and distribution networks for their products in Japan, I became familiar with the difficulties and challenges they faced. Whilst living in Chicago in the mid-1980s, I also experienced the American perspective on the so-called trade wars in which the American government claimed the Japanese employed unfair trading practices to achieve a balance of trade in its favour. The Japanese government was widely accused of practicing administrative guidance (*gyōsei shidō*), directing the energies of Japanese companies, prejudicing foreign companies' business endeavours in Japan. It is not my intention to engage in this argument save to note that one of the problems American companies demonstrated at that time, of relevance to this study, was the lack of ability or willingness to manufacture goods meeting the needs and specifications peculiar to the Japanese market. Many of the products American manufacturers tried to sell in Japan in the 1980s were designed for the American market. My own professional experiences led me to want to understand what had led to the success of German companies in Japan.

Finally, listening to my husband's stories, I also began to reflect on how knowledge about the German contribution to the Port of Kobe had become lost. Merchant histories often fall through the gap of official histories, usually written based on diplomatic records. In the case of German merchants, some repositories of records left by German merchants of their endeavours used to exist; however, most of those records were destroyed in fires, floods, and the bombing of the Second World War. The ten years spent researching and writing this book have been a wonderful journey piecing together the story contained in this work to reconstruct the contribution of two German merchants, Carl Nickel and his cousin and godson, Christian Holstein, to the building of the Port of Kobe and the development of German-Japanese trade relations.

Introduction & Background

At the second annual shareholders' meeting held for C. Nickel & Co. Limited in February 1905, the British dominated board complimented its German managing director and founder, Carl Nickel, for the "admirable manner in which he had managed the office."[1] Coming from a family steeped in the maritime trade in the independent city-state of Hamburg, Nickel arrived first in Shanghai about 1859 and then in Japan in 1860. After twenty years in Nagasaki and Yokohama supplying foreign ships, in 1880 he established a stevedoring and cargo handling company in Kobe, building a waterfront empire by the 1890s. For forty years, foreign merchants enjoyed extraterritorial protections negotiated under the unequal treaties in 1858 operating outside Japanese jurisdiction. With the end of such protections in 1899 and the signing of the Anglo-Japanese Treaty in 1902, Nickel registered his company that year in the British colony of Hong Kong as a British public company under British law. Its Kobe office was registered as a branch office under Japanese law. Japan's rapid modernization coincided with the unification of Germany in 1871, the economic rise of the German Empire and its desire to become a world power and the British fear its own imperial and commercial supremacy was under threat.[2] Nickel required not just capital but also the buy-in and protection of the British power base in Kobe to protect it from increasing competition and to mitigate a growing anti-German feeling. As Japan and Britain had signed a treaty, Nickel must have also hoped that a strengthened relationship between the British and the Japanese would compensate for the loss of extraterritorial protections in 1899 when the revised treaties were enacted.

At the AGM, the company, originally German now British with a board, management and customer base half German and half British, was described

1 "C. Nickel & Company Limited: Meeting of Shareholders," *Japan Chronicle* (Kobe), 2 February 1905, 130.

2 John E. Schrecker, *Imperialism and Chinese Nationalism: Germany in Shantung* (Cambridge, MA: Harvard University Press, 2013), 1–21; John McDermott, "'A Needless Sacrifice': British Businessmen and Business as Usual in the First World War," *Albion: A Quarterly Journal Concerned with British Studies* 21, no. 2 (Summer 1989): 263–82, https://doi.org/10.2307/4049929.

Holstein, Prue S. *The German Experience of Japan's Treaty Port System: A Case Study of C. Nickel & Co. Ltd., 1860–1923*. Taylor & Francis Group, 2025.
DOI: 10.4324/9781003706274-1

as "a business of a most complicated nature; large sums of money had to be dealt with; an enormous quantity of cargo had to be handled, and large gangs of men had to be managed."[3] However, by 1905, the company's growth was already under threat. While demand remained high, a congested customs and harbour dredging works impacted timely and safe delivery of cargoes, and a crowded port too often resulted in damaged or lost vessels and goods. Pleas from British diplomats and business leaders with the Japanese authorities for remediation of these problems went unheeded.

That same year, Nickel's cousin and godson, Christian Holstein, brought to Kobe in 1897 succeeded Nickel on the board as director and in 1906 upon Nickel's death as managing director. He continued building on Nickel's success managing the workings of a Japanese treaty port as Nickel had before him until 1914.

This work examines the experiences of two German merchants in their daily conduct of business in Japan as the Japanese government divided over its support for the presence of foreign merchants, sought to control international trade. It uses C. Nickel & Co. Ltd. as a case study to investigate how Nickel and Holstein built their stevedoring, landing and freight forwarding company into a waterfront empire in a time of rapid growth, and great change when the British as the dominant foreign power failed to police infringements of the unequal treaties and to protect foreign merchants from obstructionist policies of the Japanese authorities outside the treaties. Drawing upon archival material from Japan, Germany, and the United Kingdom together with treaty port newspapers and other sources, it shows how Nickel and Holstein navigated the commercial complexities of the Japanese treaty port partnering with their British colleagues, in the face of often hostile and anti-foreign Japanese authorities. Despite British diplomats' efforts, those efforts to protect foreign merchants' rights failed. Nickel and Holstein had to resort to their own skills, abilities and transnational connections to navigate political, mercantile, and jurisdictional obstacles to succeed until 1914, and then in Holstein's case survive in Japan from 1914 to 1923, as an "enemy alien" in the face of British opposition, during the First World War and its aftermath.

British and German Imperial Ambitions in China—The Treaties

This book places Nickel and Holstein in the context of the British imperial ambitions in full swing in China in the mid-1800s and of the German Empire

3 "C. Nickel & Company Limited: Meeting of Shareholders," 130.

which would follow suit in China in the latter part of the nineteenth century. Britain's relationship with China commenced with the British East India Company (EIC) in the 1700s and extended into the 1840s when British trade with Canton (Guangzhou) faltered and imperial Britain subdued China in the First Opium War (1839–42).[4] In 1842 Britain signed the Treaty of Nanking (Nanjing, the first of the unequal treaties); Hong Kong became a British colony and the Chinese government was forced to open five treaty ports. Shanghai was the largest. Following the Second Opium War (1856–60), twelve more treaty ports were opened.[5] The unequal treaties accorded foreigners the right of residence outside Chinese jurisdiction, low tariffs and access to China's interior and to China's rivers and coastal waters for foreign shipping companies.[6] France, the United States, the Netherlands, and later Germany signed their own unequal treaties with China. All nations were on an equal footing and formed their own relationships with the Chinese authorities competing and collaborating with each other politically and commercially in their own interests.[7]

While in Hong Kong, the British exercised absolute rule or formal imperial power, in the treaty ports, the British and the other foreign powers exercised an informal imperial power in their relationships with the Chinese leadership; a combination of influence and coercion. Jürgen Osterhammel defines imperial power as power exercised where a country, having a "dynamic capitalist centre," projects its resources, "people, technology, commodities, capital etc." into countries linked to a particular imperial system either through direct rule (formal empire) or indirect rule (informal empire), similar to a headquarters deploying entrepreneurial strategies through its overseas based subsidiary.[8] Except for the British colony of Hong Kong and later the German colony on the Shandong Province in China, no Western power established formal imperial rule in either China or Japan. Instead, they exercised an informal form of imperial power explained succinctly by Osterhammel as an

4 Jürgen Osterhammel, "British Business in China, 1860s–1950s," in *British Business in Asia Since 1860*, eds. Richard P. T. Davenport-Hines and Geoffrey Jones (Cambridge: Cambridge University Press 1989), 191.

5 Osterhammel, "British Business in China," 191.

6 Osterhammel, "British Business in China," 191.

7 Stefan Manz, *Constructing a German Diaspora: The "Greater German Empire," 1871–1914* (New York, London: Routledge, 2017), 40–41; Ghassan Moazzin, *Foreign Banks and Global Finance in Modern China: Banking on the Chinese Frontier, 1870–1919* (Cambridge, New York, NY: Cambridge University Press, 2022), 24–55.

8 Osterhammel, "British Business in China," 189.

> historical situation of some stability and permanence in which overt rule is avoided while economic advantages are secured by 'unequal' legal and institutional arrangements, and also by the constant threat of political meddling and military coercion that would be intolerable in relations between fully sovereign states.[9]

As Osterhammel explains in China, the British established a system of treaty ports as a projection of its imperial power as it sought to consolidate its commercial supremacy and global influence on the one hand and bring modernity and religion to an otherwise uncivilized country on the other.[10]

Germany was a latecomer to colonization and empire building. It had only become a nation in 1871 upon the unification of a collection of independent states, city-states, and principalities. In 1898, as part of a programme of colonial and economic expansion, Germany acquired from the Chinese the leasehold of Kiaochow in the Shandong Province for ninety-nine years and developed the Port of Tsingtao ruled by the Imperial German Navy. While Tsingtao served primarily as a base for the German naval squadron, it was also a base for key German companies to develop business and showcase German expertise in China.[11]

In Japan

In contrast to China, Japan was closed to the West for over 250 years. The Shogun Tokugawa Ieyasu, fearing the threat of Christianity, banished foreigners from Japan, allowing only the Dutch East India Company (VOC) to maintain a small trading outpost in Nagasaki. In 1853, the American Commodore Matthew Perry arrived in Japan and demanded the Japanese government reopen its borders. While the Americans forced the first of the unequal treaties on Japan opening a number of treaty ports (in addition to Hakodate and according to a fixed schedule, Nagasaki, Yokohama, and later Kobe and Osaka), the Netherlands, Russia, Great Britain and France also

9 Jürgen Osterhammel, "Britain and China, 1942–1914," in *The Oxford History of the British Empire, Volume III: The Nineteenth Century*, eds. Andrew Porter and William Roger Louis (Oxford: Oxford University Press, 1999), 148.

10 Osterhammel, "Britain and China," 146.

11 Schrecker, *Imperialism and Chinese Nationalism*, 61–62.

signed treaties in that order.[12] However when the United States of America became embroiled in the American Civil War (1861–65), the British took the lead.[13] While the British government had long been focused on China, it regarded Japan as a "minor corollary" and used the American initiative to open Japan to the West only after 1858, to strengthen its commercial and naval supremacy.[14]

Witnessing China's humiliation at the hands of the British and other foreign powers and divided in the extent to which foreigners should be allowed in Japan, the Tokugawa Shogunate—the *Bakufu* (government)—was determined Japan would not suffer a similar fate and sought to control foreign merchants within and outside the treaties. For example, foreigners in Japan were confined to a twenty-five-mile radius of the treaty port and were barred from entering the interior and dealing directly with suppliers, and while foreigners were permitted to own buildings, they could only lease land.[15] Until 1899 when the unequal treaties were revised, the extent of informal power exercised by the British and the other foreign powers in Japan lay in ensuring foreign merchants were outside Japanese jurisdiction and submitted to their own consular courts. Foreigners also had the right to manage the Foreign Settlement autonomously through a Municipal Council. However, as far as being able to exercise informal power—influencing and coercing the Japanese authorities in protecting foreigners' rights against Japanese breaches of the treaties, or other anti-foreign policies—the British failed to exercise any form of power over the Japanese in the way they had in China. After the treaties were revised, foreign merchants lost not only extraterritorial privileges having to submit to Japanese jurisdiction but continued to be banned from owning land, and were subjected to new bans on entering unopened ports without permission. The Kobe treaty port newspaper, the *Japan Chronicle*, provides evidence of the failure of British diplomatic representations through the many campaigns it conducted over decades trying to influence the Japanese authorities through its Japanese

12 Ferry de Goey, "Western Entrepreneurs and the Opening of Japanese Ports," in *Culture Power and Politics in Treaty-Port Japan, 1854–1899: Key Papers, Press and Contemporary Writings, Volume 1*, ed. James E. Hoare (Kent: Renaissance Books, 2018), 154.

13 Kurt Meissner, *Deutsche in Japan 1639–1960* (Tokyo: Deutsche Gesellschaft für Natur-und Völkerkunde Ostasiens, 1961), 9, https://oag.jp/img/1961/01/oag-mitteilung-sup-Bd-26-deutsche-in-japan-komplett-1639-1960.pdf; James E. Hoare, *Japan's Treaty Ports and Foreign Settlements: The Uninvited Guests 1858–1899*. (Kent: Japan Library, 1994), 56.

14 Payson J. Treat, Review of *Great Britain and the Opening of Japan, 1834–1858* by William Gerald Beasley, *American Historical Review* 58, no. 1 (October 1952): 120–21.

15 "The Japan Times and Land Ownership," *Japan Chronicle* (Kobe), 5 March 1902, 194.

English language readership to provide a fairer and more foreigner friendly trading environment.

German Diaspora

Little understood in the Anglophone world is that Germans had been present in the region, from at least the mid-1700s when ships from Hamburg and Prussia frequented Chinese ports and German and British merchants collaborated in China.[16] The German presence was a part of the broader German diaspora, defined as the spread or dispersion of migrants from their original homelands. German communities grew around the world differing geographically, in their political convictions, religious beliefs, and class backgrounds. Many were permanent migrants seeking new homelands while others in the merchant class, for example, were sojourners making their fortunes and retiring back to Germany.

The expansion of the British imperial spheres of influence through its network of colonies and treaty ports meant German merchant communities could be found wherever British merchants resided. In 1651 due to its naval supremacy, Britain imposed the Navigations Act forcing all cargo to be carried on British ships between British colonies and third countries.[17] German merchants commenced migrating to Britain and around the network of colonies from as early as the 1670s, bringing their transnational connections which contributed to strengthening Britain as a world power. Manz defines a "transnationalist" perspective as one whereby German merchants straddled networks within the host country connecting two or more states leading to new "transnational social spaces" that extended beyond their own nation states.[18] Thus how Nickel and Holstein came to be in China and then Japan and effectively straddle the British and German communities collaborating with British and other nationalities in Japan becomes clear.

16 Bernd Eberstein, *Preußen und China: Eine Geschichte schwieriger Beziehungen* (Berlin: Duncker & Humblot, 2007), 121; Fukuoka Mariko, "German Merchants in the Indian Ocean World: From Early Modern Paralysis to Modern Animation," in *Early Global Interconnectivity Across the Indian Ocean World, Volume 1*, ed. Angela Schottenhammer (Cham, Switzerland: Palgrave, 2019), 259–92.

17 John R. Davis, Margrit Schulte Beerbühl and Stefan Manz, "Introduction: Germans in the British Empire," in *Transnational Networks: German Migrants in the British Empire, 1670–1914*, eds. John R. Davis, Stefan Manz, Margrit Schulte Beerbühl (Leiden–Boston: Brill, 2012), 1–17.

18 Stefan Manz, *Constructing a German Diaspora: The "Greater German Empire," 1871–1914* (New York, London: Routledge, 2017), 5

Treaty Ports

While the treaty port systems in both China and Japan had similarities, there were some key differences best seen through comparing the treaty ports of Shanghai and Kobe which were both considered to be model treaty ports. In both ports, foreigners had the right to reside in designated foreign concessions or settlements outside Chinese and Japanese jurisdiction which they governed autonomously through municipal councils. Such settlements typically had their own fire brigades, police forces, clubs, Masonic Lodges, cemeteries, horse-racing tracks, taverns and bowling allies for the "lower classes" with a rigid social class structure in place. In Shanghai, there were two main foreign concessions where a mix of British and other nationalities resided alongside Chinese residents: the International Concession where the British dominated the Municipal Council and the French Concession, where the French dominated the *Conseil de Municipale*.[19] In the case of the International Concession, despite not being in the majority, the British maintained tight control of power based on their wealth.[20] In Kobe, the Foreign Settlement was home to all foreign nationalities who chose to reside there. Many, such as Carl Nickel, also chose to reside outside the foreign settlements in the Native Town. While the British dominated the Foreign Settlement in Kobe with the numbers of Germans running second, power and decision making was shared equitably by the Municipal Council governing it. The Council comprised foreign land renters, mainly English and German and foreign diplomats with one Japanese local government representative. Otherwise, until the treaties were revised in 1899, there were no Japanese resident in the foreign concession. Not all treaty port settlements in Japan were managed successfully by foreigners. Yokohama's municipal council collapsed in 1867, and the Japanese took over running the council with a foreigner as an administrator.[21]

Despite the similarities between the treaty ports, there were some significant differences in how the British handled their relationships with the host leaders in China and Japan. In China British diplomats focused much of their time on appeasing their Chinese hosts on jurisdictional matters such as the casual violence of their compatriots, or problems caused by

19 Isabella Jackson, "Who Ran the Treaty Ports? A Study of the Shanghai Municipal Council," in *Treaty Ports in Modern China: Law, Land and Power*, eds. Robert A. Bickers and Isabella Jackson (Milton Park, Abingdon, Oxon; Routledge, 2016), 40–41 (Milton Park, Abingdon, Oxon; Routledge, 2016), 43–47; Carlos Augusto Montalto de Jesus, *Historic Shanghai* (Shanghai Mercury Limited, 1909), 221–23.

20 Jackson, "Who Ran the Treaty Ports?" 45.

21 Hoare, *Japan's Treaty Ports and Foreign Settlements*, 110–11.

culturally unaware missionaries amongst other issues. Notably, "securing advantages for British business" was less of a focus presumably because the British had already established the power to enforce Chinese adherence to the treaties.[22] In Japanese treaty ports, British diplomatic correspondence showed instances where the British Minister also appeased their Japanese counterparts over disputes involving British merchants, often casting aspersions on foreign merchants' motives. However, the real focus of British diplomats and business leaders was on seeking reparations for infringements of the unequal treaties and protesting anti-foreign policies and other injustices they believed the Japanese authorities perpetrated against foreign merchants. Such diplomatic correspondence, combined with the campaigns against Japanese obstructionism conducted over many years by the *Japan Chronicle*, attest to the failure of the British power base to influence or coerce the Japanese government. The levels of frustration the British experienced in Japan dealing with the intransigence of the Japanese authorities over the forty years of extraterritoriality and then under the revised treaties is palpable in these records.

British diplomats in China were less focused on "securing advantages for British business" than in Japan because they had successfully established a collaborative relationship with the Chinese leadership, no doubt with a hint of coercion, one instance of which occurred in institution building. In 1854, the Imperial Maritime Customs Service (IMCS) was established as a joint British Chinese initiative led mostly by the British with other foreign nationals.[23] Initially the IMCS collected customs duties, but expanded its services to support trade including harbour engineering, improvement of shipping lanes, pilotage and the provision of valuable commercial intelligence and logistical support.[24] In Kobe, due to continuing resistance to the presence of foreigners in Japan amongst the Japanese leadership, British diplomats did not succeed in establishing such a relationship and had little to no success influencing their Japanese hosts in equivalent institution building. Furthermore, from the early 1870s, the Japanese government sent study missions overseas to learn how such institutions were developed. They then employed foreign experts (*o-yatoi gaikokujin*) on short-term contracts as advisors, mainly from Britain, France, the United States and

22 Osterhammel, "Britain and China," 149, 155; Robert Bickers and Isabella Jackson, "Introduction," in *Treaty Ports in Modern China: Law, Land and Power*, eds. Robert Bickers and Isabella Jackson (Milton Park, Abingdon, Oxon; Routledge, 2016), 1–21.

23 Osterhammel, "Britain and China," 156–57.

24 Osterhammel, "Britain and China," 157.

Germany.[25] The institutions most affecting foreign merchants, the Kobe Customs and the Kobe Harbour Authority, were managed by the Japanese; despite representations, the needs and preferences of locally based foreign merchants were not considered. Whereas the British cooperated with the Chinese to influence institution building, they failed to do so in Japan. The treaty port system in China lasted from 1842–1943, whereas in Japan it only lasted for forty years. In 1899 Japan regained its sovereignty, enacting the revised treaties and bringing foreigners under Japanese jurisdiction.

Adapting to an Ever-Changing Environment

Before examining how these two German merchants conducted business, the context of the period 1860–1923 is examined to understand how they navigated an ever-changing environment over a sixty-three-year time span encompassing several distinctive periods of Japan's modernization. This work commences when the arrival of foreign merchants in the mid-late 1850s met with sharp opposition from forces seeking to oust the Tokugawa Shogunate and foreigners which led to instability and threats to lives. Carl Nickel arrived in Japan in 1860, in the latter part of the Tokugawa regime, at a time of civil strife and anti-foreign feeling on the one hand while enjoying the privileges of extraterritoriality on the other. In 1868, he experienced the Meiji Restoration, an aristocratic revolution leading to the rapid modernization and industrialization of Japan, which brought a period of stability and a boom in business. Japan's success in the Sino-Japanese War in 1894 marked the rise of nationalism, and its success in the Russo-Japanese War in 1905 led to Japan's acceptance within the ranks of the great powers and an increase in international jockeying for position in the region. In 1899, both Nickel and his successor, Christian Holstein, experienced the abolition of extraterritoriality and the enactment of the revised treaties, bringing foreigners under Japanese jurisdiction. In 1902, they anticipated the benefits of the Anglo-Japanese Alliance and experienced the ensuing period of prosperity in the lead up to the First World War. Holstein then experienced the Alliance's subsequent ramifications in the outbreak of war and designation of German nationals as "enemy aliens." Thus, a focus on C. Nickel & Co. Ltd. as a company spanning this time, enables one to trace how these two German merchants dealt with and adapted to an ever-changing environment.

25 Hazel J. Jones, *Live Machines: Hired Foreigners and Meiji Japan* (Vancouver: University of British Columbia Press, 1980), 7.

While historians tend to periodize such a span of time into distinct intervals, this work focuses on the continuities between these periods as experienced within the life spans of the merchants considered here. It shows that merchants' ability to adapt or adjust to the changes varied: while some changes were anticipated and protective actions were taken in anticipation of developments in international treaties affecting merchants, equally so could adjustments to the new conditions be delayed for merchants. It demonstrates how these periods were experienced by Nickel and Holstein not always as momentous changes, but as gradual adaptations in their business practices.

Extraterritorial Privileges Versus Abilities and Skills

Examining how Nickel and Holstein managed their business in Japan from 1860 to 1923 shows that while they benefited from being outside Japanese jurisdiction until 1899, they could not rely upon British or other foreign diplomats protesting obstructionist policies deployed by Japanese authorities either before or after the end of extraterritorial protections. They had to resort to their own skills through their entrepreneurialism, innovation, collaboration, risk taking and transnational connections. They also learnt to exploit legal and administrative loopholes arising in Japanese policy making. An early example of how Nickel managed such loopholes becomes apparent when he settled in Nagasaki in 1860 as a non-treaty national with no right to do so. Merchants whose country had no treaty with Japan could only enter under the protection of a signatory country. While many Germans claimed Dutch protection initially, Nickel claimed to have American protection, although American consular records show no such record, suggesting he may have used this as a device to exploit porous borders. With the ratification in 1863 of the Prussia-Japan Treaty of Amity, Commerce and Shipping signed in 1861, Nickel is recorded in Japanese records as a Prussian.[26] This work shows the various ways Nickel and his successor Holstein applied their skills managing the efforts of the Japanese authorities to obstruct merchants under the unequal treaties and then after the treaties were revised when they introduced laws further curtailing foreign merchants' activities.

26 Sven Saaler, "150 Jahre japanisch-deutsche Beziehungen," *Unter den Augen ders Preußen-Adlers: Lithographien, Zeichnungen und Photographien der Teilnehmer der Eulenberg-Expedition in Japan, 1860–61*, eds. Sebastian Dobson and Sven Saaler (Munich: Iudicium, 2011), 38.

New Understandings About Treaty Ports

Histories on Japanese treaty ports to date provide some knowledge about the business environment in which foreign merchants operated from 1858 to 1899, but what has not been documented is how they conducted business responding to challenges and obstacles on a day-to-day basis until war commenced in 1914. The rules under which foreign merchants operated under extraterritoriality are understood; Anglophone merchants rarely spoke Japanese and communicated with their suppliers and customers through their Chinese compradors and or Japanese *bantōs*. Their club and sports activities have also been documented, and the fact they could be racist and classist in their attitudes towards their Japanese hosts are also well known.[27] This work focuses on the specific challenges two German merchants faced and how such challenges guided their business behavior, as they operated in the transnational spaces bridging the Anglophone German-Japanese divide.

Through excavating the history of a German-British waterfront empire in Japan, this research provides insights into merchants who were not British but German, often ignored by Anglophone historians. While much of the merchant experience was common across the foreign community, the experience of German merchants often differed from their British colleagues. In the broader context the German unification in 1871 saw the emergence of Germany as a global economic power. However, between 1873 and 1879 economic depression hit Germany and so German manufacturers worked harder to break into international markets increasing German exports which in turn threatened British economic supremacy.[28] From the opening of Kobe in 1868, British companies partnered with German companies to access markets they were otherwise unable to reach in collaborations lasting decades. In 1914, at the outbreak of World War One, seeking to identify German business British merchants could capture, the British government conducted an analysis of German merchants' business practices and

27 Darren Lee Swanson, "Treaty Port Society and the Club in Meiji Japan: Clubbism, Athleticism and the Public Sphere" (PhD diss., University of Sydney, 2016), http://hdl.handle.net/2123/16921; Darren Lee Swanson, "Them and Us: Perceptions of the Japanese Amongst the Foreign Community: Race Theory and Race Relations in Post-Extraterritorial Japan," *Electronic Journal of Contemporary Japanese Studies* 12, no. 1, 1–23; Harold S. Williams, *Foreigners in Mikadoland* (Tokyo: Charles E. Tuttle Company, 1963); Harold S. Williams, *Tales of The Foreign Settlements in Japan* (Tokyo: Charles E. Tuttle Company, 1958); *The Kobe Weekly Chronicle and Japan Weekly Chronicle* 1897–1920s, https://primarysources-brillonline-com.rp.nla.gov.au/browse/japan-chronicle; Kevin C. Murphy, *The American Merchant Experience in Nineteenth Century Japan* (London: Routledge/Curzon, 2003), 126–53.

28 Moazzin, *Foreign Banks and Global Finance in Modern China*, 29.

competitive strengths in Japan.[29] German merchants' success over the decades was ascribed to their willingness to meet Japanese market needs and to offering generous credit terms amongst other practices discussed more fully in chapter 9. Such findings serve not just to indicate the reasons German merchants were successful but also point to the reasons British companies valued their German business partners. In an essay written more recently, the decline in success of British trading houses in Japan which apparently accelerated in the 1880s was attributed in part to Japan's "closer commercial links with Germany, provoked by Japanese admiration for Bismarckian political institutions."[30] Such a conclusion reflects how the British, accustomed to a *laissez-faire* style of doing business with minimal government intervention, were disdainful of what is today considered good export market development practice.[31] It also ignores the close affinity that developed between German and Japanese people which had much to do with shared business values of mutual respect, prompt and timely responses and flexibility in meeting market needs.

Navigating Japanese policies and regulations the foreign community considered inimical to foreign interests, Nickel and Holstein learned to take advantage of loopholes and gaps in regulations, and to argue their way through litigating in both foreign consular and Japanese courts. Transnational connections were crucial: both Nickel and Holstein were embedded in the foreign and Japanese communities working closely with Germans, Americans, British, and Japanese. Speaking Japanese, and through transcending national origins, they were able to subvert the limitations of Japanese policy, often setting their own policies. The foreign merchant community in Japan was much more diverse than histories focusing on the British community suggest and was much more integrated into the fabric of the Japanese business world than suggested by histories focusing on the internal workings of treaty ports subject to new challenges with the abolition of extraterritoriality and the transformation of the political landscape at the beginning of the First World War.[32]

29 Memorandum by E. T. F. Crowe, 30 September 1914, Opportunities for capturing German business, FO 371/2020, The National Archives of the UK (henceforth TNA), 365–79.

30 Richard P. T. Davenport-Hines and Geoffrey Jones, "British Business in Japan since 1868," in *British Business in Asia Since 1860*, eds. Richard P. T. Davenport-Hines and Geoffrey Jones (Cambridge: Cambridge University, 1989), 222.

31 McDermott, "'A Needless Sacrifice,'" 266.

32 Robert Young, "History of Kobe" and Miss Gertrude Cozad, "Romance of Kobe," in *The Japan Chronicle, Jubilee Number 1868–1918* (Kobe: *Japan Chronicle*, 1918); Williams, *Tales of the Foreign Settlements*; Hoare, *Japan's Treaty Ports and Foreign Settlements*; Peter Ennals, *Opening a*

These two German merchants were emblematic of the many mutually beneficial German-British collaborations that commenced with the opening of the Port of Kobe in 1868, and which shaped Nickel and Holstein's commercial success until those collaborations were torn apart when the British government waged economic war against German merchants. Since those times, the story of the German merchants' contribution to the treaty port of Kobe has become subsumed into the more prominent British retelling of the history. The most comprehensive history of the treaty port in Japan is found in James Hoare's *Japan's Treaty Ports and Foreign Settlements: The Uninvited Guests 1858–1899*. It draws mainly from British diplomatic records and other English language sources. Germans are mentioned as "exceptions" to the British "rule," in the context of the Franco-Prussian war, the German government's appointment of merchant consuls frowned upon by the British professional diplomatic service, or in differences between the British and the German consular courts.[33] British diplomats left an extensive record through official correspondence whereas merchants engaged in commerce left few records of their experiences and activities. A broader history entitled *East Asia: The Modern Transformation* acknowledges the role played by German expertise in influencing Japanese studies and development of such fields as medicine, education, constitutional matters, teachings in philosophy and other areas. Such acknowledgements are made however in the context of Germany as a rival of Britain in trade and as a naval power and refers to German influence being "authoritarian" and "conservative," judgements that suggest an anti-German sentiment.[34] Thus, the lives and experiences of German merchants, despite their importance in shaping trade in the treaty ports, have remained largely unexamined in a bi-partisan manner.

The role German merchants played in building international trade in Kobe and other treaty ports is little discussed in Anglophone historical records. Two historians close to the times, Robert Young and Harold S. Williams, briefly acknowledged the contribution of Germans to the Port of Kobe. In 1918, Robert Young, the British owner of the treaty port newspaper the *Japan Chronicle*, wrote "The History of Kobe," in which he credited German merchants in Kobe with constructing the first buildings on the site of the Foreign Settlement in 1868 and with playing key roles in the

Window to the West: The Foreign Concession at Kobe, Japan, 1868–1899 (Toronto, Buffalo, London: University of Toronto Press, 2014).

33 Hoare, *Japan's Treaty Ports and Foreign Settlements*, 44–46, 50, 79, 80, 92.

34 John K. Fairbank, Edwin O. Reischauer and Albert M. Craig, *East Asia: The Modern Transformation: Volume 2* (London: George Allen & Unwin Ltd., 1965), 272, 277, 292–94, 384, 478, 544.

Municipal Council governing the Foreign Settlement.[35] Referring to the foreign community's belief in the post-war period that German commercial influence in the "Far East" had been only relatively recent, Young offers us a clue to understanding how knowledge of the German contribution had become lost. Young states that "Already in the sixties [1860s] the Germans were very strong both in China and Japan and in the early days of Kobe they were especially influential," adding that many of the old-timers had left Japan by the end of the war.[36]

Historian Harold S. Williams, an Australian who lived in Kobe from 1919 until 1986, with a brief hiatus during World War Two, was a prolific author on the treaty port communities.[37] He collected books, letters, memoirs, newspaper cuttings, photographs, and anecdotes, and wrote many books, research papers, newspaper articles and speeches on the foreign community focusing mainly on the British community. Although he collected some German material, he did not write about German merchants: the reason for this is unclear. By the time he returned to Japan after World War Two, the Occupation Forces had deported most of the German residents. Two hundred Germans were allowed to stay, mainly missionaries with some merchant families including Christian Holstein's. Fortunately for researchers, Williams bequeathed his collection of materials to the National Library of Australia, and his sources occasionally yield useful references to the German community.

The few official records that can be found about the German community in Japan are based on reports written by civil servants and diplomats, whose principal concern was the German-Japan relationship from a macro trade perspective; their concern for German merchants in Japan was secondary at best.[38] Professional German diplomats, appointed to their posts even before unification in 1871, stemmed from the German aristocracy and often regarded merchants with disdain. German merchants only appear in official dispatches where Germans served Germany's national trade interests. Germans, bridging Anglophone divides within the foreign community such as Nickel, were marginal to both communities; few records remain in either German or British consular files. Merchants themselves rarely left written memoirs.

35 Young, "History of Kobe," 14.

36 Young, "History of Kobe," 28.

37 Harold Williams Collection, National Library of Australia (henceforth HWC NLA).

38 Meissner, *Deutsche in Japan*; Otto Refardt, *Die Deutschen in Kobe* (*Alt Kobe*) (Tokyo: Deutsche Gesellschaft für Natur-und Völkerkunde Ostasiens (OAG), 1956).

In the absence of company archives and personal records, this history was reconstructed from a large collection of material such as reportage in the English language treaty port newspaper, the *Japan Chronicle*, oral histories and government records found across nine archives and four libraries in Japan, Germany, the United Kingdom, and Australia. In Japan, the National Archives of Japan Digital Archive and the National Diet Library in Tokyo, the Yokohama Public Archives, Yokohama, and the Kobe Public Archives, and Kobe Public Library in Kobe, provided invaluable primary material. In Germany the *Staatsarchiv* Hamburg in Hamburg, the *Niedersächisches Landesarchiv*, Stade, and the *Politisches Archiv des Auswärtigen Amts* (German Foreign Ministry Political Archives), the *Bundesarchiv* (National Archives in Lichterfelde), and the *Geheimes Staatsarchiv Preußischer Kulturbesitz* (Prussian Secret State Archives) in Berlin, provided both German, British, and American diplomatic records. In the United Kingdom, the Ministry of the Blockade Files at the National Archives in Kew, London provided documents relating to the First World War. In Australia, through the generosity of the National Library of Australia, I was granted a Harold S. Williams Scholarship to use its resources. The State Library of Victoria was also helpful.

The English language treaty port newspapers, the *Kobe Weekly Chronicle* and its successor, the *Japan Weekly Chronicle* (hereafter referred to as the *Kobe Chronicle* and *Japan Chronicle*), provide the most comprehensive record of events involving the two protagonists of this story and their company, C. Nickel & Co. Ltd.[39] The *Chronicle* operated initially as the *Kobe Chronicle* from the mid-1890s and was re-named the *Japan Chronicle* in 1901. It was wound up in 1941 following the outbreak of World War Two. Until the death of its founder, Robert Young in 1922, the *Japan Chronicle* served to inform the foreign community of events happening in Japan and overseas, and to report on the comings and goings of its members and their interactions with the Japanese authorities.

The *Chronicle* has been a valuable source of information on the two protagonists of this work and their company. Copies of English language newspapers, the *Japan Weekly Mail* and *Japan Gazette* and the Japanese owned *Japan Times* are also available; however, these newspapers were based in Tokyo and Yokohama respectively and rarely reported on foreign companies or individuals outside those communities. Moreover, the *Japan Weekly Mail* was subsidized by the Japanese government to promote Japan.[40]

39 *Kobe Chronicle* and *Japan Chronicle* Online, 1900–1940.

40 Peter O'Connor, "The Japan Chronicle and Its Three Editors, Robert Young, Morgan Young and Edwin Allington Kennard, 1891-1940," in *Britain and Japan Biographical Portraits, Volume 4*,

Copies of the German language *Deutsche Japan Post*, a newspaper also printed in Yokohama from 1903–14, were also available, but surviving issues were incomplete and contained no information about Christian Holstein or his company in Kobe. In contrast the *Japan Chronicle* was Kobe based and remains a greater source of information on members of the foreign community.

In addition to being a record of events, the *Chronicle* also represents "a partial voice" for the foreign community as a record of how it might have felt collectively or individually about infringements of its rights and interactions with the Japanese authorities. Young as its editor expressed his somewhat biased views as a pro-foreigner British representative, as if they were the views of the foreign community. In so doing, Young was addressing the *Chronicle*'s Japanese readership, arguing for change in the Japanese government's policies and attitudes. Despite its obvious biases, the *Chronicle* presents an invaluable window into foreigners' views of contemporary issues, and, as Hoare also notes, in the absence of personal memoirs and other records, "we have no other voices."[41] According to various obituaries written upon his death, Young was dedicated to the harmony and cohesion of the foreign community, championing the rights of foreigners regardless of nationality holding the Japanese authorities to account when he believed foreigners' rights had been infringed.[42] Young was remembered also a strong advocate for Japan regaining its sovereignty through the abolition of the unequal treaties and extraterritoriality.[43] Harold Williams records, however, that Young could be accused of anti-Japanese sentiments.[44]

While Young supported Japan's right to abolish extraterritoriality, he used the *Chronicle* to scrutinize the Japanese court system to which foreigners now had to submit. The *Chronicle* reported regularly and in detail on the many court cases involving foreigners. From 1900 to 1921, Nickel, Holstein, and their company, C. Nickel & Co. Ltd., became regularly embroiled in such cases and Young regularly used those cases to demonstrate to the foreign community the inadequacies and biases of the Japanese courts as he saw it. In scrutinizing the Japanese court system, the *Japan Chronicle*

ed. Hugh Cortazzi (London: Taylor Francis Group, 2003), 334–48.

41 James E. Hoare, "Japan's Treaty Ports and Treaty Revision: Delusions of Grandeur?" in *Culture, Power & Politics in Treaty Port Japan, 1854–1899: Key Papers, Press and Contemporary Writings, Volume 1*, ed. James E. Hoare (Kent: Renaissance Books, 2018), 254.

42 "Robert Young: A Memoir: Thursday, 9 November 1922," *Japan Chronicle* (Kobe), 16 November 1922, 632–34.

43 "Robert Young: A Memoir," 632–34.

44 Harold S. Williams, "Foreign Owned English Newspapers in Kobe: Shades of the Past," *Mainichi Daily News* (Tokyo), 21 February 1981, Folder 80, HWC NLA.

provides an important record of how conflicts between foreign merchants themselves and their Japanese counterparts were adjudicated. As Japanese court records from the earlier twentieth century were not found in any archives to supplement this research, the *Japan Chronicle* has become especially important.

Diplomatic records from the British, Prussian, and German governments provide valuable insights into the conditions of the early years in the treaty ports. *Die Preußische Expedition nach Ost-Asien Erster Band, 1864* (The Prussian Expedition to East Asia, Volume One, 1864) written by Count Frederick Albrecht zu Eulenberg provides us with a first-hand account of his voyage to Japan to negotiate the Prussia-Japan Treaty ratified in 1863.[45] He refers to his reliance upon the American Consul Townsend Harris in Yokohama for guidance on managing his Japanese interlocutors in treaty negotiations. Eulenberg's report indicates how disdainfully he and his fellow aristocratic expedition members viewed German merchants already in the treaty ports of Nagasaki and Yokohama. Max von Brandt was one such member. He became Prussia's first consul to Japan and subsequently in China. The British collection of *Correspondence with Her Majesty's Envoy Extraordinary and Minister Plenipotentiary in Japan: Presented to both Houses of Parliament by Command of her Majesty* was also invaluable.[46] The range of such reports written from 1856 to 1868 provide insights into the nature of the early trade conflicts between the British and Japanese governments and the extent to which British diplomats worked to resolve them. After the revised treaties were enacted, the Japanese courts also played a role in adjudicating commercial disputes and the *Japan Chronicle* becomes more important as a record of such events.

Japanese sources on German merchants are limited. Of importance is the late nineteenth-century work by Japanese historian Murata Seiji, *Kobe Kaikō Sanjūnen-shi* (Thirtieth Anniversary of Kobe Port), published in two volumes in 1898 which provides details on Carl Nickel and his company.[47]

45 [Albert Berg], *Die Preußische Expedition Nach Ost-Asien. Erster Band* (Berlin: Verlag der Königlichen Geheimen Oberhofbuchdruckerei, 1864), http://www.deutschestextarchiv.de/book/show/berg_ostasien01_1864. See also Mariko Fukuoka, *Puroisen Higashi Asia Ensei to Bakumatsu Gaikō* (The Prussian East-Asian Expedition and the Japanese Diplomacy in the Late Edo Era) (Tokyo: Tokyo University Press, 2013).

46 Japan. Correspondence with H. M. Envoy and Minister Plenipotentiary in Japan, 1858–68. 19th Century House of Commons Sessional Papers. https://parlipapers-proquest.com.rp.nla.gov.au/parlipapers/docview/t70.d75.1860- 036818?accountid=12694.

47 Murata Seiji, *Kobe Kaikō Sanjūnen-shi*, vol. 1, 6 May 1898 and vol. 2, 25 October 1898 (Kobe: Kaikō Sanjūnen Kinenkai—digitized copy at NLA) http://www.dl.ndl.go.jp/info:ndljp/pid/805190.

Murata notes in particular Nickel's innovativeness and risk-taking exploiting his extraterritorial privileges. Murata's account places Nickel's company in the context of the development of the stevedoring, landing and freight forwarding industry and the emergence of Japanese and other competitors at the time. Japanese newspaper sources, only just emerging in the late Meiji period, were also consulted to gauge the Japanese reactions to foreigners around the outbreak of World War One: the *Kobe Shimbun*, and the *Kobe Yūshin Nippō* were particularly helpful.

The most notable histories of the German community written by German historians, drawing on diplomatic records as well as oral histories from older Germans still living in Kobe, are Otto Refardt's *Die Deutschen in Kobe* (1956) and Kurt Meissner's *Deutsche in Japan, 1639–1960* (1961).[48] Both histories provide useful details of events and anecdotes from a German perspective. Meissner explains that Germans either came to Japan in the service of Germany, as in the case of merchants, or in the service of Japan, in the case of those *o-yatoi gaikokujin* employed by the Japanese government. He points out that German merchants were not migrants in search of a new home but apolitical sojourners retaining their German nationality, intending to retire in Germany. His book presents what he referred to as an overview of the history of the Germans in Japan, setting out "a chronicle of the comings and goings," and "of quiet and sober work," an account ultimately "poor in dramatic highpoints."[49] In delving into the detail of the history of two German merchants, my work shows that their story was full of "dramatic highpoints" and was anything but a case of "quiet and sober work."

At the time Nickel arrived in Nagasaki in 1860, already a number of significant British, Dutch, American and German trading houses had been established as well as individual merchants trying their luck. A range of histories of some of these have been written in recent times attesting to the entrepreneurialism required to be successful in Japan in the second half of the nineteenth century. All were trading houses with some holding ships agencies, and many were clients of C. Nickel & Co. Ltd. These accounts provide fascinating and varied accounts of entrepreneurialism in treaty port Japan under extraterritorial privileges and confirm in broad terms the anti-foreign forces at play as they serviced a Japanese customer base contending with obstructionist Japanese authorities.[50] However, such

48 Meissner, *Deutsche in Japan*; Refardt, *Die Deutschen in Kobe* (*Alt Kobe*).

49 Meissner, *Deutsche in Japan*. (My translation), 1.

50 Brian Burke-Gaffney, *Holme, Ringer & Company: The Rise and Fall of a British Enterprise in Japan, 1868–1940* (Leiden: Global Oriental, 2013); Alexander McKay, *Scottish Samurai: Thomas*

histories were single-nation focused, ignoring the transnational interdependent nature of treaty ports. These accounts dealt mainly with the period under extraterritoriality and being based on company archives lack impartiality. In contrast and based on third party accounts from mainly British and American sources, this work discusses how C. Nickel & Co. Ltd., a German then a British company with a multi-national workforce, conducted business as a service provider on a day-to-day basis, interacting with a multinational customer base not to mention a wide range of Japanese regulatory authorities.

Three histories written about German companies that were connected to C. Nickel & Co. Ltd. include *Yokohama Yankee: My Family's Five Generations as Outsiders in Japan*, *Handel ist Wandel: 150 Jahre C. Illies & Co.* (Changing Face of Trade: 150 Years of C. Illies & Co.) and *Zeit ist Geld: Der Kaufmann Hinrich Ahrens und die Anfänge des deutschen Handels mit Japan* (Time is Money: The Merchant Hinrich Ahrens, and the Beginnings of German Trade with Japan).[51] The first, written in English, deals with C. Nickel & Co. Ltd.'s one-time partner and then archrival Julius Helm of Helm Bros, a freight forwarding company founded in Yokohama. The other two histories in German deal with large German trading houses representing diverse product ranges and held shipping agencies—both were key clients of C. Nickel & Co. Ltd.'s. These three works outlined the backgrounds, apprenticeships, and pathways the three founders, Julius Helm, Carl Illies and Hinrich Ahrens leading them to Japan. While all three contained useful background, they lacked impartiality and did not deal with conducting business on a day-to-day basis.

To understand the treaty port system in Japan, I referred to three scholarly works, J. E. Hoare's *Japan's Treaty Ports and Foreign Settlements: The Uninvited Guests 1858–1899* mentioned earlier, Peter Ennals' *Opening a Window to the West: The Foreign Concession at Kobe, Japan, 1868–1899* and Catherine Phipp's *Empires on the Waterfront: Japan's Ports and Power 1858–1899*. Hoare's work deals with the workings of the treaty port system in Japan under extraterritoriality. Of particular use was how the British consular court system operated in the treaty port. His book does not examine the

Blake Glover, 1838–1911 (Edinburgh: Canongate Press, 2012); Kevin C. Murphy, *The American Merchant Experience in Nineteenth Century Japan* (London: Routledge/Curzon, 2003); Peter N. Davies, *The Business, Life and Letters of Frederick Cornes* (Folkestone: Global Oriental, 2008).

51 Leslie Helm, *Yokohama Yankee: My Family's Five Generations as Outsiders in Japan* (Seattle: Chin Music Press, 2013); Johannes Bähr, Jörg Lesczenski, and Katja Schmidtpott, *Handel ist Wandel: 150 Jahre C. Illies & Co.* (München: Piper Verlag GMBH, 2009); Carolin Reimers, *Zeit ist Geld, Der Kaufmann Hinrich Ahrens und die Anfänge des deutschen Handels mit Japan* (Münster: Monsenstein und Vannerdat, 2010).

workings of the ports from a commercial point of view, however, or the period after the enactment of the revised treaties in 1899. Ennals's work discusses the history of Kobe as a Foreign Concession and its social and political infrastructure. It was useful in its description of the Native Town as opposed to the Foreign Settlement and confirms the size of the German community as the second largest. His story is largely told from the British perspective. Phipps's work examines the port of Moji and its "waterfront empires." The Japanese government designated the port of Moji as a special trading port to circumvent the restrictions imposed under the unequal treaties, banning foreigners allowing Japanese companies to flourish.[52] While Phipps confirms some of my own findings regarding the challenges presented by treaty ports to foreign merchants, as foreign companies were banned, her exploration of the foreigner experience is confined to those of foreign ships upon which Japan still depended to develop its export trade. C. Nickel & Co. Ltd. established an operation in Moji after 1899.

Two private websites have been important sources of details about individual foreign merchants operating in Japan from 1856 until the end of the Meiji Era, 1911. The first is Bernd Lepach's Meiji Portraits Website, based in Leipzig.[53] Based on his collection of Meiji era stamps and envelopes, business directories, histories, and other resources, he developed a database of thousands of foreign merchants in Japan 1856–1911. The second is a database of residents of the Nagasaki Foreign Settlement run by Brian Burke-Gaffney and Lane Earns. The database has since been taken down for a software upgrade and will be rehoused in the future.

The dynamics of the foreign community in Kobe changed with the onset of World War One. Two related journal articles contributed to this analysis of the challenge Holstein, and his German management of a now British company, faced navigating the outbreak of War in 1914. John McDermott's "'A Needless Sacrifice': British Businessmen and Business as Usual in the First World War," discusses how the British government sought to protect its commercial supremacy through prosecuting economic war against overseas German merchants capturing German assets and eliminating them as competitors.[54] Philip Dehne's "From 'Business as Usual' to a More Global War: The British Decision to Attack Germans in South America during the First

52 Catherine L. Phipps, *Empires on the Waterfront: Japan's Ports and Power 1858–1899*, Harvard East Asian Monographs no. 373. (Cambridge, MA, and London: Harvard University Press, 2015), 10.

53 Bernd Lepach, Meiji Portraits Website, http://meiji-portraits.de/.

54 McDermott, "'A Needless Sacrifice,'" 263–82.

World War," investigates how the British government waged economic war on German merchants in South American countries with the cooperation of British merchants.[55] McDermott and Dehne provide useful context for how the economic war was waged by Britain on German merchants in Japan.

This study is presented in ten chapters divided into four distinct time periods. The first covers the Hamburg origins of the two German merchants and their family connections. The second explores their experiences conducting business in a Japanese treaty port under the unequal treaties and extraterritorial privileges. The third examines how they conducted business under the revised treaties and Japanese jurisdiction. The final section examines how Holstein managed his designation as "enemy alien" during the First World War and its aftermath pointing to the determination that ensured his family remained in Japan into the third generation for 140 years.

55 Phillip Dehne, "From 'Business as Usual' to a More Global War: The British Decision to Attack Germans in South America during the First World War," *The Journal of British Studies* 44, no. 3 (July 2005): 516–35, https://doi.org/10.1086/429709.

Part I

Family Origins

1. Hamburg: A Trading Port Connected to China and Japan

Abstract: Stories told by the Holstein family, combined with archival research, are used to understand how the family moved from Hamburg to Japan and remain for 140 years. Christian Holstein's family were engaged in cargo shipping and hotel businesses from the mid-1700s. Holstein and his older cousin and godfather, Carl Nickel, founder of C. Nickel & Co. Ltd. in Kobe, Japan are introduced in a time of the British Empire, before the unification of Germany, in a region well connected with Britain and the Netherlands and with growing links with China and Japan. It shows how they navigated political, mercantile, and jurisdictional upheavals in the Hamburg region leveraging transnational connections—skills required for success in a similarly turbulent and unpredictable Japan.

Keywords: memory, transnationalism, nimbleness, invasions, blockade, smuggling

This story has its roots in the early 1700s where Hamburg, an independent city state and important port, had a long tradition in trading and seafaring, well before the rise of the German Empire in 1871. From 1157 to 1611, Hamburg had been a leading member of the Hanseatic League, a loose affiliation of towns in central and northern Europe covering eight modern-day countries. It had close commercial relations with England over a five-hundred-year period until the Hanse franchise ended.[1] In the 1700s, Hamburg continued developing as a port as its merchants commenced exploration of trade in China. To this day Hamburg is the largest port in Germany and is the third largest container port in Europe.

1 Terence H. Lloyd, "The Loss of the Hanse Franchises, 1551–1611," *England and the German Hanse, 1157–1611: A Study of Their Trade and Commercial Diplomacy* (Cambridge: Cambridge University Press, 1991), 292–362. https://doi.org/10.1017/CBO9780511560279.007.

Holstein, Prue S. *The German Experience of Japan's Treaty Port System: A Case Study of C. Nickel & Co. Ltd., 1860–1923*. Taylor & Francis Group, 2025.
DOI: 10.4324/9781003706274-2

In the late 1850s, Carl Nickel, a member of an extended Hamburg family engaged in the maritime industries of seafaring, lighter owning, and cargo handling, ventured first to the treaty port of Shanghai where Germans, British, and Americans resided. Around 1860 he relocated to Nagasaki in Japan. After 250 years of self-imposed isolation, in 1854, Japan had re-opened to the West, offering business opportunities to foreign merchants on the China coast. After time spent in Shanghai, Nagasaki, and Yokohama, in 1879, Nickel then moved to Kobe, where he founded his company, C. Nickel & Co. Ltd. (later becoming Nickel & Lyons). In 1897, Nickel's cousin and godson, Christian Holstein, arrived in Kobe from Hamburg to understudy Nickel as his successor. Based on collective memories passed down through the Holstein family, combined with archival research and historical texts, this chapter explores the origins of Carl Nickel and Christian Holstein.

Collective memories constitute the memories, customs, secrets, and traditions that are used within a family to reproduce "its history [and] define its nature and qualities." Such memories are also used to express the general attitude and value system of the group and to teach by example.[2] They can never constitute a perfect record of events and personalities due to the passing of time, to members leaving the group or to differences in how members of successive generations remember. Such fragmented memories were used by the Holstein family in the form of stories to place the family in the context of the Hamburg maritime trade and to explain the entrepreneurial and resilient attributes their merchant members relied upon as they transferred business skills and knowledge to Japan. Such attributes were used to demonstrate how the two merchants managed the challenges of Japan, an unfamiliar country in a time of great social upheaval remaining in Kobe continuously as German nationals over three generations for almost 140 years.

The two protagonists of this story, Carl Nickel and Christian Holstein, were born in Hamburg in 1836 and 1875, respectively. Nickel and Holstein and their forebears lived in a region alternately occupied by the Danes, the French, and the Prussians, and earlier, the Swedes and Hanoverians. Hamburg merchants were used to changing political, mercantile, and jurisdictional imperatives. According to the family's collective memories, it was this background that made Carl Nickel and Christian Holstein so adaptable and able to weather political change to prosper in Japan.

2 Maurice Halbwachs, "The Collective Memory of the Family," *On Collective Memory*, trans. Lewis A. Coser (Chicago and London: The University of Chicago Press, 1992), 54–83.

Collective Memory Establishing Family History and Identity

When Carl Nickel left for China and Japan in the late 1850s, he joined several generations of German merchants relocating to overseas German merchant communities in China utilizing transnational connections. Germany was still a collection of states, city-states, and principalities united by a common Germanic language albeit with various dialects. During the seventeenth and eighteenth centuries the region was also subject to endless wars. Many Germans wanting to participate in international trade and avoid being drafted into military service migrated to Great Britain and its colonies from the 1600s onwards.[3] They also migrated to the Netherlands and its colonial networks. The Netherlands and Great Britain were maritime powers and controlled vital shipping. Through their Dutch and British connections, German merchants in Hamburg learnt of business opportunities in Batavia (Dutch controlled Indonesia), China and subsequently Japan and secured the means of transport, trading linkages, and extraterritorial protections they needed to explore those opportunities. Transnational linkages became a means by which German speaking merchants could participate in international trade, and, in the case of Nickel and Holstein, explained the broader context of their arrival in Japan and their alignment with the Anglophone communities. The family used collective memories to explain the toughness of character and resilience its members required to navigate the vagaries of wars and empires that allowed three generations to survive and prosper in Japan.

This story begins with two separate families living on the Elbe River, a significant trading route in the vicinity of Hamburg. While the Holstein family claimed it had originated from the Duchy of Holstein (today a part of Schleswig-Holstein), the earliest surviving records indicate they had relocated west of Hamburg to Mühlenhafen, Drochtersen in the Kehdingen region, a part of the Kingdom of Hanover having been acquired from Sweden. As a part of the British occupation post-World War Two, in 1946, the Kehdingen became a part of Niedersachsen, or Lower Saxony. From the late 1700s, subsequent generations of Holsteins moved from the Kehdingen to the docks of Altona and then Hamburg. To the east of Hamburg lived the Nickels in Billwärder Neuer Deich (today known as Billwerder or the Bille), in the parish

3 John R. Davis, Margrit Schulte Beerbühl and Stefan Manz, "Introduction: Germans in the British Empire," eds. John R. Davis, Stefan Manz, and Margrit Schulte Beerbühl, *Transnational Networks: German Migrants in the British Empire, 1670–1914* (Leiden–Boston: Brill, 2012), 9.

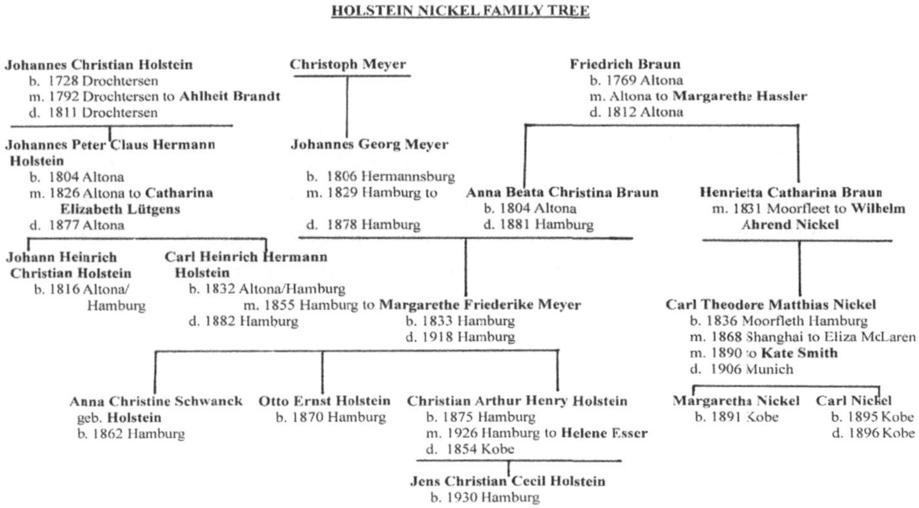

Figure 1. Holstein Nickel Family Tree. This family tree shows how the two families were connected. It also includes some other relatives referred to in the text.

of Moorfleet, a part of the city-state of Hamburg. The following family tree (figure 1) shows how, in 1829, the Nickels and the Holsteins became united in Hamburg when Carl Nickel's aunt, Anna Braun, one of two daughters of the sea captain Friedrich Braun, married into the Meyer family. Their daughter, Maria Margarethe Friederike Meyer, Nickel's first cousin, subsequently married into the Holstein family, and became Christian Holstein's mother. Christian was Nickel's first cousin once removed. The families were close with Nickel becoming Christian's godfather and mentor. Several generations of the Braun, Meyer and the Holstein families were engaged in seafaring, and in the lighter owning and cargo handling business, and in the case of the Holsteins, the inn business servicing the maritime trade as well. Carl Nickel and Christian Holstein continued the freight handling and hotel businesses in Japan: Nickel established the Falcon Hotel in Nagasaki in 1870, and Christian Holstein founded the luxury Tor Hotel in Kobe in 1908.

Two political events were incorporated into the Holstein family's collective memory as being particularly significant, although they would have been significant for many German families. From the early 1600s until 1712, the Kehdingen and Bille regions were subjected to foreign invasions and wars.[4]

4 Christopher Clark, *Iron Kingdom: The Rise and Fall of Prussia, 1600–1947* (London: Penguin Books, 2007), 19; Conversations with Jens Holstein.

The first such event was the Thirty Years' War (1618–48), a partly religious war which embroiled some twenty-five powers and was dubbed the biggest catastrophe in German history. Holstein family stories include a distant and unnamed ancestor from the Duchy of Holstein fighting in the Thirty Years' War. While specific details have been lost, the family retains in its possession a helmet and two Swedish halberds from the period and uses this experience to explain an inherent toughness of character. The second event was the Great Northern War (1700–12). After the Thirty Years' War, the Swedes and the Danes remained in the Kehdingen region fighting to control the Elbe, a major trading river. Some fifteen powers were involved in the Great Northern War challenging Swedish supremacy. Sweden was forced out of the northern German region in 1712 when the coalition it had formed with the Duchy of Holstein-Gottorp was defeated. The family story has it that the earliest member of the Holstein family, recorded living in the Kehdingen region, had participated in the Great Northern War on the side of the Swedes and at the end of the war settled in the area.[5] After the Swedes were expelled, the Kingdom of Hanover took control of the region. Under the Hanoverians, peace reigned, the population rebuilt, and prosperity returned until between 1795 and 1814, when the region suffered the consequences of the French takeover of the Netherlands and subsequently Napoleon's economic warfare and military occupation of Hamburg and other Hanseatic cities.[6]

Although these family stories may owe much to myth, archival records show that during the time of peace, in 1727 or 1728, the earliest verifiable Holstein ancestor, Johann Christian Holstein, was born in Drochtersen at Mühlenhafen, one of two major ports in the Kehdingen region.[7] As many records were destroyed in a church fire around 1772, no official record of his birth or the name of his father remains. However, a Hinrich Holstein was born in October 1725 to a Johann Friedrich Holstein only three years prior to Johann Christian's birth suggesting they could have been brothers.[8]

5 Letter from Otto Holstein, Idar-Oberstein, Germany to his brother, Christian Holstein, Kobe, Japan, 22 September 1940 (in private hands, hereafter Letter Otto Holstein, 22 September 1940).

6 Katherine Aaslestad, "Paying for War: Experiences of Napoleonic Rule in the Hanseatic Cities," *Central European History* 39, no. 4 (December 2006): 641. https://10.1017/S0008938906000215.

7 Holstein Family *Ahnenpaß*, prepared in 1940 as a record of so-called Aryan ancestry required by the Nazi Party, held in private hands. Each entry was verified by the Registry in Idar Oberstein, Germany. Due to a fire, church births, marriages and death records have only survived from the years 1715–26, 1746, 1751–52, 1759–63 and 1765–71, hence no birth registration for Johann Christian Holstein was found. *Niedersächsisches Landesarchiv*, Stade, Germany.

8 Birth Registration: Hinrich Holstein 1 October 1725, Sig.: Rep.84 Nr. 97, *Niedersächsisches Landesarchiv*, Stade (hereafter Birth Registration: Hinrich Holstein).

Johann Friedrich is noted on the birth register as an *Arbeitsmann* or labourer having been born on the "other side of the Elbe" presumably in the Duchy of Holstein.[9] Johann Christian married for the first time in the late 1740s and had two daughters. Records show that he remained in Drochtersen as a shipper and lighter owner until his early 60s.[10] Like Johann Christian, Hinrich also became a shipper residing in Dornbusch, a town near Drochtersen. Hinrich died in 1765 at the age of thirty-five after producing two daughters and no sons.[11]

The Holsteins' Lives as Shippers

Shipping cargo in the Kehdingen region has a long history. Gerd Bahr, a local historian and published author from Bützfleth, also descended from a shipper family, recorded that shipping cargo occurred as early as the 1300s and remained an important industry until 1862. In 1663, some seventy-five shippers lived in the region, and many were based in Drochtersen.[12] In 1718, there were ten harbours with locks from Wischhafen southwards to Bützfleth. The two main harbours in the region were Mühlenhafen, where the Holsteins lived, and Gauensieke.[13] Lighters continued transporting cargo until 1862, when a road built through the Kehdingen region allowed stagecoaches to connect towns, and rail transportation of cargo gradually rendered the lighter obsolete and the harbours disappeared. While the Port of Gauensieke still exists, all that remains of the Port of Mühlenhafen are a few puddles in lush green pastures bounded by the old dyke to the south, and by a newer dyke built to the north some kilometres away, reflecting the changing course of the Elbe River. A handful of old shippers' homes remain behind the original dyke on the old canals and are reminders of these early origins.

Apart from birth, marriage and death records providing a limited range of details, almost no other public records remain about Johann Christian

9 Birth Registration: Hinrich Holstein. (My translation); Letter Otto Holstein to Christian Holstein, 22 September 1940.

10 Letter Otto Holstein, 22 September 1940.

11 Letter Otto Holstein, 22 September 1940.

12 Gerd Bahr, unpublished notes, historian and writer in Plattdeutsch, https://de.wikipedia.org/wiki/Gerd_Bahr, "Über die Entwicklung der Kehdinger Küsten und Flußschifffahrt," May 2013, provided in a private meeting on 6 June 2013.

13 Bahr, unpublished notes; Else Alpers, *Kehdingen Bilderbogen, Land an der Niederelbe gestern und heute* (Stade: Bei Friedrich Schaumburg, 1972) 24.

Holstein's life as a shipper or the lives of other shipping families. Histories of the Kehdingen region and the few records available in the Niedersächsisches Landesarchiv in Stade suggest that shipping businesses were family owned and operated, with shippers sailing long distances alone. They were often away for months at a time, living in flat-bottomed wooden *Ewern* or lighters, delivering their cargoes and interacting with people of many nationalities. Bahr describes the qualities of "self-confidence, toughness and tenacity rooted in his native soil" which the shippers demonstrated as they contended with the solitary nature of the work as well as damaging storm tides.[14] In his stories, he shows that life was not easy. Bahr maintained that shippers required "nimbleness" responding to opportunities, leveraging the extensive networks throughout the northern European region to succeed.[15] In the days before land transportation, before the invention of the railway system, the Elbe River connected the Kehdingen marshlands to the ports of Hamburg and Altona. When Dutch and Friesian settlers arrived in the region in the 1200s, they drained the marshlands and built dykes to hold back the flood tides and storm surges of the North Sea. They also constructed a network of channels used by lighters to ship produce from the hinterlands to market.[16] The lighters sailed between the towns and cities along the Elbe River, to Hamburg and Altona and as far away as Berlin and Bohemia, then a part of the Habsburg monarchy today known as the Czech Republic.[17] The channels also allowed lighters to trans-ship goods onto ocean going vessels anchored in the Elbe River bound for the Netherlands, Belgium, Denmark, Sweden and Great Britain. The shippers in the Kehdingen region spoke *Plattdeutsch* or Lower German, a language which was one of the languages spoken on the docks of Hamburg and Altona reflecting the intermingling of the shippers with English, Dutch, and Danish speakers over the centuries. It is still common along the east and north Friesian coastline.[18]

Some shippers' houses from the 1700s remain in Mühlenhafen located near canals for ease of access for loading cargoes onto lighters. Such houses reflected the self-sufficiency required for a shipper's family to live while the head of the family was away for lengthy periods, particularly in the harsh winters. They were typical in the northern Lower Saxony region—"A" shaped timber framed with space for a barn for the animals, a hay loft and

14 Bahr, unpublished notes.
15 Bahr, unpublished notes.
16 Alpers, *Kehdinger Bilderbogen*, 8.
17 Alpers, *Kehdinger Bilderbogen*, 25.
18 Bahr, unpublished notes.

an oven to dry meat in the roof space and storage for potatoes in the cellar. The living space for the family was located at the back of the structure. The Holstein family most likely lived in such a house: the death of Johann Christian's first wife Anne, in 1788, was recorded as resulting from a fall from the hay loft in her home.[19]

The Holstein family in Japan was proud of its family crest. The crest consists of an oak tree, placed on a shield with the motto in Latin *Frangas non Flectes*, "Break but not bend." The Holstein family memory held that the oak tree was representative of the Duchy of Holstein, the origins of the family, as well as the resilience of the family in the face of political and economic disturbances, an unpredictable and inhospitable environment, and the arduous way of earning a living. How, when and by whom the crest was devised is unknown.

German Merchants Building Transnational Connections

During the 1700s, as the shipping business boomed, the lives of German merchants and shippers became entwined with those of their Dutch and British counterparts as the Netherlands and Great Britain held the monopoly of the international cargo carrying trade. While Germany and its citizens were mired in the Thirty Years' War (1618–48), these two nations had been building maritime and colonial empires. The Netherlands commenced its colonial expansion during the late 1500s in the Dutch East Indies (today Indonesia) and the British engagement with India commenced when the British East India Company (EIC) entered India in 1612 and ruled India as a colony from 1757. The British government took over from the EIC in 1858 and ruled until Independence was granted in 1947.

In China from the mid-1700s, the EIC also had a foothold in Canton (Guangzhou) China which was also taken over by the British government. Following the first Opium War (1839–42) Britain negotiated the Treaty of Nanjing, establishing a British colony in Hong Kong and five treaty ports in Canton (Guangzhou), Amoy (Xiamen), Foochow (Fuzhou), Ningpo (Ningbo) and the largest, Shanghai. A further twelve treaty ports were negotiated following the Second Opium War. These Chinese treaty ports attracted merchants of other nationalities with each nation subsequently signing its own treaty with the Chinese leadership placing the treaty ports effectively under the "informal rule" of multiple imperial powers. However, despite

19 Letter Otto Holstein, 22 September 1940.

the numbers of British, Britain's naval power and its role in having forced the unequal treaties upon China for the following one hundred years the Chinese treaty port system lasted, British informal rule would change shape and form.[20]

In 1651, in an anti-competitive act, the British imposed the Navigations Act forcing all cargo to be carried on British ships. This act also resulted in German merchants and shippers migrating to Britain, its colonies and treaty ports to participate in international trade, and was the basis for some of their earliest collaborations with their British counterparts.[21] While Anglo focused histories do not mention the presence of German merchants in Anglo dominated ports, two non-Anglo historians, Bernd Eberstein and Fukuoka Mariko, confirm the presence of German merchants in China at least from the 1780s onwards.[22] Thus a pattern of Germans collaborating with their British counterparts, continued in northeast Asia until the outbreak of World War One.[23] While details have been lost, family stories suggest that the Holsteins had such British connections, whether through relatives moving to Britain, or through shipping and servicing the mariner trade, most likely a combination of the two. Astute German merchants certainly saw the potential of trade in Asia.

Early Trade Between Hamburg, Prussia, and China

Three forces emerged in northern Germany potentially challenging the monopoly held by the Netherlands and Great Britain in international trade. The first was the status of Hamburg as an independent city-state,

20 Jürgen Osterhammel, "British Business in China, 1860s–1950s," in *British Business in Asia Since 1860*, eds. Richard P. T. Davenport-Hines and Geoffrey Jones (Cambridge: Cambridge University Press, 1989), 189–216; Jürgen Osterhammel, "Britain and China, 1942–1914, in *The Oxford History of the British Empire, Volume III: The Nineteenth Century*, eds. Andrew Porter and William Roger Louis (Oxford: Oxford University Press, 1999), 153; Robert Bickers and Isabella Jackson, "Introduction," *Treaty Ports in Modern China: Law, Land and Power*, eds. Robert Bickers and Isabella Jackson (Milton Park, Abingdon, Oxon; Routledge, 2016), 1–21.

21 Davis, Schulte Beerbühl and Manz, "Introduction: Germans in the British Empire," 9.

22 Bernd Eberstein, "Kaufleute, Konsuln, Kapitäne: Frühe deutsche Wirtschaftsinteressen in China," Catalogue for an exhibition held on Tsingtao at the German Historical Museum, 1998, 11, http://www.dhm.de/archiv/ausstellungen/tsingtau/katalog/auf1_1.htm, accessed 2021; Fukuoka Mariko, "German Merchants in the Indian Ocean World: From Early Modern Paralysis to Modern Animation," in *Early Global Interconnectivity Across the Indian Ocean World, Volume 1*, ed. Angela Schottenhammer (Cham, Switzerland: Palgrave, 2019), 259–92.

23 Davis, Schulte Beerbühl and Manz, "Introduction: Germans in the British Empire," 9.

a significant trading port with a growing shipping industry. With the end of the Thirty Years War in 1648, Hamburg began to flourish as the focus of European trade moved to the Atlantic Seaboard and it developed into a leading German port and a centre of shipbuilding. Hamburg had a long and close relationship with Portugal with Portuguese ships docking in Hamburg delivering Chinese cargoes of porcelain and tea and raising an early awareness of the potential offered by trade with China.[24] The second force was Prussia. By the 1700s, Prussia had the military wherewithal to compete with the Dutch East India Company, (*Vereenigde Oostindische Compagnie* or VOC 1621–1791) and the British East India Company (EIC 1600–1874). Once peace reigned on German soil in the 1700s, both King *Friedrich Wilhelm* of Prussia (ruled 1713–40) and his son, King *Friedrich der Große* (ruled 1740–86) tried to challenge the dominance of the Netherlands and Great Britain. During this period, the groundwork was being laid for successive generations of German merchants to move to northeast Asia to engage in trade and commerce. The third force was the Danish which, from the fifteenth century until 1864, ruled the Duchies of Schleswig and Holstein separately, and specifically the port of Altona, located next door to Hamburg.

Early German-British Collaborations in China

As the Danes and Prussians sought to break the British monopoly, sustained trade between China and the northern German states grew along with early British-German collaborations. In 1787, 1825 and 1829, Prussia, Hanover and Hamburg respectively appointed British merchants as merchant consuls to service and protect the interests of German ships and merchants who were appearing in China from the mid-1700s. Those British appointed were former employees of the EIC, who without such appointments would have been expelled from China by the EIC to prevent them becoming competition. As Eberstein makes clear, from 1779 until 1840, at least five British merchants running their own trading houses acted as consuls for the Prussian Government.[25] These appointments ended when the Prussian Government realized that the British representatives prioritized developing

24 Bernd Eberstein, *Hamburg China: Geschichte einer Partnerschaft* (Hamburg: Christians), 1988, 25.

25 Bernd Eberstein, *Preußen und China: Eine Geschichte schwieriger Beziehungen* (Berlin: Duncker & Humblot, 2007), 116–18,

their own businesses in cotton and opium over advancing Prussian trade.[26] Once German merchants established their own companies in China, from the 1820s onwards, they were then appointed as consuls.[27] Such evidence points to the earliest collaborations in China between German and British merchants out of mutual necessity, a practice which would continue in Japan until the outbreak of World War One. Such collaborations were also crucial to the development of the German company C. Nickel & Co. at the centre of this book.

Political Turbulence and the Threat of the French

After decades of peace in the Kehdingen, political and historical tides in the wider region offered Johann Christian Holstein new business opportunities prompting him and his family to move to Altona in 1795. Aaslestad argues in part, that from 1792–1806, the French Wars and resulting French conquests around Europe benefited the north German coastal economies. With the French takeover of Amsterdam from 1795, there was a flight of capital and merchants to the neutral Hanseatic ports such as Hamburg. Although the Hanseatic League had ended, nine German towns including Hamburg, Bremen and Lübeck retain references to their Hanseatic past to this day. Hamburg for example, is also known as the Free and Hanseatic City of Hamburg. As the Anglo-Hanoverian alliance with the Austrians, Prussians and the Dutch Republic had failed to defeat the French, the French now controlled the Netherlands. Amsterdam had been the leading port in Europe, but under French control and with the bankruptcy of the VOC in 1798 British goods had to be diverted to Hamburg. Hamburg was now the "emporium" of goods and financial centre of Europe.[28]

Napoleon's Advance Brings Opportunities and Threats

At the age of sixty-seven, Johann Christian Holstein left Drochtersen with a second family and established himself in Altona.[29] After the death of his

26 Eberstein, *Preußen und China*, 116–18.

27 Eberstein, "Kaufleute, Konsuln, Kapitäne," 11–12; Fukuoka, "German Merchants in the Indian Ocean World," 268. Fukuoka also provides more details of Anglo-German collaborations, 268.

28 Aaslestad, "Paying for War," 646.

29 Holstein Family *Ahnenpaß*; Letter Otto Holstein, 22 September 1940.

first wife, he remarried in 1792 to a considerably younger woman, Ahlheit Brandt. Ahlheit was the daughter of the pastor of Drochtersen, and by 1795 had borne Johann Christian two sons, Johann Christian (II) and Johann Hinrich.[30] Under Danish rule, Altona had become a centre of Danish shipping and trade and benefited from being next door to Hamburg. From 1792–99, ships were being sent from Canton, Calcutta, Madras, Manila, Bombay and Batavia direct to Hamburg with it becoming an important transshipment port for Asian products. Britain now replaced France as a major supplier of goods, in particular sugar and coffee.[31] Moving to Altona offered Johann Christian unprecedented business opportunities.[32]

Johann Christian's taking advantage of new opportunities was understood in the family collective memory to be evidence of a family trait of merchant nimbleness to which local historian Gerd Bahr also referred regularly in his histories of the region. There is archival evidence that Johann Christian arrived in Altona with financial means: his registration as a *Bürger* or officially designated citizen in 1797, was a process reserved for those with wealth and property.[33] Johann Christian became the proprietor of an inn called the Dornbusch Keller, servicing the seafaring trade on the Groβe Elbstraße on the docks of Altona.[34] In the 1811 Address Book for Altona, he is listed as an innkeeper and handler of green produce, suggesting he still owned a lighter and transported produce.[35] In 1797 in Altona, he and his wife had a daughter and then in 1804, a third son, Johann Peter Claus Hermann Holstein, grandfather to Christian Holstein.[36]

Until 1806, France accepted Hamburg's neutrality as a trading port when again the political tides turned, this time against Hamburg.[37] In 1799 General Napoleon Bonaparte rose to political prominence as First Consul of France and then in 1804 became Emperor of France. In 1806 the

30 Marriage Registration: Johann Christian Holstein 17 August 1792. Sig.: Rep. 84 Nr. 98 Bl. 198 V. Film Number: 1189000, Niedersächsisches Landesarchiv, Stade, 360.

31 Aaslestad, "Paying for War," 646–47; Silvia Marzagalli, "Port Cities in the French Wars: The Responses of Merchants in Bordeaux, Hamburg and Livorno to Napoleon's Continental Blockade, 1806–1813," *The Northern Mariner*/Le Marin du Nord V1, no. 4 (October 1996): 66–67.

32 Marzagalli, "Port Cities in the French Wars," 66–67.

33 The status of *Bürger* was conferred upon eligible men along with the right to vote and to own land. *Bürger* records are held in the Staatsarchiv *Hamburg*; Holstein *Ahnenpaβ*.

34 Letter Otto Holstein, 22 September 1940.

35 Places of residence have been traced through births, death and marriage registrations and the Hamburg Address Book accessed through the Staatsarchiv Hamburg at http://agora.sub.uni-hamburg.de/subhh-adress/digbib/view?did=c1:39310&sdid=c1:39349&hit=2 Updated 2021.

36 Holstein *Ahnenpaβ*.

37 Aaslestad, "Paying for War," 647.

Prussian loss against Napoleon at the Battle of Jena led to the peaceful surrender of Hamburg and to its occupation by French forces.[38] To safeguard their businesses, Hamburg merchants for the most part cooperated with the French but became increasingly marginalized.[39] As Aaslestad argues, while Napoleon is credited with introducing legal reforms throughout his Empire, his occupation of Hamburg and the northern German coast between 1806 and 1814 devastated its economy. Having failed to defeat the British militarily, Napoleon occupied Hamburg to wage economic warfare against Britain. In 1806 he imposed the Continental Blockade to prevent British ships from arriving in Hamburg and in 1807, he banned British goods altogether forcing Hamburg into bankruptcy.[40] Napoleon damaged economic infrastructure, subjected the population to economic hardship, heavy taxation, and conscription, not to mention requiring local people to billet, feed and support his military forces. The population was also expected to support other forces such as the Cossacks or Prussians arriving to fight Napoleon.[41] In 1806, Napoleon's imposition of the Continental Blockade and quest to defeat the British economically was at the expense of northern Germany, and Hamburg, a process which affected Johann Christian Holstein as we will see.[42]

In the meantime, over the next four years the rapidly changing times provided Johann Christian with another advantageous business opportunity. As Napoleon sought to restrict the entry of goods from Britain and its colonies, the merchants and shippers of Altona and Hamburg responded by smuggling British goods. British goods were diverted to the then Danish ports of Tönning on the Atlantic or North Sea coast and Glückstadt on the Elbe River. Goods were then conveyed to Hamburg through a network of marshy channels, mudflats, river deltas, coastal islands and sand dunes, which were difficult for the French authorities to monitor.[43] Furthermore, as Marzagalli demonstrates, the laxity in French customs and other controls combined with the inadequate numbers of officials and their susceptibility to corruption, allowed smuggling to flourish.[44] With the close proximity of Altona to Hamburg, it was easy for thousands of individuals to transport

38 Aaslestad, "Paying for War," 649.
39 Aaslestad, "Paying for War," 644.
40 Aaslestad, "Paying for War," 649–50.
41 Aaslestad, "Paying for War," 641, 642, 644–45, 649.
42 Aaslestad, "Paying for War," 646.
43 Aaslestad, "Paying for War," 650–51.
44 Marzagalli, "Port Cities in the French Wars," 68–69.

goods in small quantities crossing the customs line daily.[45] Correspondence from Christian Holstein's brother Otto written in 1940 repeats stories told by their uncle, Johann Heinrich Christian, about how Johann Christian had engaged in smuggling using his lighter.[46] As Johann Christian continued to use his lighter throughout this period, with his access to business connections and flows of information through his inn, one can imagine him becoming willingly involved in the carrying of a load of "contraband" goods hidden below a cover of green produce, with his knowledge of the waterways allowing him to circumvent lax French customs controls.

At the end of 1810, Napoleon imposed stricter enforcement of French legislation to end bribery and corruption diverting trade flows yet again and impacting the lives of the citizens of Hamburg and Altona and that of Johann Christian. Economic warfare destroyed Hamburg's commerce, ruined livelihoods, and forced many into poverty.[47] In 1810, Johann Christian's wife, Ahlheit, died an untimely death, and with the loss of his business he returned to Drochtersen in 1811 at the age of eighty-three to live with his daughter from his first marriage in a house he had placed in her name. He died later that year. Johann Christian's death registration described him as *Inshausling*, an old German word indicating he was homeless and bankrupt, potentially having succumbed to the effects of Napoleon's Continental Blockade.[48] Before returning to Drochtersen, Johann Christian left his youngest son, Johann Peter Claus Hermann, aged seven, behind in Altona in the care of a family called Hinsch.[49]

While Johann Christian was described as *Inshausling*, according to Otto Holstein's letter to his brother Christian, their uncle, Johann Heinrich Christian, brother of their father, Carl Hermann, had passed on a family secret suggesting that a substantial inheritance lay in the Netherlands. Otto recounted a story heard from their uncle that one of the two older sons of Johann Christian had been involved in a fight over a ship and, under threat of death, had been forced to flee to the Netherlands where he allegedly availed himself of this so-called wealth.[50] While this detail is unverifiable, I found evidence of the two older sons pointing to a different scenario of potential relevance to younger generations of the Holstein family: Johann Christian

45 Marzagalli, "Port Cities in the French Wars," 69; Aaslestad, "Paying for War," 651.

46 Letter Otto Holstein, 22 September 1940.

47 Aaslestad "Paying for War," 654.

48 Death Registration: Johann Christian Holstein 6 February 1811 Sig.: Rep.84 Nr. 99 Bl. 101 V, *Niedersächsisches Landesarchiv*, Stade; Holstein *Ahnenpaß*; Letter Otto Holstein, 22 September 1940.

49 Letter Otto Holstein, 22 September 1940.

50 Letter Otto Holstein, 22 September 1940.

(II) and his brother Johann Hinrich Holstein, both recorded as being born in Drochtersen as sons of Johann Christian and citizens of Hanover and having married in their early twenties in 1819 and 1817 respectively. They were also recorded in the British Immigration records as having arrived in London in 1836 and 1846 respectively.[51] Johann Hinrich is furthermore recorded in London as a sugar baker, having joined many of his compatriots in migrating to England to take advantage of jobs and higher wages being offered by the booming British cane sugar refining industry.[52] While this could suggest that neither brother had accessed a lost Holstein fortune, this also suggests the existence of family connections in England for successive Holstein generations of shippers in Germany, and possibly the origins of the Holstein family crest.

From archival records, published histories and collective oral and written memories, we have a sense of the lives of the earlier generations of the Holstein family and their engagement in shipping and commerce in Hamburg and its surrounds, leading up to Carl Nickel and Christian Holstein's respective moves to Japan. The family used these stories not just to affirm their identity as German nationals, but also to show the attributes of entrepreneurship and resilience the family believed equipped them for succeeding in Japan in the face of the adversities that beset them.

Early Lives of the Two Protagonists

Christian Holstein, who spent nearly sixty years in Japan, was thus born into a family with a history of entrepreneurship in shipping and cargo handling. The Births and Marriages Registry at the *Staatsarchiv Hamburg* reveal that Johann Christian's youngest son, Johann Peter Claus Hermann, who was brought up in Altona, married and had two sons, Johann Heinrich Christian (born 1826) and Carl Heinrich Hermann (born 1832). Both sons lived much of their lives at Johannisbollwerk, on the docks of Hamburg. The eldest son pursued a career in seafaring and the youngest, Carl Heinrich Hermann, entered the cargo shipping business. Carl Holstein married Maria Margaretha Friederike Meyer in 1855 and had six children, of which the

51 Lists of Aliens arriving at English ports. The National Archives of the UK: Public Record Office FGO 83/21–2.

52 Sugar Refiners & Sugarbakers Database compiled by Bryan Mawer, http://www.mawer.clara.net/sugarbbio.html, 2000; Hörst Rössler, "Sugarbakers, Farmers, Goldminers: From Hanover via London to New Zealand," *Transnational Networks: German Migrants in the British Empire, 1670–1914*, eds. John R. Davis, Stefan Manz and Margrit Schulte Beerbühl (Leiden–Boston: Brill, 2012), 101–2.

youngest was Christian Holstein (born 1875). It was Christian who took his knowledge of lightering to Japan to work for his older relative, Carl Nickel. Maria Meyer also came from a family with ties to shipping, and she and her husband lived near members of her family, in Johannisbollwerk, on the Hamburg Docks. The *Staatsarchiv Hamburg* also tells us that both Johann Heinrich Christian and Carl Heinrich Hermann had financial means and were granted *Bürger* status in 1850 and 1854 respectively. While there are no records that provide other details of the families' lives, it is understood within the family that Carl Heinrich Hermann was making a comfortable living from shipping as an owner of a lighter business at the time of his death in 1882 in Johannisbollwerk.

The first protagonist of this book, Carl Theodore Matthias Nickel, was born the second of six children on the fringes of Hamburg in 1836, four years after his cousin-by-marriage, Carl Heinrich Hermann Holstein, father of Christian Holstein. Carl Nickel was born in Billwärder Neuer Deich (today Billwerder) in the parish of Moorfleet, located east of Hamburg on the Elbe Islands in the Elbe River. It was a part of the extended Hamburg Port, within a ten-kilometre walking distance of Christian Holstein's family at Johannisbollwerk. Very little is known of Nickel's earlier life and that of his forebears, or of the influences that shaped his character and impacted his life choices. The Billwärder, like the Kehdingen region, had also been devastated by successive wars, and "plundered" by Napoleon in his occupation of northern Germany. Nickel was at least the second generation of his family to be born in Billwärder—his father, an *Arbeitsmann* (labourer), had been born there about 1812, so presumably his grandparents at least on the Nickel side had lived there through Napoleon's occupation. As a labourer, his father may have been an agricultural worker but could also have worked on the docks as a stevedore. There was an understanding within the family that the relationship between Carl Nickel and the Holstein family had been close. He was a first cousin to Maria Holstein, Christian Holstein's mother and was appointed godfather to Christian, her youngest son. Within the family he was referred to as *Onkel* Nickel.

Referred to in later years as Captain Nickel, it is possible he left Hamburg and went to sea and by the time he arrived in Shanghai had become a ship's captain. Records show he sailed a few times between Shanghai and Nagasaki in Japan, and he may well have worked for a foreign shipping company, either British or American.[53]

53 Johannes Bähr, Jörg Lesczenski, and Katja Schmidtpott, *Handel ist Wandel: 150 Jahre C. Illies & Co.* (München: Piper Verlag GMBH, 2009), 20. By 1862, Hamburg had the third largest shipping

In 1882, Carl Heinrich Hermann died at the age of fifty, leaving his youngest son Christian fatherless at the age of seven. According to collective family memories, Carl Nickel, was appointed not only as Christian's godfather but also as his mentor. At the time of Carl Holstein's death, Nickel had been in Japan for twenty-two years. He had arrived in Japan in 1860 and had settled in Kobe in 1879 where he founded a successful stevedoring, landing and freight forwarding company. As Nickel did not have any living sons in 1897, at the age of twenty-two, Christian Holstein was sent to Japan to join him and become his successor.

This chapter has shown how the Holstein and the Nickel families operated over successive generations adapting to an ever-changing environment and how the accumulated experience passed down the generations in the form of family memories prepared Nickel and Holstein for the challenges they faced in Japan. The collective memories of the waves of foreign occupations and turbulence of the north German region most likely prepared Nickel and Holstein for the civil unrest and subsequent frictions between the Japanese authorities and the foreign community they encountered in Japan. An understanding of the Port of Hamburg, the state of Prussia and the respective interconnections with Great Britain leading to British-German collaborations in Japan is important in establishing the origins of such collaborations that would both benefit Carl Nickel and Christian Holstein and then have adverse consequences for Holstein in later years.

fleet operating in China after the British and the American fleets.

Part II

Unequal Treaties & Extraterritoriality

2. Nagasaki: Civil Unrest and Consular Jurisdiction

Abstract: Carl Nickel arrived in Nagasaki in 1860 from Shanghai illegally claiming to have American protection. Germany was not yet a unified nation, and the Prussia-Japan Treaty providing Nickel legal status was only enacted in 1863. Unhappy with having the unequal treaties forced upon it, the Japanese government found ways to control and obstruct foreign business either by design or through lack of experience in dealing with foreign merchants. British and Prussian diplomats regarded their compatriot merchants somewhat disdainfully. Nickel relied on his own devices managing loopholes often subverting those obstructions. He built his business working with his American colleagues negotiating a treaty port where the British power base lacked the influence over the Japanese government it had in China.

Keywords: treaties, protection, extraterritoriality, obstructive, anti-foreign, Prussia

In 1859, the twenty-three-year-old Carl Nickel arrived in Shanghai and from 1860 commenced exploring business opportunities in Nagasaki. Ten years after the British opened Shanghai in 1849 as a treaty port, it had become a cosmopolitan city attracting merchants not just from Britain and British colonial India but also from around Europe. While most companies were British and Indian, they also included French, American, Dutch and Danish amongst others, and some belonging to German speaking merchants.[1] Pustau & Co., Carlowitz & Co., and Siemssen & Co. significant German trading houses present in Canton (Guangzhou) and Singapore for decades were also in Shanghai alongside smaller German businesses. The British and to a lesser extent, the French exercised an informal imperial rule over Shanghai

1 *The Hongkong Directory: With List of Foreign Residents in China*, 1859, Printed at the "Armenian Press," Hong Kong, 1859, https://archive.org/details/hongkongdirectooounkngoog/page/n8/mode/2up, 2024, 8–9.

Holstein, Prue S. *The German Experience of Japan's Treaty Port System: A Case Study of C. Nickel & Co. Ltd., 1860–1923*. Taylor & Francis Group, 2025.
DOI: 10.4324/9781003706274-3

managing the International and the French concessions respectively where a mix of nationals resided. In Shanghai, prior to the unification of Germany, a German merchant acted as consular agent for Prussia and two English merchants acted as consul and vice-consul for Hamburg and Bremen.[2] In 1858, a year before Nickel arrived in Shanghai, the Sino-British treaty of Tianjin was signed permitting foreign ships to participate in coastal trading in China.[3]

Nagasaki on the other hand, had only just been opened as a treaty port in 1858 when the unequal treaties were forced upon Japan by the foreign powers. While Nagasaki was viewed as an opportunity to expand trade to Japan, it was also seen as a "wild frontier." It had been opened in a time when anti-foreigner sentiment amongst Japanese towards foreign merchants was strong with threats to foreigners' safety. Britain's first diplomat to Japan, Sir Rutherford Alcock, recorded these times in his reports to the British Parliament.[4] From 1858–64 Alcock served first as Consul and then as Her Majesty's Envoy Extraordinary and Minister Plenipotentiary to Japan.[5] He had already served in several treaty ports in China—Amoy, Fuzhou, and Shanghai from 1846 to 1855 where Britain acted informally as an imperial power developing a cooperative relationship with the Chinese authorities that benefited its merchant classes. As Nickel had experienced British influence in Shanghai as an informal power, it is reasonable to assume that he, as a German merchant, aligned himself with his Anglophone counterparts hoping to benefit from a relationship between Britain and Japan similar to that in China. Unlike many of his German compatriots, he had not aligned himself with the Dutch; he was known as an "anglicized" German.[6]

2 Fukuoka Mariko, "German Merchants in the Indian Ocean World: From Early Modern Paralysis to Modern Animation," in *Early Global Interconnectivity Across the Indian Ocean World, Volume 1*, ed. Angela Schottenhammer (Cham, Switzerland: Palgrave, 2019), 259–92.

3 Bert Becker, *France and Germany in the South China Sea, c. 1840–1930: Maritime Competition and Imperial Power*. Cambridge Imperial and Post-Colonial Studies (Cambridge: Palgrave Macmillan, 2021), 62.

4 Japan. Correspondence with H. M. Envoy and Minister Plenipotentiary in Japan, 1858–68. 19th Century House of Commons Sessional Papers. https://parlipapers-proquest-com.rp.nla.gov.au/parlipapers/docview/t70.d75.1860–036818?accountid=12694 (hereafter Japan; Correspondence with H. M. Envoy and Minister Plenipotentiary in Japan, 1858–68).

5 Sir Rutherford Alcock, *Capital of the Tycoon: A Narrative of a Three Year's Residence in Japan Vols. I & II.* (London: Longman, Roberts & Green, 1863); Japan; Correspondence with H. M. Envoy and Minister Plenipotentiary in Japan, 1858–68; Sano Mayuko, "Disturbed Reciprocity: Rutherford Alcock's Diplomacy and Merchant Communities in China and Japan," in *Chronicling Westerners in Nineteenth-Century East Asia*, eds. Robert S. G. Fletcher and Robert Hellyer (London: Bloomsbury Publishing, 2022), 21–42.

6 Kurt Meissner, *Deutsche in Japan, 1639–1960* (Tokyo: Deutsche Gesellschaft für Natur-und Völkerkunde Ostasiens, 1961), https://oag.jp/img/1961/01/oag-mitteilung-sup-Bd-26-deutsche-in-japan-komplett-1639-1960.pdf, 18

Only a few records remain suggesting how Nickel came to be in Nagasaki. In the 1890s he was referred to as Captain Nickel, suggesting he may have captained a merchant ship, perhaps when coastal trading in China was opened to foreign shipping.[7] His grandfather, Friedrich Braun, had also been a ship's captain. As a ship's captain, Nickel would have moved regularly between Shanghai and Nagasaki dealing with trading houses and merchants seeking to consign cargoes with him, building the connections for his future ships chandlery, butchery and trading business in Nagasaki. The opening up of coastal trading in China to foreign shipping may have been what attracted Nickel to Shanghai.

Third party accounts in treaty port newspapers, German and British historical accounts, and Japanese records provide insights into the period 1860 to 1875, which straddled the last decade of the Edo Era (Tokugawa Period (1603–1868)), a period of civil strife and anti-foreign sentiment, and the first seven years of the Meiji Era (1868–1911) when relative peace was established. The Meiji Era commenced in 1868 following a political revolution of the elite, which set in train the modernization and industrialization of Japan. Business was precarious for foreign merchants in such a dynamic environment and especially for German merchants with ad-hoc consular arrangements, who were non-treaty residents until the Prussia-Japan Treaty was ratified in 1863. Throughout this period, Nickel managed his presence in Nagasaki working with his British and American counterparts learning to exploit the limits of the Japanese authorities' ability to control foreign merchants' activities. Before examining Nickel's trajectory, it is important to understand that the 1850s was not the first time Japan encountered Germans. To provide context for Nickel's arrival in Nagasaki, some earlier and little-known engagements between Germans and Japanese are described that already contributed to what would become a growing respect the Japanese would have for German merchants and technology.

Japan's Closure to the West and Its Early Exposure to German-Speakers

Despite Japan being closed to the West for 250 years, the Japanese authorities became exposed to German technology and know-how throughout this period. In 1634, the Shogun Tokugawa Ieyasu closed Japan (a period known

7 "The Late Mr. Charles Sutton: A Will Case at Yokohama," *Kobe Chronicle*, 30 May 1900, 460. Carl Nickel is referred to as Captain Nickel.

as *Sakoku* 1634–1854), expelling the Spanish and Portuguese who had been trading and proselytizing in Japan for over a hundred years. In the minds of the Tokugawa Shogun and his *Bakufu* or military government, the acceptance of Christianity amongst the peasant classes and the promise of an after-life threatened the Shogun's grip on power. Only Dutch traders were permitted to remain in Nagasaki, confined under Japanese guard to a small trading enclave on Deshima Island if they did not smuggle or proselytize.[8] Deshima was initially run by the Dutch East India Company, *Vereenigde Oostindische Compagnie* (VOC), until its bankruptcy in 1798, and then by the Dutch government, and had a close trading relationship with Batavia (Indonesia) then a Dutch colony. Deshima became Japan's "window" to the West through which it gained exposure to Western peoples, goods, ideas, and technological developments. Despite other Europeans being banned from entering Japan (Korean and Chinese traders were permitted), the VOC illicitly employed other nationalities including Germans. German medical professionals, naturalists, seamen and mercenaries, plus an array of "barbers and teeth pullers," masqueraded as Dutch to the Japanese authorities.[9] Two German physicians were engaged to look after elite Japanese families, Engelbert Kaempfer (in Japan from 1683 to 1693) and Philipp Franz von Siebold (in Japan from 1823 to 1829). This exposure marked the beginnings of German influence in Japan in the fields of medicine, natural sciences, pharmacology, and military armaments.[10] Early exposure of Germans to Japan also allowed for the emergence of so-called "Japan experts" in Germany who helped inform Germans' growing awareness of Japan's potential as a trading partner as Japan reopened.[11]

The Re-Opening of Japan, the Unequal Treaties, and the Prussia-Japan Treaty

Japan reengaged with the West from 1853, when the American government sent Commodore Matthew Perry to force the Japanese government to end its seclusion. By the 1850s, the annexation of California, the rise of Shanghai as a trading centre and the transcontinental railway in the United States made

8 James E. Hoare, *Japan's Treaty Ports and Foreign Settlements: The Uninvited Guests 1858–1899* (Kent: Japan Library, Curzon Press Ltd. 1994), 53.

9 Meissner, *Deutsche in Japan*, 1–2.

10 Meissner, *Deutsche in Japan*, 5–8.

11 Holmer Stahncke, *Die diplomatischen Beziehungen zwischen Deutschland und Japan, 1854–1868* (Wiesbaden: Franz Steiner Verlag, 1987), 63.

the China market more attractive to the United States of America (USA). In 1854 Commodore Perry negotiated the Treaty of Kanagawa to secure access for American whaling fleets and American vessels to refuel on their way to China. Although Townsend Harris, the first American Consul, is credited with signing the first of the unequal treaties with Japan followed by the Netherlands, Russia, Great Britain and France in that order, it was the British who introduced and refined the concept of extraterritorial protections (already in use in China) outside of Japanese jurisdiction.[12] As Germany did not yet exist, German merchants only became treaty nationals when the Kingdom of Prussia negotiated the Prussia Japan Treaty of Amity, Commerce and Shipping in 1861, and it was ratified in 1863 allowing Germans to reside under Prussian protection.[13]

As happened in China, the unequal treaties were negotiated to the benefit of foreign merchants and were forced upon the Japanese authorities using gunboat diplomacy.[14] The foreign powers believed that "the Japanese were 'Orientals' and what little was known of their legal system indicated that it was as savage as that of China."[15] The treaties bound the Japanese government to opening five treaty ports. The ports of Kanagawa (subsequently moved to Yokohama), Nagasaki, and Hakodate were opened initially. The Tokugawa government promised that Hyogo (Kobe) and Osaka would be opened in 1863, but this was delayed by political turmoil until 1868.[16] Once opened, the Japanese government prepared land for foreign settlements to be governed by "their own [consular] authorities."[17] Unlike in China, in Japan foreigners were restricted to a twenty-five-mile radius of the treaty port, were banned from entering the interior without permission and were not permitted to own land. To ensure the Japanese government's adherence to the treaties and to protect the foreign community from anti-foreign actors, the British and the Americans maintained a naval presence in the treaty ports.[18]

12 Ferry de Goey, "Western Entrepreneurs and the Opening of Japanese Ports," in *Culture Power and Politics in Treaty-Port Japan, 1854–1899: Key Papers, Press and Contemporary Writings Volume 1*, ed. James E. Hoare (Kent: Renaissance Books, 2018), 154; Hoare, *Japan's Treaty Ports and Foreign Settlements*, 56.

13 Sven Saaler, "150 Jahre japanisch-deutsche Beziehungen," in *Unter den Augen ders Preußen-Adlers: Lithographien, Zeichnungen und Photographien der Teilnehmer der Eulenberg-Expediction in Japan, 1860–61*, eds. Sebastian Dobson and Sven Saaler (Munich: Iudicium, 2011), 38.

14 Hoare, *Japan's Treaty Ports and Foreign Settlements*, 54–55.

15 William Gerald Beasley, *Great Britain, and the Opening of Japan* (London: Luzac, 1951), 201–2; See also Hoare, *Japan's Treaty Ports and Foreign Settlements*, 54.

16 Hoare, *Japan's Treaty Ports and Foreign Settlements*, 6.

17 Hoare, *Japan's Treaty Ports and Foreign Settlements*, 52.

18 Hoare, *Japan's Treaty Ports and Foreign Settlements*, 15.

Although Commodore Perry's mission to re-open Japan was an American initiative, Germans were also unofficially involved, further confirming their long-term presence in the region. Attached to Perry's flotilla was the German ship *Greta*, chartered by a German company, Pustau & Co., based in the then Canton, Singapore and later Shanghai to supply coal to Perry's expedition.[19] On board was supercargo Friedrich August Lühdorf, who brought with him a range of goods, firearms, clocks, glassware, textiles, and sugar to sell to the Japanese. Lühdorf became the first recorded German to pave the way for German mercantile undertakings in Japan, albeit as a member of an American expedition.[20]

Perry's actions ultimately lead to the development of official diplomatic relations between Japan and Prussia, albeit some years after Nickel and his German merchant colleagues had become well established in Japan. Perry's actions were widely reported in the newspapers in Berlin, the base of the Prussian government and in the independent city-state of Hamburg, home to shipbuilding and trading houses already established in Asia. In 1854, the Prussian consul in San Francisco, Kirchhoff, sent a copy of Perry's Treaty of Kanagawa to Berlin, where it was deemed to be a treaty of friendship rather than a trade treaty.[21] Perry's treaty was three weeks old when Reinhard Ritterhaus, a German merchant in Singapore, joined several German merchants petitioning the Prussian ministry to conclude a commercial treaty with Japan.[22]

Based on their knowledge of Japan, two Germans cautioned the Prussian government on how to approach negotiating a trade treaty with Japan in a way that is important to understand how the German merchants subsequently conducted business in Japan. The German "Japan hand," Philip Franz von Siebold, had worked for the VOC on Deshima as a medical professional and had been expelled by the Japanese government in 1829 for possessing a map of Japan. In engaging with Japan, von Siebold advocated for understanding the differences in state structures and political processes and "the Japanese politics of negotiation." He advised that the British and French acted in Japan as they did in their own colonies

19 Bernd Eberstein, "Kaufleute, Konsuln, Kapitäne: Frühe deutsche Wirtschaftsinteressen in China," Catalogue for an exhibition held on Tsingtau at the German Historical Museum, 1998, 10, http://www.dhm.de/archiv/ausstellungen/tsingtau/katalog/auf1_1.htm, accessed 2021.

20 Stahncke, *Die diplomatischen Beziehungen*," 70; Holmer Stahncke, *Friedrich August Lühdorfs Handelsexpedition nach Japan*, Deutsche Gesellschaft für Natur- und Völkerkunde Ostasiens, no. 39 (Tokyo: OAG aktuell, 1988); Meissner, *Deutsche in Japan*, 10.

21 Stahncke, *Die diplomatischen Beziehungen*, 57.

22 Stahncke, *Die diplomatischen Beziehungen*, 56.

of India and Indochina respectively, negotiating out of self-interest, in what he termed a "series of capture and conquest politics." In his view, the "Americans had no influence" no doubt due to the Civil War (1861–65). He considered the Russians and the Dutch were positive models in the way they adapted to Japanese market needs.[23] A later German "Asia hand," Richard Carlowitz, the first German to be appointed Consul for Prussia 1847–69 in Canton, believed that merchants should understand what trade meant for the Japanese. He considered that apart from wine and spirits, the Japanese had little need for European goods. His company Carlowitz & Co. became a significant German trading house in China and Japan. These insights can be seen as early indications of German merchants' willingness to identify and accommodate Japanese market needs which was, as later noted by a British diplomat, a practice superior to British business practices. British merchants expected to sell what they already manufactured.[24]

In 1860 the Prussian government sent the Eulenberg Mission under the leadership of Count Friedrich Albrecht zu Eulenberg to conclude trade treaties with Japan, China, and Siam (Thailand). Lacking a navy and a merchant fleet, and with no overseas colonies, Prussia had been slow to act having minimal interest in trade.[25] However, the government had become concerned Japan might be divided among the European powers and, by initiating such a trade treaty acting on its own behalf and that of a range of German city-states and principalities, saw a chance to take the lead in the eventual unification of Germany in 1871.[26] The Mission arrived in Japan in 1861, visiting Nagasaki and Yokohama, and concluded the Prussia-Japan Treaty that year. During negotiations, Eulenberg requested the inclusion of Hamburg, and its shipping fleets, in the treaty. Prussian and Danish ships (Denmark occupied the Port of Altona next-door to Hamburg) had been trading in Canton since the 1830s, if not earlier, and by 1862, Hamburg had the third largest fleet of merchant ships in China after Great Britain and the United States. Eulenberg also requested the inclusion of thirty other German principalities and states. Overwhelmed, the Japanese authorities denied the Prussian request, eliminating Hamburg and the rest of what is

23 Stahncke, *Die diplomatischen Beziehungen*, 63. (My translation).

24 Bernd Eberstein, *Preußen und China: Eine Geschichte schwieriger Beziehungen* (Berlin: Duncker & Humblot, 2007), 121; Stahncke, *Die diplomatischen Beziehungen*, 56–57.

25 Stahncke, *Die diplomatischen Beziehungen*, 56, 60.

26 Johannes Bähr, Jörg Lesczenski, and Katja Schmidtpott, *Handel ist Wandel: 150 Jahre C. Illies & Co.* (München: Piper Verlag GMBH, 2009), 20.

now Germany for the time being.[27] The treaty was ratified in 1863. From that moment, merchants like Nickel could reside in Nagasaki under extraterritorial protection as Prussian subjects. The treaty was then upgraded in 1869 with the formation of the Northern German Confederation, including Hamburg, and was further upgraded upon the unification of Germany in 1871.[28]

Nagasaki: A Wild Frontier

The Nagasaki that Nickel contended with in 1860, with its social tensions and dangers for all pioneer foreign merchants, could be described as a wild frontier. In this context a "wild frontier" is defined as "geographic zones of interaction between two or more cultures ... [and] places where cultures contend with one another and with their physical environment to produce a dynamic that is unique to time and place."[29] Nagasaki represented a wild frontier for two reasons. First, foreign merchants arrived as civil war was brewing. They faced daily threats to life and property from *samurai* (the Japanese warrior class) wanting to overthrow the Tokugawa military government, restore the emperor to power and throw foreigners out of Japan. The two main *samurai* clans behind this movement, the Satsuma and Chōshū clans, were based near Nagasaki. With their cry "*Sonnō jōi,*" "revere the emperor, throw out the foreigners," their presence was a threat to the foreign community: foreigners could be killed or maimed at the slightest provocation. While there were many such incidents reported in British official correspondence, the one best illustrating this was the Namamugi Incident. On 14 September 1862 in Yokohama, Charles Lennox Richardson, a merchant from Shanghai, was out riding with friends when they encountered the retinue of the regent of the *Daimyo* (lord) of the Satsuma clan on the Tōkaidō Highway. The foreign party failed to show respect, and Richardson was cut down by a Satsuma *samurai* and died shortly after.[30] From 1859, the British Consul in Nagasaki, George Morrison,

27 [Albert Berg], *Die Preußische Expedition Nach Ost-Asien. Erster Band* (Berlin: Verlag der Königlichen Geheimen Oberhofbuchdruckerei, 1864), http://www.deutschestextarchiv.de/book/show/berg_ostasien01, 1860, 340.

28 Saaler, "150 Jahre japanisch-deutsche Beziehungen," 38.

29 E. Taylor Atkins, "Jammin' on the Jazz Frontier: The Japanese Jazz Community in Interwar Shanghai," *Japanese Studies* 19, no. 1 (1999): 5–16. https://doi.org/10.1080/10371399908727663, 6.

30 Despatches of HBM Consulate Nagasaki to Sir Rutherford Alcock, British Consul-General, Japan, June 1859–December 1863, Harold Williams Collection, National Library of Australia

born in Macau, China the son of a British missionary, reported that in the wake of the incident, the foreign settlement in Nagasaki, twelve hundred kilometres from Yokohama, was on high alert. As Consul, he had placed a British naval vessel in readiness for evacuating foreigners should tensions escalate.[31] This sense of unease continued until the end of the Shimonoseki Campaign in September 1864, another prolonged conflict between the Chōshū clan and the British Navy, involving Nickel, which will be discussed shortly.[32]

Second, Nagasaki felt like a wild frontier because the Japanese authorities were ill-equipped for managing relations with foreign merchants under the treaties. As Consul, Morrison spent his time trying to resolve conflicts and ensure the Japanese authorities' adherence to the letter of the unequal treaties. The tone of his correspondence reflected his frustration with the Japanese authorities' ignoring the foreign community's demands. One case involved the Consul's request of the Japanese Customs for trade statistics. Unlike in China where the Imperial Maritime Customs Service (IMCS) willingly provided such information, Morrison reported the Japanese response as being "excuses and delays."[33] A second case involved his protesting the Japanese authorities' punishing Japanese merchants who had dealt with foreigners, another practice considered obstructionist. Morrison reported that even where such a case was "indisputable," "the invariable excuse was that the sufferer has been punished for breach of some … petty offense."[34] While this may have been true in part, the British and other foreign consular representatives failed to appreciate the local Japanese government's lack of experience dealing with foreign merchants under conditions forced upon them. Moreover, the authorities often had to defer to the Tokugawa Administration in Edo (Tokyo), the *Bakufu* for decision-making. As messengers travelled on foot between Nagasaki and Edo, it could take weeks to seek the *Bakufu*'s determinations.

Nagasaki's location far from Edo, the Tokugawa government's seat of power, worked both to the advantage and disadvantage of the foreign community. On one hand, when foreign consuls requested the protection of the

(henceforth HSW NLA), Call Number: 1083.

31 Despatches No. 5, 14 April 1863, January–July 1863, HSW NLA, 144–45.

32 Despatches No. 5, 14 April 1863, January–July 1863, HSW NLA, 144–45.

33 Despatches No. 13, 27 February 1861, January-June 1861, 87; Jürgen Osterhammel, "Britain and China 1842–1914," in *The Oxford History of the British Empire, Volume III: The Nineteenth Century*, eds. Andrew Porter and William Roger Louis (Oxford: Oxford University Press, 1999), 156–57.

34 Despatches No. 19, 2 March, 1861, January-June 1861, 89.

Japanese Governor of Nagasaki from rogue samurai or advocated for their rights to a fairer trading environment, the Governor had to wait for the *Bakufu*'s decisions, allowing foreigners to take matters into their own hands. On the other hand, as the Chōshū and Satsuma clans opposed the *Bakufu* the latter could not control the threat posed by these clans to foreign interests. In his reports to the British Legation in Yokohama, Morrison acknowledged the British residents in Nagasaki should "take steps to safeguard commercial interests" by arming themselves, while also urging them to remember "the importance of avoiding anything in language or action to excite the ill-will of the people;" he also advised that the British Naval Commander in Chief "would provide for general security and defense."[35]

Between 1859 and 1863, treaty ports shifted from a pioneer to a more cosmopolitan lifestyle as suggested though Kurt Meissner's descriptions of German merchants. Of those pioneer Germans arriving in Japan, Meissner differentiated between two groups. On the one hand, he referred to some "wild Germans" arriving in Japan from the US (presumably straight from the Californian "wild west"), describing them evocatively as "trailblazers" wearing "seaboots," "flannel shirts" and "heavy jackets carrying revolvers," surrounding their properties "with palisades" against attack from disaffected Japanese samurai. On the other hand, he describes German merchants arriving from China or Batavia as honourable businessmen who could afford the cost of a ship's passage, which he stated was not inexpensive.[36] These two opposing images suggested class distinctions were visible amongst German merchants working for trading houses and those engaged in the labour-intensive businesses of butcheries, blacksmithing and cargo handling. By 1863 life in the treaty ports had visibly changed: in Yokohama, for example, Meissner described the "palatial" buildings that had been constructed alongside "an attractive quai where people could promenade," and where elegantly dressed gentlemen would "shudder at the sight of an early settler still wearing a flannel shirt."[37] One wonders whether Nickel, as one such trailblazer, initially wore the garb of the pioneer settler in Nagasaki, and then adapted his wardrobe to the more cosmopolitan life of the treaty port in Shanghai on one of his frequent visits.

A certain lawlessness existed in the 1860s amongst Germans (and possibly other foreign merchants) who were predominantly young single men, which was tolerated by Japanese officials. Meissner described German merchants

35 Despatches No. 5, 14 April 1863, January–July 1863, 144–45.

36 Meissner, *Deutsche in Japan*, 11. (My translation).

37 Meissner, *Deutsche in Japan*, 5. (My translation).

as a sturdy and wild lot, who liked to gallop through the settlement when work was finished and occasionally got up to pranks. He recorded that local Japanese officials, considering those young Germans to be uneducated, laughed at their antics and did their best to avoid incidents.[38] Zielke records that a group of German merchants with the knowledge of their bosses threw the Japanese Customs house (presumably a light wooden structure) into the sea.[39] In later years, Nickel reflected on those wild days, recounting "some lively stories … of the early days when foreigners used to sell arms secretly to the Japanese and English gunboats … of the way business was conducted in the Dutch Settlement … and camphor, wax and bronzes secretly exported."[40]

Instead of being sympathetic to the trials German merchants faced, Prussian officials condemned such wild behaviour. Count Eulenberg wrote disparagingly of the "silly rascals who live in Yokohama with no right to do so" (without the protection of a treaty nation) and of "a young green merchant" from Hamburg, who was "a thorn in his side." The latter had possibly been hopeful of some Prussian government support for protecting German merchant interests in Japan.[41] A colleague of Eulenberg's in Edo called his own countrymen in Japan "scum of the earth."[42] Such comments reflected the classist views of elite diplomats towards merchants, who, being associated with money making, were relegated to the lower echelons of society. Count Eulenberg did not appreciate that in 1860, one year after the treaty ports were opened, merchants saw their environment as one where survival of the fittest reigned, and where courage was required to succeed. Eulenberg's comments also suggest that in concluding a treaty, the aims of the Prussian government had little to do with protecting the rights of German merchants in Japan and more to do with advancing the prestige of the Prussian government as it sought to unite Germany.[43]

Vulnerability of Germans as Non-Treaty Residents

Without Prussian consular protection, German merchants were vulnerable to deportation. In 1860, Eulenberg recorded that Japanese authorities had

38 Meissner, *Deutsche in Japan*, 27–28. (My translation).

39 Erich Zielke, "Konsul Louis Kniffler: Der Pionier des Deutschen Japanhandels," *Journal of Business History* 25, no.1 (1980): 7. https://doi.org/10.1515/zug-1980-0101. (My translation).

40 "Local and General," *Japan Chronicle* (Kobe), 24 May 1906, 629.

41 Meissner, *Deutsche in Japan*, 11. (My translation).

42 Meissner, *Deutsche in Japan*, 11. (My translation).

43 Stahncke, *Die diplomatischen Beziehungen*, 60.

discovered that some British merchants in Yokohama were Germans under British protection, and ordered the British Consul, Sir Rutherford Alcock, to deport all non-treaty citizens.[44] Alcock stopped providing protection for foreign nationals of non-treaty powers, except those employed by British trading firms and ordered British captains to cease conveying them from Shanghai to Nagasaki.[45] As this order coincided with the arrival of the Eulenberg Mission in Yokohama, Count Eulenberg forestalled their deportation as part of the Prussia-Japan Treaty negotiations.[46] The Japanese officials were reluctant to negotiate with their Prussian counterparts, but with the help of the first American Consul, Townsend Harris, and facing Prussian gunboats, they were soon persuaded. As a result, German merchants continued to do business in Yokohama and Nagasaki.[47]

Sir Rutherford Alcock shared his Prussian colleagues' disdain for the merchant classes. In his reports to the Houses of Parliament he noted that foreign merchants were "profiting by the present moment to the utmost; regardless of Treaties or future consequences ... in defiance of Japanese laws and edicts."[48] He also noted that "indiscreet conduct [of some] foreign residents" resulted in regular "dispute and irritation between Japanese officials of all grades and the foreign traders."[49] Alcock recorded his appreciation for the patience of Japanese officials, and wondered at the "rarity of such retaliative acts of violence," adding that it was "a striking testimony in their favour."[50] However, he did attribute some of the foreigners' bad behaviour to Japanese officials' decisions to restrict the goods foreigners could export,

44 [Albert Berg], *Die Preußische Expedition Nach Ost-Asien*, 346; Michael Rauck, "Die Beziehungun zwischen Japan und Deutschland, 1859–1914" (PhD diss., Friedrich-Alexander-Universität Erlangen-Nürnberg 1988): 23. The original reference: according to details of American Resident Minister in Edo from 30 May 1860 quoted *San Francisco Herald* 8 August 1860 respectively. HA 186011, 412.

45 Rauck, "Die Beziehungun, 1859–1914," 23. Original reference: Offizier vom Dienst, Die preußiche Expedition nach Ost-Asien, Bd. 1, 1864, 163, 293f.

46 Berg, *Die Preußische Expedition nach Ost-*Asien, 347.

47 Berg, *Die Preußische Expedition nach Ost-Asien*, 347; Mariko Fukuoka, "Prussia or North German? The Image of 'Germany' during the Prusso-Japanese Treaty Negotiations in 1860–1861," in *Mutual Perceptions and Images in Japanese-German Relations, 1860–2010*, eds. Sven Saaler, Kudō Akira and Tajima Nobuo (Leiden, The Netherlands: Brill, 2017), 69–72.

48 Japan. Correspondence No. 37. Mr. Alcock to Lord J. Russell, Yedo, 10 November 1859, Japan, Correspondence with H. M. Envoy and Minister Plenipotentiary in Japan, 1860. 19th Century House of Commons Sessional Papers, https://parlipapers-proquest-com.rp.nla.gov.au/parlipapers/docview/t70.d75.1860-036818?accountid=12694._78–79 (hereafter Correspondence No. 37. to Lord J. Russell).

49 Correspondence No. 37. to Lord J. Russell, 78–79.

50 Correspondence No. 37, to Lord J. Russell, 78.

to charge high exchange rates for the local currency needed to purchase goods, and to the authorities prohibiting Japanese merchants from dealing with foreign merchants.[51] These were on-going bones of contention for the foreign community and suggest some of the ways the Japanese authorities subverted the unequal treaties imposed upon them over which the British were powerless to act. This suggests Alcock appeased the Japanese government rather than confronting it over infringements of merchants' rights as he saw his role as building relations between his government and the Japanese authorities as he had in China.[52]

By the time Nickel arrived in Nagasaki, the German community was already a significant part of the foreign community.[53] By 1861 there were at least twelve German merchants in Nagasaki, possibly more.[54] Meissner counted between six and nine German companies across Yokohama and Nagasaki as well as individual German ships chandlers, gold dealers, auctioneers and shop owners.[55] In the same period, the British Consul reported that there were twenty-five British residing in Nagasaki including merchants, smaller traders, compradors (agents for a foreign company) and a butcher.[56] While the British predominated, the numbers of Germans were not insubstantial.

German Merchants Choosing Protection of a Treaty Power

Until 1863, German merchants residing in Japan had to seek the protection of a treaty power. Whereas in Yokohama some German merchants claimed British protection, in Nagasaki over half of German merchants claimed Dutch protection.[57] Many had worked in Batavia alongside the Dutch

51 Correspondence No. 41. Alcock to Lord J. Russell, Dec. 6, 1859. Japan. Correspondence with H. M. Envoy and Minister Plenipotentiary in Japan, 1860. 19th Century House of Commons Sessional Papers. https://parlipapers-proquest-com.rp.nla.gov.au/parlipapers/docview/t70.d75.1860-036818?accountid=12694, February 2021, 89.

52 Sano Mayuko, "Disturbed Reciprocity," 21–24.

53 China Directory for 1862, Japan/Nagasaki, Hong Kong: Shortrede & Co. For 1862 Germans are listed according to the country from which protection was obtained, Harold Williams Collection, National Library of Australia (henceforth HWC NLA).

54 Bernd Lepach, Meiji Portraits Website, http://meiji-portraits.de/, Leipzig, Germany, 2021; Brian Burke-Gaffney, Nagasaki Institute of Applied Science and Lane Earns, University of Wisconsin–Oshkosh, USA: Nagasaki Foreign Settlement Website, http://www.nfs.nias.ac.jp/, June 2017. (This website has since been taken down to be rehoused in the future.)

55 Meissner, *Deutsche in Japan*, 14.

56 Despatches No. 5, 5 January 1861, January–June 1861, 82.

57 Despatches No. 16, 1 February 1860, January–June 1860, 43.

previously and already had established connections with the Dutch trading post on Deshima Island in Nagasaki. Such German merchants established businesses on Deshima, working with Dutch trading houses, tapping into their networks with the Nagasaki government, utilizing Dutch ships to secure consignments and cargo space and employing Dutch speaking Japanese. Only three Germans claiming British protection in Nagasaki were recorded. William Kagermann, Hermann Trotzig a German Swede, who subsequently moved to Kobe in 1868, and Hermann Grauert who arrived under British protection, in 1857, but then moved to Yokohama joining a Dutch delegation.[58]

Three German merchants with close links to the Dutch in Batavia founded the earliest German trading houses in Japan. Carl Julius Textor worked in Batavia from 1846 to 1856 before transferring to Deshima under Dutch protection and in 1859 founded Textor & Co. in Nagasaki and then in Yokohama.[59] In 1859, Edward (Everhard) Grösser, arrived in Nagasaki under Dutch protection establishing Grösser & Co. importing metals, textile dyes, paints, and cement, representing insurance companies and manufacturers and exporting Japanese glassware. In 1864 Grösser relocated to Yokohama where he opened a branch. In 1868 both German companies were amongst the first companies to establish branches in Kobe.

The third German merchant and founder of the most significant German trading house in Japan was Louis K. Kniffler. Coming from an affluent family, Kniffler had moved to Hamburg about 1850. In 1853 he was sent by one German company to work for another German firm based in Batavia since 1848.[60] In Batavia, Kniffler joined Martin H. Gildemeister in business. After going bankrupt they left for Nagasaki in 1858 arriving under Dutch protection.[61] In 1859 Kniffler established his company, L. Kniffler & Co. on Deshima and soon opened a branch in Yokohama. The company became a large exporter of Japanese products—silk, tea, beeswax, plant wax, rapeseed, copper, and coal. It also became a significant importer of armaments (representing Krupp), communications, and transportation infrastructure. The company was a major beneficiary of the Prussia-Japan treaty. By 1865, of the eighteen ships arriving in Yokohama for German companies, Kniffler

58 Nagasaki Foreign Settlement Website, http://www.nfs.nias.ac.jp/page042.html#HLG 2017; The China Directory for 1862 (Nagasaki, Japan, Hong Kong: Shortrede & Co. 1862) (hereafter China Directory 1862), 51.

59 Nagasaki Foreign Settlement Website, http://www.nfs.nias.ac.jp/page019.html#CJT, 2017.

60 Zielke, "Konsul Louis Kniffler," 2–3.

61 Nagasaki Foreign Settlement Website, http://www.nfs.nias.ac.jp/page042.html#OH, 2017 and http://www.nfs.nias.ac.jp/page042.html#MHG, 2017; Zielke, "Konsul Louis Kniffler," 3.

had commissioned 50 per cent of the tonnage.[62] That year Louis Kniffler was appointed the first Prussian Consul in Nagasaki, the first of a number of German merchant consuls representing Prussian interests.[63] Merchant consuls were able to further their business interests building connections within the Japanese government, and securing contracts for infrastructure, armaments and other equipment until in 1871 with the unification of Germany, a professional diplomatic service was introduced. L. Kniffler & Co. went bankrupt in early 1881 and was taken over by one of its staff members, Carl Illies to form C. Illies & Co.[64] In later years in Kobe, C. Illies & Co. became closely associated with Carl Nickel and Christian Holstein. The company remains to this day based in Hamburg.

While most German merchants in Japan chose Dutch protection, a handful in Nagasaki arrived in 1859 under American protection including a close Hamburg friend of Nickel's, Carl Gustav Wilckens who subsequently became an American. From 1860 onwards, Carl Nickel, Gustav Reddelien and Oscar Hartmann arrived claiming American protection.[65] Nickel's claim has been confirmed in the Japanese House to House Checks. The Tokugawa Shogunate conducted monthly house to house checks as part of a longstanding practice of "population governance, social control and the maintenance of social order" and to keep tabs on foreigners.[66] While Nickel claimed to have American protection, possibly because his friend Wilckens had taken American citizenship, there is no evidence in American consular records that he had done so, suggesting that his claim may have been unfounded, if useful to establish the validity of his residence in Nagasaki.[67]

The absence of extant official records in either German or American consular archives around this time for Nickel suggests that he operated in a fluid and multi-national business environment. Although Reddelien and Hartmann entered under American protection, they formed business

62 Zielke, "Konsul Louis Kniffler," 4.

63 Zielke, "Konsul Louis Kniffler," 5.

64 Meissner, *Deutsche in Japan*, 14.

65 Nagasaki Foreign Settlement Website, http://www.nfs.nias.ac.jp/page042.html#OH and http://www.nfs.nias.ac.jp/page042.html#GR, 2017.

66 Nagasaki Kyōryūchi Gaikokujin Meibō (Names and Populations of Foreign Residents in Nagasaki aka House to House Checks) October 1862 to March–May 1870, #14-12-7 compiled by the Nagasaki Bugyōsho (printed by Nagasaki Prefectural Library 2002), Nagasaki Museum of History and Culture (hereafter Nagasaki Kyōryūchi Gaikokujin Meibō); David Chapman and Karl Jakob Krogness, eds. *Japan's Household Registration System and Citizenship: Koseki, Identification and Documentation* (London and New York: Routledge, 2014), 1.

67 Lepach, Meiji- Portraits, http://meiji-portraits.de/, 2021; Nagasaki Kyōryūchi Gaikokujin Meibō; Email to author from Lane Earns, the Nagasaki Foreign Settlement Website, 26 August 2014.

partnerships with Dutch and other Germans and once the Prussia-Japan Treaty came into being, they came under the purview of the Prussian Consulate. Nickel and Wilckens, doing business in the transnational spaces between the German and Anglophone communities, remained outside the Prussian Consulate's purview. They were also outside the purview of the British and American consular reporting responsibilities.[68]

As a further measure of the fluidity of the multinational environment, by 1863, all German merchants became anglicized to an extent having to speak English daily. The banks and insurance companies they dealt with were English as were the British and American ships captains upon whom they relied for cargo space. While Hamburg ships could ply the China coast, they could not dock in Japanese ports until the Prussia-Japan Treaty was upgraded in 1869 to include Hamburg. Meissner describes how until 1869, German ships had to unload in Shanghai, and the German merchants had to work closely with their Shanghai correspondents and the captains of British ships to secure consignments and cargo space for on-forwarding freight to Japan.[69]

Nickel's Arrival in Nagasaki

Carl Nickel's obituary in 1906 suggests he arrived in Shanghai about 1859 and then, sometime in 1860, commenced exploring opportunities in Nagasaki.[70] While indications are that Nickel arrived in China operating as a ship's captain, it is not known exactly how he came to be in Shanghai; his itinerary to Shanghai and the nature of his travel documents remains unknown.[71] Passports were in use around this time in Hamburg: until 1850, they were issued for a specific destination by the Hamburg Senate and from the 1850s were issued by the Hamburg Police Department.[72] Because of the Crimean War (1854–56), however, there was a need to retain potential soldiers so leaving Hamburg was strictly supervised.[73] Nickel was of military service

68 A review of Prussian, British and American diplomatic correspondence held in the *Geheimes Staatsarchiv Preußsicher Kulturbesitz* (Prussian Secret State Archives) revealed no mention of Carl Nickel, suggesting he was outside the purview of the Prussian Consulate in Nagasaki.

69 Meissner, *Deutsche in Japan*, 18.

70 "Death of Mr C. T. M. Nickel," *Japan Chronicle* (Kobe), 16 August 1906, 213.

71 "The Late Mr. Charles Sutton," 460.

72 Email to author from Christine Heitmann, *Staatsarchiv Hamburg*, 1 August 2017.

73 John Thorpey, *Invention of the Passport: Surveillance, Citizenship, and the State* (Cambridge, New York: Cambridge University Press, 2000), 75.

age, and as there is no record of his passport application in the Hamburg Archives, he may have left Germany without one.

Details around Nickel's arrival in Nagasaki suggest that despite the Japanese government's prohibitions on the entry of non-treaty foreigners, Japanese borders were porous: foreign merchants could move in and out of Japan rather freely. Two pieces of evidence point to this. First, shipping passenger lists published in the *North China Herald* record one paid passage for Nickel from Nagasaki to Shanghai in April 1862.[74] He most likely moved between Shanghai and Nagasaki more than once before settling in Nagasaki, suggesting he had been a ship's captain. According to the British Consul in Nagasaki, George Morrison, with the right timing and connections it was possible for diplomats and merchants to "hitch a passage" (and save money) on one of the many British and American naval and merchant vessels sailing between the ports.[75] As four-fifths of Nagasaki's trade was with Shanghai in the early 1860s, movement of merchants between the two ports was frequent.[76]

Nickel's claim to have American protection may have been the result of close American connections, notably his friend Gustav Wilckens. From what we do know of Nickel's life and the lives of other German merchants, he most likely developed such connections in Shanghai or possibly in the United States (US). The lives of two of his contemporaries, German merchants Louis Kniffler and Hinrich Ahrens, show that it was common practice in the mid-nineteenth century amongst young Hamburg merchants to undertake apprenticeships in Germany and overseas. As the Port of Hamburg had strong connections with Great Britain, the Netherlands and the US, such apprenticeships were undertaken in those countries. Histories written about C. Illies and Co. and H. Ahrens & Co. refer to their founders' early careers working for German companies in Germany and then in Batavia or in Britain respectively that enabled them to develop the networks they utilized in Japan.[77] It is well possible that Nickel completed such an apprenticeship with a British or American company, possibly in shipping, through which he acquired American connections. In February 1873, the Shanghai press reported Nickel on one of his regular visits to Shanghai over the years, was one of two judges of a Man of War's boat race held in Shanghai between two cutters belonging to American ships in service of the American Asia

74 "Latest Shipping Intelligence, Passengers," *North China Herald* (Shanghai), 5 April 1862, 54.

75 Despatches No. 5, 16 August 1859, June–December 1859, 11.

76 Despatches No. 5, 14 April 1863, January–June 1863, 144–45.

77 Bähr, Lesczenski, and Schmidtpott, *Handel ist Wandel*, 21–23; Carolin Reimers, *Zeit ist Geld: Der Kaufmann Hinrich Ahrens und die Anfänge des deutschen Handels mit Japan* (Münster: Monsenstein und Vannerdat, 2010), 20–45.

Squadron in China (1867–74), the USS Iroquois and USS Saco.[78] The USS Iroquois had been one of several American and British ships that arrived in Kobe for the opening of the treaty port on 1 January 1868. Nickel's association with this boat race suggests he had developed a strong association with either or both the American Navy and an American merchant shipping company prior to arriving in Nagasaki. As a ship's captain he would have moved between Nagasaki and Shanghai on a regular basis trading on his own account arriving in Nagasaki with capital and connections.

Upon arrival in Nagasaki, Nickel moved into Ōura, the foreign settlement where his American connections helped shape his future business endeavours. The Japanese House to House Checks confirm his various addresses, businesses, and the names of his early associates. In October 1862, Carl Nickel and Carl Gustav Wilckens were both listed as Americans living at 12 Ōura, Nagasaki, a property leased by British national R. Arnold, a former employee of the Imperial Maritime Customs Service who had moved from Shanghai to Nagasaki in 1861. In July 1863, Nickel, listed as a Prussian (no longer allegedly under American protection) and Wilckens were now registered as living at 40 Sagarimatsu, a property leased by Americans, the Lake Brothers.[79] Meissner records Nickel and Wilckens as "slaughterers and ships chandlers."[80] Not only were they sharing accommodation and business interests in Lot 40 Sagarimatsu in 1863, they lived next door to David Holmes Tillson, an American in Lot 41. Tillson worked for George and Edward Lake, who had opened their company Lake & Co. in 1860 and, until 1921, were involved variously in the hotel business, in slaughtering/butchery, in ships chandlery and general trading.[81] Three butchery and ships chandlery businesses were located next to each other right on the wharf (the third was Smith and Breen). Nickel's close friendships with both Wilckens and Tillson helped him, and his business in Nagasaki and later Kobe. Moreover, the range of businesses the Lake Brothers were engaged in also provided the template for the businesses Nickel would also try over the next fifteen years: butchery, ships chandlery, the hotel business, coal, and stevedoring and cargo-handling.

Nickel established his company, Carl Nickel & Co. with his business partner, Gustav Wilckens.[82] Wilckens had become leaseholder of the property

78 "Man of War Boat Race," *The N.C. Herald and S.C. and C. Gazette*, 27 February 1873, 186.

79 Nagasaki Kyōryūchi Gaikokujin Meibō.

80 Meissner, *Deutsche in Japan*, 17.

81 Nagasaki Foreign Settlement Website, http://www.nfs.nias.ac.jp/page030.html#GL, 2017.

82 The Chronicle and Directory for China, Japan, and the Philippines for 1865. *Japan Chronicle* (Kobe), HWC NLA, 242.

Lot 40 in Sagarimatsu and sub-let the premises to Nickel.[83] Wilckens must have also arrived in Nagasaki with means. He held the lease for two other properties, sub-letting one to Smith and Breen.[84] The numbers of commercial and naval vessels entering the Port of Nagasaki, as well as the network of Chinese treaty ports within the vicinity of Nagasaki, would have ensured a strong demand for meat.

In addition to his American connections, Nickel associated with German merchants. He was a contemporary of Louis Kniffler, Nickel's senior, only by ten years. He also knew two of Kniffler's employees who were also from Hamburg, August Evers and Carl Illies. Both worked in Nagasaki before moving to Kobe in 1868. Nickel was also a contemporary of Hinrich Ahrens, although as Ahrens lived in Yokohama, one can only assume they knew one another. The company Nickel formed in 1880 in Kobe had a decades-long working relationship with both C. Illies & Co. and H. Ahrens & Co. Nickel was also a contemporary of Thomas Blake Glover, who through Glover & Co. represented Jardine Matheson & Co., and who also owned the Takashima coal mine.[85] While there is no record of a working relationship with Glover, it is possible; Nickel established himself as a coal merchant in Yokohama between 1874 and 1879 as indicated by business directories for those years.[86]

Nickel and the Shimonoseki Campaign

From 1864 onwards, further clues to Carl Nickel's life and the dangers he faced appear in a handful of records. In 1864, Nickel was involved in an incident during the Shimonoseki campaign, in the politically turbulent period leading up to the 1868 Meiji Restoration. Lead by Britain, the Shimonoseki Campaign was jointly waged by the treaty powers between July 1863 and September 1864 against the Chōshū Clan, loyalists of the emperor. Soldiers of the Chōshū domain tried to force foreigners to leave Japan by firing on foreign and

83 Nagasaki Foreign Settlement Website, http://www.nfs.nias.ac.jp/page019.html#GW, 2017; The China Directory, 1862, 52; Montague Paske-Smith, "Supplement No. 3, Reproduction of List of Foreign Hongs and Residents and Plan of the Foreign Concessions in Nagasaki, 1867," in *Western Barbarians in Japan and Formosa in Tokugawa Days, 1603–1868* (Kobe: J. L. Thompson & Co. (Retail) Ltd. 1930).

84 "Supplement No. 3," in *Western Barbarians in Japan and Formosa.*

85 Alexander McKay, *Scottish Samurai: Thomas Blake Glover, 1838–1911* (Edinburgh: Canongate Press, 2012), 120–21.

86 Japan Directories 1874–79, E206-1, E206-2, and E206-3, Kobe Public Archives (KPA).

Japanese ships sailing through the Straits of Shimonoseki, into the Inland Sea, an important shipping route. From 3 to 16 July 1864, Nickel, two business associates from Shanghai and his Japanese servant were travelling on the *Monitor*, an American merchant ship registered in Shanghai carrying cargo from Hakodate to Nagasaki.[87] The ship ran into trouble: the coal secured by the *Monitor* in Hakodate was poor quality and to conserve supplies its sailors had to burn "bulkheads, berths and every piece of wood that could be found to make the coal last as long as possible … all the spare hemp rigging, water-casks, lower deck hatches."[88] In distress, the ship's captain pulled into Furukawa Bay in what was then the Nagato Domain, a part of the Chōshū clan's territory, mooring near the towns of Kiwado and Senzaki (now part of Nagato-city), hoping to secure coal. There the *Monitor* was met by Japanese officials who had to deal with the captain through Nickel's Japanese servant. The captain identified all his passengers as American and requested "coal, water and fresh provisions."[89] The next day at dawn, instead of the officials returning with supplies, the *Monitor* found itself being fired upon by "a battery of four guns, about 12-pounders … [which] continued firing until we got up steam … about one hour after the firing commenced."[90] A volley of shots followed the *Monitor* as it headed out of reach of Japanese fire. The *Monitor* then opened fire "on the town [Kiwado] with shell from two 14-pounder Parrots guns … setting the town on fire."[91] Gunfire continued from the Japanese side but "fell short" while the *Monitor* steamed out of the harbor with only a few hours of coal left. Twenty-two bullets had hit the side of the ship. The ship headed for Tsushima Island where again they received no help from the local Japanese but were able to chop sufficient wood to return to Nagasaki. In 1865, the British Consul, Sir Rutherford Alcock, included in his reports to the House of Commons a "declaration and protest," to the Japanese authorities about the *Monitor* being fired upon. Although Nickel was not hurt, this incident illustrates the precariousness of the environment in which Nickel was operating.

87 Inclosure 3 in No. 57, Protest of the Master of the United States' ship "Monitor," Yokohama, 23 August 1864. Japan. Correspondence with H. M. Envoy and Minister Plenipotentiary in Japan, 1858–68. 19th Century House of Commons Sessional Papers, https://parlipapers-proquest-com.rp.nla.gov.au/parlipapers/result/pqpdocumentview?accountid=12694&groupid=100358&pgId=4397d38e-54ce-4138-803b-bf68e0978064&rsId=1772D192605, 69–70 (hereafter Protest of the Master of the United States' ship "Monitor").

88 Protest of the Master of the United States' ship "Monitor," 70.

89 Protest of the Master of the United States' ship "Monitor," 70.

90 Protest of the Master of the United States' ship "Monitor," 70.

91 Protest of the Master of the United States' ship "Monitor," 70.

Financial Security and a Wedding

Signalling that Nickel had achieved financial security, in November 1868 aged thirty-two, he married Eliza McLaren in Shanghai, where the couple celebrated with friends. The *Nagasaki Times* recorded Nickel making three trips on paid passages to Shanghai from Nagasaki between November and December 1868. On his trip back to Nagasaki on 30 November, he was accompanied by his new wife. The *Nagasaki Times* records his wedding notice, "Married. At the Church of Our Saviour, Shanghai on November 26, 1868. Carl T.M. Nickel to Eliza McLaren both of Nagasaki."[92] In a male dominated foreign community, he was fortunate to have met his wife-to-be without having to return to Europe to find a bride. Eliza McLaren was thirty, she was British and as there was an R. McLaren, a sawyer employed by Glover & Co. in Nagasaki, it seems she was either his daughter or his widow.[93]

Meiji Restoration and Merchants Leave Nagasaki for Kobe

Business in Nagasaki did not live up to expectations, and many merchants left Nagasaki for Yokohama or Kobe. From 1858 until the late 1860s, Japan's trade with the West had been mostly out of Yokohama. Yokohama had shorter shipping distances from product source with easier access to the political capital, Edo (Tokyo) for resolving treaty disputes. Nagasaki, on the other hand, had no hinterland of its own from which to source product and was heavily dependent upon Shanghai as a transhipment point. Nickel's friend Tillson moved to Kobe in 1868, the day the Port opened, where he established his own butchery and ships chandlery.

While the Meiji Restoration in 1868 ended Tokugawa rule and ushered in Japan's modernization, it brought peace and stability on the one hand but caused several foreigners financial pain on the other. Associated with the Meiji Restoration were significant changes to the feudal structure and the way the feudal lords or *daimyo* generated incomes. In 1868, *daimyo* had to relinquish their titles, lands, and sources of income and, as many *daimyo* bought goods from foreign merchants on credit, they were unable to pay

92 "Nickel departed for Shanghai on the *Costa Rica*," *Nagasaki Times*, 7 November 1868, 78; "Nickel returned from Shanghai to Nagasaki on the Orissa," *Nagasaki Times*, 21 November 1868, 86; "Mr and Mrs Nickel returned from Shanghai to Nagasaki on the *Feloong*," *Nagasaki Times*, 5 December 1868, 94.

93 Nagasaki Foreign Settlement Website, http://www.nfs.nias.ac.jp/page002.html, 2017; Email to author from Lane Earns, 26 August 2014.

their debts, sending some foreign merchants into bankruptcy. Foreign merchants were also affected by rapidly changing market conditions not to mention currency exchange manipulations.[94]

With the death of his partner, Gustav Wilckens, on 28 January 1869 of an unspecified illness, Nickel's situation also changed.[95] Wilckens began winding up his affairs early in 1868. In April, he transferred the premises at 40 Ōura to Nickel, who then sold it to a local shoemaker.[96] That month, according to the Japanese April–July 1868 House to House Checks, Nickel was registered as the leaseholder of Lot 31 A/B Ōura with his soon-to-be wife, Eliza.[97] During this time, Nickel's company continued trading. He was listed in the Shipping List of January 1869 as the agent/consignee for the *Sarah*, an American brig of 186 tons arriving in Nagasaki on 23 December 1868 from Chefoo, China (Yantai) destined for Yokohama.[98] Chefoo, on the Shantung Peninsula (Shandong), was a smaller treaty port negotiated by the British in China in 1858 following the Second Opium War. As Shantung Peninsula was known for its coal resources, Chefoo had become a coaling station.[99] This is also the first and only evidence so far discovered that Nickel was dealing with a treaty port in China outside of Shanghai. It was located next door to what would become the German leasehold on the Shantung Peninsula in 1898 in a quasi-colony Germany hoped would deliver benefits like those the British enjoyed with its colony of Hong Kong.[100] Being a consignee meant that Nickel would need to cover the cost of his purchases while waiting to sell the goods. The timing of revenue needed to make loan repayments is critical to avoiding insolvency. Nickel's partner, Wilckens, died a month after the ship's arrival. Because of Nickel's new property investments and without Wilckens's continued financial backing, it is possible he wound up his company in anticipation of suffering a cash squeeze.

Despite some of his contemporaries leaving Nagasaki, Nickel remained entering the hotel business. From May 1870 he returned to Germany reportedly for a "well-earned rest."[101] Upon his return to Nagasaki he established the Falcon Hotel with a bowling saloon in Lot 31 Ōura, Sagarimatsu and

94 Harold S. Williams, *The Story of Holme Ringer & Co., Ltd. in Western Japan 1868–1968* (Tokyo: Charles E. Tuttle Company, 1968), 20.

95 Nagasaki Foreign Settlement Website, http://www.nfs.nias.ac.jp/page019.html#GW, 2017.

96 Email to author from Lane Earns, 26 August 2014.

97 Email to author from Lane Earns, 26 August 2014; Nagasaki Kyōryūchi Gaikokujin Meibō.

98 The Nagasaki Shipping List, 6 January 1869, KPA.

99 John E. Schrecker, *Imperialism and Chinese Nationalism: Germany in Shantung* (Cambridge, MA: Harvard University Press, 2013), 16.

100 Schrecker, *Imperialism and Chinese Nationalism*, 1–2.

101 "Death of Mr C.T.M. Nickel," 213; Nagasaki Kyōryūchi Gaikokujin Meibō.

Naminohira. While his wife ran the hotel, Nickel worked as a shipping clerk for the Pacific Mail Steam Ship Company generating a back-up income.[102] We also know from his adjudication of the Man of War's boat race held in Shanghai in 1873 that he continued to visit Shanghai. In 1873, he transferred the hotel into his wife's name and in 1877 sold it for $525 to a Mr Thomas. We have little other information about Carl and Eliza's lives in Nagasaki save for one incident. The Nagasaki press reported in January 1871 that the landlady of the Falcon Hotel, Mrs Carl Nickel, who "had been constantly annoyed by … goats breaking into her garden," through "incautious use of firearms" had shot a little Japanese boy who was passing at the time "nearly resulting in [his] death."[103] Eliza having a gun in her possession suggested a lingering insecurity felt within the foreign community.

During his time in Nagasaki, like his early pioneer merchant colleagues, Nickel faced considerable challenges and adversity in one of the first treaty ports opened in Japan. Foreign merchants contended not just with physical threats from samurai wanting to rid Japan of foreigners but also with a Japanese administration they believed was obstructive and anti-foreign as it got around the treaties imposing restrictive laws and practices. Whereas Sir Rutherford Alcock, the British Minister, arguably prioritized the relationship with the Japanese government over the interests of the foreign merchants, the British Consul in Nagasaki, George Morrison, regularly advocated for merchants' interests and safety with limited results. Certainly, the Japanese administration was inexperienced in handling conflicts with foreign merchants arising out of the unequal treaties. Finally, the evolving political situation left some foreigners in financial straits with the commencement of the Meiji Restoration with many, seeing no further business opportunities in Nagasaki, departing for the newly opened Treaty Port of Kobe. Still seeing such opportunities, Nickel remained in Nagasaki together with his wife, Eliza, in the hotel and bowling alley business. Nickel was embedded in the Anglophone community operating from the periphery of the foreign community in the transnational spaces bridging British, German, and Japanese business interests. Whilst in Nagasaki, he learnt it was possible to avoid, evade or negotiate Japanese regulations and other attempts to curtail the activities of foreign merchants. In the next chapter we will see how, after spending a short period in Yokohama, he moved to Kobe and built a waterfront empire under the benefits of extraterritorial protections.

102 The Chronicle & Directory for China, Japan & the Philippines 1872, The Hiogo (Kobe) Directory, 311–12, and The Nagasaki Directory, 310 (Kobe: Hong Kong Daily Press), HWC NLA, 311–12.
103 "Mrs Nickel shoots Japanese boy in an accident," *The Nagasaki Express*, 28 January 1871, 218.

3. Kobe: Building a Waterfront Empire

Abstract: In 1880, Carl Nickel founded his freight forwarding and cargo handling business, C. Nickel & Co. in Kobe. This chapter shows how Nickel grew his business benefiting from the rapid economic growth following the Meiji Restoration in 1868 and the expansion of the Port of Kobe. Exploiting extraterritorial privileges under the terms of the unequal treaties outside Japanese jurisdiction, Nickel was also innovative and entrepreneurial, living on the periphery of the foreign community and utilizing his transnational connections employing a multi-national workforce collaborating with his American and British counterparts. He submitted to the British consular courts for the most part to protect and advance his business interests. In 1897, he brought his cousin and godson to Japan as his successor.

Keywords: extraterritoriality, port, jurisdiction, Germans, entrepreneurial, multi-national

In 1874 Carl Nickel moved to Yokohama where he operated as a stevedore and coal merchant until 1879 when he relocated to Kobe. This period coincided with the consolidation of the Meiji government, the transformation of the treaty ports, and a period of peace and dramatic economic growth. In Kobe, Nickel established C. Nickel & Co., which by 1890s became a successful and powerful stevedoring and cargo handling company. He achieved success exploiting not only extraterritorial privileges but also his entrepreneurial skills and transnational connections. From 1858 to 1899, foreign merchants benefited from extraterritorial protections outside Japanese legal jurisdiction, a concession of the unequal treaties much detested by the Japanese authorities. In the eleven years since its establishment, the Port of Kobe developed rapidly, and Nickel's company benefited from this growth and explosion of trade. This chapter places Nickel in the context of the German community in Kobe, a part of a network of German communities throughout northeast Asia, where Germans and British worked side by side. Nickel hoped

Holstein, Prue S. *The German Experience of Japan's Treaty Port System: A Case Study of C. Nickel & Co. Ltd., 1860–1923*. Taylor & Francis Group, 2025.
DOI: 10.4324/9781003706274-4

to benefit from the British power base protecting foreigners' interests under the unequal treaties. This chapter provides an insight into the day-to-day management of Nickel's business under extraterritorial protection.

New Opportunities in Yokohama

Nickel moved to Yokohama where the increasing presence of foreign navies presented new business opportunities. Whilst in Nagasaki, he had visited other Japanese treaty ports and had been to Kobe as early as August 1868.[1] Following the death of his partner, Gustav Wilckens, Nickel faced challenges with a shipping consignment threatening his finances. Having accumulated some capital from his hotel business, he was ready to explore new opportunities. Yokohama had become a base for the British, American, French, Russian and German naval vessels.[2] From the end of the 1850s, foreign navies were deployed in Japan to protect foreigners from civil unrest and to enforce the Japanese government's adherence to the unequal treaties. However, as European powers including the newly unified Germany sought to expand their influence, their navies were deployed to the northeast Asian region to support diplomatic and commercial aspirations.[3] In 1875 Nickel was listed in the business directory as a stevedore and coal dealer most likely servicing those foreign navies.[4] The little that is known of Nickel's life in Yokohama has been traced through business directories. From 1875 to 1879, he resided in Yokohama at various addresses.[5] Around 1877 his wife Eliza arrived in Yokohama and managed two hotels: the "Retreat" from 1878–81 and the "Commercial" in 1882 where she also resided.[6] She died in Yokohama

1 "Nickel departed for Hiogo (Kobe) on the Feloong," *Nagasaki Times*, 15 August 1868, 30.

2 The *Japan Herald*, the *Japan Gazette* and the *Japan Chronicle* all published business directories. In the Kobe Public Archives (KPA), directories for each of the years 1868–1900 have been kept, but not all from the same publishing house. The Japan Herald Directory & Hong List for Yokohama, 1870 records the British, French and US navies in Yokohama (Yokohama: *Japan Herald*, 1870) E206-1, KPA, 3; The Japan Directory 1882 records the Japanese Navy, the British, French, German and Russian Squadrons in China and Japan and the United States Naval Force on the Asiatic Station (Yokohama: *Japan Gazette*, 1882) E206-4, KPA, 13–19.

3 Ian H. Nish, *The Anglo-Japanese Alliance: The Diplomacy of Two Island Empires* (London: The Athlone Press, 1966), 14.

4 Hong List and Directory 1875 (Yokohama: *Japan Gazette*, 1875), E206-1 KPA, 29.

5 Hong List and Directory 1875, 29. Carl Nickel is first recorded at 121B Yokohama; The Japan Directory (Yokohama: *Japan Gazette*, 1879) E206-3, KPA, 46. Carl Nickel is last recorded at 168 Private Residence, Rising Sun.

6 "Mrs Nickel, Manager, 108 The Retreat," Hong List and Directory 1878 (Yokohama: *Japan Gazette*, 1878) E206-2 KPA. 40; "Mrs Nickel, 31 'The Commercial,'" Japan Directory 1882 (Yokohama

in 1883 of unknown causes aged forty-seven and childless and is buried in the Yokohama Foreign Cemetery.[7]

Whilst in Yokohama, Nickel formed a significant connection with the German merchant, Julius Helm. Nickel's stevedore and coal business was located in the same building as Helm's private residence, so their paths may well have crossed around then.[8] Born in Rosow in 1840, Helm arrived in Yokohama via the United States (US) around 1869.[9] He spent several years in Wakayama, working as military advisor to Carl Koppen, a German sergeant employed to help turn the samurai of the former *Daimyo* (Lord) of Wakayama into a modern army.[10] Helm then returned to Yokohama to work for J. D. Carroll & Co. Storekeepers, Ships Chandlers and General Commission Agents.[11] Around 1878, he established a drayage company in Yokohama and in 1881 expanded it to become a Landing and Shipping Agent.[12] In 1892, he formed Helm Bros. Landing, Hauling and Shipping Agents with his brother Paul.[13] To expand his business, Helm later travelled to Kobe and partnered briefly with Nickel in Nickel's company in 1894 as will be seen.

Kobe

Based in Yokohama, Carl Nickel knew foreign navies were calling into Kobe. Nickel's old friend David Holmes Tillson who relocated to Kobe from Nagasaki when the Port opened most likely prompted Nickel's visits to Kobe from 1868 onwards. There are no records of Nickel taking a paid passage between Yokohama and Kobe, so he most likely "hitched" a free ships' passage through his shipping connections, while still maintaining a residence in

Japan Gazette, 1882) E206-4 KPA, 28.

7 "Eliza Nickel, death 1883," *The Japan Weekly Mail,* 2 June 1883, 1, Yokohama Public Archives (YPA); Patricia McCabe, *Yokohama, Japan: Gaijin Bochi, the Foreigners' Cemetery* (London: British Association for Cemeteries in South Asia, 1994), https://www.bacsa.org.uk/shop/cemetery-record-books/yokohama-japan-gaijin-bochi-the-foreigners-cemetery/#, 87. The name on her tombstone was Nichel, E. N. British died 1883.

8 "J. Helm, resident at 121B" and "C.T.M. Nickel, Stevedore and Coal Dealer," Hong List and Directory 1875 (Yokohama: *Japan Gazette*, 1875) E206-1 KPA, 29.

9 Bernd Lepach, Meiji Portraits Website, http://meiji-portraits.de/meiji_portraits_h.html#20090527093325890_1_2_3_15_1, 2017.

10 Leslie Helm, *Yokohama Yankees: My Family's Five Generations as Outsiders in Japan* (Seattle: Chin Music Press, 2013), 48–49.

11 Hong List and Directory 1875, E206-1 KPA, 29.

12 Hong List and Directory 1878, E206-1 KPA, 42 and Japan Directory 1881, E206-4 KPA, 31.

13 Meiji Portraits Website, http://meiji-portraits.de/meiji_portraits_h.html#20090527093325890_1_2_3_15_1, 2017.

Yokohama.[14] In 1879, Nickel moved to Kobe, leaving his wife in Yokohama, perhaps relying on her income as a hotel manager allowing him to take risks exploring new business ventures.

The Treaty Port of Kobe was opened by the Japanese government on 1 January 1868, and Sir Harry Parkes, the British Minister to Japan and successor to Sir Rutherford Alcock, entered Kobe together with a detachment of the Nineth Infantry Regiment along with British, American, Dutch, and French amongst other nationalities and twenty-five Germans. Under the unequal treaties, the Japanese government provided land for a foreign settlement to be governed by the foreign community.[15] It selected fifty hectares bounded by Nishi-Machi (Division Street) in the west, Ura-Machi in the north, Higashi-Machi (Ikuta River) in the east and Kaigan-dōri (the Bund or embankment at the sea front) in the south. Within eighteen months, this area was transformed from a "sand patch" flanked by a fishing village with the Japanese Customs House the only solid building, into a thriving treaty port with buildings, offices, residences, and *go-downs* (warehouses), a recreational ground, a clubhouse, and a foreign cemetery located nearby. The Bund was lined with impressive buildings, a promenade along the foreshore and a park where German brass bands played on summer evenings.[16]

German Merchants Already Influential

Nickel arrived to find German companies already established in Kobe's Foreign Settlement offering him a potential customer base. When the Japanese government initially offered 126 lots for 'sale' (as perpetual leaseholds; foreigners were forbidden to own land) British merchants purchased sixty-three lots, the largest number, and German merchants purchased twenty-five lots, the second largest. Of the twelve prestigious waterfront lots, three were sold to German trading companies.[17] Although the Kobe foreign

14 The Japan Directory 1879, E206-3 KPA, 46.

15 Treaty between Great Britain and Japan. Signed at Yedo, 26 August 1858. Treaties and Conventions, Concluded between Japan and Foreign Nations 1854–1870 (Yokohama: Daily Japan Herald Office 1871), Harold Williams Collection, National Library of Australia (henceforth HWC NLA), 57–61.

16 Otto Refardt, *Die Deutschen in Kobe* (*Alt Kobe*) (Tokyo: Deutsche Gesellschaft für Natur-und Völkerkunde Ostasiens (OAG), 1956), 19–20; "Reminiscences of Kobe, the Port's Beginnings," *Japan Chronicle* (Kobe), 9 January 1901, 25.

17 Refardt, *Die Deutschen in Kobe*, 20. As discussed in a later chapter, foreign merchants could not own property. Under the provisions of the unequal treaties, foreigners could purchase a perpetual leasehold in the Settlement with the Japanese government as landlord. In the Native Town they could only lease from Japanese landlords.

community was dominated by the British, Germans came second in each year from 1870 until 1896 except in 1880 when the Americans outnumbered the Germans by one. By 1896 the foreign population numbered at most 1,000 including 515 British and 141 Germans.[18]

The Foreign Settlement, like the International Settlement in Shanghai, was governed by a municipal council. As both the Shanghai Municipal Council (SMC) and the Kobe Municipal Council (KMC) were considered model councils and were closely connected, it is useful to make some comparisons to understand the exercise of power.[19] The SMA and the KMC both collected land tax, provided a police force and a fire brigade and planned for maintenance and repairs and other works to keep the concessions up to standard.[20] The makeup of the councils differed, however. The KMC comprised a chairman and vice-chairman (often but not always British), foreign consuls from Britain, the US, the Netherlands, France, Prussia (later the German Empire), Russia and other nationalities, a representative from the Japanese government, plus three representatives elected by the land renters of the Settlement, one of whom was consistently German.[21] There were no Japanese residents. In the case of the SMC, while it had jurisdiction over a much larger and more diverse population including a substantial Chinese population from 1865, despite representing only 3 per cent of the community, wealthy British landowners held the concentration of power. Seven British, one German and one American served on the council.[22] Whereas the SMC reflected the British determination to maintain control over the International Settlement, out of proportion to its numbers, the KMC was more equitable in its representation of the diversity of its Foreign Settlement. German representation on the KMC was also greater than that of the SMC. Furthermore, not all British and Germans resided in the International Concession in Shanghai. Some resided in the French Concession located separately but near the International Concession. It had its own *Conseil d'Administration Municipale* dominated by the

18 Peter Ennals, *Opening a Window to the West: The Foreign Concession at Kobe, Japan, 1868–1899* (Toronto, Buffalo, London: University of Toronto Press, 2014), 148.

19 Isabella Jackson, "Who Ran the Treaty Ports? A Study of the Shanghai Municipal Council," in *Treaty Ports in Modern China: Law Land and Power*, eds. Robert Bickers and Isabella Jackson (Milton Park, Abingdon, Oxon; Routledge, 2016), 43–47.

20 Jackson, "Who Ran the Treaty Ports?" 43–47.

21 Ennals, *Opening a Window to the West*, 45.

22 Jackson, "Who Ran the Treaty Ports?" 43–47.

French.[23] In Kobe, some foreigners like Nickel chose to live in the Native Town outside the Foreign Settlement, renting from Japanese landlords as discussed in chapter 7. While the SMC existed from 1854 to 1943, the KMC only lasted thirty-one years until 1899 when it reverted to Japanese control under the revised treaties. Reflecting the autonomous nature of the SMC and KMC, the *Japan Chronicle* later referred to the KMC as a "little self-governing republic" resonating with Hoare's description of how foreigners living in Shanghai had run the SMC as "an autonomous state within the Chinese Empire, in which the Chinese Government lost its jurisdiction."[24]

In Kobe, German merchants' wealth in the Settlement ensured their influence on the KMC. While the role of chairman was mostly filled by British, two German merchants, Max Militzer and Thuiscon Lenz, served as chairman of the Council.[25] August Evers, the Prussian consul and subsequently consul of the Northern Confederation of German States in Kobe, served on the Council for thirty-one years from its inception in 1868 to 1899.[26] Evers was a merchant consul initially representing L. Kniffler & Co. and subsequently his own firm, Simon Evers & Co. Nickel, Militzer, Lenz, and Evers had all lived in Nagasaki contemporaneously. Of the three land renters one place was reserved for a German merchant. Charles Braess and Charles Lange-Delacamp both served on the council for extended periods. The *Japan Chronicle*'s obituaries for August Evers (1904) and Charles Braess (1911) affirmed the high esteem in which the foreign community held them.[27] Evers was praised as "a man of sterling qualities and high business integrity."[28] Charles Braess was in turn acknowledged as "a very popular member of the foreign community ... of sterling character, [doing] a lot of charitable work."[29] The Municipal Council Superintendent

23 Carlos Augusto Montalto de Jesus, *Historic Shanghai* (Shanghai: The Shanghai Mercury Limited, 1909), 221–23.

24 "Robert Young: A Memoir: Thursday, 9 November 1922," *Japan Chronicle* (Kobe), 16 November 1922, 632; James E. Hoare, *Japan's Treaty Ports and Foreign Settlements: The Uninvited Guests 1858–1899* (Kent: Japan Library, Curzon Press, 1994), 54.

25 Japan Directory 1882 (Yokohama: *Japan Gazette*, 1882), E206–4 KPA, 98.

26 "Death and Funeral of Mr Aug. Evers. Interesting Career of Old Resident. Touching Tribute at the Graveside by Mr Krien (German Consul General in 1904)," *Japan Chronicle* (Kobe), 9 June 1904, 709.

27 "Death of Mr C. Braess," *Japan Chronicle* (Kobe), 9 February 1911, 225; "Death and Funeral of Mr Aug. Evers," 709–10.

28 "Death and Funeral of Mr Aug. Evers," 709–10.

29 "Death of Mr. C. Braess. Funeral Service at Kasugano," *Japan Chronicle* (Kobe), 9 February 1911, 225.

was a German-Swede: Herman Trotzig served the Council for thirty years from the early 1870s until the end of extraterritoriality in 1899 when control of the KMC passed to the Japanese government. Trotzig was retained by the Japanese as an advisor for twenty years until his death in 1919.[30]

The influence of German merchants in the Settlement was felt institutionally and culturally. From 1868 to 1870 German trading houses such as L. Kniffler & Co., Textor & Co., and Grösser & Co., already established in Nagasaki and Yokohama, were now in Kobe.[31] In 1869, German merchants established the first foreign club in Kobe, the Union Club, catering to Germans as well as Swiss, Dutch, Norwegian and Swedish nationals. Its "luxurious" building was the envy of the community.[32] The club became the precursor to the Concordia Club which was opened in October 1879 and became a meeting place for the foreign community after Second World War.[33] In 1872, German merchants established the *Deutsche Gesellschaft für Natur-und Völkerkunde Ostasiens* (Society for East Asian Natural History and Anthropology or, as the British referred to it, the German Asiatic Society). The society still provides a forum for speakers on Japan and East Asia and is known by its acronym, OAG.[34]

German-British Partnerships

From 1868 onwards British companies offering a range of products and services formed partnerships with German merchants reflecting more broadly Germany's growing importance to Britain as an economic partner.[35] In Kobe advertisements placed in business directories and in the *Hiogo News* from 1868 onwards show British insurance companies for example

30 "Death of Mr Herman Trotzig: A Sixty Years' Resident of Japan," *Japan Chronicle* (Kobe), 24 July 1919, 144.

31 A list can be compiled from articles on the three land sales between 1868–70 from the following sources: *Japan Gazette*, Yokohama, September 1868, KPA, 6; the *Hiogo News* (Kobe), 3 June 1869, KPA, 381 and *Hiogo News* (Kobe), 18 May 1870, KPA, 158.

32 German Community: Extract from *Geschichte des Club Concordia Festschrift zum 50 Jährigen Stiftungfest* 1879–1929, Papers of Harold Williams, Subject Files Series 1 Folder 47, HWC NLA.

33 Hoare, *Japan's Treaty Ports and Foreign Settlements*, 50.

34 Refardt, *Die Deutschen in Kobe*, 24. Contains membership list of the OAG in 1879. Also refer the OAG website, https://oag.jp/.

35 John McDermott, "'A Needless Sacrifice': British Businessmen and Business as Usual in the First World War," *Albion: A Quarterly Journal Concerned with British Studies* 21, no. 2 (Summer 1989): 263. https://doi.org/10.2307/4049929.

announcing appointments of German agents.[36] On 19 May 1869 the *Hiogo Daily News* announced: the Royal Insurance Company, Liverpool, Fire & Life Branches appointed Schultze, Reis & Co. agents in Hiogo (Kobe) and Osaka; the Home & Colonial Marine Insurance Company Limited appointed Gutschow & Co. its Japan agents; and the North British and Mercantile Fire Insurance Company appointed Charles Thorel & Co. its authorized agents.[37] Later British commentary in 1914 indicated retrospectively that British insurance companies valued the diverse business and client portfolios of German trading houses enabling them to reach markets they could not access on their own.[38]

Partnerships between British and German companies were also found in the banking industry. British commentary in 1914 ascribes the strength of German commercial influence in Japan to German companies with the backing of both British and German banks offering longer lines of credit than their British counterparts.[39] From 1864, the British Hong Kong Shanghai Banking Corporation (also known as Hongkong Bank but hereafter referred to as HSBC) was established in Hong Kong and Shanghai about 1864 or 1865 initially to provide treaty port merchants with trade finance and subsequently financing Chinese infrastructure projects. By 1885 it had become the largest bank operating in China.[40] It opened branches in Yokohama in 1866 and in Kobe in 1869 and by 1879 was the only foreign exchange bank in Japan.[41] As an international bank, HSBC had a multi-national board including four German directors, heads of significant German companies in Hong Kong and Shanghai reflecting its strong German customer base. These appointments ensured that HSBC was able to compete with the German Deutsche-Asiatische Bank (DAB) when it was finally established in Shanghai in 1889. The DAB tried to establish a branch office in Yokohama in 1872 to service those German merchants dependent upon HSBC but had to close in

36 The Chronicle & Directory for China, Japan & the Philippines 1872, The Hiogo (Kobe) Directory (Kobe: Hong Kong Daily Press), HWC NLA, 311–12.

37 Such advertisements appeared regularly in the *Hiogo Daily News* throughout the 1880s and 1890s.

38 Letter on behalf of the British Insurance Companies to the Secretary of Board of Trade, 1 December 1914, FO 371/2019, The National Archives of the UK (henceforth TNA), 182–83.

39 Memorandum by E. T. F. Crowe, 30 September 1914, Opportunities for capturing German business, FO 371/2020, TNA, 365–79.

40 Frank H. H. King, *The Hongkong Bank in Late Imperial China, 1864–1902: On an Even Keel: Volume 1 of The History of the Hongkong and Shanghai Banking Corporation* (Cambridge: Cambridge University Press, 1987), 6, 20.

41 King, *The Hongkong Bank in Late Imperial China*, 151, 288.

1875.[42] It was not until 1905 that the DAB reestablished a branch in Yokohama.[43] While HSBC and the DAB were competitors, they also collaborated in joint financing of large projects. While little has been written about DAB's history in Japan, it seems that to compete with the DAB, HSBC was willing to offer the same generous credit terms German merchants offered their Japanese clients that British merchants were otherwise unwilling to offer.

As a further measure of their wealth, German merchants in Kobe also served alongside their British counterparts as directors and key funders on the boards of new companies formed such as the Kobe Ice Company and the Hiogo Gas Company (subsequently becoming Kobe Gas Co.). Germans were also represented on the boards of the International Hospital, and the Hiogo and Osaka Chamber of Commerce, later to become the Kobe Foreign Board of Trade.[44]

Thus, when Nickel arrived in Kobe, he found a client base already valuing German mercantile skills. The diversity of merchant experience in the treaty ports, and the interconnectedness of the businesses represented, can only be understood when considering a company such as that built by Nickel through transnational connections. Literature on such transnational collaborations across British and German companies has been limited. However, research conducted by Frank King into HSBC and Ghassan Moazzin into DAB in China and Japan confirm how important such collaborations were.[45] The interconnectedness of German and British companies reveals business patterns integral to the development of the treaty port, but such transnational partnerships cannot be found in the records of national archives, especially where they collect diplomatic records of national representatives. And yet, this transnational collaboration was crucial to the size and success of the Port of Kobe.

42 Ghassan Moazzin, "A German Bank in China: Early Contact of German Bankers with China from the 1870s to the 1880s," *Foreign Banks and Global Finance in Modern China: Banking on the Chinese Frontier 1870–1919* (Cambridge, New York, NY: Cambridge University Press, 2022), 28.

43 Bernd Lepach, Meiji-Portraits: http://meiji-portraits.de/meiji_firms_d.html, 2024.

44 The Japan Directory 1882 (Yokohama: *Japan Gazette*, 1882), E206-4 KPA, 97, 99, 100. Of twenty-two member companies of the Hiogo and Osaka Chamber of Commerce, nine were German. One-quarter of directors for the International Hospital (99) and the Hiogo Gas Company (97) and two out of five directors of the Kobe Ice Company (100) were German.

45 In China: Moazzin, "A German Bank in China"; King, *The Hongkong Bank in Late Imperial China*; In Japan: Ennals, *Opening a Window to the West.* Ennals acknowledges the German community as the second largest in Kobe until 1899, 148, 151. His references to German contributions are however too generalized to add variation to a mainly British context, 106. In dealing with significant German companies, detail and accuracy are lacking, for example, 123. L. Kniffler & Co. was not transient. It became C. Illies & Co., and the name of the subsequent owner was incorrect. It was Carl Ilies.

Kobe: Part of a Network of German Communities

Kobe was not the only treaty port in the northeast Asian region dominated by the British and where the German merchant community played an important role working alongside the British. Communities of German merchants formed in China well before Germany's unification; the most significant being in the British Colony of Hong Kong and in the Chinese treaty port in Shanghai. The following compares such communities with Kobe's bearing in mind that British control or influence with the host authorities ranged from absolute colonial rule in Hong Kong to informal imperial rule in Shanghai to having negligible influence in Kobe outside the running of the Foreign Settlement.

German merchants lived under absolute British rule in the British Colony of Hong Kong working with British companies in what Becker characterized as *participatory colonialism.*[46] Some twenty German companies with headquarters or branch offices operated in Hong Kong mainly in import/export, slightly fewer than British equivalents. A wide range of small German businesses and services were also evident.[47] The German community in Hong Kong was on an equal footing with the British, playing an important role in trading, partnering, and investing with their British counterparts. Germans were appointed as directors on the boards of the Hong Kong Chamber of Commerce, the British bank, HSBC, and the largest dockyard in East Asia, Hong Kong & Whampoa Dock Company serving the British Navy.[48] Under British rule, German merchants thrived; the colony was not subject to interference or obstruction from the Chinese authorities that might have occurred elsewhere in Chinese treaty ports or as did occur from Japanese authorities in Japanese treaty ports. The British in Hong Kong also benefited. Even though the German presence relative to other foreign nations in Hong Kong was small, its outsized wealth and influence contributed substantially to Hong Kong's economic success as the British sought to develop the colony as "a hub of East Asian shipping, trade and finance."[49]

The nature of C. Nickel & Co.'s connections with Hong Kong during the late nineteenth and early twentieth century are not known. From 1899, as Britain saw the rise of the German Empire as a threat to its commercial

46 Bert Becker, *France and Germany in the South China Sea, c. 1840–1930: Maritime Competition and Imperial Power*, Cambridge Imperial and Post-Colonial Studies (Cambridge: Palgrave Macmillan, 2021) 50.

47 Becker, *France and Germany in the South China Sea*, 49.

48 Becker, *France and Germany in the South China Sea*, 50.

49 Becker, *France and Germany in the South China Sea*, 48.

supremacy, Nickel along with fellow Germans Julius Helm and Charles Lange-Delacamp registered their companies as British public companies in Hong Kong (as will be discussed in the next chapter) possibly as a protective measure against the loss of extraterritorial protections. The onset of the First World War changed this dynamic when the British government seeking to capture German business forced British companies to end their partnerships with Germans with some limited success, as will be seen in chapter 9.

Whereas Osterhammel, Bickers and Jackson view treaty ports as being dominated by British informal rule, Manz takes a transnational approach referring to a "sphere of European informal imperialism" in China reflecting the relationships developed between the foreign powers as well as with the Chinese authorities.[50] As with other nations, Germany signed its own treaties, first as Prussia in 1861 and then as Germany after 1871 developing its own diplomatic relationship with the Chinese authorities. As an example of the exercise of German informal power, when German banks prior to the establishment of the DAB tried to break HSBC's monopoly in securing Chinese loans with the Chinese government in 1885, they appealed to the German minister in Beijing, Max von Brandt, for help. He advocated for a German bank in China for some time and used his influence with the Chinese authorities to achieve this.[51] Nevertheless, the British were the dominant power in the major Chinese treaty ports and had established long and cooperative relationships with their Chinese hosts, for example, in establishing the Imperial Maritime Customs Service (IMCS), so where their interests coincided the British can be said to have exercised informal rule on behalf of other foreign powers.

While the treaty ports of Shanghai and Kobe were closely connected, too little research has been conducted into the German community in Shanghai and its relationships with their British counterparts to be able to adequately compare it with its counterpart in Kobe. We have some sparse details. In 1898 there were one hundred and seven German companies operating in China compared to one hundred and fifty English companies.[52] In 1914, there were six hundred German men living in Shanghai: mostly merchants and clerks working for some thirty important German import-export companies. British companies however outnumbered German companies two to one.[53]

50 Stefan Manz, *Constructing a German Diaspora: The "Greater German Empire," 1871–1914* (New York, London: Routledge, 2017), 40.

51 Moazzin, "A German Bank in China," 38–41.

52 Manz, *Constructing a German Diaspora*, 39.

53 Manz, *Constructing a German Diaspora*, 39, 40–41.

The German community was sizeable, and as Shanghai had a close treaty port relationship with Kobe, it can be assumed that the German community in Shanghai was as important to its British counterparts in Shanghai as it was in Kobe.

Taking its lead from the British colonization of Hong Kong, from 1898 to 1914, Germany held territory it acquired in China through taking a leasehold from the Chinese government in Kiaochow (Jiaozhou Bay) in Shantung Province (Shandong Province), and its Port of Tsingtao (Quingdao).[54] Of the population of two thousand residing in Tsingtao, mainly naval personnel, less than two hundred were German merchants representing German companies based elsewhere in China. As the German leasehold was an integral part of the rise of the German Empire, Kiaochow will be discussed in more detail in chapter 4.

Residing in the Native Town

In Kobe, under the terms of the unequal treaties, foreigners were free to reside in the Foreign Settlement, taking a perpetual lease from the Japanese government, or rent from Japanese landlords in the Native Town on less favourable terms. Nickel chose the latter. The Native Town was located between Division Street, the western boundary of the Foreign Settlement and the town of Hyogo, and was home to Japanese, Chinese and foreigners servicing the mariner trade. As the spelling of Hyogo can be interchangeable with Hiogo, the former spelling is used to refer to the town and the latter when it is used as a part of a name. As the Foreign Settlement had no port facilities, the Native Town offered access to the port facilities of Hyogo, and ships' supplies, lower rents and a cheap workforce of Japanese and Chinese day labourers. In 1879, Nickel co-located at No. 18 Native Town with his American friend David Tillson, to set up his own business.[55]

Nickel chose to live on the periphery of the Foreign Settlement for reasons not just connected with Tillson and the convenience of Hyogo's port. As observed earlier, in a foreign population in Kobe of 1,000, there was a class distinction between those servicing the mariner trade and those running trading houses in the Settlement. The latter saw themselves as members of a social elite and held leadership positions in the running of the Municipal

54 John E. Schrecker, *Imperialism and Chinese Nationalism: Germany in Shantung* (Cambridge, MA: Harvard University Press, 2013), 1.

55 Japan Directory Hyogo 1880. (Yokohama: *Japan Gazette*, January 1880), E206-3 KPA, 96.

Council, and in organizations such as the Hiogo and Osaka Chamber of Commerce. They were also listed amongst the guests of official functions held by leaders of the foreign community, the Governor of Kobe, Japan Post, the Harbour Master, and similar august Japanese authorities. However, certain foreign visitors to the port recorded their impressions of life within the foreign community in Kobe and suggested that even these so-called elites were 'riffraff.' One such commentator, Richard Gordon Smith, a British gentleman traveller who was in Kobe from the late 1890s to the early 1900s, and who lived apart from the foreign community, refused to participate in club life mixing with "remittance men and other socially undesirable expatriates."[56] As for Nickel, he probably felt more at home in the Native Town with its "mechanics and blacksmiths ... ship's chandlers and ... sailor's hostels and grog shops," an atmosphere similar to that of his native Hamburg and the Ōura Settlement in Nagasaki, away from the pretension of some of his foreign contemporaries.[57] As business grew, Nickel bridged the "social divide" using his transnational skills and his long established connections within the Foreign Settlement to source his clients, and to access the local Japanese government and British power structures.

Founding C. Nickel & Co. and Key Transnational Connections

Tracing Carl Nickel's company through business directories and newspapers from 1879–99 reveals how rapidly C. Nickel & Co. grew. While Japanese historian Murata Seiji claimed in 1898 that Nickel formed his stevedoring, landing and customs clearance company around 1880, the company's name only appears in local business directories in 1890.[58] In the years from 1882 to 1888, Nickel is recorded variously as a stevedore and customs agent as well as conducting a coal merchant business. In 1888 he placed front page advertisements in the *Hyogo News* offering a towing service: "The Tow Boat KATE is now ready to TOW Ships, in or out: Cargo Boats etc. to order."[59] In 1890, he listed C. Nickel & Co. with an expanded range of services—Stevedore,

56 Victoria Manthorpe ed., *The Japan Diaries of Richard Gordon Smith* (London: Viking/Rainbird, 1986), 12.

57 Ennals, *Opening a Window to the West*, 36.

58 Japan Directory, Hyogo, 1890 (*Japan Gazette*, Yokohama 1890), E206–12 KPA, 129; Murata Seiji, *Kobe Kaikō Sanjūnen-shi, Volume 1, 6 May 1898 and Volume 2, 25 October 1898* (Kobe: Kaikō Sanjūnen Kinenkai—digitized copy at NLA), http://www.dl.ndl.go.jp/info:ndljp/pid/805190, 224.

59 *The Hyogo News*, 3 July 1888, KPA, 1.

Landing and Shipping Agents, Auctioneers, and a new company, the Kobe Towing, Landing and Lighter Company Limited. In 1891, Nickel added a storehouse and shipping yard located at Ono, east of the Foreign Concession and according to Murata, held the monopoly of handling foreign cargo in Kobe, using a large workforce of Japanese stevedores and labourers.[60]

In Kobe, Nickel reconnected with many colleagues he had known in Shanghai, Nagasaki and Yokohama who had relocated to Kobe. The nature of his transnational connections and the impact of collaborations between foreign merchants on companies such as C. Nickel & Co. reveal the vital importance of such personal relationships, particularly amongst German and British, to successful business deals in Kobe under extraterritoriality.

The first of significance to Carl Nickel's success was his American friend, David Tillson. Tillson arrived in Kobe in 1868 and entered a partnership in the Foreign Settlement with another Nagasaki contact, William Warren, forming Warren, Tillson & Co., Compradores, Storekeepers, Navy Contractors and General Commission Merchants.[61] Twelve months later, this company failed, and Tillson moved out of the Settlement to 18 Native Town to establish his own business, D. H. Tillson & Co. Butchers, Bakers, and Compradores, with a slaughterhouse located in Ono.[62] When he arrived in Kobe, Nickel joined Tillson and although listed as a staff member of Tillson's company, he was building his own business. Tillson's death in Kobe in 1882 ended their association.[63]

Arguably the most important of Nickel's relationships to the eventual success of C. Nickel & Co. was with the British Jacob Lyons, an employee and later junior partner. Lyons, thirty years Nickel's junior, was a British Jew who had lived in Japan since at least 1886. He was first listed as a foreman in C. Nickel & Co. in 1890 and around 1893 was promoted to Superintendent. In 1896, he left to establish the Kobe Water Company, which in 1897 he sold to C. Nickel & Co., returning as junior partner.[64] In January 1898, he left a second time to form his own company, J. Lyons & Co., Stevedores, Landing & Shipping Agents, now competing with Nickel. An obituary written in 1916

60 Murata, *Kobe Kaikō Sanjūnen-shi, Volume* 2, 224.

61 Advertisement for opening of the business. *The Hiogo News*, no. 1. 23 April 1868, KPA, 4; Notice of winding up of Warren & Tillson Co.; *The Hiogo News*, 26 January 1870, Establishment of D. H. Tillson Co., KPA, 31.

62 Hong List and Directory 1872. *Japan Gazette*, Yokohama 1872, Hiogo, E206-1 KPA, 50.

63 Death Notice {David Holmes Tillson}, *Rising Sun & Nagasaki Express*, 4 February 1882, 3.

64 "Charges of Embezzlement: Messrs Nickel Proceed Against an Employee," *Kobe Chronicle*, 25 September 1897, 248.

described Lyons at the age of fifty as a "valuable assistant" to Carl Nickel in his stevedoring business, a man of "strong physique and untiring energy." He was also noted as being "kind-hearted and generous" and had "helped many men who appealed to him when in difficulties; a much-loved member of the British community."[65] Apart from Lyons' experience and competence, it seems his value to Nickel lay in his popularity and ability to connect with the British community. Nickel, on the other hand, while respected by the British for his business acumen, was considered something of an outsider, someone people other than his closest friends found hard to warm to. Nickel as a person will be explored in more detail later in this chapter.

As Nickel's company grew, he needed capital to ward off increasing competition. In 1894 he took on fellow German, Julius Helm, as a business partner. As noted earlier, Helm arrived in Kobe from Yokohama around 1894. He initially set up his own branch office but closed it and took a share of his largest competitor, C. Nickel & Co.[66] Helm's partnership with Nickel ended in late 1895 or early 1896 when Helm acquired the stevedore company, Jack Yong & Co., another long-time competitor of Nickel's in Kobe.[67]

The story of Jack Yong's business further demonstrates the dynamics of Kobe's rapidly changing business landscape. Jack Yong, a Hong Kong Chinese with British citizenship, first appeared in Yokohama directories in 1872, the same year Julius Helm's name appeared.[68] Moving to Kobe in 1874, he joined the British company Samuel & Samuel as managing stevedore.[69] Samuel & Samuel was a British company established in Kobe, holding a range of agencies in insurance, shipping and energy companies amongst others.[70] In 1891, attempting to end C. Nickel & Co.'s monopoly of foreign cargo handling, Samuel & Samuel established the Kobe Lighter & Drayage Co. under Jack Yong's management. This company subsequently failed, and Yong took over his former employer's business renaming the company Jack Yong & Co.[71] Allowing Yong's takeover may have reflected Samuel & Samuel's acknowledgement of the competitive nature of stevedoring, and the higher priority it placed on its other businesses.

65 "Death of Mr J. Lyons: A Thirty-Year's Resident," *Japan Chronicle* (Kobe), 4 May 1916, 721.

66 Japan Directory 1894. Zainichi Gaikokujin Kikan Meikan Dai 16 ban 1894, Kobe Directory, E206-16 KPA, 141; Helm, *Yokohama Yankees*, 79.

67 Helm, *Yokohama Yankees*, 79.

68 Japan Herald Directory Hong List for Yokohama 1870 (Yokohama: *Japan Herald*, 1870), E206-1 KPA, 12.

69 The China Directory 1874 (Hong Kong: *China Mail* Office, 1874), E206-1 KPA, 4.

70 Meiji Portraits Website, http://meiji-portraits.de/meiji_firms_s.html, 2017.

71 Murata, *Kobe Kaikō Sanjūnen-shi, Volume* 2, 253.

The importance of close relationships is reflected in the collaboration, at Nickel's expense, between the German Helm and the British Chinese Yong at the outbreak of the Sino-Japanese War, 1894–95. As war broke out, the Japanese government announced the end of Chinese extraterritoriality gained through the China-Japan Treaty in 1871. While some Chinese left Kobe, a number remained to protect their business interests.[72] Yong asked Helm to buy his business to avoid anti-Chinese reprisals.[73] Helm sold his share in C. Nickel & Co., acquired Yong's business and in early 1897 sold it back to Yong.[74] Helm benefited significantly through acquiring partnerships in both Nickel's and Yong's companies, learning much about the industry and benefiting his own company when he re-established his branch office in Kobe and he and Nickel became lifelong rivals. C. Nickel & Co. subsequently took over Yong's company in the early 1900s. As these changing relationships demonstrate, Nickel's company grew in a highly competitive environment, where foreign merchants at times collaborated and at others competed.

Extraterritoriality and Consular Jurisdiction

Despite the loss of Helm's capital, with careful management of his relationships, Nickel's company continued to grow throughout the 1890s. In 1898, C. Nickel & Co. was appointed comprador for the Japanese owned Nippon Yūsen Kaisha (NYK) shipping line, and Nickel employed a former NYK employee, the Danish Georg C. Kreidner, to run that arm of the business.[75] NYK was founded as a Japanese company in 1885 and employing many foreigners, built a fleet of fifty-eight steamships. Today it is a global logistics enterprise with over 800 container ships, bulk carriers, tankers and so on.[76] By 1899 Nickel's company became so successful that it secured a number of substantial companies as key clients, for example the American company Standard Oil and British companies, Dodwell, Carlill & Co. and Butterfield Swires, two Shanghai based large general import/export trading houses and

72 Hoare, *Japan's Treaty Ports and Foreign Settlements*, 67.

73 Helm, *Yokohama Yankees*, 79.

74 Helm, *Yokohama Yankees*, 79–80.

75 Japan Directory 1898. Zainichi Gaikokujin Kikan Meikan, Dai 20 ban 1898, Kobe Directory, E206-20 KPA, 135; Japan Directory 1898, E206-20 KPA, 135.

76 Catherine L. Phipps, *Empires on the Waterfront: Japan's Ports and Power 1858–1899*, Harvard East Asian Monographs no. 373 (Cambridge, MA, and London: Harvard University Press, 2015), 158; History of Nippon Yūsen Kaisha Website, https://www.nyk.com/english/profile/history/; Meiji Portraits Website, http://meiji-portraits.de/meiji_portraits_k.html, 2017.

agents for shipping lines operating across north Asia.[77] In addition, Nickel had at least three German key clients, two trading houses and ships' agents, H. Ahrens & Co. and C. Illies & Co, and a third trading house dealing in tea and silk, Delacamp & Co. By the first decade of the 1900s, half the business handled by C. Nickel & Co. was British and half German.[78] Evidence of the company's steady growth is also seen in the frequent changes of address, between 1891 and 1894. The address 3 Native Bund, where C. Nickel & Co. moved in 1894, was renamed 3 Kaigan-dōri in 1903 and became the company's permanent address until 1916.[79]

Nickel's success can be ascribed not only to his transnational connections, but also to his ability to innovate, revolutionizing the cargo-handling business under extraterritorial privileges. When he arrived in Kobe, the cargo carrying industry comprised large numbers of individual lighter owner-operators, *hashike-bune* or cargo carrying lighters, mostly Japanese with a handful of foreigners.[80] With the increasing numbers of foreign ships arriving in the port, the American *Hatoba* or wharf, only twenty metres long, was too small to accommodate passengers and cargo. Ships had to be loaded and unloaded lying at anchor in the harbour. Nickel was the first to employ Japanese day labourers as stevedores, conveying them in his lighters to and from the ships, squeezing the smaller owner-operators out of business.[81] Being outside Japanese jurisdiction, Nickel exploited large numbers of labourers for the cheapest possible rates and managed them in an uncompromising manner; being poor and uneducated, they could not sue him in either the consular courts or in the Japanese courts. They could however strike, as explored in chapter 6 on Nickel's relationship with his Japanese employees.

Under extraterritoriality, a foreigner could not be prosecuted by the Japanese authorities and was answerable to the laws of his own country. Nickel further exploited his extraterritorial privileges: for example, in November 1890, due to overcrowding in the port and a rise in accidents, the Japanese Customs and Marine Police banned boat owners (*hashike-gyōsha*) from anchoring inside the port when not working, except in the case of bad weather. Nickel ignored this ban, operating his lighters when he pleased,

77 "An Alleged Breach of Contract: Nickel v. Lynn," *Kobe Chronicle*, 26 April 1899, 322; "Claim for Damaged Cargo: Interesting Questions," *Kobe Chronicle*, 16 October 1897, 17.

78 "Nickel & Lyons Limited: Second Annual General Meeting," *Japan Chronicle* (Kobe), 29 April 1915, 647.

79 Japan Directory 1894, Kobe Directory. E206-16 KPA, 141.

80 Murata, *Kobe Kaikō Sanjūnen-shi, Volume* 2, 223–24.

81 Murata, *Kobe Kaikō Sanjūnen-shi, Volume* 2, 224.

much to the ire of the Japanese *hashike*. A Japanese commentator noted the harbour authorities "were usually indulgent towards foreign merchants" and continued to allow C. Nickel & Co. to operate and anchor within the port. However, Nickel's defiance of Japanese laws was not without consequences. On 12 July 1891, over 400 angry *hashike-gyōsha* and their crew crowded into Zenshōji Temple in Motomachi-dōri, a public gathering place, to protest to the police about Nickel continuing to operate despite the ban. While, their anger was not directed against Nickel specifically, as a precaution, he slipped away from Kobe to Osaka.[82] Nickel also entered the tugboat business without the permissions required.[83] In that sense, extraterritoriality was a boost to Nickel's business since it allowed him to ignore the Kobe Harbour Authority's rules. It is no wonder that the Japanese government was keen to revise the unequal treaties and to abolish extraterritoriality. As later made clear, Japan's objective of achieving treaty revision was to regain its sovereignty and achieve recognition as a world power.[84]

Choosing to Submit to the British Consular Courts

Nickel also took advantage of extraterritoriality through having disputes adjudicated by the British consular courts. There is no extant evidence that as a German national he resorted to the German consular courts: until the 1870s, the German consular courts had been run by merchant consuls. Since they lacked formal legal knowledge and, continuing to run their own companies, had inherent conflicts of interest, Nickel may have considered them to be unqualified and insufficiently impartial. Furthermore, appeals lodged in Berlin meant long delays, high costs and difficulties in bringing witnesses from Japan.[85] In contrast, the British consular court system, while not perfect, was the most sophisticated in use in Japan. By 1865, the British had a system of circuit courts in place in China and Japan with the Supreme Court based in Shanghai, not too far from Kobe. In March 1865, the British promulgated the China and Japan Orders in Council as the basis of British jurisdiction in Japan, which also allowed foreigners breaking Japanese laws to be prosecuted. British consular officials were professionals who

82 Murata, *Kobe Kaikō Sanjūnen-shi, Volume 2*, 236–37.

83 Murata, *Kobe Kaikō Sanjūnen-shi, Volume 2*, 236–37.

84 I. H. Nish, "Japan Reverses the Unequal Treaties: The Anglo-Japanese Commercial Treaty of 1894," in *Culture, Power & Politics in Treaty Port Japan, 1854–1899: Key Papers, Press and Contemporary Writings, Volume I*, ed. James E. Hoare (Kent: Renaissance Books, 2018), 348–60.

85 Hoare, *Japan's Treaty Ports* and Foreign Settlements, 58.

studied for the Bar and the Japanese language.[86] Non-British citizens such as Nickel could resort to the British courts where there was a conflict in jurisdiction and with the agreement of the foreign national's own consular service, although this latter requirement was not rigorously enforced.[87] Where consular jurisdictions were unclear, the treaty powers preferred to cooperate with each other rather than risk losing extraterritoriality.[88]

Many foreign merchants resorted to the British consular court to settle their disputes. The *Kobe Weekly Chronicle* reported regularly on such court cases and on C. Nickel & Co. in the context of those courts, as the following examples demonstrate. Two cases brought by Nickel to the British consular court in 1897 and 1898 are indicative of his expectations of the court. The first case Nickel submitted concerned the payment of "squeezes and commissions," today known as kickbacks. The *Kobe Chronicle* reported on this case to campaign against such practices, claiming the low wages paid by steamship companies meant that "it was well known that captains and officers of many ships levied a sort of blackmail on those who supply necessaries" to sailing vessels and steamships.[89] In 1897, the *Kobe Chronicle* reported that Nickel accused Frederick Da Silva, employed by the Kobe Water Company he acquired from Jacob Lyons, of embezzling money. Da Silva had collected "monies" for water delivered to steamships in the Harbour presumably paying the kickbacks.[90] According to the *Chronicle*, the court, while not condoning the paying of kickbacks and acknowledging that it was possible Da Silva had paid himself a commission, decided there was no evidence he had. Rejecting Nickel's claim, it stated it was his responsibility to know about this practice and to instruct Da Silva accordingly.[91]

In the second dispute the *Japan Chronicle* reported that in April 1899, Nickel sued Captain Lynn, Master of the British barque *Glencona*, for a breach of a contract for the supply of ballast that had not been written down. According to the *Chronicle's* reportage, "it was the custom for ships like the *Glencona* [arriving with a cargo of oil] to be loaded with ballast on the return journey" and Nickel claimed he had Lynn's agreement to supply twelve hundred tons.[92] He also claimed that it was "not custom to have

86 Hoare, *Japan's Treaty Ports and Foreign Settlements*, 57.

87 Hoare, *Japan's Treaty Ports and Foreign Settlements*, 71.

88 Hoare, *Japan's Treaty Ports and Foreign Settlements*, 70, 74.

89 "Charges of Embezzlement," 247–48.

90 "Charges of Embezzlement," 247–48; "Squeezes and Commissions," *Kobe Chronicle*, 9 October 1897, 286.

91 "Squeezes and Commissions," 286.

92 "An Alleged Breach of Contract: Nickel v. Lynn," 321

written agreements" for such orders. Standard Oil & Co. had employed C. Nickel & Co. as the landing agent to unload kerosene oil from the *Glencona*. However, it seems Lynn was somewhat devious, having Nickel prepare the empty hold at his cost, but not telling Nickel he had ordered ballast from Nickel's competitor, J. Lyons & Co. Nickel showed the customs permit for the ballast, he had obtained based on his understanding with Lynn as proof of the contract. Lynn however countered, suggesting Nickel had taken out such a permit "in anticipation of the business being obtained" to manipulate Lynn into giving Nickel the job of loading the ballast.[93] With no written evidence of a contract, the British court ruled that contracts for goods above the value of £10 should be written and not verbal. These disputes reveal not only the competitive nature of the stevedore, freight forwarding business by the end of the 1890s, but also a rapidly growing business in an increasingly busy port. Operators such as Nickel had to shift from relying upon personal relationships, common understandings, and gentlemen's agreements to seeking the consular courts' arbitration of such disputes. While such a shift might signal Nickel's need to see regulated and codified business arrangements in treaty ports, as seen in subsequent court cases, it also signals the potential for Nickel doing whatever it took to prevail over his competition and other claimants.

Carl Nickel, The Man, and the Arrival of His Successor

So far how Carl Nickel did business under extraterritoriality collaborating with his Anglophone counterparts has been shown. Despite the success of his company, a sense of the man himself is harder to discern. What is clear is that while Nickel was connected to the establishment, he was not a part of it. He remained on the periphery of not just the German but also the foreign community. The *Japan Chronicle* reported on the many grand dinners held in Kobe by the foreign community: farewelling key foreign business leaders leaving the port on vacation or permanently; or held by Japanese dignitaries in honour of foreign merchants. Reportage occupied at least a full page of the newspaper if not two and listed the key foreign participants and the speeches made almost verbatim. While Nickel's British and German contemporaries were listed as guests and benefactors, Nickel's name was only once mentioned. In 1900 his name appeared on the guest list of a grand dinner held to farewell Governor Ōhmori who was to become Minister for

93 "An Alleged Breach of Contract: Nickel v. Lynn," 322.

Home Affairs.[94] Even when Nickel retired from his role as director and managing director of C. Nickel & Co. Ltd. and departed Kobe in May 1906 to vacation in Germany, there were no reports of a grand formal dinner being held in his honour. This absence suggests that despite his business success over twenty-seven years in Kobe and forty-six years in Japan, he was not a member of the establishment.[95]

Nickel left no personal records, and so it is by his absence from the lists of eminent participants in the port's glittering social events, and by other empty spaces that his status can be guessed at. Given Nickel's age of sixty-three by 1899, his long presence in Kobe, his wealth, and his notoriety, one might have expected to find his name associated with such institutions as the Hiogo and Osaka Chamber of Commerce which became the Kobe Foreign Board of Trade, the Masonic Lodge, the Kobe Club, the Concordia Club or the Kobe Racquet and Athletics Club. Whereas several of his German contemporaries' names are listed, Nickel's name is not. While this could reflect his need to consolidate his business in a highly competitive environment, it could also reflect his status as an outsider in a community defined by class hierarchies. While representatives of the larger trading houses tended to have a higher social standing, Nickel in contrast appeared more accustomed to environments where differing social classes intermingled, from his earliest associations with shipping and the slaughtering and ship chandlery business in the Ōura Settlement in Nagasaki and the Native Town in Kobe.

Nickel's lack of close identification with Kobe's foreign community suggests a tough, uncompromising and at times abrasive character that did not place a high priority on pleasing others. Glimpses of such traits can be found in his domination of the foreign cargo trade by 1890, his dealings with the Kobe Harbour Authority, his dealings with ships' captains, the way he handled *oyakata* (labour contractors) and strikers, and in the prosecution of his claims in court when logic suggested he had little justification. When Jacob Lyons left C. Nickel & Co. a second time, there was a suggestion of conflict between the two men. The *Japan Chronicle* had stated in Lyons' obituary that he had been of great use to Nickel and had been a much-loved member of the foreign community. Perhaps Lyons had been a foil for Nickel's abrasiveness.

During this period of rapid growth, Nickel and his company did play a strong civic role. He was a supporter of the Mission to Seamen, an institution

94 "Dinner to Mr Ōhmori: Presentation of an Address," *Kobe Chronicle*, 14 November 1900, 416.
95 "Local and General," *Japan Chronicle* (Kobe), 24 May 1906, 629.

established to assist seafarers finding themselves abandoned in Kobe without means. He provided the use of his launch to ferry members to foreign community picnics. He was a founding member of the Japan Red Cross and is listed as the only German national contributing to the fund for widows and orphans of British soldiers in the Transvaal War in South Africa in 1899, a war considered by the British community as a "family feud between Dutch and British."[96] In January 1896 sharing news from the *Hiogo News* in Kobe on a personage well known in Shanghai, *The North China and South China Herald* reported that the "foreign and native staff" of C. Nickel & Co. had presented Nickel with a "handsome testimonial in recognition of his popularity and generosity as an employer of labour for twenty-five years."[97] Apart from providing evidence that Nickel was well regarded by those close to him, he also had status as a man with deep and warm personal connections in Shanghai. Ships' passenger records indicate he travelled regularly to Shanghai and judging by the various newspaper reports, he was well known and regarded with affection.[98] Reports on his role as judge in a Man of War race between two American cutters in Shanghai in 1873 outlined in chapter 2 and in 1887 of him having a horse racing in the Kaiser Cup at the Shanghai Paper Hunt Club Races, which finished last, both suggest that perhaps in Shanghai Nickel was not such an outsider in that port![99]

Further evidence for Nickel's formidable character can be found from his personal life. He found a working partner in his first marriage to the English Eliza McLaren held in Shanghai in 1868, a marriage which lasted until her death in Yokohama in 1883. At the time of her death, however, she and Nickel were living separately. Possibly Nickel's entrepreneurialism took its toll on the marriage. In 1890, Nickel remarried to San Francisco-born Kate Smith, widow of Oliver Smith. Smith, a ship's pilot who had died in Kobe in 1888, had been a close friend of Nickel's since Nagasaki days. Nickel named his tow-boat *Kate* in 1888 after his wife-to-be, suggesting

96 "Relief Fund Second List," *Kobe Chronicle*, 13 December 1899, 507.

97 "Award to Nickel of Testimonial," *The N. C. Herald and S. C. & C. Gazette* (Shanghai), 10 January 1896, 34.

98 Two examples, 1) Mr Nickel was a judge at a Man-of-War Boat Race in Shanghai held between a cutter belonging to the *Saco* and that of the *Iroquois*, two American naval vessels. The cutters had been built in Kobe, further emphasizing the close ties between the two ports and Nickel's potential involvement in the cutters' construction, *North China Herald* (Shanghai), 27 February 1873, 186; 2) "Nickel's horse racing in the Kaiser Cup at the Shanghai Paper Hunt Club Races came last," *The North China Herald* (Shanghai), 23 March 1887, 326.

99 "Nickel's horse racing in the Kaiser Cup at the Shanghai Paper Hunt Club Races came last," 326.

a romantic streak.[100] Upon their marriage, Nickel took responsibility for supporting her two daughters from her first marriage.[101] Nickel and Kate had their own children: a girl, Margarethe Kathe Karolina, whom he called Maggie, and a boy, Carl William Theodor. His son died tragically in 1896 at eighteen months and is buried at Shukogahara Cemetery in Kobe. Two years later the couple separated. In his last will and testament written days before his own death in Munich on holidays in July 1906, Nickel stated that he and his wife had separated around 1898 for "conduct of my wife having done acts which would justify ... divorce," suggesting a bitter breakup. Nickel went on to express his wish that his wife "not exercise the parental power over my daughter [fifteen at the time] but that a Guardian be appointed ... as the moral conduct of my wife gives rise to the most serious apprehensions."[102] He denied his wife the right to bring up their daughter. Nevertheless, he provided for her and his two stepdaughters, as well as for his biological daughter and for a handful of business associates and friends. His will suggested that while he was uncompromising, he was still cognisant of his duties and responsibilities. Through her marriage to Nickel, Kate and her two daughters had taken German nationality and had relocated from Japan to Hamburg sometime in the early 1900s. Kate died in 1911.[103]

With his advancing years, Nickel must have been thinking about planning for a successor. In August 1897, at the age of twenty-two, Nickel's godson and cousin, Christian Holstein, arrived in Japan. With Holstein's arrival, the future of the company under German management was secured for the foreseeable future. Upon his arrival Holstein assumed a clerical position and by 1899 replaced Jacob Lyons at the head of the directory list of employees.[104] As Lyons was the most senior manager at a crucial time in the company's development, if he had harboured ambitions of succeeding Nickel, they appear to have been dashed with the arrival of a family member. Lyons left for a second time to form his own company.[105]

100 Death certificate Kate Emily Nickel died Hamburg 5 May 1911 (born: Law, widowed: Smith) BN 332-5, SA 8008, *Staatsarchiv, Hamburg* (hereafter Death Certificate Kate Emily Nickel), 399; "The Late Mr Charles Sutton: A Will Case at Yokohama," *Kobe Chronicle*, 30 May 1900, 460.

101 Last Will and Testament of Carl Nickel, 23 July 1906, England & Wales National Probate Calendar Index of Wills and Administration 1861–1941, London, UK (hereafter Last Will and Testament of Carl Nickel). Obtained through the Probate and Wills Office, London, UK.

102 Last will and Testament of Carl Nickel.

103 Death certificate Kate Emily Nickel; "The Late Mr Charles Sutton," 460.

104 Japan Directory 1899. Zainichi Gaikokujin Kikan Meikan, Dai 21 ban 1899, Kobe Directory, E206-21, KPA. 151.

105 "Trial Trip of a New Launch," *Kobe Chronicle*, 8 January 1898, 52.

Part III

Revised Treaties

4. Transitioning to Japanese Jurisdiction

Abstract: In 1899 foreigners' self-rule and extraterritorial privileges ended with the enactment of the revised treaties. Foreigners now submitted to the Japanese courts which they believed to be anti-foreign and biased. The Japanese government continued subverting the revised treaties, maintaining its ban on foreign land ownership and introducing further restrictions on foreigners, most notably banning them from coastal trading. This chapter shows how Nickel and Holstein continued challenging boundaries set by Japanese authorities, litigating their claims through the Japanese courts to grow and expand their business. Under the Anglo-Japanese Alliance signed in 1902, hoping for greater British influence with the Japanese government, they took their company public, registering it as British and appointing a British chairman and some British directors.

Keywords: courts, bribery, jail, by-laws, alliance, *Chronicle*

In 1899, the Japanese government enacted the revised treaties ending extraterritoriality, allowing it to regain full sovereignty and control over foreign merchants. Thus ended the extraterritorial privileges foreign merchants had enjoyed over the previous forty years. Foreign merchants now had to submit to Japanese jurisdiction, causing fear and angst amongst the foreign community. Adding to the community's concern, the Japanese government enacted legislation by-passing the revised treaties. Practices that had been long accepted in the treaty ports and, internationally, under the unequal treaties were quietly negated by these new laws with consequences for foreign companies.

Until now extraterritorial privileges had played a strong part in Carl Nickel's success. With their removal, foreign merchants not only lost a competitive advantage, but also had to learn to navigate the Japanese court system in a business environment where Japanese competition had increased substantially. How Nickel met the challenges of transitioning from a position of

Holstein, Prue S. *The German Experience of Japan's Treaty Port System: A Case Study of C. Nickel & Co. Ltd., 1860–1923*. Taylor & Francis Group, 2025.
DOI: 10.4324/9781003706274-5

privilege to having to submit to the Japanese courts from 1900–6 is the focus of this chapter and is dealt with in three ways. First, by focusing on an 1897 corruption scandal, it examines how the foreign community foreshadowed problems submitting to the Japanese courts. Then, it shows how Nickel handled the Japanese court system analysing amongst others, the *Hamburg* Case brought against C. Nickel & Co. in the courts. The *Japan Chronicle* reported extensively on this case arguing that the Japanese government introduced by-laws getting around the treaties to ban foreign companies from participating in coastal trading. Finally, this chapter discusses how, facing the loss of extraterritoriality, Nickel acted to protect the future of his company.

How the foreign community enjoyed their free time with clubs at the centre of social life and how racist they could be at times towards their Japanese hosts is well documented.[1] Many British and American merchants were unable or unwilling to learn Japanese, and operated a step removed from their Japanese suppliers and customers using their Chinese *compradors* and Japanese *bantōs* to conduct negotiations, handle deliveries, complaints and any other matters requiring knowledge of the Japanese language.[2] Very little is known, however, about how individual foreign merchants ran a business in Meiji Era Japan on a day-to-day basis interacting with the various Japanese authorities. The foreign community was very unhappy transitioning from consular jurisdiction to submitting to the Japanese courts because it believed the courts were biased against foreigners. While little is known about how merchants in general approached the transition, this story shows that Nickel and Holstein did so pragmatically. Due to the opaqueness of the Japanese court system and lax policing of the new laws by the Japanese authorities, Nickel and Holstein continued to work their way around the system, not always risk free, however.

Between 1900 and 1906, C. Nickel & Co. grew substantially. In 1903, C. Nickel & Co. Ltd., recently taken public, acquired the stevedoring businesses of Jack Yong & Co. and Ah Chung & Co. with the former reported as a "valuable acquisition."[3] By 1905, the company "had built a fleet of 77

1 Darren Lee Swanson, "Treaty Port Society and the Club in Meiji Japan: Clubbism, Athleticism and the Public Sphere" (PhD diss., University of Sydney, 2016), http://hdl.handle.net/2123/16921; Harold S. Williams, *Foreigners in Mikado Land* (Tokyo: Charles E. Tuttle Company, 1963); Harold S. Williams, *Tales of The Foreign Settlements in Japan* (Tokyo: Charles E. Tuttle Company, 1958); *The Kobe and Japan Chronicles* 1897–1920s.

2 Kevin C. Murphy, *The American Merchant Experience in Nineteenth Century Japan* (London: Routledge/Curzon, 2003), 126–53.

3 "Trade and Commerce: Shares and Companies in Japan," *Japan Chronicle* (Kobe), 2 November 1905, 578.

lighters, 27 various boats, 8 steam launches totalling 6,266 tons … valued at ¥255,000."[4] While the amount of ¥255,000 (¥953,579,182 in 2019 terms) is equivalent to £4,994,269 in today's terms, the investment required today to build comprehensive land and sea transport systems would be much higher.[5] By 1906, the company had forged links beyond the Port of Kobe embracing Yokohama, Nagasaki, Shanghai, Tsingtao, and Hong Kong and possibly further afield. In 1904, one of its British directors, Mr F. J. Lias, was recorded as being absent in England working "in the interests of the company," so it can be assumed that the company had English connections as well.[6]

Fearing the Loss of Extraterritoriality

The foreign community was becoming increasingly anxious about how the revised treaties might affect their businesses. Such anxieties provide insights into the kind of daily issues confronting business owners in the treaty ports, and foreign expectations of the probity of Japanese authorities. In 1897, reporting on a scandal involving the Kobe Customs house, the *Kobe Chronicle* used this case to express its concern for how the revised treaties and the loss of extraterritoriality would affect foreign merchants. The *Chronicle* revealed that in 1896, Japanese Customs House officials and Japanese and Chinese employees of both foreign and Japanese companies were found guilty of embezzling duties paid by foreign and Japanese merchants on imports and exports by "forging receipts for the amounts paid [by the companies] as duty and appropriating the money."[7] The *Kobe Chronicle* complained that the Kobe Customs House would not accept "cheques on foreign banks" only cash, so "the way was … opened by which the frauds could be carried out …

4 "Trade and Commerce: Shares and Companies in Japan," 578.

5 This and subsequent Yen conversions to 2019 equivalents are based on website: https://yaruzou.net/hprice/hprice-calc.html. Conversion to British pounds at 2019 values was conducted on 14 April 2024; Estimating current values for currency from this period is difficult due to the ever-fluctuating exchange rates which was a complaint of foreign merchants due partly to lack of experience of the foreign exchange dealers, and partly because foreigners took enormous profits arbitraging the Mexican dollar, see also Simon James Bytheway, Martha Chaiklin, "Reconsidering the Yokohama 'Gold Rush' of 1859," *Journal of World History* 27, no. 2 (June 2016): 281–301. Company profile obtained for Nickel & Lyons, a company today in Japanese hands shows the complexity of a modern-day logistics company in the businesses of port and land transport, oil, fat and chemical transport as well as import/export business. https://www.nickel.co.jp/english/ 2025.

6 "C. Nickel & Co. Limited: Annual Meeting," *Japan Chronicle* (Kobe), 4 February 1904, 137.

7 "The Kobe Customs House Frauds: Findings of the Preliminary Judge," *Kobe Chronicle*, 26 March 1898, 263; "Scandal in the Kobe Customs," *Kobe Chronicle*, 4 December 1897, 472.

with impunity."[8] In the *Chronicle*'s view this scandal was "one more proof of widespread corruption of the Japanese public service."[9] Upon hearing of the resignation of the Superintendent of Customs, Mr Egawa, over the scandal, the *Chronicle* reflected that those in "contact with him had always found ... [him] a courteous and obliging officer."[10] This suggested that the *Chronicle* deemed some Japanese officials as being worthy of respect.

The *Chronicle* reported that C. Nickel & Co. had been one of thirteen foreign firms "unknowingly" involved in this scandal. One of its Japanese employees, Hara Jinzaburō, superintendent of the company's Japanese stevedores at the Customs House, had been one of thirty-nine charged and sentenced to jail while a second employee, Kawada Hyōjirō, was acquitted.[11] As a result of Hara's involvement, C. Nickel & Co. and other foreign companies were asked by Kobe Customs to hand over their books so that the monies that had been embezzled could be traced, a request which the *Chronicle* deemed preposterous.[12] The *Chronicle* thus used the Kobe Customs scandal to illustrate to the foreign community what could happen when foreigners had to submit to the Japanese courts. With access to their books, foreign businessmen saw the potential for Customs to claim that they had been involved in the embezzlement, and to demand unpaid duties from them.[13] Such was the concern of the foreign community about the loss of extraterritoriality and the corruption of Japanese officials, that the *Chronicle* reported on a "remarkable rumour" circulating in April 1898,

> According to this rumour, the Customs authorities have resolved to ... recover money, of which their own officials and others recently defrauded the nation by proceeding against foreign firms ... [on the basis] the duties have not been paid![14]

Given the concern about rampant corruption foreign companies claimed to experience in Kobe, the reporter added "it is fortunate foreign firms still have the protection of their own [consular] Courts."[15]

8 "The Customs-House Frauds: Heavy Sentences," *Kobe Chronicle*, 30 July 1898, 74.

9 "Scandal in the Kobe Customs," 472.

10 "The Custom House Scandal," *Kobe Chronicle*, 18 December 1897, 502.

11 "Claim for Damaged Cargo: Interesting Question," *Kobe Chronicle*, 16 October 1897, 319; "The Customs-House Frauds: Heavy Sentences," 74.

12 "The Kobe Customs Scandal," *Kobe Chronicle*, 8 January 1898, 28.

13 "Kobe's Curious Customs," *Kobe Chronicle*, 7 April 1898, 300.

14 "Kobe's Curious Customs," 300.

15 "Kobe's Curious Customs," 300.

The Revised Treaties

Following protracted negotiations between the Japanese government and each of the treaty powers, the revised treaties were enacted on 17 July 1899. After forty years, the Japanese government had ended the unequal treaties and extraterritorial privileges regaining its sovereignty.[16] While foreign merchants complained about the Japanese authorities' obstructionism, they had still enjoyed forty years of relative advantage over their Japanese competition outside Japanese jurisdiction.[17] Foreign merchants now had to litigate or defend themselves in the Japanese courts, while remaining sceptical about the Japanese court system handling their cases impartially. The *Japan Chronicle*, formerly the *Kobe Chronicle*, reflected the foreign community's beliefs that "their subjection to Japanese law will involve them in serious dangers and disabilities."[18] The *Chronicle* reported extensively on court cases involving foreign merchants including Nickel and his company, revealing its own bias against the Japanese court system. Nevertheless, in the absence of extant legal records, the *Chronicle*'s reportage provides valuable information about how decisions made by the Japanese government were understood by the *Chronicle* to affect the competitiveness of foreigners' businesses in general and how one foreign company managed the loss of extraterritoriality, as will be shown.

The revised treaties were negotiated and signed between the Japanese government and each of the foreign powers, commencing with the British in July 1894.[19] The treaties were negotiated by professional foreign diplomats, keen to increase trade between Japan and their respective countries. They had to balance the needs of manufacturers wanting to trade directly with Japanese suppliers against the needs of foreign merchants based in Japan, who had acted as middlemen, and who were more concerned about compensation for the loss of extraterritoriality.[20] Under the unequal treaties, foreign merchants were restricted to a twenty-five-mile limit around the treaty port

16 Douglas Howland, *International Law and Japanese Sovereignty: The Emerging Global Order in the 19th Century* (Basingstoke: Palgrave MacMillan, 2016), 60.

17 Correspondence No. 41, Alcock to Lord J. Russell, Dec. 6, 1859. Japan. Correspondence with H. M. Envoy and Minister Plenipotentiary in Japan, 1860. 19th Century House of Commons Sessional Papers. https://parlipapers-proquest-com.rp.nla.gov.au/parlipapers/docview/t70.d75.1860-036818?accountid=12694, February 2021, 89.

18 Robert Young, "The Case of the Foreign Residents in Japan: 'Nineteenth Century' for August," *Kobe Chronicle*, 2 October 1897, 273.

19 Young, "The Case of the Foreign Residents in Japan," 273.

20 James E. Hoare, *Japan's Treaty Ports and Foreign Settlements: The Uninvited Guests 1858–1899* (Kent: Japan Library, Curzon Press, 1994), 140.

and, denied access to the interior, could only deal with Japanese suppliers outside this limit through Japanese intermediaries. In exchange for forfeiting extraterritoriality, foreign merchants in Japan were now permitted to enter the interior and deal directly with Japanese suppliers. Nevertheless, having to submit to the Japanese courts and their potential bias against foreigners remained a concern for foreigners, not to mention the dangers for foreigners of being incarcerated in the insanitary conditions of Japanese jails.[21]

Bypassing the Revised Treaties

At the same time it was negotiating the revised treaties, the Japanese government drew up laws and by-laws bypassing some of the provisions in the revised treaties. Under the unequal treaties, a master of a foreign vessel required Japanese government permission to enter ports not yet opened to trade, the only exception to this rule was if their vessel was in a distressed state when they could dock for repairs. With the opening of the interior, foreign companies had also hoped for access to coastal trading. However, just prior to the enactment of the revised treaties, the Japanese government introduced the Shipping Law banning foreign shipping concerns from entering unopened ports, thereby banning foreign ships from coastal trading.[22] In focusing on developing international trade, foreign diplomats had not anticipated the Japanese government devising laws separately subverting the rights of those merchants already accepted under the unequal treaties and supposedly expanded under the revised treaties. In the *Hamburg* Case, these new laws would mean that long-standing practices suddenly became illegal either through oversight or intention, in a set of new circumstances that greatly affected C. Nickel & Co.

Learning to Deal with Japanese Courts

Despite the foreign community's apprehensions about submitting to the Japanese courts as expressed in the *Kobe Chronicle*, Nickel was quick to build his experience of handling disputes through the courts, finding some

21 Hoare, *Japan's Treaty Ports and Foreign Settlements*, 140; Young, "The Case of the Foreign Residents in Japan," 273.
22 "The Hamburg Case," *Japan Chronicle* (Kobe), 18 March 1903, 234; "The Penalty of Entering an Unopen Port," *Japan Chronicle* (Kobe), 30 July 1902, 98; "The Hamburg Case," 234.

advantages. The *Kobe Chronicle* reported on two separate occasions in March and May 1900 where Nickel applied to the Kobe Local Court to attach two foreign steam launches against money owed to him by their respective owners. Attachment is a legal process by which a creditor requests a court to have an asset of a debtor transferred to the creditor or sold so that a debt can be recovered. Both steam launches had collided with Nickel's lighters, and in both cases, Nickel was granted the attachments as compensation for the damages sustained.[23] Given that the defendants were British Hong Kong Chinese and Russian respectively, it was difficult for Nickel to prosecute these cases through any one consular court. Issues of jurisdiction had mitigated against compelling citizens of one nationality to appear in the court of another.[24] Resorting to the Japanese court may have allowed Nickel to achieve satisfaction where cases involved parties of another nationality, potentially a positive outcome of moving to Japanese jurisdiction. These two cases were amongst the first cases reported in the *Kobe Chronicle* involving foreign parties before a Japanese court, demonstrating Nickel's preparedness to embrace the new system. These cases also suggest that Nickel was able to navigate a liminal jurisdictional space, and that he did not share the foreign community's fears and concerns.

Christian Holstein, only recently arrived in Japan in 1897, also had an early exposure to the Japanese courts, and was able to exploit inconsistencies in the application of Japanese laws in the early years of post-treaty revision. From March to May 1901 Holstein, at that time sub-manager of C. Nickel & Co., appeared before the Kobe Ward Court charged with "an infraction of the customs law," avoiding customs tax on a shipment of jewellery.[25] As reported in the *Kobe Chronicle*, C. Nickel & Co.'s steam launch, the *Bismarck*, was conveying cargo and passengers between the *hatoba* (wharf or pier) and various ships within the Kobe Harbour. In this instance, the *Bismarck* was conveying a jewellery shipment from a ship to Kobe Customs. Under the law, Customs required the shipper to have a permit for removing goods from the ship and landing them at Customs within a specified period. Holstein argued (defending himself in German, though he would soon gain competent Japanese) that he had obtained two copies of the permit from Customs. Customs denied issuing these to him.[26] Holstein also stated that

23 "Application to Attach a Steam-Launch: Nickel & Co. vs Jack Yong & Co.," *Kobe Chronicle*, 21 March 1900, 234; "Attachment of a Russian Steam Launch," *Kobe Chronicle*, 16 May 1900, 419.

24 Hoare, *Japan's Treaty Ports and Foreign Settlements*, 80–81.

25 "Alleged Infraction of the Customs Law: A Foreigner Summoned," *Kobe Chronicle*, 27 March 1901, 272.

26 "Alleged Infraction of the Customs Law," 272.

the law was unclear on the exact amount of time considered reasonable before goods had to be landed as some goods could remain on their steam launches for over a month.[27] The court fined Holstein ¥10 (about ¥43,209 or £226). He appealed this decision, arguing that as the *Bismarck* had to convey passengers as well as cargo, it could take time for the goods to reach Customs and that any failure to pay customs tax was due to the law being unclear. The Appeals Court quashed the lower court's decision acquitting Holstein on insufficient evidence.[28] These events demonstrate loopholes in the laws which Nickel and Holstein could exploit effectively in a Japanese court setting, and they highlight the important and practical ways in which the merchants negotiated the legal infrastructure of Meiji ports and commerce.

Critiquing the Japanese Courts

The *Japan Chronicle* reported on many court cases involving foreigners, becoming a self-appointed scrutinizer of the Japanese courts. It campaigned against what it saw to be inequities in the Japanese legal system and what it perceived to be the court's bias against foreigners. Revision of the Japanese legal system commenced around 1873, introducing Western concepts of jurisprudence largely influenced by German legal experts, and was completed by 1899.[29] Nevertheless, by 1899, many foreigners still believed Japan lacked the legal and judicial systems to support Japanese jurisdiction over the foreign community.[30] The editor of the *Japan Chronicle* questioned the Japanese judiciaries' willingness to enforce or abide by the spirit of the revised treaties and criticized the quality of Japanese judges and the processes around examining witnesses. It considered the salaries offered judges were too low to attract the experience required, leaving judges susceptible to bribery and to political and commercial vested interests. It maintained that judges' knowledge of law was inferior to that of barristers, and whereas in the west competent barristers became judges, in Japan good judges were more likely to become barristers.[31] As judges could not

27 "The Alleged Infraction of the Customs Law: Second Hearing. Judgement," *Kobe Chronicle*, 3 April 1901, 293.

28 "Alleged Violation of the Customs Law: Acquittal on Appeal," *Kobe Chronicle*, 1 May 1901, 394.

29 Hoare, *Japan's Treaty Ports and Foreign Settlements*, 81–82; Young, "The Case of the Foreign Residents in Japan," 272.

30 Howland, *International Law and Japanese Sovereignty*, 66.

31 "Foreigners and the Revised Treaties: A Japanese Legal Comment," *Japan Chronicle* (Kobe), 27 August 1902, 209; "The Japanese Law Courts: Their Constitution and Procedure," *Japan*

afford to "associate with and entertain men even in the same official rank as themselves," their "knowledge of business methods remains restricted."[32] Moreover, a judge was guaranteed a position for life, making it difficult to remove them unless they broke the law and so in the *Chronicle*'s opinion, "the incapable remained."[33]

The *Chronicle* also criticized procedures around witness examination resulting in cases being "unnecessarily drawn [out] owing to ... delays ... due to a system which has proved unworkable."[34] It explained that only the judge could question witnesses; the defence had limited rights to cross-examine them. Defence had to seek permission to summon witnesses (which was often denied) and then had to submit the questions to be asked to the judge. The witness was given the list of questions having "ample time" to prepare their responses. As cross-examination of witnesses was limited, the accuracy of testimony could not be verified. Witnesses could also refuse to answer questions that were not on the list. A new list of questions had to be submitted, and adjournment sought to allow for the time this would take. Comparing this to the British system, the *Chronicle* explained that in British courts, counsel questioned witnesses directly with no limits on cross-examination.[35] Understanding how the *Chronicle* viewed the processes in the Japanese court is important to understanding its criticisms of the courts' handling of witnesses and the evidence provided. The foreign community continued to press for changes and modifications to Japanese laws and the courts' judicial decisions, with changes only occurring slowly as Japanese judges built "a body of precedent law to follow."[36]

As Robert Young was the British editor and owner of the *Kobe* and *Japan Chronicles*, his thoughts, beliefs, and objectives become important to this work. Robert Young was born in London in 1858 to a church-going family and became interested in Positivism, "a philosophical system recognizing only facts and observable phenomena."[37] He attended programmes with the "South Place Religious Society renamed the Ethical Society in 1887,"

Chronicle (Kobe), 3 September 1902, 226.

32 "The Japanese Law Courts," 226.

33 "The Japanese Law Courts," 226.

34 "The Japanese Law Courts," 226.

35 "The Japanese Law Courts, 226, 334–47.

36 Hoare, *Japan's Treaty Ports and Foreign Settlements*, 84.

37 Peter O'Connor, "The Japan Chronicle and Its Three Editors, Robert Young, Morgan Young and Edwin Allington Kennard, 1891–1940," in *Britain and Japan Biographical Portraits, Volume 4*, ed. Hugh Cortazzi (London: Taylor Francis Group, 2003), 335; *The Australian Pocket Oxford Dictionary*, Fifth Edition (Melbourne: Melbourne University Press).

associating increasingly with Atheists and human rights activists. This put him at odds with "Victorian England" and the conservative Japanese elites he would associate with in Japan.[38] Arriving in Kobe in 1888, Young entered the newspaper business managing the *Hiogo News*, purchasing it in 1897 and renaming it the *Kobe Chronicle*. In 1902, it became the *Japan Chronicle* and by 1905, the newspaper had become the best-selling English-language newspaper in Japan, targeting a constituency that included not just a foreign but also a wider Japanese readership. Young was also seen as "invariably liberal, often radical and sometimes socialist," and as a "pacifist" concerned with "truth and justice."[39] His newspaper provided a forum not only for his own leftist views but also for leading left-leaning thinkers both Japanese and Western.[40]

While it is easy to dismiss the *Chronicle*'s reportage as being anti-Japanese and biased in favour of the foreign community's interests, a more nuanced picture of Young's views on Japan emerges from an article written in the *Chronicle* upon his death in November 1922. The unnamed author suggested the *Chronicle*'s reportage should be viewed in the context of Young's appreciation for Japan's achievements of rapid modernization on the one hand and his desire to influence that process "to ensure a just system" on the other.[41] Young advocated for treaty revision and the abolition of extraterritoriality, maintaining that Japan had "the right and the capacity to rule in her own house." He considered extraterritoriality had been a useful privilege while it lasted but that it "was inimical to Japan's progress and dignity."[42] While Young supported the abolition of extraterritoriality, he could not support "the lack of equity and reciprocity" inherent in the revised treaties, in particular the continuing ban on foreigners owning land and the exclusion of foreigners from coastal trading.[43] Young believed that foreign diplomats negotiating the treaties had sacrificed "the interests of foreign residents in Japan" to the interests of home-based manufacturers.[44] He advocated for foreigners to own land, to engage in coastal trading, for justice for foreigners in the Japanese courts and against foreigners being incarcerated in the "insanitary" conditions

38 O'Connor, "The Japan Chronicle and Its Three Editors," 335.

39 "Robert Young: A Memoir: Thursday, 9 November 1922," *Japan Chronicle* (Kobe), 16 November 1922, 632–34; O'Connor, "The Japan Chronicle and Its Three Editors," 336.

40 O'Connor, "The Japan Chronicle and Its Three Editors," 336.

41 "Robert Young: A Memoir," 632–34.

42 "Robert Young: A Memoir," 632–34.

43 O'Connor, "The Japan Chronicle and Its Three Editors," 337–38.

44 "Robert Young: A Memoir," 632–34.

of Japanese jails.[45] Young, considered elements of the Japanese authorities were anti-foreign, and, believing the solidarity of the foreign community was crucial, advocated for "international friendship ... especially the British and the German, the two strongest in the port on friendly terms."[46] Young had a German brother-in-law, Emil Junker, who arrived in Kobe in 1886 and married Young's wife's sister in 1900 and became a teacher of German at the Kobe Higher Commercial School.[47] The importance of Young's support for British-German relations will be seen in subsequent chapters in the way the *Chronicle* reported on cases involving members of the German community, C. Nickel & Co. Ltd., and Holstein during the First World War.

As Harold Williams wrote in 1981, the *Japan Chronicle* served the community "faithfully and well defending individuals of all nationalities" against injustice it perceived within the Japanese system. However, Williams added, even Young's "closest friends" considered that the *Chronicle* suffered from its "constant criticism of the Japanese."[48] O'Connor also records that Young accused his media competitors, the *Japan Times* and the *Japan Weekly Mail*, owned by his nemesis Captain Francis Brinkley, of the "indiscriminate promotion of Japanese causes" for which he claimed they were paid by the Japanese government. He records that Young himself accepted Japanese government monies "to argue the case for ending extraterritoriality," which not only contradicted Young's claim to the moral high ground over his competitors but also suggested he was torn between his support for the revision of the treaties and advocacy for the rights of the foreign community.[49] Finally, like many of his British compatriots in Kobe, Young spoke little to no Japanese.[50] One wonders, if he had spoken Japanese and not had to deal through interpreters, he might have had a more nuanced appreciation of the Japanese authorities' position regarding the foreign community on various issues.

45 Young, "The Case of the Foreign Residents in Japan," 273.

46 "Robert Young: A Memoir," 633. For more on the role of the *Japan Chronicle* in Japanese Society, see also Tomiko Kakegawa, "The Japan Chronicle and Its Editors: Reflecting Japan to the Press and the People, 1891–1940," *Japan Forum* 13, no. 1 (2001): 27–40, https://doi.org/10.1080/09555800020027647.

47 Meiji-Portraits, http://meiji-portraits.de/meiji_portraits_j.html#20090527093346125_1_2_3_3_1, 2024.

48 Harold S. Williams, "Foreign Owned English Newspapers in Kobe: Shades of the Past," *Mainichi Daily News*, 21 February 1981. Extract found in file on Kobe Newspapers & Journals, Folder 80, Harold S. Williams Collection, National Library of Australia.

49 O'Connor, "The *Japan Chronicle* and Its Three Editors," 337.

50 O'Connor, "The *Japan Chronicle* and Its Three Editors," 337.

The Confiscation of the *Hamburg*

The first major case exposing Nickel to the shortcomings of the revised treaties, the Shipping Laws and the Japanese court system was the *Hamburg* Case. In May 1901, the *Hamburg* was towing the British ship the *Dumfriesshire* through the Inland Sea to Tsuchio/Habu, Innoshima Island in Hiroshima (136 nautical miles from Kobe) "to be repaired and overhauled."[51] While towing the ship, the *Hamburg*'s rope became entangled with its propeller. Although the rope was removed at sea, both Lorenz H. Petersen, a C. Nickel & Co. employee on board the vessel, and Christian Holstein waiting in Habu, ordered the tugboat to dock there to check for damage.[52] While the *Dumfriesshire* already had permission from the Itosaki Marine Office to dock in Habu, the *Hamburg* did not. Whether Petersen or Holstein had been aware the laws around distressed ships entering an unopened port had changed is unknown. As they had no choice, they may have been relying on the laxity in policing such laws.[53] Nevertheless, the Itosaki Marine Office charged the alleged boatswain or captain, Takeda Tōkichi with infringing the Shipping Law.[54] On 6 November 1901, Takeda was tried and convicted and was fined the sum of ¥200 (¥864,177 or £4526), a considerable sum for a Japanese boatswain. The *Hamburg* was to be confiscated.[55]

The *Kobe Chronicle* first reported the *Hamburg* Case as an "Infringement of the Shipping Law," and the case ran from October 1901 until March 1903.[56] It became a *cause célèbre* as the *Japan Chronicle* used the case to campaign against the promulgation of the Shipping Law on 8 March 1899 which bypassed the revised treaties.[57] While the revised treaties now permitted foreigners to trade in any part of Japan, the *Chronicle* asserted the Shipping Law was framed just before the revised treaties were enacted "to provide for the retention of the coasting trade in the hands of the Japanese."[58] The *Japan Chronicle* reported that the *Hamburg* was supposed to have infringed Article 3 which stated:

51 "The Hamburg Case: Text of Judgement," *Japan Chronicle* (Kobe), 6 August 1902, 130. Innoshima is an island in Hiroshima Prefecture near Itosaki. The port/s names of Tsuchio/Habu no longer exist.

52 "The Hamburg Case: Text of Judgement," 130.

53 "The Penalty of Entering an Unopen Port," 98.

54 "The Hamburg Case," 233–34.

55 "Infringement of the Shipping Law," *Kobe Chronicle*, 6 November 1901, 452.

56 "Infringement of the Shipping Law," 452.

57 "The Penalty of Entering an Unopen Port," 98.

58 "The Penalty of Entering an Unopen Port," 98,

> Only Japanese ships are allowed to enter Japanese ports other than open ports, or to carry goods or passengers between Japanese ports; unless otherwise provided by law or treaty, or in order to avoid the perils of sea or capture, or by the permission of the competent Minister in case of war or civil commotion.[59]

The *Chronicle* speculated separately that the true purpose of the Shipping Law was "to guard against smuggling by foreign vessels running into ports where there is no Customs-house and no Customs guard."[60]

From 1899, the Shipping Law immediately impacted the operations of businesses like C. Nickel & Co. While much of its operations were conducted within the harbour limits, its towing business took its vessels beyond the harbour. Until 1899, foreign tugboat operators could tow ships between ports with permission, and if they encountered difficulties, could enter an unopened port with the full assistance of the Japanese authorities.[61] If a foreign vessel was charged with unlawful trade or smuggling it could be prosecuted by the Japanese authorities in the British consular court with illegal entry of an unopened port under the Order in Council of 1865 which covered unlawful trade. Any person engaging in unlawful trade was deemed guilty of a misdemeanour with the punishment being up to two years prison plus a fine not exceeding Mexican $10,000.[62] Prior to the revised treaties, a distressed vessel entering an unopened port was protected under Japanese law.

According to the *Japan Chronicle* the Japanese drafters of the Shipping Law changed the chief offence from unlawful trade to mere entry into an unopened port by a foreign vessel, ignoring the needs of distressed vessels. During the *Hamburg* Case, the *Japan Chronicle* questioned how the court determined that Japan's interests could be injured by a distressed foreign vessel entering an unopened port, when there was no evidence of trade or smuggling. A law intended to prevent smuggling should have been more

59 "The Hamburg Case," 233–34.

60 "The Hamburg Case," 233–34.

61 "Foreigners and the Revised Treaties: A Japanese Legal Comment," 209.

62 "The Penalty of Entering an Unopen Port," 98. From 1854–68, the *Bakufu* Administration supported a silver standard economy making the silver Mexican dollar the official foreign currency in use. It seems the Mexican dollar was still in use in the 1890s. For more details on Japanese currency and foreign exchange systems, see E. S. Crawcour and Kōzō Yamamura, "The Tokugawa Monetary System: 1787–1868," *Economic Development and Cultural Change* 18, no. 4, part 1 (July 1970): 489–518; "Kobe's Curious Customs," 300; Simon James Bytheway and Martha Chaiklin, "Reconsidering the Yokohama 'Gold Rush,'" 281–301.

specific. The *Chronicle* considered that the provisions of the Shipping Law were not based on principles of "equity" and "mutual benefit" and used the *Hamburg* Case to illustrate these concerns.[63] As Nickel had secured permission for the *Dumfriesshire*, he had obviously been aware of the need for permission to enter an unopened port for the ship he was towing. However, it did not occur to him that the *Hamburg* was now in breach of the new Shipping Law and potentially subject to confiscation.

To avoid having the *Hamburg* confiscated, the *Chronicle* reported that Nickel appealed to the Osaka Appeal Court, claiming that it was Lorenz Petersen, a German national, who had been master of the *Hamburg* and not Takeda, who was only the steersman. Perhaps his thinking was that a German national might get away with pleading ignorance of the change in law. The defence argued that under German law, it was illegal to appoint non-German nationals as masters of German vessels, and as Takeda did not have the required training, he could not have been the master.[64] The court accepted this evidence and quashed Takeda's conviction.

A new trial to determine Petersen's culpability commenced in the Kobe Lower Court. The *Chronicle* reported that Petersen's counsel, Dr Masujima, invoked the German-Japanese Treaty signed in 1871 whereby "any ship of war or merchant vessel ... compelled by stress of weather, or by reason of any other distress, to take shelter in a port ... was at liberty to refit ... procure necessary supplies ... and put to sea again."[65] He applied for two expert witnesses to attest to the distressed state of the vessel, but the prosecution rejected his request claiming bias.[66] The court called its own expert witnesses, a qualified ship's master, Captain T. Kasuga, and an engineer with the Osaka Tekkōjo (Iron Works), Mr Y. Iyeiri. When questions put to them had not been answered by the next day, Dr Masujima questioned the witnesses' impartiality, claiming "there was something suspicious."[67] Despite his protests, the court determined that "the *Hamburg* did not experience serious inconvenience ... [justifying] her being described as a 'vessel in distress.'"[68]

The *Japan Chronicle* detailed a series of missteps where Dr Masujima in trying to navigate the Japanese court system misjudged its processes.

63 "The Penalty of Entering an Unopen Port," 98.

64 "The Hamburg Case: Procurator Recommends Acquittal," *Japan Chronicle* (Kobe), 19 February 1902, 156; "The Hamburg Case: Hearing of the Appeal," *Kobe Chronicle*, 11 December 1901, 563.

65 "The Hamburg Case: New Trial," *Japan Chronicle* (Kobe), 25 June 1902, 584.

66 "The Hamburg Case: New Trial," 584.

67 "The Hamburg Case: Another Adjournment: Value of Expert Evidence. Judgement," *Japan Chronicle* (Kobe), 30 July 1902, 105.

68 "The Hamburg Case: Text of Judgement," 130.

In lodging an appeal on Petersen's behalf, Masujima had understood from the small size of the fine imposed on Takeda, that the court viewed this case as a misdemeanour and not a crime. As a misdemeanour, "it was quite legal for an attorney to appeal by the power-of-attorney form placed in his hands by the appellant."[69] However, the court deemed the appeal invalid because Dr Masujima had appealed and not Petersen in person. Masujima appealed the technicality in the Court of Cassation but failed again due to another unanticipated breach. The court upheld the Osaka Appeal Court's decision on the basis that the time in which the accused could appeal in person had "now expired."[70] Petersen was convicted, and the confiscation of the *Hamburg* restated.[71] The *Chronicle* protested that despite the "lightest fine laid down in the Shipping Law … [being] inflicted," the court viewed this as a criminal act, where the appellant had to appear in person. The *Chronicle* also criticized the unnecessary delays in the way witnesses were examined.[72] Finally, referring directly to the *Hamburg* Case, it criticized the lack of an Admiralty Court with nautical expertise: claiming that "The judges who hear such cases have little or no acquaintance with nautical terms, and are mostly ignorant of the parts of a ship."[73] The *Chronicle* opined that the court was determined to rule against C. Nickel & Co. because of its rigid adherence to the so-called technical breach, regardless of confusion over the definitions, meanings and intentions understood by both parties.

Inconsistencies in Policing Foreigners

Examining the *Hamburg* case reveals key concerns of both the foreign community and the Japanese authorities. Foreigners believed that the Japanese government had circumvented the revised treaties by introducing the Shipping Law to prevent foreign companies from coastal trading. Foreign diplomatic negotiators had also not anticipated that conventions around distressed foreign vessels pulling into a port unopened to trade without permission were no longer supported under the new Shipping Law. The reporting on this case also revealed the confusion even Japanese lawyers experienced trying to interpret the application of the law and the correct

69 "The Hamburg Appeal: Claim the Appeal is Illegal," *Japan Chronicle* (Kobe), 1 October 1902, 317.
70 "The Hamburg Case," 233–34.
71 "The Hamburg Case: Another Adjournment," 105.
72 "The Japanese Law Courts," 226.
73 "The Japanese Law Courts," 226.

court procedures, confirming the foreign community's poor opinion of the court's ability to adjudicate fairly on its interests.

The *Hamburg* Case was also used to highlight the ad hoc way the Japanese authorities administered and policed the Shipping Law. Some eight months after the case had commenced, in June 1902, the *Japan Chronicle* reported that when Nickel "obtained permission for his steam launches to cruise in waters of unopened ports in the Inland Sea east of Akashi Channel," he (now) had to secure permission not only from the Ministers of Communications and the Navy but also from the Minister of Finance who also controlled Customs.[74] The *Chronicle* did not comment on this new layer of approvals, but having to obtain permission from three different government bodies must have added to the time and costs involved. A few days later, the *Chronicle* reported that the *Hamburg* had been forbidden by the authorities to tow a sailing ship, the *Professor Koch*, through the Kii Channel. It was reported that "The master received a notice from the Japanese authorities prohibiting him from taking the tugboat beyond the harbour limits ... the privilege of towing ships beyond the harbour limits being ... reserved to Japanese tugboats."[75] The management of C. Nickel & Co. reportedly said that the *Hamburg* had been towing ships through this channel for the past twelve months and although they knew there was a law prohibiting foreign vessels from doing this, "the law had never ... been enforced against the *Hamburg*."[76] The *Japan Chronicle* stated that Nickel had referred this prohibition to the German Consul, citing this action as another example of foreign steam launches being restricted from operating outside harbour limits. While from 1899 the Shipping Law had prohibited foreign tugboats from towing foreign vessels, the Japanese authorities' policing of these laws had only commenced around June 1902, reflecting an inconsistent and confusing application of the laws by the authorities in different ports. The *Chronicle* concluded such a rigid application was "a doubtful law in order to prevent competition of foreign tax payers with Japanese, [which] does not add to the dignity of Japanese Administration."[77] Nickel, understanding how loosely the application of the law worked between the Japanese authorities and the courts, worked around these restrictions as he had always done until the Japanese authorities decided to tighten their policing of the laws. This latest instance could also suggest

74 "Local and General," *Japan Chronicle* (Kobe), 18 June 1902, 564.

75 "Regulations Respecting Tugboats," *Japan Chronicle* (Kobe), 25 June 1902, 592.

76 "Regulations Respecting Tugboats," 592.

77 "Regulations Respecting Tugboats," 592.

lobbying by the Japanese tugboat industry trying to eliminate a major competitor.

By the end of 1902, the *Japan Chronicle* reported that the *Hamburg* Case had been brought to the attention of the Minister for Justice Baron Kiyoura, who had confirmed that the provision made within the Shipping Law as applied to the *Hamburg* was intended to prevent smuggling. He was quoted saying that confiscation of a foreign tugboat without cargo was unjust and that the court should give latitude. It was also reported that the Minister of Communication would bring a bill to the Diet altering the law.[78] This statement confirmed for the *Chronicle* that C. Nickel & Co. had not been suspected of smuggling. However, these pronouncements had no effect on the outcome of the *Hamburg* Case. By March 1903, the Court of Cassation confirmed the rejection of Dr Masujima's appeal based on his misinterpreting court processes.[79] The *Japan Chronicle* accused the Japanese courts of "elevating the letter of the law into a fetish, while totally ignoring its spirit or intention" and expressed the view that the case "must be argued between governments diplomatically."[80] Nickel could have resorted to diplomatic intervention, but there is no record that he did so and the *Hamburg* was confiscated.

The case continued to be a *cause célèbre* for the *Japan Chronicle*, and Dr Masujima himself entered the debate. In August 1902, the *Japan Chronicle* reported that Masujima had published an article in the *Japan Register and Messenger* using the *Hamburg* Case "as a text for questioning the way the Japanese government was carrying out the Treaties." He wrote:

> The interpretation which the Japanese authorities place upon any disputed provision indicates that in their opinion the Treaty was framed for the purpose of restricting the rights of the stranger within the gates and so point after point is strained to apply against the foreigner ... In their view, the kernel of the Treaty is for the Japanese, the shell for the foreigner.

Furthermore, Dr Masujima maintained that "foreigners sojourning among us are entitled to as many privileges as Japanese subjects ... enjoy."[81] Masujima's difficulties interpreting the law, and the court's processes in the *Hamburg*

78 "Local & General," *Japan Chronicle* (Kobe), 19 November 1902, 509.

79 "The Hamburg Case: Judgement of the Supreme Court. Conviction Confirmed," *Japan Chronicle* (Kobe), 18 March 1903, 247.

80 "The Hamburg Case," 234.

81 "Foreigners and the Revised Treaties: A Japanese Legal Comment," 209.

Case, led him to believe that the Treaties were interpreted by the Japanese authorities to curtail the rights and privileges of foreign residents and that he considered the confiscation of the *Hamburg* was unjust.

Despite Baron Kiyoura's stated intention of having the ambiguities of the Shipping Law addressed in November 1902, another steam launch was reportedly detained in April 1903 for infringing the Shipping Law. A launch owned by Messrs Helm Bros. Limited in Yokohama had been moored on the coast of Kamoimura while transferring its cargo to a lighter, which was then conveyed into a port closed to foreign trade. As the lighter's return was delayed, the launch entered the unopened port without permission and was immediately detained. The captain was interrogated before being allowed to return to his vessel and sail for Yokohama. Somewhat tongue-in-cheek, the *Japan Chronicle* reported that the Japanese authorities intended to "prosecute the captain for the heinous offense committed."[82]

Protecting The Company Post-Extraterritoriality

As the *Hamburg* Case played out in the Japanese court system, Nickel was already thinking about how to protect his company in the changing political and commercial environment. As a German owned company in a dominant market position handling in equal measure German and British cargoes, without extraterritorial protections and having to submit to the Japanese courts, C. Nickel & Co. increasingly became a target for Japanese competition.[83] To ward off his competitors, Nickel needed more capital plus access to a power base that could advocate on his company's behalf.

Furthermore, as a German company already handling substantial British business, C. Nickel & Co. found itself increasingly enmeshed in a web of international tensions operating in Japanese and Chinese ports. In 1902, the Anglo-Japanese Alliance was signed, confirming Britain's continuing role in theory as the dominant foreign power with access to the Japanese government. The Anglo-Alliance was a strategic alliance. From the British perspective, it was a means for Britain to share "the burden of maintaining Pax Britannica in the Far East" that Britain had assumed since 1860 with Japan.[84] The Alliance was also aimed at preventing the foreign powers

82 "Seizure of a Foreign Launch near Yokohama," *Japan Chronicle* (Kobe), 7 May 1903, 414.

83 "C. Nickel & Co. Ltd.: Third Annual Meeting," *Japan Chronicle* (Kobe), 25 January 1906, 116.

84 Ian H. Nish, *The Anglo-Japanese Alliance: The Diplomacy of Two Island Empires 1894–1907* (London: The Athlone Press, 1966), 1.

from carving up China, then under a weak rule following Japan's defeat of China in 1895. The words of British explorer and writer Colquhoun in 1902—"China, defeated and humbled ... unable to defend herself, and but for the jealousies of the Powers would be a carcass for the wolves"—confirm British concern.[85] Japan, on the other hand, saw the Alliance with Britain as a way to limit Russia's ambitions in Manchuria and Korea.[86] As Germany had taken a leasehold in China, in Kiaochow (Jiaozhou Bay) in the Shantung (Shandong) Province in 1898, both Britain and Japan informally sought Germany's inclusion in the Alliance. In exchange for joining the Anglo-Japanese Alliance, Germany sought Britain's adherence to the Triple Alliance of Germany, Austro-Hungary and Italy. It is also believed that Germany feared encirclement by Russia and so did not want to antagonize Russia.[87] The British rejected this invitation. With the ending of extraterritorial rights in 1899, Nickel and no doubt other merchants saw the signing of the Anglo-Japanese Alliance as a way for Britain to reassert its authority defending the interests of the foreign community.[88]

With Germany's economic rise and colonial expansion, Nickel also saw a growing anti-German feeling amongst his British contemporaries that could affect his business. In 1898, Germany's leasehold of the Kiaochow and the development of the Port of Tsingtao, now the base for the German Far Eastern Squadron, changed the balance of power in northeast Asia.[89] Since unification in 1871, Germany had been developing its export markets and had been building a network of colonies. In addition to colonies in Africa, Germany had acquired colonies in the Pacific Ocean which could help strengthen German merchant shipping in the region. With Germany's acquisition of the Kiaochow Bay (Jiaozhou Bay) came control of the large resource province of Shantung (Shandong), especially coal, with a population of twenty million people.[90]

Details on the leasehold of Kiaochow and the Port of Tsingtau are limited. As Manz explains, while Kiaochow was a part of the German diaspora, it was never intended to be a colony for German migrants. It was a concession

85 Archibald Ross Colquhoun, *The Mastery of the Pacific* (New York: The Macmillan Company, 1902), 404.

86 Nish, *The Anglo-Japanese Alliance*, 1.

87 Nish, *The Anglo-Japanese Alliance*, 125; Thomas G. Otte, *The China Question: Great Power Rivalry and British Isolation, 1894–1905* (Oxford: Oxford University Press, 2007).

88 Nish, *The Anglo-Japanese Alliance*, 19.

89 John E. Schrecker, *Imperialism and Chinese Nationalism: Germany in Shantung* (Cambridge, MA: Harvard University Press, 2013), 1.

90 Colquhoun, *The Mastery of the Pacific*, 404.

obtained from China under a ninety-nine-year lease and, unlike other German colonies which were controlled by the German Ministry for Foreign Affairs, was occupied and managed by the Imperial German Navy.[91] The Navy's intention was to build a model city and port in Tsingtao and to exploit Shantung Province's natural resources to display German achievements in the "Far East." Some 2,000 civilians lived there of which 1,855 were German and 1,183 were male, the majority of which were associated with the German Far Eastern Naval Squadron.[92]

John Schrecker explains that Kiaochow was a joint initiative of the Imperial German Navy and German commercial interests supporting "the rapid expansion of German [merchant] activity in China." German merchants believed a powerful navy ensured a commercially strong nation based no doubt on their observations of the basis for British commercial success in its colony of Hong Kong.[93] By the early 1900s, there were some 1,500 German troops and some 200 Western civilians, although the break down by nation is not given.[94] Most of the companies established in Kiaochow were branches of German companies long established on the China coast, and the community, including foreigners, were all subject to German law.[95] Neither Manz nor Schrecker provide any more details that enable a comparison with Kobe such as how many British merchants were active in Tsingtao or whether they worked in partnership with German companies. King indicates that in Tsingtau, it was the German firms who were keen for an agent from the Hong Kong Shanghai Banking Corporation (HSBC), indicating evidence of German-British collaboration.[96]

Rather than focusing on the commercial aspects of Kiaochow, Schrecker focuses on the leasehold of Kiaochow as a product of an imperialistic Germany and its "drive for the status of a world power in the 1890's [which] precipitated these acts of imperialism." He focuses on Germany's desire to create a German sphere of influence in China to both contribute to China's development and to compete with the British.[97] He does not place Kiaochow in the context of the general jostling within China by all of the major foreign powers as they

91 Stefan Manz, *Constructing a German Diaspora: The "Greater German Empire," 1871–1914* (New York, London: Routledge, 2017), 38–40.

92 Manz, *Constructing a German Diaspora*, 40.

93 Schrecker, *Imperialism and Chinese Nationalism*, 1.

94 Schrecker, *Imperialism and Chinese Nationalism*, 61–62.

95 Schrecker, *Imperialism and Chinese Nationalism*, 61–62.

96 Frank H. H. King, *The Hongkong Bank in the Period of Imperialism and War, 1895–1918: Wayfoong, the Focus of Wealth, Volume II of The History of the Hongkong and Shanghai Banking Corporation* (Cambridge: Cambridge University Press, 1988), 531.

97 Schrecker, *Imperialism and Chinese Nationalism*, 1–2.

sought to take advantage of China's defeat by the Japanese in 1895 and carve out their own spheres of influence. He does not examine the extent to which those other powers posed a threat to China or to Britain's interests for that matter. Schrecker also does not refer to Britain's leasing of Weihaiwei from 1898–1930 or mention Japan's acquisition of the Liaodong Peninsula and what became known as Port Arthur (Lüshunkou District of Dalian). Japan was forced by the European powers to return Port Arthur to China, which the Chinese then leased to Russia. He does however assert that the German government was sensitive to competing political interests in the region. In seeking a leasehold rather than annexing Kiaochow, Germany did not want to antagonize China and wanted to protect Chinese sovereignty. Germany also sought to negotiate with Britain and Russia to appease their concerns.[98] Paradoxically, he writes Britain "rather welcomed the idea of a German buffer between the Russian zone in Manchuria and the centre of England's activities in the Yangtze Valley."[99] Over time, Schrecker explains that the Chinese and Germans developed a growing closeness through the efforts of Max von Brandt, Germany's diplomatic representative to China. Furthermore, the Chinese used Germany as a counterweight to the power and influence exerted by the British.[100] Schrecker only suggests at the end of his book that further research into the imperialistic ambitions of other powers should be conducted to assess whether other nations posed a threat to China. The German leasehold ended when the Japanese laid siege to Tsingtao in October 1914.[101]

The rise of the German Empire presented C. Nickel & Co. Ltd. not just with opportunities but also threats. Through the presence of Germans in Japan over decades, the Japanese authorities gained a sense of a cultural compatibility, leading to Japan's adoption and adaptation of a range of German systems across military, legal, educational and other spheres. Nickel must have been aware that due to the growing affinity between Germans and Japanese in addition to Germany's economic growth and growing network of colonies, an anti-German feeling was growing wherever Germans and British coexisted and that Britain was becoming fearful of losing its economic supremacy. As C. Nickel & Co. Ltd.'s customer base was primarily British and German, Nickel foresaw difficulties for a fully German-owned company managing its British customer base in the context of increasing tensions.

98 Schrecker, *Imperialism and Chinese Nationalism*, 35.
99 Schrecker, *Imperialism and Chinese Nationalism*, 35.
100 Schrecker, *Imperialism and Chinese Nationalism*, 7–8.
101 Schrecker, *Imperialism and Chinese Nationalism*, 250.

In 1902, Carl Nickel listed C. Nickel & Co. Limited on the Hong Kong Stock Exchange as a British public company. The company's headquarters was now in Alexander House on Hong Kong Island with the Kobe office designated a branch office.[102] He appointed to his board influential business leaders in the foreign community. The inaugural chairman was Australian born Victor Thiennette de Berigny (owner of Berigny & Co., an insurance company, who also floated the Oriental Hotel in Kobe). Amongst his directors were British born Frederick J. Bardens (Manager of Samuel & Samuel, the British trading, shipping and insurance company introduced in chapter 3 and chairman of Hyogo and Osaka Chamber of Commerce), and Alf Woolley (agent for Peninsula & Navigation Steamship Company and Marine Insurance Co.). Two German directors included Nickel, also managing director, and Franz J. Popert (Ahrens & Co.).[103] In 1905, Nickel's successor and cousin, Christian Holstein, joined the board along with John S. Happer, the American head of Standard Oil in Japan. Holstein succeeded Nickel as managing director upon the latter's retirement.[104] With the appointment of influential foreign community leaders on his board, Nickel might have hoped to be able to resort to British diplomatic recourse in the face of the Japanese courts' intransigence in such cases as the *Hamburg*. He might have also seen such action as a way of forestalling anti-German sentiment towards his company.

While C. Nickel & Co. Ltd. was listed as a British Company, the *Japan Chronicle* pointed out that the Kobe branch of the company was also registered in Japan "as a juridical person under Japanese law ... so that ... they would have a status in Japanese law ... as if registered as a Japanese concern."[105] The *Chronicle* cited Article 258 of the Japanese Commercial Code: "A foreign company which sets up a principal office in Japan or which makes it its principal object to do business in Japan, must, even though it is formed in a foreign country comply with the same provisions as a company formed in Japan."[106] By listing his company on the Hong Kong stock exchange and as a Japanese juridical person, Nickel secured protection under British law through registration in the British colony of Hong Kong and protection under Japanese law for his branch office in Kobe. Nickel was not the first German national to do so. His one-time partner and now rival Julius Helm,

102 Title Registration for C. Nickel & Co.'s Kaigan-dōri, 3-chome property, 1895–1913. Kobe Chihō-Hōmukyoku (Kobe Land Registry Office) 1–1, Hatoba-chō, Chuo-ku, Kobe.

103 "C. Nickel & Co. Limited: Annual Meeting," 137.

104 "C. Nickel & Co. Ltd.: Third Annual Meeting," 116.

105 "Nickel & Co. Limited: Statutory Meeting," *Japan Chronicle* (Kobe), 25 February 1903, 166; "Commercial Firms Under the New Treaties," *Kobe Chronicle*, 30 July 1898, 69.

106 "Commercial Firms Under the New Treaties," 69.

also a German based in Yokohama, had already registered his company, Helm Bros. as a British company in 1899.[107] These initiatives were consistent with the transnational nature of the stevedoring business and the ability of both Nickel and Helm to straddle the British and German merchant communities and reflected the benefits they hoped for in aligning their businesses with British informal power.

Through the *Hamburg* Case, the impact of the loss of extraterritoriality on foreign shipping interests becomes clear. We also learn that the Japanese government enacted the Shipping Law to get around the revised treaties to ban foreign companies from coastal trading. Past practices of pulling into an unopened port in a distressed state under the unequal treaties were no longer permitted, leaving foreign companies vulnerable to having vessels confiscated. Despite the new laws, Nickel, and Holstein, aware of lax policing by Japanese authorities, continued plying their tugboats along the coast until policing policies were tightened two years later. The opaque and inflexible practices of the Japanese courts in administering the law were also a problem for the most seasoned of Japanese lawyers representing a foreign company. However, despite the changed landscape, Nickel continued to ignore or circumvent such restrictions and fight his company's cases in court accepting the risk that success might elude him. Finally, we understand what prompted Nickel to register his company as a British public company aligning his company with the British informal power base and influence with the Japanese authorities hoping it would be protected in the absence of extraterritoriality. If British diplomats or its British board advocated on behalf of C. Nickel & Co., they were unable to overcome a Japanese court determined to apply the law in the literal sense, possibly pressured by competitive interests. While this chapter showed how Nickel and Holstein dealt with the laws bypassing the revised treaties and navigated opaque court processes in the post-extraterritoriality environment, the next chapter shows how they had to deal with the consequences of an under-regulated and chaotic harbour as foreign trade exploded.

107 Leslie Helm, *Yokohama Yankee: My Family's Five Generations as Outsiders in Japan* (Seattle: Chin Music Press, 2013), 80.

5. Operating in the *Hatoba*

Abstract: The Japanese management of the rapidly growing Kobe Harbour, the locus of operation for C. Nickel & Co. Ltd., did not meet the foreign community's expectations. While it expected the Japanese authorities to mitigate increasing congestion and lack of infrastructure in the harbour and its associated risks, the Japanese authorities left it to private companies to remediate those problems. Rather than establishing speed controls and rights of way, the authorities also deferred to the Japanese courts for adjudicating disputes over damage and loss of vessels, cargoes and lives after the fact. How Nickel managed the risks in the harbour is the focus of this chapter. While he suffered losses, he also proved adept at turning risks into opportunities to develop new businesses.

Keywords: harbour, Customs, risks, transition, steam, courts

The rapidly growing Kobe Harbour was C. Nickel & Co. Ltd.'s locus of operation. It conveyed cargoes, stevedores and passengers between the piers or wharves (*hatoba*) and ships moored in the harbour, conducted customs clearance and towed foreign vessels beyond the harbour confines for which permission had to be obtained. The company's own launches and lighters had to navigate a melee of vessels criss-crossing a harbour with few speed, rights of way or other controls, landing cargoes in a chaotic Customs House exposed to the weather and leaving passengers to clamber over numerous sampans, lighters, and launches already moored at the American *Hatoba* or having to jump into knee deep water to make their way to the shore.

With its deep waters, mild climate, access to the Inland Sea and position in central Japan, Hiogo/Kobe had been a port since 710 CE facilitating coastal trade and trade with China.[1] It commenced operating as an international port when Kobe was opened as a treaty port in 1868. As

1 Kobe Trade Information Office: https://cityofkobe.org/about-kobe/history/

Holstein, Prue S. *The German Experience of Japan's Treaty Port System: A Case Study of C. Nickel & Co. Ltd., 1860–1923*. Taylor & Francis Group, 2025.
DOI: 10.4324/9781003706274-6

the present Kobe Ports and Harbor's Office explains from 1868 to 1907, the existing wharves were not large enough to accommodate increasing numbers of ships, so the loading and landing of cargo and passengers had to be conducted offshore where ships lay at anchor.[2] From the 1870s, the transition from sailing ships to the introduction of steam driven vessels led to a rapid increase in shipping fleets, of tugs, launches and steam powered merchant ships, with larger ships increasing cargo and passenger carrying capacity and shortening travel times. Moreover, the growth in the Port of Kobe coincided with and benefited from not just an "explosion" in shipping but also in world trade.[3] From 1870 to 1913, the volume of trade worldwide increased three times.[4] By 1912, Kobe Customs records that the Port of Kobe accounted for 40 per cent of Japan's entire trade with imports exceeding exports.[5] However, while major ports overseas such as London, Hamburg, Antwerp, Rotterdam and others were expanded and infrastructure upgraded to accommodate the explosion in shipping, in Kobe the harbour facilities went unremedied for forty years, and the explosion of trade only compounded congestion in the harbour and the risks taken on by such companies as C. Nickel & Co Ltd..[6]

In China and arguably Japan, treaty ports evolved from being just "a point of access" for foreign merchants to becoming an important link in a modern transport network and infrastructure engaged in the broader circulation of goods and people.[7] Furthermore, shipping infrastructure in Chinese treaty ports was a part of British semi-colonialism: due to Britain's dominant position in shipping and shipping facilities in British concessions, British firms ensured the infrastructure kept up with the needs of expanded trade.[8] It also helped that Chinese treaty port harbours were brought under the auspices of the Imperial Maritime Customs Service (IMCS), a joint British-Chinese initiative formed in 1854, administered by European nationals employed by the Qing dynasty which had ruled China

2 Kobe Ports and Harbors' Office: https://www.pa.kkr.mlit.go.jp/kobeport/en/pdf/thedevelopmentofkobeport.pdf.

3 John Darwin, *Unlocking the World: Port Cities and Globalization in the Age of Steam, 1830–1930* (London: Penguin, 2022), 297–99 & 304.

4 Darwin, *Unlocking the World*, 150.

5 Kobe Customs—History of the Kobe Port, https://www.customs.go.jp/kobe/english/e_kobekou.htm/e_kobekou.htm.

6 Darwin, *Unlocking the World*, 150–51.

7 Anne Reinhardt, "Treaty Ports as Shipping Infrastructure," *Treaty Ports in Modern China: Law, Land and Power*, eds. Robert Bickers and Isabella Jackson (Milton Park, Abingdon, Oxon; Routledge, 2016), 101–2.

8 Reinhardt, "Treaty Ports as Shipping Infrastructure," 101–2.

from 1644 to 1911. Always more than a revenue-collection agency, the IMCS had extensive responsibilities including the management and improvement of ports and harbours.[9] In contrast, in Kobe, Japan, where harbours and customs facilities were governed by the Japanese, the foreign community's advocacy for improvements to facilities led by the British went ignored for years. It was not until 1906, when a branch office of the Special Construction Department of the Ministry of Finance was established, and the first stage of harbour construction works commenced in 1907 in Kobe. Construction has over the decades resulted in the extensive port development extending from Osaka along the thirty-kilometre landfill along the coastline to Akashi and beyond seen today.[10]

The growth in shipping in Kobe Harbour occurred in tandem with Japan's role on the world stage. Upon defeating China in 1895, Japan joined the ranks of the great powers jostling for influence in China. Despite the port facilities not keeping up with the needs of increasing numbers of ships, Kobe became an important transhipment point for goods around Japan, China, and the German held Port of Tsingtao.[11] By the beginning of the twentieth century, C. Nickel & Co. Ltd., a hybrid British-German company servicing merchant ships bound for Japanese and Chinese treaty ports and beyond, was a company operating in the middle of a growing web of diplomatic tensions.

Exploring the challenges C. Nickel & Co. Ltd. faced conducting business in Kobe's harbour provides insights into how foreign companies thrived or struggled in this dynamic period of Japanese history, in a port (and a country) that was only just adapting to the demands of modernization. Examining Nickel's company in this period through the reportage of the *Japan Chronicle* allows us to trace the transformation of the treaty ports in Japan. This chapter investigates how the company, now a British company under German management, negotiated its position as a powerful player in the port, and as part of a community feeling increasingly under siege by the strengthening hold of the Japanese government on its national economy and its international trade.

9 Jürgen Osterhammel, "Britain and China, 1942–1914," in *The Oxford History of the British Empire, Volume III: The Nineteenth Century*, eds. Andrew Porter and William Roger Louis (Oxford: Oxford University Press, 1999), 156–57.

10 Kobe Ports and Harbors' Office: https://www.pa.kkr.mlit.go.jp/kobeport/en/outline.html, 2024.

11 "The Glut at the Customs: Views of a Cotton Expert. Views of Landing Agents," *Japan Chronicle* (Kobe), 24 August 1905, 241–42.

A Port Struggling to Keep Up

By the early 1900s the Kobe Harbour and Kobe Customs had grown organically without the authorities anticipating the ramifications of rapid and chaotic growth. The Harbour Regulations for Open Ports, promulgated for the first time in 1898, did not address the increasingly congested harbour, or the escalating bottlenecks at Kobe Customs.[12] It was left to the courts to adjudicate disputes arising from the challenges of a congested port. The foreign community still struggled with the loss of extraterritoriality and were diffident about the Japanese court system, considering the court processes to be slow, opaque, and biased. The *Japan Chronicle* regularly reported to its readers the foreign community's perceptions about the inadequacies of the Japanese Harbour Master, the Kobe Customs, and the Japanese court systems. In so doing, it not only informed its foreign readership of the consequences of the loss of extraterritoriality, but it also represented the foreign community's views to senior Japanese decision makers and business leaders who also read the *Chronicle*.

After listing on the Hong Kong Stock Exchange, C. Nickel & Co. Ltd. continued to flourish. As C. Nickel & Co. had been a private company prior to 1902, there was no published financial data. However, with its listing in 1902, the company held annual general meetings (AGM) reporting to its shareholders which the *Japan Chronicle* covered for its readership, so, although the company's files are no longer available, an idea of the company's performance can be gleaned.[13] At the second AGM held in 1904, the board noted, "the flotation of the company (in 1902) had proved to be a sound enterprise."[14] Despite the complexities of the business, the cargoes to be handled and the "large gangs" of men to be managed, the company was "flourishing."[15] The *Chronicle* also reported that the company, with its significant fleet of vessels, had introduced a marine insurance department intending to become its own underwriters, signifying not just a measure of

12 "Harbour Regulations for Open Ports: Imperial Ordinance No. 139," *Kobe Chronicle*, 17 September 1898, 234.

13 The *Japan Chronicle* reported on the AGMs for C. Nickel & Co. Ltd. and its successor, Nickel & Lyons, from 1903–15. See for example, "C. Nickel & Co. Ltd.: Third Annual Meeting," *Japan Chronicle* (Kobe), 25 January 1906, 116; "C. Nickel & Co. Ltd.: Seventh Annual General Meeting," *Japan Chronicle* (Kobe), 30 December 1909, 1177; "Nickel and Lyons Limited: First Annual Meeting," *Japan Chronicle* (Kobe), 16 April 1914, 642.

14 "C. Nickel & Company Limited: Meeting of Shareholders," *Japan Chronicle* (Kobe), 2 February 1905, 130.

15 "C. Nickel & Company Limited: Meeting of Shareholders," 130.

financial success but also the company's desire to better control the costs of damaged and lost vessels and cargoes.[16]

At the same time, the AGM reports also signalled a growing concern about the harbour's infrastructure and the potential impact on the company's profits. In 1904, the *Japan Chronicle* noted that due to the congested customs compound "boats laden with cargo ... were ... occupied for days ... discharging ... [and were] kept in the harbour doing nothing, to the great inconvenience of ship-owners."[17] In 1906, the board reported that a decline in profit for 1905 had not been

> due to any deterioration of their business—it was directly the result of the deficient Customs accommodation at the Hatoba, which had resulted last year in a glut of merchandise ... Owing to the lack of proper appliances, the Customs could not deal with the amount of goods ... and the company had ... to pay demurrage.[18]

At the same time, business was booming: one British shareholder, a Mr Noel, pointed out that "the past year [1905] had been a phenomenal one" to the extent that "the stevedore business was so attractive in Kobe that other companies were starting in the line."[19]

An Influential Board

Listing as a British company, C. Nickel & Co. Ltd. benefited from a board connected to the broader merchant community increasing its access to capital and in theory to the British and Japanese power structures. From 1902 to 1914, the board appointed men of influence and power within Kobe's foreign community to represent its interests to its stakeholders and potential clients, mainly British and German.[20] Directors were typically "Asia-hands" engaged in trade, insurance and shipping businesses in northeast Asia and were predominantly British.[21] Two well-respected British chairmen of the

16 "C. Nickel & Company Limited: Meeting of Shareholders," 130.

17 "C. Nickel & Company Limited: Meeting of Shareholders," 130.

18 "C. Nickel & Co. Ltd.: Third Annual Meeting," 116.

19 "C. Nickel & Co. Ltd.: Third Annual Meeting," 116; Bernd Lepach, Meiji-Portraits: http://meiji-portraits.de/meiji_portraits_n.html, 2024.

20 "Nickel & Lyons Limited: Second Annual General Meeting," *Japan Chronicle* (Kobe), 29 April 1915, 647.

21 "C. Nickel & Co. Ltd.: Annual General Meeting," *Japan Chronicle* (Kobe), 2 January 1908, 15.

board were Frederick J. Bardens (chairman of the provisional board from 1902 to 1903) and Alf Woolley (chairman from 1907 to 1913).[22] Frederick Bardens had arrived in Japan in 1886 and represented Samuel & Samuel in Kobe until 1905.[23] As seen in chapter 3, Samuel & Samuel had established the Kobe Lighter and Drayage Company to break Nickel's monopoly during the 1890s, subsequently becoming Jack Yong & Co. and then acquired by C. Nickel & Co. in 1900.[24] Alf Woolley, also British, had been in Japan since 1890 representing the Peninsular & Oriental Steam Navigation Co. (today P & O).[25] Bardens served as chairman of the influential Hyogo and Osaka General Chamber of Commerce (1900–5) and Woolley served as chairman of its successor, the Kobe Foreign Board of Trade (from 1905–8 at least). The Kobe Foreign Board of Trade and its predecessor represented sixty-six foreign member companies, and from at least 1900 lobbied the Japanese government to make improvements to the Kobe Harbour and Kobe Customs.[26] These connections highlight how beneficial it was for Nickel to be well-connected with other foreign businesses.

In addition to British representatives on the board, two positions were reserved for German directors, the managing director, and a non-executive director. Nickel was initially the managing director and later, in an arrangement established prior to taking his company public in 1902, his relative Christian Holstein. The second position on the board was held successively by German nationals Franz J. Popert and H. Hoffmann, representatives of two key clients, Norddeutscher Lloyd and Ahrens & Co. respectively.[27] In 1906, an American, John S. Happer, who represented another key client, the Standard Oil & Co., joined the board.[28] Born in China in 1863, Happer was highly respected within the foreign community and aside from his

22 Meiji-Portraits: http://meiji-portraits.de/meiji_portraits_b.html#20090527093402531_1_2_3_13_1; http://meiji-portraits.de/meiji_portraits_w.html#20090527093525140_1_2_2_12_1, 2024.

23 Meiji-Portraits, http://meiji-portraits.de/meiji_portraits_b.html#20090527093402531_1_2_3_13_1, 2021.

24 "Trade and Commerce: Shares and Companies in Japan," *Japan Chronicle* (Kobe), 2 November 1905, 577.

25 "Obituary: Mr. Alf Woolley," *Japan Chronicle* (Kobe), 30 December 1920, 906.

26 "Hyogo and Osaka General Chamber of Commerce: Annual Meeting," *Japan Chronicle* (Kobe), 11 February 1903, 123; "Hiogo & Osaka Chamber of Commerce: Annual General Meeting," *Japan Chronicle* (Kobe), 2 March 1905, 255.

27 Meiji-Portraits Persons: http://meiji-portraits.de/meiji_portraits_p.html; http://meiji-portraits.de/meiji_portraits_h.html, 2024.

28 Meiji-Portraits Persons, http://meiji-portraits.de/meiji_portraits_h.html#20090527093325890_1_2_3_32_1, 2024; Japan Directory 1916 (Yokohama, *Japan Gazette*), 1916. Happer is listed as a director of Tor Hotel Ltd.

business dealings was also acclaimed as a collector of Japanese *ukiyoe* or wood-block printing. Until his death in Tokyo in 1936, Happer remained closely associated with Holstein, reflecting the ongoing importance of connections and influence in the business dealings of foreign merchants in Kobe. In 1908, Happer and Holstein were co-promoters in building the luxurious Tor Hotel in Kobe, both becoming directors. For C. Nickel & Co. Ltd., these connections were important to ensure the joint buy-in of the British and German merchant communities to support the success of the company.

Death of the Founder and His Legacy

At the end of July 1906, just after he retired, aged seventy-two, Carl Nickel died while on vacation in Germany.[29] The board and management of C. Nickel & Co. Ltd. anticipated his impending retirement in the first quarter of 1906 by appointing Holstein to the board of directors in 1905.[30] In 1906, Holstein, then aged thirty-one, succeeded Nickel as managing director.[31] With Nickel's sudden death, the board noted, somewhat dispassionately, that the equal profit sharing arrangement made between Nickel and the company for five years from 1902 would cease, thus improving the company's position and that of its shareholders.[32] The dry tone of this report confirms what had become apparent in chapter 3, that although Carl Nickel was respected and acknowledged in Kobe in the monopoly he held as the "king of *sutebe-gyō* (stevedoring business as termed by a local Japanese Kobe historian), the wider foreign community viewed him with antipathy.[33]

Nickel's obituary was also telling about how the foreign community regarded him. As seen in chapter 3, when high-profile foreigners died, detailed obituaries were often written in the *Japan Chronicle* providing a record of their lives in Japan and praising their contributions to the foreign community. In contrast, and despite his forty-six years in Japan, Nickel's obituary was short. It acknowledged the sadness "his many old friends in

29 "Death of Mr C. T. M. Nickel," *Japan Chronicle* (Kobe), 16 August 1906, 213.
30 "C. Nickel & Co. Ltd.: Third Annual Meeting," 116.
31 "C. Nickel and Company Ltd.: Annual Meeting," *Japan Chronicle* (Kobe), 27 December 1906, 816.
32 "C. Nickel and Company Ltd.: Annual Meeting," 816.
33 Email from Rick Taniguchi, 1 May 2017 Re: Span of Kobe Port. Mr Ryōhei Taniguchi belongs to the Kobe Gaikokujin Kyoryūchi Kenkyūkai (Kobe Foreign Settlement Research Society). Established in 1998, it has 130 members.

this country" felt. It mentioned the timeline of his arrival in Japan and Kobe via Shanghai and that he had "made a comfortable fortune" out of the stevedoring business.[34] While the *Japan Chronicle* published many articles about Nickel during his twenty-five years in Kobe, personal information given in his obituary was scant. Nickel's obituary did not expand on his depth of experience and knowledge of Japan, his adventures during the early days of Nagasaki, his contribution to revolutionizing the Japanese stevedoring industry and his civic role and charitable acts as outlined in chapter 3. It relied upon the knowledge of one informant, most likely Holstein, and reflected a man who lived life on his own terms, choosing to remain on the periphery of the foreign community.[35]

Operating in the Port

As seen in chapter 4, C. Nickel & Co. Ltd.'s operations were limited to the Kobe Harbour unless it obtained the required permissions to move beyond the harbour. The boundaries of the harbour were laid down by Imperial Ordinance No. 77 on 14 September 1892 and reconfirmed in 1898.[36] The port extended from Point Wada in the west to the former mouth of the Ikuta River at Ono Bay in the east forming a horseshoe shape in the centre. While foreign companies were confined to operating within these harbour limits, their Japanese competitors were free to operate between Kobe and Osaka, to the east and beyond.

Until 1898, Nickel and other foreign merchants operated in a largely unregulated port. Under Imperial Ordinance No. 139 in September 1898, this changed ahead of the enactment of the revised treaties with new regulations around the entry and use of the port.[37] The Harbour Regulations were reported in the *Kobe Chronicle* translated into English. They reconfirmed the boundaries of the harbour and the limits of foreign merchants' activities. They

34 "Death of Mr C.T.M. Nickel," 213.

35 "Death of Mr C.T.M. Nickel," 213.

36 Original script signed by the emperor, 1892, Imperial Ordinance No.77, Expansion of Vessels Mooring Area in Kobe Port, Japan Centre for Asian Historical Records, https://www.jacar.archives.go.jp/aj/meta/MetSearch.cgi?SUM_KIND=MetaSummary&SUM_NUMBER=20&IS_KIND=SimpleSummary&IS_SCH=META&IS_STYLE=eng&DB_ID=G0000101EXTERNAL&GRP_ID=G0000101&IS_START=1&IS_EXTSCH=&DEF_XSL=default-en&IS_SORT_KND=ASC&IS_SORT_FLD=&IS_TAG_S1=InfoSDU&IS_KEY_S1=A03020128700&IS_NUMBER=20&ON_LYD=on, 2021.

37 "Harbour Regulations for Open Ports: Imperial Ordinance No. 139," 234.

focused on the obligations of ships' captains of vessels entering or leaving the port to notify the Harbour Master and to berth where directed. To avoid obstructing free navigation, vessels had to remain lit at night for safety. In case fires broke out, the ship's bells were required to signal for assistance, although how that assistance was provided was not stated. Ships were also required to adhere to quarantine directives, prepare for bad weather when notified, and prevent waste and debris from being thrown into the harbour.[38]

With these developments, foreign merchants, including Nickel, found themselves beholden to laws formed by Japanese authorities for the first time since arriving in Japan, something they were not used to, and so they viewed these laws with ambivalence. The *Japan Chronicle* suggested as much when it reported on a banquet held by the Harbour Master Captain Tashiro in April 1899, an occasion bringing Japanese government officials together with foreign businessmen operating in the harbour.[39] A number of C. Nickel & Co. Ltd.'s key clients such as Standard Oil, Delacamp & Co., Ahrens & Co. and C. Illies & Co. attended, but C. Nickel & Co. Ltd. and their other stevedore and freight forwarding colleagues were not listed. Speaking positively about the regulations and about his relationship with foreign merchants, Captain Tashiro undertook to "interpret and carry out the Harbour Regulations in a liberal manner ... to prevent friction and inconvenience." The aim was "to preserve order ... so that accidents and injury to life and property may be prevented ... to facilitate the trade of the port."[40] The British Consul, John Carey Hall, replied on behalf of the foreign community, "The necessity of the Harbour Office and Harbour Regulations has long been felt want at the open ports" and were "long needed and warmly welcomed." Possibly anticipating little real improvement and reflecting a veiled cynicism felt amongst some merchants in dealing with Japanese authorities, Hall continued:

> We foreigners ... for the last thirty or forty years, [were] under a highly abnormal condition of things, where we were not brought ... directly into contact with executive authority; while ... we have managed to get on so well in the absence of Regulations ... we recognise that such a state of affairs could not be perpetual ... we can assure you that ... mistakes will not arise from bad intentions ... but from the difficulty ... in accommodating ourselves to the new conditions.[41]

38 "Harbour Regulations for Open Ports: Imperial Ordinance No. 139," 234.
39 "The New Harbour Office: Banquet at the Tokiwa Kwadan," *Kobe Chronicle*, 5 April 1899, 257.
40 "The New Harbour Office," 257.
41 "The New Harbour Office," 257.

Despite mutual assurances of cooperation, the foreign community became more entrenched in its beliefs that the Japanese authorities should be introducing regulations mitigating the risks of doing business in the port. The regulations did not address the frequent accidents and expensive loss of vessels, cargoes and sometimes lives. There were no regulations providing for speed controls or rights of way. In one article, the *Chronicle*, complaining about the constant speeding of Japanese steamers, commented that the Harbour Master "does not seem to have the necessary power to interfere."[42] Moreover, issues around poor infrastructure—such as inadequate cargo loading and landing facilities or cranes at shore, the lack of water borne fire-fighting equipment, the absence of derricks for recovering sunk and damaged vessels, and the lack of adequate policing and traffic control—remained bones of contention for foreign operators. Moreover, it was often left to the Japanese courts to adjudicate on disputes occurring, as will be seen shortly.

Amongst the many challenges of a congested harbour was the size and positioning of the *hatoba* in the port, making loading and landing passengers and cargoes not only costly, but also perilous. There were four piers. No. 1 *Hatoba*, located on the eastern boundary of the harbour at Ono was the location of the Eastern Customs House where foreign cargoes had to be delivered for assessment. It was also designated for unloading imported cargo. No. 2 *Hatoba* was known as the American *Hatoba* and was used for the loading of export cargoes and passengers. It only measured twenty metres in length and was regularly crowded with lighters. No. 3 *Hatoba* at Minatogawa/Kawasaki was the location of the Western Customs House and where export cargoes were loaded. The *hatoba* were all too small to accommodate the increasing volume of ships, so most ships had to lie at anchor in the harbour whilst passengers and cargo were loaded and unloaded, often in rough seas. C. Nickel & Co. Ltd.'s steamers, launches and lighters joined the constant flow of vessels day and night as they conveyed passengers, stevedores and cargo between ships and the piers. The potential for accidents, loss of vessels and cargoes, not to mention lives, was ever-present.

Added to the melee of vessels criss-crossing the harbour were the dangers of ship-board fires, collisions and typhoons. Ship-board fires occurred frequently: the most common causes, according to newspaper reports, were sabotage by disgruntled foreign crews, highly flammable cargoes and Japanese stevedores smoking illegally whilst loading or unloading cargoes. In April 1901, the *Kobe Chronicle* reported that the American sailing ship, *R. D. Rice*, consigned to the Standard Oil Company and still loaded with some

42 "Japanese Steamers Again," *Kobe Chronicle*, 13 February 1898, 109.

thirty-three thousand cases of kerosene oil, was destroyed by fire whilst anchored at the company's oil station at Yokoya (now Uozaki). Standard Oil was a regular client of C. Nickel & Co. Ltd., and Nickel's stevedores were unloading the cargo. The Kobe Water Police and other boats helped to rescue the crew. The *Chronicle*, implying criticism of the Harbour Authority's lack of risk mitigation, reported that as Nickel was on hand, it was left to him and his crew to try to extinguish the fire "as soon as he could get near the ship." The *Chronicle*'s reportage referred to the absence of water based equipment for fighting fires and reminded its readership that the Foreign Settlement's Fire Brigade only fought land-based fires.[43] According to the English translation of the Harbour Regulations, responsibility for extinguishing the fire was not specified: regulations stated only that "the ships bell should be rung" until assistance arrived.[44] As the *R. D. Rice* was responsible for removing the burning barrels of kerosene floating in the harbour and threatening ships anchored nearby, not to mention cleaning up leaking oil threatening fish, Nickel was commissioned to perform these tasks.

Because this fire occurred in 1901, still within the transition period following the enactment of the revised treaties, the *Japan Chronicle* reported that the American consular court claimed jurisdiction, and that after its investigation, the crew was hastily returned to the United States. The *Chronicle* suggested the fire was caused by disgruntled American crew and that the American Consulate was keen to remove the guilty parties from Japan rather than have them confined in a Japanese jail.[45] In this transition period, the Kobe Harbour Authority left it to the foreign parties to remedy the situation and relied upon the cooperation of companies such as C. Nickel & Co. Ltd. to put out the fire and clear away the debris.

"Out of Adversity Comes Opportunity"[46]

Such disasters enabled C. Nickel & Co. Ltd. to make money, salvaging ship's parts for sale at auction or repairing vessels in its Shinzaike shipyard, meaning

43 "An Oil Ship Destroyed by Fire: Burnt to Water's Edge," *Japan Chronicle* (Kobe), 1 May 1901, 400; "The Burning of the Ship R. D. Rice: Inquiry at the American Consulate. The Vessel Scuttled," *Japan Chronicle* (Kobe), 8 May 1901, 416; "Harbour Regulations for Open Ports: Imperial Ordinance No. 139," 234.

44 "Harbour Regulations for Open Ports: Imperial Ordinance No. 139," 234.

45 "Local and General," *Japan Chronicle* (Kobe), 8 May 1901, 411; "The Burning of the Ship R. D. Rice: Inquiry at the American Consulate," 416.

46 Attributed to Benjamin Franklin.

competition for such business was both fierce and costly. As reported in the *Japan Chronicle*, C. Nickel & Co. Ltd. and its competitors volunteered their services in remediating ship-board fires hoping to win the salvaging contract. In August 1903, the *Chronicle* reported that the ship the *Tonkin*, whose agents were the French Messageries Maritimes, suffered a "disastrous" fire in Kobe Harbour requiring "the combined resources of the Harbour" to be extinguished. The *Chronicle* reported that C. Nickel & Co. Ltd., the Kawasaki Dockyard Company, the Kobe Pier Co., Nippon Yūsen Kaisha, the P&O Co., J. Lyons & Co., the Kobe Water Police, and local fire brigades all assisted providing their services free of charge. The *Chronicle* further reported that Kawasaki Dockyard Company won the salvaging contract and subsequently included their charges for fighting the fire in their final bill. Taking the moral high ground, the *Chronicle* questioned the company's effort to recoup its costs fighting the fire, stating that most companies assisting had been "animated simply by a wish to render assistance ... and save property" with no thought of making a profit.[47] Those companies unsuccessful in winning the salvage contract, such as C. Nickel & Co. Ltd., were expected to cover their own costs.

Japanese Authorities Take No Responsibility for Mitigation

Illegal smoking on board ship among so-called "coolies," a pejorative term used by the foreign community referring to unskilled Japanese and Chinese day labourers employed as stevedores, was the bane of foreign merchants' lives. The origins and meaning of "coolie" and the relationship between C. Nickel & Co. Ltd. and its "coolie" workforce will be discussed further in chapter 6. In 1905 the *Japan Chronicle* reported that some twenty foreign shipping agents wrote to the governor of Kobe, Governor Hattori, about the frequency of fires amongst flammable cargoes handled by day labourers. The letter referred to five fires between 8 March and 9 July 1905 alone, four of which had occurred on board ship and the fifth at Customs.[48] According to the *Chronicle*, the foreign shipping agents believed it was the Japanese authorities' responsibility to exercise

> stricter supervision ... over coolies, that these men shall be ... examined before they proceed to work ... and that ... pipes or cigarettes ... shall be taken away and ... handed back ... when they leave work[49]

47 "The Claim Against the Tonkin," *Japan Chronicle* (Kobe), 16 September 1903, 268.

48 "Fire in Kobe Harbour," *Japan Chronicle* (Kobe), 3 August 1905, 136.

49 "Fire in Kobe Harbour," 136.

There was no reporting of any response from the Japanese authorities.

Three years later, the problem of Japanese day labourers smoking while handling cargo remained unchecked.[50] In March 1908, C. Nickel & Co. Ltd. was engaged by the agent of the Danish and Swedish East Asiatic Company's steamer *Cathay* to unload a cargo of carbonate of soda when fire broke out on the deck. One of the casks brought up from the hold was discovered to be alight, possibly due to a day-labourer smoking illegally below deck. The burning cask could not be thrown overboard, as C. Nickel & Co. Ltd.'s lighters were moored alongside the *Cathay* to receive the cargo. It had to be placed on the deck. According to breathless reportage in the *Japan Chronicle*, the cask suddenly exploded and sparks flew overboard, igniting the one hundred and nine kilograms of carbonate of soda already on board Nickel's lighter, burning it "to the water's edge in a few minutes."[51] As the company had supplied the labour force in this case, the Harbour Authority may have considered the fire was C. Nickel & Co. Ltd.'s responsibility and not its own. This case demonstrates not only the risks foreign companies such as C. Nickel & Co. Ltd. faced, but also how the Harbour Authority placed the onus on foreign and Japanese companies to mitigate all dangers fire posed to their vessels, cargo, and lives.

Typhoons also posed a serious threat to vessels in the harbour and the following reportage highlights the reliance the Harbour Authority placed on companies such as C. Nickel & Co. Ltd. to conduct salvage operations. Typhoons regularly created havoc. The harbour afforded little protection, and infrastructure for recovering vessels was lacking. Vessels could be thrown against the retaining walls and destroyed, and cargoes could be found floating in the water. In August 1902, a "typhoon-like storm" hit Kobe. The propeller of the North German Lloyd's launch, the *Lloyd*, became fouled helping a distressed *sampan*, and the Lloyd was blown onto the seawall.[52] The *Lloyd's* agents, H. Ahrens & Co., engaged C. Nickel & Co. Ltd. to salvage it. It reportedly took the Company nearly nine days to erect a derrick to lift the vessel from "the broken seawall," patch the bottom where it was ripped open and tow it to its shipyard for repairs. Although C. Nickel & Co. Ltd. was technically compensating for the harbour's lack of infrastructure, it was able to charge for repairs at its shipyard at Shinzaike, thus providing some compensation for the risks the company had taken.[53]

50 "Fire in Kobe Harbour," 136.

51 "Fires in Kobe," *Japan Chronicle* (Kobe), 19 March 1908, 351.

52 "The Typhoon: Steam Launch Stranded at Kawasaki," *Japan Chronicle* (Kobe), 13 August 1902, 151.

53 "The Stranded NDL Launch," *Japan Chronicle* (Kobe), 20 August 1902, 174.

The greatest risk C. Nickel & Co. Ltd. faced in a congested harbour was collision of vessels, with associated costs of damage or loss of those vessels, cargoes, and lives. The Harbour Authority left it to the Japanese courts to adjudicate on claims arising over collisions with the courts, often apportioning the blame to both parties. The *Japan Chronicle*'s reportage indicated the foreign community held the Japanese authorities responsible for the safe management of the harbour in general. As the spokesperson for the foreign community, the *Chronicle*'s focus as usual was on the bias of the Japanese court processes against foreigners.

Jurisdictional Ambiguities of the Harbour

The following case demonstrates C. Nickel & Co. Ltd.'s experience of some of the jurisdictional ambiguities of the harbour. In October 1902 according to the *Japan Chronicle*'s sources, a launch owned by the Japanese Union Tugboat Company of Osaka, the *Zuiken-maru*, reportedly "going at full speed" at night, ran into and sank C. Nickel & Co. Ltd.'s steam launch, the *Cruiser*. Launches owned by the Kobe Pier Company, the Nippon Yūsen Kaisha, as well as C. Nickel & Co. Ltd. rescued crew and passengers from the *Cruiser*. Two passengers drowned and two others were missing. It was reported that seeing the *Cruiser* heading to the American *Hatoba*, the *Zuiken-maru*, which was heading across the harbour, blew its whistles to which the *Cruiser* replied and kept going. Neither vessel stopped. The *Zuiken-maru* struck the *Cruiser* amidships with such force it sank in ten minutes. The *Cruiser* was raised from the harbour six days later and taken to C. Nickel & Co. Ltd.'s shipyard for repairs, but it was too badly damaged.[54] As the rules and regulations on speed limits and the giving of right of way had not been clearly stipulated by the Harbour Authority, it was left to the Japanese court to apportion blame.[55] Fourteen months later, the court determined that the Union Tugboat Company pay two-thirds of the costs and C. Nickel & Co. Ltd. bear the remaining one third, stating that the latter's launch was "also responsible in some degree."[56] Judging by those cases reported in the *Japan Chronicle* and, in the absence of rules laid down by the Kobe Harbour Authority, while C. Nickel & Co. Ltd. had some satisfaction in winning

54 "Steam Launch Collision in the Harbour: Two Men Drowned. Four Men Reported Missing," *Japan Chronicle* (Kobe), 15 October 1902, 387.

55 "A Collision in Kobe Harbour," *Japan Chronicle* (Kobe), 13 January 1904, 47.

56 "A Collision in Kobe Harbour," 47.

compensation through the courts there was no onus placed on the Kobe Harbour Authority to stipulate rules of right of way or penalties for not observing those rules. This prompted C. Nickel & Co. Ltd. in 1904 to create its own marine insurance department.[57] By 1907, "half of the insurance of the company's fleet (of launches and lighters) was now carried by the company itself, while half was insured in local marine insurance offices."[58]

A costly consequence of accidents for the company lay also in the claims for personal injury. In 1909 C. Nickel & Co. Ltd. was sued in the Kobe Local Court by Anami Kumeo, a tailor aged twenty-seven, claiming compensation for injuries received in a collision which he said were due to the "carelessness on the part of C. Nickel & Co. Ltd.'s employees."[59] He was boarding a steamer, the *Nanyetsu-maru II*, from a lighter when C. Nickel & Co. Ltd.'s steam launch, the *Oyama-maru,* collided with the *Nanyetsu-maru II*, throwing him off the vessel and crushing him. He was in the hospital for over a month and returned to work believing he had recovered but he had to stop working when pain reoccurred.[60] He filed a claim in the Kobe Local Court for the substantial sum of ¥8000 (¥28,516,305 or £149,351), including salary foregone over the next twenty years, and an amount for pain suffered.[61]

By now experienced in Japanese courts' practices and believing claims could be over-stated, C. Nickel & Co. Ltd. attacked the claim from all angles. The company denied responsibility, claiming it had not heard that Anami had been injured because of a "mistake" on the part of the *Oyama-maru.* It expressed doubt "whether the plaintiff's alleged incapacity ... resulted from the accident" or whether the amount claimed was correct.[62] Furthermore, the company denied it even owned the steam launch *Oyama-maru* and had not employed the captain or crew.[63] It said it had leased the vessel from a former employee Ishida Satoru, who had proven his loyalty to the company in other ways over the years. As Ishida was still in the company's employ in 1914 as the company's chief *bantō*, he could have been running the *Oyama-maru*

57 "C. Nickel & Company Limited. Meeting of Shareholders," 130.

58 "C. Nickel & Co. Ltd. Annual General Meeting," 15.

59 "Claim for Compensation for Injuries: Anami Kumeo v. Messrs. Nickel & Co.," *Japan Chronicle* (Kobe), 22 September 1910, 531; "Claim for Compensation for Injuries: Anami Kumeo v. Messrs. Nickel & Co.," *Japan Chronicle* (Kobe), 10 November 1910, 840.

60 "Exemption from Court Expenses: Action Against Messrs. Nickel & Co.," *Japan Chronicle* (Kobe), 28 April 1910, 725.

61 These Yen conversions to 2019 values and others in this chapter are based on the website: https://yaruzou.net/hprice/hprice-calc.html. Conversion to British pounds was conducted on 14 April 2024.

62 "Claim for Compensation for Injuries," 531.

63 "Claim for Compensation for Injuries," 531.

as a side business.[64] In any case, Anami's counsel disputed this claim as a ruse for C. Nickel & Co. Ltd. to avoid its obligations.[65] In December 1910 the court dismissed Anami's claim, ruling that as the vessel was registered in Ishida's name, C. Nickel & Co. Ltd. was not responsible.[66] In May 1911, Anami then sued Ishida for ¥8000, and the court delivered its judgement against Ishida, awarding Anami ¥ 4000 (¥14,258,152 or £74,676) of the sum claimed with interest.[67] Claiming the vessel was in the name of a so-called former Japanese employee may have reduced C. Nickel & Co. Ltd.'s fine.

As well as dealing with the consequences of collisions, C. Nickel & Co. Ltd.'s management also complained about poor harbour infrastructure causing damage to cargoes, for which it was held responsible. As the *hatoba* were too small to accommodate ships, they had to be anchored in the harbour. Japanese stevedores had to load cargoes from the wharf onto lighters, which transported them and the cargo across the harbour to the relevant steamship. Upwards of ten or more lighters could be moored alongside the ship. This was a high-risk process, not just the risk of collision, but also the risk of lighters being swamped in rough seas, and lives and cargoes damaged or lost. The *Japan Chronicle*'s reporting on some of the court cases involving C. Nickel & Co. Ltd. indicated the level of risk, time, and money the company spent fighting lawsuits brought against it by consignees or insurance companies for the losses or damages incurred. The following case before the Japanese court is illustrative. In April 1901, the Tokyo Marine Insurance Company sued Dodwell & Co. and C. Nickel & Co. Ltd. for damages to raw cotton while the cargo was being landed.[68] Mitsui Bussan had imported the raw cotton from the United States. It had been shipped on the *Breconshire* by Dodwell & Co. and landed by C. Nickel & Co. Ltd. The Tokyo Marine Insurance Company contended that the bales had fallen overboard during discharging, as the lighter had been overloaded, and the two defendants had been careless: judgement was awarded in its favour.[69] A month later the defendants challenged the decision claiming that the damage was not

64 "Domiciliary Searches in Kobe: Charges Not Yet Stated. Mr Holstein Arrested," *Japan Chronicle* (Kobe), 12 November 1914, 891.

65 "Claim for Compensation for Injuries," 840.

66 "Claim for Compensation for Injuries: Sequel to a Collision in Kobe Harbour," *Japan Chronicle* (Kobe), 25 May 1911, 904.

67 "Claim for Compensation for Personal Injury: Sequel to an Accident in Kobe Harbour. Judgement," *Japan Chronicle* (Kobe), 18 April 1912, 689.

68 "Claim for Damage Done in Discharging Cotton: Action in the *Kobe Chiho Saibansho*," *Kobe Chronicle*, 24 April 1901, 372.

69 "Claim for Damage Done in Discharging Cotton," 372.

caused by their negligence. "At the time, the sea was running very high, and a steamer passing [nearby] caused the water to wash into the lighter," and that the consignees, Mitsui Bussan, had initially accepted the cotton without objection.[70] No outcome of this case was recorded but the case illustrates the inadequacies of the *hatoba* and the perils of high seas.

As well as an inadequate *hatoba*, foreign merchants complained that the Kobe Customs office was crowded and chaotic, and created constant challenges for landing agents such as C. Nickel & Co. Ltd. All goods arriving in the port had to be landed and stored at Customs for assessment for duties before being delivered to consignees. In the latter part of 1905, the *Japan Chronicle* wrote several articles based on interviews with merchants, consignees, and landing agents. It was generally agreed by all interviewees that blame for the problems of damaged or lost cargoes could not be placed on Kobe Customs alone, and that all parties were responsible for working together.[71] The following quotes provide a picture of the effects of the congestion and the burdens landing agents felt they were being unfairly forced to shoulder:

> There used to be system [whereby] certain goods [were] consigned to certain sheds [for] iron [for] flour and so forth ... this system ... has ... fallen through and the authorities ... have lost control. Due to the lack of space and lack of proper supervision, the goods have to be dumped ... anywhere ... the goods get mixed in places where there was no protection from rain and sun for which consignees had no redress.[72]

Instead of it being a responsibility shared between all the parties, Kobe Customs regarded the loss and damage to goods as solely the responsibility of landing agents. One interviewee explained that in the past shipping companies had been responsible for delivering cargo to consignees. Now they appointed landing agents to be responsible for landing and delivering cargo.[73] Any claims consignees had for damage to cargoes, shortages, mistakes in delivery and misidentification of goods went straight to the landing agents, who considered they were too busy minimizing demurrage and labour costs.[74] Landing agents in turn criticized Kobe Customs for not

70 "Claim for Damage Done in Discharging Cotton: A Re-Hearing," *Kobe Chronicle*, 22 May 1901, 468.

71 "The Glut at the Customs: Views of a Cotton Expert. Views of Landing Agents," 241–42.

72 "The Glut at the Customs: Views of a Cotton Expert. Views of Landing Agents," 241.

73 "The Glut at the Customs: An All-Round View," *Japan Chronicle* (Kobe), 14 September 1905, 340.

74 "The Glut at the Customs: Views of a Cotton Expert. Views of Landing Agents," 241.

taking responsibility, claiming Customs should take leadership and set down clear rules.[75] One landing agent reportedly said, "The responsibility for any damage or delays arising ... has never been fixed [by Kobe Customs] either by means of commercial documents or by the customs of the port."[76] In fact,

> [the] rules governing the ... customs of the port [were] so vague ... that from a legal standpoint neither of the parties handling goods from a steamer until [they were] delivered to the consignees can be made responsible in a clear and direct way.[77]

He went further, saying that consignees also bore some responsibility:

> We have lighters coming in and we have to discharge the cargo as best we may. If the consignees had one or two men at the landing place to look after the goods and identify and classify the various marks, there would be very little trouble. As it is the goods have to be dumped down anywhere [and] the goods get mixed.[78]

Kobe Customs had different ideas about their responsibility for the management of Customs. The Japanese Vice-Minister of Finance was reportedly quoted saying "the Customs are responsible for nothing except the collection of duties," absolving Customs from responsibility for establishing and policing rules.[79]

The lack of proper supervision of lighters on the one hand and unchecked silting up of the harbour on the other also impacted the landing agent's ability to land cargoes in a timely manner. As noted by one landing agent, without appropriate supervision,

> empty lighters cannot get out and full ones cannot get in ... it sometimes requires 30 men to get out a boat ... at great expense ... There are constantly boats lying there ... full up ... What they wait there for we do not know.[80]

In the views of the landing agents, Kobe Customs should have been managing the traffic flow of lighters as they had apparently done in the past. "There

75 "The Glut at the Customs: Views of a Cotton Expert. Views of Landing Agents," 241.
76 "The Glut at the Customs: Views of a Cotton Expert. Views of Landing Agents," 241.
77 "The Glut at the Customs: Views of a Cotton Expert. Views of Landing Agents," 241.
78 "The Glut at the Customs: Views of a Cotton Expert. Views of Landing Agents," 241.
79 "The Glut at Customs. An All-Round View," 340.
80 "The Glut at the Customs: Views of a Cotton Expert. Views of Landing Agents," 242.

… ought to be an official at the camber whose duty it should be to regulate the traffic."[81] "It used to be the police, but they have given up."[82] Moreover, delays were also caused due to the landing area not being regularly dredged. During "low tide … lighters will be stuck in the mud." Such chaos in the landing area took its toll on one landing agent in particular:

> We landing agents have … a very hard time of it. I myself have been "on the go" from early in the morning until late at night, and although I … sleep almost as soon as my head is on the pillow, I have of late had visions of coolies, lighters, lighters, coolies night after night.[83]

Kobe Customs was criticized for the lack of infrastructure such as a floating crane and the inadequate supervision of day labourers it employed where "the irresponsible coolie reigns supreme; unchecked and undirected, he works his will on valuable cargo."[84] The problems within Customs and the harbour were further compounded from 1904 onwards by the Russo-Japanese war (1904–5). Not only had "public works throughout the country come to a standstill" due to the need to fund the war, but also

> fifty to seventy-five percent of the boats … used for landing purposes have been taken away [for] the war, and we have … been compelled to use most unsuitable junks, paying the rates and demurrage of those boats, which the coolies dislike to discharge … although we have our own, of course we charter others … Most of the best coolies, boatmen and tally clerks have also gone to the front.[85]

One landing agent said that what took a week to discharge 5,000 tons before the war could now take a month. Fearing the worst, he warned that "if something is not done quickly, the Port of Kobe will be put on the blacklist of all the steamship companies, and the expansion of trade … will be seriously hampered."[86]

81 "The Glut at the Customs: Views of a Cotton Expert. Views of Landing Agents," 242.
82 "The Glut at the Customs: Views of a Cotton Expert. Views of Landing Agents," 242.
83 "The Glut at the Customs: Views of a Cotton Expert. Views of Landing Agents," 242.
84 "The Glut at the Customs: Views of a Cotton Expert. Views of Landing Agents," 241–42; "The Glut at Customs: An All-Round View," 340.
85 "The Glut at the Customs: Views of a Cotton Expert. Views of Landing Agents," 242.
86 "Customs Facilities in Kobe," *Japan Chronicle* (Kobe), 31 August 1905, 257; "The Glut at Customs: Another Point of View," *Japan Chronicle* (Kobe), 7 September 1905, 318.

Foreign Merchants Lobby for Harbour Works

At C. Nickel & Co. Ltd.'s second AGM held in 1905, it was decided that Alf Woolley, both chairman of its board and chairman of the Kobe Foreign Board of Trade, would "approach Customs with a view to remedying [the congested conditions]."[87] He argued that it was the duty of the Japanese government to ensure the quick handling and disposal of goods arriving at the port and to make rules to get goods cleared quickly. He advocated for the improvement of the harbour and better accommodation at the Customs.[88] According to the *Kobe Chronicle*, improvements for the harbour had been mooted since at least 1898, but due to funding constraints, little had happened.[89] The *Chronicle* reported that at the Kobe Foreign Board of Trade's AGM in March and another meeting in June of 1905, the board had "repeatedly brought before the authorities the necessity of extending the accommodation at the Customs," but that "the question … had not advanced very far."[90] In 1905, the Committee acknowledged that there was "little hope of any material change being made … owing to the country being at war."[91] In August 1905 the *Chronicle* reported that Kobe Customs had issued new regulations with "the object of expediting the landing and delivery of cargo."[92] It was also acknowledged that without an expansion of accommodation for goods awaiting duty assessment and collection by consignees, such new regulations would make little difference.[93] Harbour infrastructure thus continued to be the bane of foreign merchants' lives.

As the Kobe Foreign Board of Trade's efforts lobbying Kobe Customs had been unsuccessful, the board of C. Nickel & Co. Ltd. took matters into its own hands. In 1906, the *Japan Chronicle* reported that Holstein, now managing director and sharing his godfather's entrepreneurialism, had taken direct action to prevent further losses. He had twelve drays built to deliver cargo by land to consignees which, according to the board "had proved (to be) a

87 "C. Nickel & Company Limited: Meeting of Shareholders," 130.

88 "Hiogo & Osaka Chamber of Commerce: Annual General Meeting," *Japan Chronicle* (Kobe), 2 March 1905, 255.

89 "Landing Facilities at Kobe," *Kobe Chronicle*, 22 October 1898, 334; "Hyogo and Osaka General Chamber of Commerce: Annual Meeting," 123–24.

90 "Hiogo & Osaka Chamber of Commerce: Annual General Meeting," 256; "Kobe Foreign Board of Trade: Extraordinary General Meeting," *Japan Chronicle* (Kobe), 15 June 1905, 721.

91 "Hiogo & Osaka Chamber of Commerce: Annual General Meeting," 255–56.

92 "The Kobe Customs. New Regulations," *Japan Chronicle* (Kobe), 31 August 1905, 258.

93 "The Glut at the Customs: Another Point of View," 318.

paying concern. Consignees now received their cargo much more promptly than before."[94]

Kobe Harbour Works Scheme Underway in 1907

Following the end of the Russo-Japanese War in September 1905, the *Japan Chronicle* reflected the Japanese authorities' recognition that the Kobe Harbour needed improvement, announcing the Kobe Harbour Works Scheme was getting underway in 1907. With its natural depth and tidal nature, it considered that Kobe Harbour could become "the principal port in Japan if not of the Far East."[95] The Mayor of Kobe, Mr Minakami, lobbying the National Diet in January 1907 for additional funding for the Kobe Harbour Works Scheme, emphasized the need for Kobe Harbour to capitalize on "the increased competition between Japanese and foreign shipping" as well as "the completion of the Panama Canal" to expand foreign trade. By September 1907, the *Japan Chronicle* reported that the scheme was "in full swing" with the loan "successfully negotiated and that the renovation would take seven years."[96]

With the commencement of works, however, shipping agents and stevedores voiced concerns about interim arrangements made for loading and unloading goods. In October 1907, Kobe Customs closed off access to the landing place at Ono where it was located with "Lighters now to be taken across the bay to the Minatogawa Customs [Western Customs] ... where there is room for only a few lighters to discharge simultaneously." "Consequently ... stevedores have their lighters glutted with cargo." The *Japan Chronicle* summed up the situation by saying, "It takes longer to get your goods from the ship to godown than ... across the Pacific from America."[97]

In response to such adverse temporary arrangements, the Kobe Foreign Board of Trade appointed a sub-committee "to thoroughly investigate the matter." The sub-committee comprised two representatives for each of the merchants, marine insurance firms and shipping firms, one of which was P&O of which Alf Woolley was the representative as well as being the chairman of C. Nickel & Co. Ltd. The two foreign stevedores represented

94 "Hyogo and Osaka General Chamber of Commerce: Annual Meeting," 123–24; "C. Nickel and Company, Ltd.: Annual Meeting," 816.

95 "Harbours and Ports," *Japan Chronicle* (Kobe), 21 December 1905, 798.

96 "The Kobe Harbour Works," A Remarkable Situation: Some Official Correspondence. Wednesday, October 23," *Japan Chronicle* (Kobe), 31 October 1907, 568.

97 "The Kobe Harbour Works," 568.

were Christian Holstein and Jacob Lyons of J. Lyons & Co.[98] The task force presented a letter with their findings to Kobe Customs requesting the Onohama Compound be kept open for landing cargo while the breakwater was being built. It explained how the arrangements made by the Japanese authorities caused double-handling, where cargoes were taken out of lighters, inspected by Customs and then re-loaded and towed back again across the harbour to Ono where the godowns or warehouses were, adding to costs and stress.[99] The alternative was to transport cargoes at great cost for three miles from the mouth of the Minato River through "the busiest parts of Kobe to [Customs at] Ono ... by road."[100] In yet another failure of British-led advocacy and to the ongoing consternation of the sub-committee, Saito Shigetaka, Director of Imperial Customs of Kobe, rejected their requests, keeping the Onohama Compound closed.[101]

Until the decision to undertake the Kobe Harbour Works Scheme in 1907 which had been long advocated for by foreign business leaders such as Holstein, the Kobe Harbour and Kobe Customs facilities grew unchecked causing congestion, the risks of which were left for foreign companies to mitigate. While the foreign community considered the Japanese authorities had abrogated their responsibility for ensuring a safe and efficient operating environment, the Japanese authorities saw their role as merely collecting taxes. Any disputes arising out of the congestion caused were left to the Japanese courts to adjudicate with companies such as C. Nickel & Co. Ltd. having to adopt their own risk mitigation strategies. Managing the unregulated nature of the Kobe Harbour represented significant risks to C. Nickel & Co. Ltd.'s day-to-day operations. The other contributing factor to the risks the company had to manage was that of its large unskilled workforce, mainly day labourers, which were also known as "coolies." The relationship between C. Nickel & Co. Ltd. and its "coolie" workforce is the subject of the next chapter.

98 "The Kobe Harbour Works," 568.
99 "The Kobe Harbour Works," 568–70.
100 "The Kobe Harbour Works," 569.
101 "The Kobe Harbour Works," 570.

6. Managing a Japanese Workforce

Abstract: The success of C. Nickel & Co. Ltd. relied upon a constant supply of a cheap labour, both Japanese and Chinese, some 2,000 to 3,000 per day being required when a ship entered the harbour to be loaded or unloaded. The relationship between C. Nickel & Co. Ltd. and its large unskilled workforce, referred to in those times in the pejorative "coolie," as well as with its smaller permanent skilled Japanese workforce is examined in the context of the rise of nationalism amongst the "coolie classes" and the loss of extraterritorial privileges. Just as C. Nickel & Co. Ltd.'s relationships could be exploitative, violent and antagonistic on the one hand, they could also be relationships of trust and collaboration on the other.

Keywords: "coolies," violence, nationalism, racism, extraterritoriality, courts

C. Nickel & Co. Ltd.'s success was not just due to how it managed the risks of doing business in a congested port, it was also due to how it managed a large, casual, and unskilled Japanese workforce that was starting to feel empowered. C. Nickel & Co. Ltd.'s Japanese and Chinese workforce was a crucial part of its success. It could require 2,000 to 3,000 day labourers whenever ships entered the harbour to be loaded or unloaded of cargo. This chapter explores how the company managed its relationship with what was increasingly considered to be an unruly workforce and how this changed after the end of extraterritoriality as Carl Nickel continued to build his company.

While the company employed skilled and unskilled Japanese labour on a long-term basis, most of its employees were day labourers employed as required as stevedores. Such day labourers were the mainstay of the stevedore and freight forwarding industry; large numbers could be required in any one day, and supply of cheap unskilled labour was plentiful. With no records left by such workers or indeed by merchants, and the lack of archival materials relating to the many court cases where the nature of the

Holstein, Prue S. *The German Experience of Japan's Treaty Port System: A Case Study of C. Nickel & Co. Ltd., 1860–1923*. Taylor & Francis Group, 2025.
DOI: 10.4324/9781003706274-7

boss-worker relationship was frequently negotiated, the *Japan Chronicle* remains an important record of these relationships. The *Chronicle* reported extensively on labour disputes dealt with in the Japanese courts, especially when it sought to show how ill-equipped the Japanese court system was to adjudicate disputes impartially between foreign bosses and their workforce. As shown previously, the *Chronicle* believed the court was inherently biased against foreigners in favour of Japanese complainants. The nature of conflict between foreign managers and their unskilled workforce and between labourers themselves is explored in this chapter. I show that C. Nickel & Co. Ltd.'s relationship with its unskilled workforce was multifaceted, fluid, and changeable, characterized by violence in part but also by trust and collaboration. In the following pages, this relationship is placed in the context of the foreign community's attitudes towards Japanese unskilled labour and how the relationship changed with the revised treaties.

Foreign Merchants and Japanese Unskilled Labour

To understand the relationship between C. Nickel & Co. Ltd. and its unskilled workforce, the *Japan Chronicle*'s liberal use of the word "coolie," the name most used to denote such day labourers, needs to be understood. Up until 1920s, the *Japan Chronicle* used "coolie/s," conveying the classist and racist views of the foreign community and the Japanese elites towards the poorer classes available for such unskilled, manual labour. The term was used not just to refer to unskilled workers or day labourers including stevedores, but also to those employed longer-term as well as those, either self-employed or unemployed, just "hanging" around Japanese ports on the off chance of finding work, such as rickshaw drivers, construction workers or stevedores. The term conjured images of an undifferentiated mass of unskilled, uneducated, unwashed, often homeless labourers living hand to mouth. Japanese and Chinese "coolies" were often portrayed as lacking agency in managing their own lives, inviting the contempt of both the foreign community and elite Japanese, and were often badly treated by their employers. The *Chronicle* frequently reported on the violent way foreign bosses handled their workers, implying that by nature they were insubordinate, and required discipline.[1] Working conditions for unskilled workers were often dirty and dangerous. They were paid extremely low wages and had to put up a bond against

1 "Charge of Assault: A Foreigner Sent to Prison for Fifteen Days," *Japan Chronicle* (Kobe), 2 April 1902, 278.

poor performance, refundable upon termination of their employment. They were punished with spontaneous beatings, non-payment of wages or refusal to refund the performance bond.[2] While the *Japan Chronicle* uses the term "coolie" liberally, it is used here only when it is a direct quote from the *Chronicle*, or to emphasize the contempt implied amongst nineteenth-century foreigners and educated Japanese for all categories of unskilled employed and unemployed workers. Otherwise, I differentiate where possible between the various categories of unskilled workers used in the harbour. It should be kept in mind that a foreign stevedore was seen as a more worthy and skilled worker than his Japanese equivalent.

The use of the term "coolie" in nineteenth-century Japan originated in the colonial experience the British brought to the treaty ports of China and Japan. The Oxford Dictionary defines the term "coolie" as an "unskilled native labourer in some Asian countries [perhaps] from Kuli, an indigenous tribe of Gujarat in India."[3] During the eighteenth and nineteenth centuries, with the end of the slave trade with Africa, the British used "coolies" as indentured labour in India and China for public works, working on plantations and in other industries, wherever unskilled, plentiful and cheap labour was required.[4] The British introduced the word to Japan in the late 1850s to refer to unskilled, mostly manual day labourers, today known in Japanese as *hiyatoi rodosha*. As the Port of Kobe was being developed by foreign merchants and Japanese alike, the availability of work attracted such unskilled labour across a range of industries: construction, road works, railways, mining, transportation, and as stevedores on the docks. Foreign merchants thus had access to cheap labour which under extraterritorial privileges they could exploit without fear of prosecution.

The writings of a range of Japanese and European commentators visiting Kobe in the late nineteenth early twentieth century confirm the classist and racist attitudes the foreign community held about Japanese "coolies." Japanese historian Murata Seiji, writing in 1898, referred to them as "*hadaka rōdōsha*" [naked labourers] and called them a "disgrace."[5] In his book written in 1890, *Things Japanese*, Basil Hall Chamberlain, a professor of Japanese at

2 "Claim for Salary," *Japan Chronicle* (Kobe), 4 June 1902, 518.

3 *The Australian Pocket Oxford Dictionary*, Fifth Edition (Melbourne: Melbourne University Press).

4 Nitin Varma, "Contractors, Contracts, Coolies," *Coolies of Capitalism: Assam Tea and the Making of Coolie Labour* (Berlin, Boston: De Gruyter, 2017).

5 Murata Seiji, *Kobe Kaikō Sanjūnen-shi*, Volume 1, 6 May 1898 and Volume 2, 25 October 1898 (Kobe: Kaikō Sanjūnen Kinenkai—digitized copy at NLA), http://www.dl.ndl.go.jp/info:ndljp/pid/805190. 243.

Tokyo Imperial University and a British Japanologist, mentioned "coolies" to illustrate the game of chess they played while waiting for work, the clothing they wore or lack thereof, and the tendency of others to lump them in with "hucksters" as undesirable members of the community.[6] As late as 1920, Sydney Greenbie, an American photographer, wrote about Japanese day labourers briefly in his book *Japan, Real and Imaginary*, likening them to insects:

> Go through one of the great dockyards [in Japan] ... to see this same clinging, swarm activity in full swing ... There seems to be no order, no plan, no arrangement, just a mass of workers, each attacking a job with the instinct of ant and bee.[7]

The Growth of Nationalism and a New Assertiveness Amongst Unskilled Labour

While such depictions might suggest a compliant workforce, in the late 1800s, a trade in Japanese "coolies" developed where they were transported around the north Asian region broadening their life experience, and according to the *Chronicle*, resulting in a change in behaviour towards foreigners in Kobe. Reflecting on "coolies" returning to Kobe after a period of travel, the editor of the *Kobe Chronicle* suggested that such Japanese workers were becoming a threat to foreigners' safety in Kobe. In 1898, the *Chronicle* lamented that prior to the Sino-Japanese War of 1895 "strangers [to Kobe] met with nothing but civility and courtesy [from coolies]."[8] After the war, the *Chronicle* fumed,

> the attitude of the coolie class towards foreigners of all ranks, of every age, and of either sex, [had become] a serious menace to the reputation for public security hitherto enjoyed by Japan ... [with increased] reports of ... violence, insult, and molestation.[9]

The *Chronicle* reported that this newfound assertiveness also gave "coolies" licence to call foreigners racist epithets such as *ketojin* (red head) or *chikushō*

6 Basil Hall Chamberlain, *Things Japanese,* Sixth edition (London: Kegan Paul, Trench, Trubner & Co. Ltd., Kobe: Japan Chronicle Press, 1939), 106, 139–40, 272.

7 Sydney Greenbie, *Japan, Real and Imaginary* (New York: Harper & Brothers, 1920), 134–35.

8 "The Coolie Question," *Kobe Chronicle,* 12 February 1898, 109.

9 "The Coolie Question," 108.

(dumb animal) or to throw stones and carry out other forms of assault. Georges Bigot's cartoon "Heaving the Foreigner Over the Cliff for Fun," dated 24 August 1897, describes this anxiety: a group of "coolies" observe foreigners walking in their direction when one of them says, *"Ohé Ohé! Ijin ga kita, ijimeté yarō, wakarané kara"* ("Hey, look at that. There are some foreigners. Let's give them hell, because they're clueless.")[10] The foreign community may well by the late 1890s have developed a nostalgic and misguided view of the past as a much safer and settled period; as we saw from Nickel's early days in Kobe, that was certainly not the case. Nevertheless, the *Kobe Chronicle* and its successor, the *Japan Chronicle*, reported regularly on incidents involving "coolies" which were widely read by the foreign community.

According to the *Kobe Chronicle* and the *Japan Chronicle*, Japan's defeat of China in the Sino-Japanese War of 1894–95 and the nationalism the victory engendered amongst the so-called "coolie" class was in the foreigners' view the cause of a change in "coolies" behaviour towards them. With Japan's victory in the Sino-Japanese War came the growth of nationalism in Japan across all classes.[11] The politicization of unskilled workers commenced with the Sino-Japanese War and the Boxer Rebellion of 1900 where the Japanese army imported them into China mainly for "carriage and transport purposes."[12] German troops in North China also imported such workers to assist them in establishing their colonial occupation of the Shantung (Shandong) Province in China. In 1900, the *Kobe Chronicle* reported that a Shanghai-based German merchant had received an order from the German War Office for the engagement of 8,000 Japanese "coolies" for the German troops in North China, in the newly acquired German territory, Kiaochow.[13] The *Chronicle* further reported that "2,000 more coolies are wanted for the German troops in North China and that keen competition is … on between the emigration companies and the coolie agents."[14] The *Kobe Chronicle* reported that through their participation in Japan's operations in China, they witnessed Japan defeating the powerful Qing Dynasty that had been previously revered, engendering a belief "that [now] all foreign nations were … [including the Chinese] to be regarded with the contempt that the conqueror feels for the

10 Aaron Herald Skabelund, *Empire of Dogs: Canines, Japan and the Making of the Modern Imperial World.* (Ithaca & London: Cornell University Press, 2011), 74.

11 Makito Saya, *The Sino-Japanese War and the Birth of Japanese Nationalism* (Tokyo: Kodansha, 2009), 163.

12 "Japanese Coolies for China," *Kobe Chronicle*, 8 August 1900, 123.

13 "Japanese Coolies for China," 123.

14 "Local and General," *Kobe Chronicle*, 5 September 1900, 207.

conquered."[15] Furthermore, through Japan's ascendancy into the ranks of world powers, such labourers witnessed the competition amongst the foreign powers in China and their relative weaknesses, as those powers tried to carve up China for their own purposes. According to the *Chronicle*, these processes translated into "coolies" losing the respect they had previously shown members of the foreign community. Focusing on a growing sense of nationalism amongst the so-called "coolie" class and its consequences for the foreign community, the *Kobe Chronicle* wrote:

> They [coolies] got their heads stuffed with the notion that Japan was the greatest country on ... earth, and that ... the proper thing ... to do was to assert ... the greatness of the country in their own proper persons. Hence, when ... they returned to Japan, hapless foreigners in the Treaty Ports ... soon began to have a bad time of it.[16]

Foreshadowing difficulties foreign bosses might experience managing the new levels of cockiness amongst its unskilled workforce, the *Chronicle* wrote that at the end of the Sino-Japanese war these workers,

> Returned ... [to Japan] with the glamour of successful warriors about them, with considerable savings ... or they were well paid ... with the habits of confirmed gamblers ... and a steady dislike for settled work[17]

In addition to the poorer classes being portrayed as disrespectful and aggressive towards foreigners, such Japanese workers were also portrayed as drunken, violent, and murderous louts, gamblers, and thieves. The *Chronicle* recounted many incidences of senseless violence, many involving day labourers employed by C. Nickel & Co. Ltd. One night in September 1903, Tada Ganjirō, the head foreman of the labourers in C. Nickel & Co. Ltd.'s employ, was murdered by a former employee, Yoshimoto Kankichi. Yoshimoto had been dismissed for drinking and disorderly conduct but would drop by the office asking for money and to be taken back. Tada told him he was not required, whereupon Yoshimoto stabbed him five times with a sword "he was known to carry around with him."[18] It was dark, and no-one saw what

15 "The Coolie Question," 109.
16 "Military Coolies," *Kobe Chronicle*, 5 September 1900, 205.
17 "The Coolie Question," 109.
18 "The Murder of a Coolie in Kobe: Further Particulars," *Japan Chronicle* (Kobe), 23 September 1903, 297.

had happened. The bloody body remained under the windows of C. Nickel & Co. Ltd. until 3:00 a.m. awaiting the arrival of the judge and prosecutor.[19] Another incident occurred on the evening in July 1908, when a man was severely injured at the boarding house C. Nickel & Co. Ltd. provided for its workforce, in Nakayamate-dōri, 7-chome. Sano Sōtarō, twenty-eight, and a man known as Torako were gambling early in the evening. Sawada Mankichi, twenty-four, seeing Torako's elation over his win, asked to borrow some money for alcohol. Sano, angry he had lost, threw a tobacco firebox at Sawada, redeemed a short sword from the pawnshop and returned to the boarding house. A fight ensued where Sawada cut Sano badly leaving him in a critical condition and went to the police station.[20] The depiction of these incidents in the *Japan Chronicle* focused on the spontaneity and senselessness of crimes amongst drunken "coolies," probably reinforcing the foreign bosses' views that such labourers required strict discipline justifying the use of violence.

Furthermore, the *Chronicle* reported in a perfunctory manner on theft by day labourers, with the underlying suggestion such labourers were despicable and untrustworthy individuals. In May 1901, a Japanese employee of C. Nickel & Co. was arrested stealing twenty-five fathoms of Manila rope from the *R. D. Rice*, the steamer destroyed by fire mentioned in chapter 4. Further thefts involving C. Nickel & Co. Ltd. workers included items such as cloth valued at ¥636 (¥2,642,591 or £13,840), forty-two rolls of *habutai* silk and a block of copper valued at ¥20 (¥66,240 or £335). There was clearly a thriving trade in stolen goods, encouraged perhaps by the poverty of such workers; the Japanese local authorities who policed them had as little sympathy for their plight as foreign merchants. No wonder then that occasionally such employees of foreign merchants were tempted to join the ranks of the better off: in February 1905, a newly employed Fujii Masaji was working in the C. Nickel & Co. Ltd. office in the Eastern Customs compound. He was reported to have received ¥2,030 (¥7,591,238 or £39,758) from Bowden Bros. as payment of duty on sheet lead and subsequently absconded with the funds. He reportedly bought a watch, hat, etc. and neatly dressed, had gone to a licenced house in Shinchi, Osaka, where he was caught trying to change a ¥100 note (¥373,953 or £1,959) into cash.[21] It appears Fujii desired to briefly

19 "The Murder of a Coolie in Kobe," 297.

20 "Sanguinary Affray at a Boarding House: Stevedore Coolies Again," *Japan Chronicle* (Kobe), 30 July 1908, 169.

21 "Kobe Youth's Temptation," *Japan Chronicle* (Kobe), 9 March 1905, 286.

experience the lifestyle of his bosses as he viewed them. Such thefts must have represented a significant cost of doing business for C. Nickel & Co. Ltd.

Japanese "coolies" were not the only threat to public safety concerning the foreign community: unemployed drunken foreign sailors, at times referred to as beachcombers, were also considered a threat to law and order in and around the ports. Foreign sailors regularly arrived in the port, were paid off by the ship's captains and then left stranded. At the Annual Meeting of the Kobe Seamen's Institute, where members discussed the need for supporting such men, it was observed that: "these men would be thrown on the town ... [and could be found] on the beach ... forced to beg on the streets ... or at your residence on the Hill during your absence at your office."[22] But while the foreign community considered unemployed sailors a threat, it also viewed them as its responsibility as reflected in the following quote:[23]

> it would be a reproach ... a disgrace to the foreigners in the port if they did not provide ... respectable accommodation ... some place ... to stay for a short time ... be kept away from the grog shops and other questionable haunts.[24]

The Mission to Seamen had been established to provide relief to unemployed sailors and had been renamed the Kobe Seamen's Institute in 1903. The foreign community had taken over the running of the Kobe Seamen's Institute from the Salvation Army in 1907, and Christian Holstein was a member of the board and a long-time financial supporter.[25]

Unskilled Labour: The Mainstay of the Freight Forwarding Industry

Since the establishment of the then C. Nickel & Co. in the early 1880s, the company had relied upon large numbers of Japanese and Chinese day labourers employed as stevedores to load and unload cargo. By the 1890s, the company could require upwards of 2,000 to 3,000 per day for their irregular and high-volume cargo business. The company tapped into the large pool of unskilled labourers provided by *oyakata* (also known as "coolie" bosses

22 "The Kobe Seamen's Institute: Annual Meeting," *Japan Chronicle* (Kobe), 5 May 1910, 774.
23 "The Kobe Seamen's Institute: Annual Meeting," 774.
24 "The Kobe Seamen's Institute: Annual Meeting," 774.
25 "The Kobe Seamen's Institute: Annual Meeting," 774.

or contractors) under short term contracts on low wages.[26] In addition, C. Nickel & Co. employed one hundred stevedores for its regular business and a further one hundred specialist stevedores for key clients. While the term "coolie" referred mainly to stevedores within the company, it also covered nightwatchmen and boat watchmen (*sendō*), foremen and *oyakata*, the "coolie" bosses who provided "coolies" on contract. Reinforcing the generally held view in the foreign community that such workers were an undifferentiated mass, many were identified by number rather than by name, though these may also have been a practicality for the administration of their employment and pay.[27]

Nickel, as a pioneer of *sutebe-gyō* (stevedoring business), was innovative in employing large numbers of Japanese unskilled day labourers as stevedores, a practice considered to be "revolutionary" in the Port of Kobe.[28] Until Nickel introduced this practice, loading and unloading of cargo had been conducted by individual owner-operated lighters, manned by one or more stevedores, with many such lighters converging on foreign ships in the hope of winning business. C. Nickel & Co. as a *tsumioroshi-gyōsha* (cargo carrying company) offered a more efficient service conveying large numbers of stevedores and cargo between ships moored at anchor in the harbour and the piers. Its success relied upon securing a substantial workforce at short notice when large ships arrived in port, taking a contract with an *oyakata* for the numbers of workers required and squeezing the *oyakata* for the cheapest rates. An incident in 1883 demonstrating the pressures the *oyakata* were under is on record. A riot occurred when one hundred Japanese "coolies" claimed ¥5500 (¥32,788,517 or £171,726) of missing wages from one *oyakata*, a Hamaguchi Gonshirō.[29] The case was brought before the Kobe Local Court which ruled in the stevedores' favour. While the circumstances surrounding the shortfall in wages Hamaguchi paid were not reported, this case suggests that such bosses had to supply stevedores to companies such as C. Nickel & Co. at wage rates that were unprofitable unless they underpaid their workforce. This incident also indicates that in the years prior to the enactment of the revised treaties, while stevedores could not take their foreign bosses to the Japanese courts, they could at least sue their Japanese *oyakata*.

26 Murata, *Kobe Kaikō Sanjūnen-shi, Volume* 2, 622.

27 "A Foreigner Charged with Assault. Sentenced to 15 Months Imprisonment," *Japan Chronicle* (Kobe), 18 March 1903, 247.

28 Murata, *Kobe Kaikō Sanjūnen-shi, Volume* 2, 224.

29 Murata, *Kobe Kaikō Sanjūnen-shi, Volume* 2, 622.

Managing a Japanese Workforce under Extraterritorial Privileges

Taking full advantage of extraterritorial privileges, Nickel knew his workforce and their *oyakata* could not protest his uncompromising treatment of them. He also knew he had the support of the Hyogo governor and the police. In November 1892, contractors attempted to break C. Nickel & Co.'s stranglehold over the international cargo market. "Coolie" leaders Fujino Seihachi, Ikemoto Kentarō and Sekiura Seigorō, protesting the "arrogance" of C. Nickel & Co. Ltd., tried to poach Nickel's employed labour, who were paid only eighteen sen (one yen corresponds to one hundred sen and cannot be calculated in today's terms) a day, by offering them twenty-five sen a day, and dispatching them directly to foreign ships. Given Nickel's notoriety in Shanghai, the *North China Herald* in Shanghai reported on the same dispute adding some more detail to the story. It reported that in December 1892 a strike by Japanese stevedores had been organized by a "native" (Japanese) stevedoring association in Kobe that "wanted to get the monopoly of the business and succeeded by intimidation in stopping all business for a day or more." C. Nickel & Co. reportedly appealed to the Governor of Hyogo. Outside labourers were brought in under police protection and the strike collapsed. According to the *Herald*, strikers were only "too glad to be allowed to work for Messrs. Nickel and Co."[30]

Foreign Bosses and New Rights for Unskilled Japanese Workforce

With the ending of extraterritoriality in 1899, the legal situation changed for Nickel and his company. In having to now submit to the Japanese courts, they lost the discretion shown in the above incidents in dealing with their workforce. The company could now be sued in the Japanese courts by its workers for poor working conditions, alleged misdemeanours, and crimes. The *Japan Chronicle* reported in detail on those court cases, not least because they helped provide evidence for its accusations of the Japanese court's bias against foreigners. During the period 1901–11, the *Chronicle* reported on twenty separate court cases (including appeals) in which C. Nickel & Co. Ltd. and its workforce fought each other over better wages and working conditions or sought redress and compensation for injuries sustained during outbursts of violence. Some of these cases ran for one or more years, invariably going to appeal.

30 "Nickel breaking a strike in 1892," *The N. C. Herald and S. C. & C. Gazette*, 2 December 1892, 821.

Three court cases involving the same person, reported by the *Japan Chronicle*, speak to the relationship between workers and foreign bosses and were no doubt part of its broader interest in condemning the violence of treaty port culture. In the first case, in January 1902, Richard Metcalf was charged with assaulting a Chinese worker named Su.[31] Metcalf had been employed by C. Nickel & Co. Ltd. to oversee Japanese and Chinese stevedores unloading the British steamer, *Olympia*. When reportedly asked by Metcalf for a boat-note or shipping order, Su had refused reportedly claiming, "there was no need of showing it to him [Metcalf]."[32] Metcalf stated in court that as time was running out "before work would be stopped," the Chief Officer of the *Olympia* had ordered Metcalf to seize the note whereupon Su attacked him. In defending himself Metcalf injured Su, putting him off work for six days. Despite a Japanese worker, Maebara Yasutarō, supporting Metcalf's claim of self-defence, the court sentenced Metcalf to fifteen days imprisonment with hard labour, plus damages and court-costs. From subsequent reports, it seemed Metcalf was known to be violent, which may have raised doubts about his statement. Metcalf appealed the conviction, but by the time it was heard in May he had disappeared without serving his sentence.[33] Five months later in September 1902 the Kobe Water Police discovered Metcalf working on another British steamer, the *Diomed*, and arrested him on a new charge of assaulting another Chinese stevedore (unnamed). Back in court March 1903, Metcalf admitted to not having served his sentence for an earlier charge.[34] His disappearance suggests that like many foreigners he was keen to avoid serving time in a Japanese jail, which foreigners considered highly unsanitary.

In the second case involving Metcalf, another Chinese labourer on the American steamer *Lyra* was tallying bags of flour on deck when he claimed Metcalf told him to go below deck as he was in the way.[35] The Chinese worker apparently did so but then reappeared. The Chinese claimed Metcalf struck him causing him to fall overboard on to a lighter. He was off work for twenty days. The court determined Metcalf had bullied the Chinese prior to causing his injuries and he was again convicted

31 "A Foreigner Charged with Assault," *Japan Chronicle* (Kobe), 29 January 1902, 80.

32 "A Foreigner Charged with Assault," *Japan Chronicle* (Kobe), 19 March 1902, 263.

33 "Disappearance of a Foreigner," *Japan Chronicle* (Kobe), 30 April 1902, 400; "The Charge of Assault Against a Foreigner," *Japan Chronicle* (Kobe), 7 May 1902, 426.

34 "Arrest of a Foreigner in Kobe Harbour," *Japan Chronicle* (Kobe), 17 September 1902, 273.

35 "Foreigner Charged with Assault: Sentenced to 15 Months Imprisonment," *Japan Chronicle* (Kobe), 18 March 1903, 247.

and sentenced to fifteen months in prison.[36] In the third case Metcalf appealed to the Osaka Court of Appeal which decided that despite being cautioned, the Chinese had provoked Metcalf into violence. The court also deemed that as Metcalf had been convicted of similar offences in the past, the accusation was "not improbable." Offering Metcalf some latitude for extenuating circumstances, the Osaka Appeal Court reduced Metcalf's sentence from fifteen to nine months imprisonment.[37] The Metcalf case reveals that foreign bosses such as Metcalf were not averse to using spontaneous physical punishment when they considered their workers were insubordinate and needed discipline.

Seeking to remind the foreign community of the on-going levels of violence between foreign bosses and their workers, the *Japan Chronicle* continued to report on such violence between foreign foremen and Japanese and Chinese workers. Such brief reports demonstrate not just the levels of violence existing between foreign bosses and their workers, but that violence was the option of first recourse. They also show that the Japanese courts, instead of taking sides, sought to mediate the disputes through apportioning blame for such incidences in some way to both parties.

The threat of casual workers breaking into mass violence against a foreign boss was also ever present. The *Japan Chronicle* reported extensively on a case tried in the Kobe Local Court on the assault on C. Nickel & Co. Ltd.'s Manager, Christian Holstein, and a Japanese labourer, Nakagawa Kanematsu. Because this case involved an assault on a senior member of the foreign community, the *Chronicle* took close interest, especially as it considered in such cases that the Japanese court's sentencing was often far too lenient. In February 1909, Holstein was watching the discharge of cargo from the German steamer, the *Slavonia*, when he saw some workers using hooks. He told them from the deck to stop using them, presumably to not damage the cargo. According to the *Japan Chronicle*, thinking that "the men were wilfully disobeying his orders," Holstein went down into the hold "snatching" away the hook and returned to the deck. It was reported that the five accused "coolies," Nagaoka Teiji, Motoyama Fukumatsu and Tomita Kakutarō, all aged twenty-three, Goto Kikuzō, aged twenty, and Yoshizawa Shōtarō, aged eighteen, all of Kobe, followed Holstein and assaulted him, "some with sticks ... some with their fists, inflicting injuries

36 "A Foreigner Charged with Assault: Sentenced to 15 Month's Imprisonment," 247.

37 "The Charge of Assault Against a Foreigner: Appeal to the Osaka Court," *Japan Chronicle* (Kobe), 20 May 1903, 445.

to his head and face."[38] Nakagawa, trying to restrain them, was beaten and injured as well. By this time, some fifty men had assembled, so it was difficult to tell who had struck whom first. One of the accused claimed he struck Holstein in self-defence, others claimed they had not been present. The five accused were eventually charged and convicted of assault, and were sentenced to three months imprisonment, suspended for three years, on the basis they were still young and "had the opportunity of retrieving their conduct."[39]

The *Japan Chronicle* used this case to express its disapproval of the court's decision, noting that as this was "not the first time Mr Holstein has been assaulted, the sentence certainly does not err on the side of severity: it merely amounts to what would be known in England as binding over to keep the peace."[40] The *Chronicle* reported that the court was aware of numerous prior assaults of Holstein by "men of this type who are known to be of extremely violent character," and it advocated for severer sentences to reduce such violent assaults.[41] While foreigners mostly did not speak Japanese and interacted with Japanese suppliers, customers or workers through Japanese-speaking intermediaries, this case shows that Holstein, as a senior level foreign manager, dealt directly with his Japanese workers speaking Japanese.[42] This case also indicates that the relationship between the company and its casual workforce was not always based on trust or respectful communication, and resulted in the violent behaviours Holstein experienced. The *Japan Chronicle* was however more focused on the violent nature of the Japanese workforce than on the need to improve relations between foreign bosses and their casual Japanese workforce.

Whereas the cases referred to above dealt with spontaneous violence occurring between foreigners and their workforce, the following case study offers a different perspective. It is an example of premeditated violence exercised by independent Japanese workers, still referred to pejoratively as "coolies," as a stand-over tactic over a foreign boss or business client. Four Japanese men were trying to stop Holstein as the managing director of C. Nickel & Co. Ltd. from taking action prejudicial to their own stevedoring

38 "Coolie Affray at Kobe: Foreigner Assaulted. Sentence on Coolies," *Japan Chronicle* (Kobe), 8 April 1909, 562.

39 "Coolie Affray at Kobe: Foreigner Assaulted. Sentence on Coolies," 562.

40 "Coolie Affray at Kobe: Foreigner Assaulted. Sentence on Coolies," 562.

41 "Stray Notes," *Japan Chronicle* (Kobe), 29 April 1909, 652.

42 Kevin C. Murphy, *The American Merchant Experience in Nineteenth Century Japan* (London: Routledge/Curzon, 2003), 126–53.

business interests.[43] The *Japan Chronicle* reported that one Saturday evening in December 1907 around 7:00 p.m. "eight Japanese rushed into Messrs. Nickel & Co.'s offices ... demanding to see the manager, Mr Holstein" whereupon they drew revolvers.[44] Failing to find Holstein, "the murderous gang rushed through ... [the] premises upstairs and down, firing revolvers wildly, the bullets now ... embedded in the walls."[45] Told by Japanese staff that Holstein was at the American *Hatoba* where he was visiting C. Illies & Co., they went there to look for him.[46] Later asked by a journalist about the reason for the attack, Holstein suggested "some labour organization ... had formed a vague ... idea that if the manager of Messrs. Nickel & Co. were killed ... the business ... would be diverted ... to the advantage of those ... [who] so callously plotted the murder."[47] All four intruders were arrested by the Kobe police: they were Yamanouchi Tajirō, a labour contractor aged thirty-one, and labourer, Hayashida Otokichi, also thirty-one, who were both engaged in contracting labour for the loading of cargo on steamers from lighters. Also arrested were Sakaya Kamekichi, thirty-two, a labour foreman employed by C. Nickel & Co. Ltd., and Kikuyo Kikumatsu, a labourer aged twenty-one employed by Hayashida. Much to the consternation of the *Chronicle*, despite being armed the four were only charged with unlawful entry, and were allowed out on bail despite Yamanouchi, Hayashida and Sakaya, having been found guilty of minor crimes previously.[48] It was also revealed that they all had an ongoing relationship with C. Nickel & Co. Ltd. Sakaya was an employee of the company and used to contract out stevedoring work to Yamanouchi and Hayashida, who owned a small stevedoring business, receiving a 5 per cent commission. In addition to his other duties for C. Nickel & Co. Ltd., and to justify his use of a gun, Sakaya claimed he was responsible for frightening away professional *gorotsuki*, or individual Japanese extortionists known to be making a living through protection rackets.[49] The most junior member of the four, Kikuyo, said he also visited C. Nickel & Co. Ltd. to collect orders for *bento* (lunch boxes) for delivery the following day.[50]

43 "Armed Attack on a Stevedore's Office: Extraordinary Incident," *Japan Chronicle* (Kobe), 26 December 1907, 822.

44 "Armed Attack on a Stevedore's Office: Extraordinary Incident," 822.

45 "Armed Attack on a Stevedore's Office: Extraordinary Incident," 822.

46 "Armed Attack on a Stevedore's Office: Extraordinary Incident," 822.

47 "Armed Attack on a Stevedore's Office: Extraordinary Incident," 822.

48 "The Recent Armed Attack in Kobe: Prisoners at Large," *Japan Chronicle* (Kobe), 20 February 1908, 229.

49 "The Recent Armed Attack in Kobe: Trial of Accused. Judgement," *Japan Chronicle* (Kobe), 12 March 1908, 317.

50 "The Recent Armed Attack in Kobe: Trial of Accused. Judgement," 317.

Sakaya's claim that he needed a gun to ward off *gorotsuki* on behalf of his foreign employers provides an important insight into Kobe business culture at the time. In February 1908 an article described an unnamed foreign merchant's encounter with

> a prepossessing individual sprawling over the table in his bantō's [Japanese clerical interface between the company and its clients] office ... engaged in animated conversation ... It was noticed that lying before the visitor ... was a letter in Japanese characters with the mark of blood in one corner.[51]

The *Chronicle* went on to say,

> It is extraordinary how the Japanese people tolerate these *gorotsuki* who manage to extort money from all classes by means of threats, the victims being afraid to report [the blackmail] to the police ... We understand there is quite an army of *gorotsuki* in Kobe at the present time.[52]

Revealing the potential effect of C. Nickel & Co. Ltd.'s business tactics on local Japanese companies, the four accused claimed they had gone to the office to merely request that the manager "not monopolize the lightering business of Kobe, as they would lose their work should the firm carry out the plan."[53] In contrast, a C. Nickel & Co. Ltd. employee Tatamiya Torakichi testified that he had gone to Yamanouchi's home to inform him that the company would be taking over the work previously contracted out to Yamanouchi and Hayashida. Torakichi added that the men all then agreed to attempt to intimidate Holstein with guns into abandoning the business. Despite relying on their pre-existing relationship with C. Nickel & Co. Ltd., and discussing their disagreement cooperatively, the four threatened violence as a first resort in the face of intransigent management to achieve their aims. As the *Japan Chronicle* reported, despite being armed, they were only charged with unlawfully entering the premises. The court acquitted Yamanouchi, Hayashida and Kikuyo, stating that they had the right to seek an interview and that their actions were in the normal course of trying to dissuade Holstein from taking over their business. Because Sakaya had fired a gun, he was sentenced to three months imprisonment with hard labour.

51 "'Gorotsuki' in Kobe: A Growing Danger," *Japan Chronicle* (Kobe), 13 February 1908, 197.
52 "'Gorotsuki' in Kobe: A Growing Danger," 197.
53 "Armed Attack on a Stevedore's Office: Extraordinary Incident," 822.

In its coverage of the judgement, the *Chronicle* expressed disappointment at the lenient sentencing, reflecting the foreign community's belief that the Japanese courts did not appropriately punish Japanese "coolies" for violent crimes against foreigners. The *Chronicle* contrasted the Japanese approach with that of American and British courts, both of which interpreted the possession of arms as intent to threaten to kill. In the *Chronicle*'s view, Japanese courts only considered threats of violence as the intention of bodily harm where harm was caused.[54]

Labourers also brought to the courts claims against C. Nickel & Co. Ltd. for dismissal with unpaid wages and bonds not reimbursed. The following cases show that despite the relatively small amounts being claimed, C. Nickel & Co. Ltd. was prepared to go to considerable cost to fight such cases based on a principle of not paying employees for poor performance. C. Nickel & Co. Ltd. and most likely other foreign companies took advantage of the unlimited supply of workers in the port looking for work, to terminate workers for poor performance without monies owing, when they could be easily replaced. Furthermore, while the revised treaties may have given these labourers the right to sue foreign employers in the Japanese courts, their rights were still limited as such foreign companies had the resources and wherewithal to tie plaintiffs up in the courts at great expense with no guarantees of winning.

In a case demonstrating the efforts Carl Nickel would go to win, in March 1902, he was personally sued in the Kobe Ward Court by one Tajima Yujirō for the sum of ¥24 (¥99,720 or £522), the balance of salary and bond due to him upon termination of his employment.[55] Nickel argued that Tajima had been discharged for neglect of duty and it was the firm's practice not to pay salary. The court disagreed with Nickel, ordering him to pay a total of ¥23.70 (¥99,720 or £522) plus return deposit money of ¥2 (¥8,310 or £44), a paltry sum for Nickel, but significant for Tajima. Court costs were to be borne by both parties.[56] Six months later, in September 1902, Nickel appealed this judgement, claiming that he had not personally employed Tajima, and was "not the man to be sued." It was explained that in December 1901, Nickel had formed a *goshi-kaisha* or partnership of limited liability with two other unnamed partners under the trade name of C. Nickel & Co.[57] All employees

54 "Peaceable Persuasion," *Japan Chronicle* (Kobe), 19 March 1908, 343.

55 The successive reporting on this case identified the claimant as Tanaka Yujiro, Tadero Fujiro and Tajima Yujiro reflecting the difficulty the English language press must have had in correctly representing Japanese names.

56 "Peaceable Persuasion," 343.

57 "The Claim for Salary by a Japanese: Nickel v. Tajima. The Appeal," *Japan Chronicle* (Kobe), 17 September 1902, 270.

of the previous firm had been engaged by the new firm and their wages paid by them. Tajima had been dismissed on 20 February, and as he had not performed "a day's work in February," had no claim. Tajima counter claimed that as he had been unable to work after 1 February, he had sent a substitute and had paid him out of his own pocket, showing his passbook as evidence. Nickel's counsel discredited the passbook, and the witness called in support of Tajima. After three hearings, the court quashed the original decision of the Kobe Ward Court and ordered that Nickel pay only the ¥2 deposit fee and one quarter of the court costs. In appealing the case, Nickel showed his determination to not pay Tajima as well as put Tajima to additional expense by dragging the court case out.

In a similar case confirming C. Nickel & Co. Ltd.'s motives and desire to win at all costs, in June 1904 Kihira Tatsuzo claimed unpaid wages of ¥18 (¥69,720 or £365) and ¥3 (¥11,620 or £61) deposit money from Holstein, sub-manager of C. Nickel & Co. Ltd. Before proceedings commenced, the judge advised Kihira that Holstein had written to the court saying he would pay the wages but not refund the deposit money. The judge advised Kihira to accept this offer and not dispute the ¥3 (£61). Kihira refused, suggesting how important this amount was to him.[58] The hearing proceeded and as Holstein did not appear, judgement was given in Kihira's favour. Holstein protested the decision and after several adjournments, in September, the hearing was resumed. Taking his lead from Nickel, Holstein changed tack protesting that he was not the legal representative of the company and therefore not liable. The substitution of a company for the individual suggests not only a way of broadening the case against the plaintiff by involving additional third parties but also a way of dragging the court case out to the detriment of the plaintiff. There are no further records of this case, but given the small amount, even the *Japan Chronicle* regarded this dispute as a waste of time.[59] Such case studies however remind us that the company placed such low value on the employment of such casual workers that it sought to win regardless of cost. Complainants were considered worthy of exploitation and severe punishment.

The following is an example of a case that went in C. Nickel & Co. Ltd.'s favour. On 24 March 1908, Lo Si Pin claimed he had been discharged from C. Nickel & C. Ltd. without proper notice and demanded ¥27 (¥92,553 or £485) salary as compensation plus the ¥25 (¥85697 or £449) deposit made by him during his service in the firm. In response, C. Nickel & Co. Ltd.

58 "Claim for Wages: Plaintiff and Judge's Advice," *Japan Chronicle* (Kobe), 16 June 1904, 742.
59 "Claim for Wages: Plaintiff and Judge's Advice," 742.

claimed the amount of salary owing was ¥18.19 (¥61,702 or £323) adding that as the company dismissed Lo due to incompetence and negligence, he was not entitled to the deposit money. Lo had been responsible for tallying a quantity of sugar, but his calculations resulted in a shortage of nineteen bags valued at ¥295.35 (¥1,011,230 or £5296) for which the firm would have to compensate the customer. Lo had agreed to pay ¥140 (¥479,906 or £2513) against the loss suffered but had not fulfilled the agreement. Lo's claim was dismissed as he had caused his employer financial damage through his negligence and had not repaid the funds lost.[60]

Each of the above court cases were for relatively small amounts and today, would be best handled by some other form of mediation. Judging by the numbers of hearings and appeals per case, however, C. Nickel & Co. Ltd. fought them vigorously. It would have been difficult for the Japanese court to assess the extent to which C. Nickel & Co. Ltd. had been justified in terminating their employees' contracts and in withholding wages and the bonds due to poor performance. One can only imagine that employment practices were arbitrary in the treaty ports and access to an abundant supply of day labourers made them both exploitable and expendable.

Loyalty Between Foreign Bosses and Japanese Workers

Not all the *Japan Chronicle*'s reporting on C. Nickel & Co. Ltd. and its relationship with its workforce portrayed Japanese unskilled workers as unruly and undisciplined or disloyal. The *Chronicle* reported on unskilled workers coming to their foreign bosses' rescue when attacked violently by other labourers. The *Chronicle* also provides evidence that some of C. Nickel & Co. Ltd.'s employees who had been with the company for many years were treated as loyal and trusted partners. As such they could be enlisted to help Nickel and Holstein undermine Japanese courts' attempts to impose hefty fines on the company. In chapter 5, when Anami Kumeo sued C. Nickel & Co. for compensation for injuries received due to a collision with a C. Nickel & Co. Ltd. owned vessel, the company transferred ownership to one of its Japanese employees, Ishida Satoru, allowing it to avoid responsibility for the accident and to reduce the fines incurred.[61] The company and its managing directors also utilized their trusted relationships to thwart the

60 "Negligence of Employés: An Important Point," *Japan Chronicle* (Kobe), 9 April 1908, 459.

61 "Claim for Compensation for Injuries: Sequel to a Collision in Kobe Harbour," *Japan Chronicle* (Kobe), 25 May 1911, 904.

Japanese authorities' restrictions on foreigners owning land, as will be seen in chapter 7. The relationship between C. Nickel & Co. and certain employees was a close, respectful, and mutually beneficial one. As seen in chapter 3, in 1896, it was reported that Nickel had been presented by his staff with a "testimonial in recognition of his popularity and generosity as an employer ... for twenty-five years." Presumably it was his permanent staff who regarded him highly.[62]

Most of the *Japan Chronicle*'s reportage involving its employees portrayed C. Nickel & Co. Ltd. as having a combative relationship with its workforce. The *Chronicle* no doubt selected those cases that served its purpose of reminding the foreign community of two things. First, organized workers were represented as a growing threat to the lives and interests of foreigners and their businesses in Kobe. Second, as seen in chapters 4 and 5, the *Japan Chronicle* reminds the foreign community that they could not expect justice at the hands of the Japanese courts because of their inherent bias against foreigners. Through the reportage of the *Japan Chronicle* which refers to manual day labourers by the pejorative term "coolies," how foreigners, and C. Nickel & Co. Ltd. justified their exploitation and poor treatment of the lowest paid Japanese and Chinese workers can be seen. The cases discussed above provide evidence that C. Nickel & Co. Ltd.'s foreign bosses believed they were entitled to handle their workforce roughly, and even after the end of extraterritoriality, this attitude did not change. As several of the cases dealt with violence meted out by foreign bosses in response to perceived insubordination, it can be assumed that they considered the casual workforce to be by nature, insolent, insubordinate and/or aggressive in their attitudes towards foreigners. The Japanese court system sometimes took the view that blame and responsibility should be shared, considering that where foreign bosses had a history of violence, they could have provoked their workers into insubordination and aggression. In any case, the funds expended by C. Nickel & Co. Ltd. fighting their claimants, which must have become a significant cost of doing business, were offset against profits made exploiting a cheap and abundant supply of labour. Buried within other reportage of the *Chronicle* are clues indicating that Nickel and subsequently Holstein did have close and trusting relationships with long-term members of their workforce. Such employees helped Nickel and Holstein mitigate fines imposed where the company was sued for negligence or to circumvent the Japanese ban on land ownership.

62 "Award to Nickel of Testimonial," *The N. C. Herald and S. C. & C. Gazette* (Shanghai), 10 January 1896, 34.

Chapter 7 explores further costs of doing business through the Japanese government's ban on foreigners owning land in Japan and its refusal to properly register foreign leasing arrangements and how C. Nickel & Co. Ltd. managed those limitations.

7. Securing Land Tenure

Abstract: From the opening of the treaty ports, the Japanese authorities prohibited foreigners from owning land. They feared the foreign merchants' wealth would put prices out of reach of the Japanese. In the Foreign Settlement, foreigners could take a perpetual lease, while being permitted to own the buildings. Those residing in the Native Town could only lease from Japanese landlords for twenty to twenty-five years, leaving them feeling vulnerable to the whims of those landlords. In the case of disputes, foreigners had to resort to the Japanese courts. In this chapter, how Nickel and Holstein controlled their properties and the innovative ways they circumvented the Japanese prohibition on foreign land ownership is discussed. These strategies were not without risks, however.

Keywords: registration, courts, lease, superficies, treaties, loopholes

How the "nimble" and ever-adaptive Carl Nickel conducted business after the loss of extraterritoriality has become clear: submitting to Japanese jurisdiction, to changes to the Shipping Law subverting the revised treaties, to a congested Kobe harbour and customs, and to an unruly Japanese workforce. A further obstacle to doing business was the Japanese ban on foreigners owning land. Whereas in the treaty Port of Shanghai, foreigners were permitted to own land, in Japan, the government banned foreign land ownership.[1] Even though Japanese residents in Europe and parts of the US already had the right to own land, the Japanese refused to reciprocate. Foreign residents considered land ownership was the key to securing their business interests: not only securing their investment in constructing the buildings they required, but also in building equity they could use to borrow funds to expand their business and in turn invest in Japan's

1 Isabella Jackson, "Who Ran the Treaty Ports? A Study of the Shanghai Municipal Council," in *Treaty Ports in Modern China: Law, Land and Power*, eds. Robert A. Bickers and Isabella Jackson (Milton Park, Abingdon, Oxon; Routledge, 2016), 45.

Holstein, Prue S. *The German Experience of Japan's Treaty Port System: A Case Study of C. Nickel & Co. Ltd., 1860–1923*. Taylor & Francis Group, 2025.
DOI: 10.4324/9781003706274-8

future. Land ownership for foreign merchants in the treaty ports of Japan became a fundamental goal British diplomats pursued on behalf of their constituents over seventy years, from 1856 until 1926, when the Alien Land Law allowing foreigners to own land was finally enacted. In no other aspect of doing business in Kobe was Nickel and his successor, Holstein's, ability to push boundaries better displayed than in the ways they circumvented the Japanese government's ban on foreign land ownership, to acquire and control their investments in land and buildings for commercial, residential and investment purposes. This was however not without risk.

This chapter traces how Nickel circumvented the Japanese government's restrictions on foreign land ownership, adopting innovative strategies to secure their property needs. Examining Japanese land registration records in Nagasaki and Kobe before and after 1899, the strategies used to control their land, both under extraterritoriality and after the enactment of the revised treaties and loss of extraterritoriality, are revealed. Furthermore, how Holstein managed the risks associated with the investment properties he acquired, defending his interests in the Japanese courts, is also explored. In the absence of other documents, the *Chronicle*'s reportage once more becomes important in tracing how, Holstein, in defending his investments, continued to challenge the legislative constraints the Japanese government imposed on foreigners, both in and outside the Japanese court system.

Foreigners' Rights to Lease but not Own Land

The unequal treaties signed from 1858 onwards accorded foreigners the right to lease land in the treaty ports. The treaties stated that foreign "citizens may permanently reside" in the treaty ports and towns of Hakodadi (Hakodate), Kanagawa (Yokohama), Nagasaki, and in in Yedo (Tokyo) from 1862, and from 1863 in Kobe and Osaka. Due to civil war in Japan, Kobe was not opened to foreign merchants until 1868. The treaties stated that

> they [foreigners] have the right to lease ground and purchase the buildings thereon and may erect dwellings and warehouses ... The place which ... subjects shall occupy for their buildings ... shall be arranged by the foreign Consul and the Japanese authorities.[2]

2 *Treaties and Conventions Concluded between Japan and Foreign Nations: Together with Notifications and Regulations Made from Time to Time, 1854–1870: Notification: Arrangements for the Establishment of Foreign Settlements at the Port of Hiogo and of Osaka* (published by Sir Harry S Parkes, Her Britannic

While the unequal treaties did not specifically prohibit foreigners from owning land, this prohibition was formalized in legislation introduced by the Japanese government in 1874.[3] The treaty between Great Britain and Japan (signed in 1858) laid down broad prescriptions around where foreigners could live with the details around the Japanese government's provision of a dedicated foreign settlement being elaborated on in subsequent notifications.[4] The British Minister, Sir Harry S. Parkes (serving from 1865 to 1883), issued notifications from time to time clarifying further elements of the treaty for British subjects. Such notifications were specific to a particular treaty port, were published in English and dealt with a range of additions and clarifications agreed to between the British Minister and the Japanese government.[5] In the case of Hiogo (Kobe) and Osaka, a notification, entitled "Arrangements for the Establishment of Foreign Settlements at the Port of Hiogo and of Osaka," was published by Sir Harry S. Parkes on 17 May 1867 in Osaka, "for the general information of Her Majesty's subjects." This notification detailed the Japanese government's plans for preparing the ground for the foreign settlement and for auctioning off that land to foreigners. The auction was further explained as being necessary for the Japanese government to recoup its costs.[6] A municipal council run by the foreign community themselves was established to govern the Settlement. It charged foreign land renters an annual rent which covered the land tax payable to the Japanese government, plus the costs of maintaining roads and drains, lighting and of law and order for which the council was responsible. The Japanese government was responsible for providing the warehouses, a cemetery for foreigners and, according to treaty arrangements, promised to keep in good order the sea and river walls, parapets and landing places including maintaining the depth of water.[7]

The basis upon which foreigners could live in the Kobe Foreign Settlement was explained in a document entitled "Foreign Settlements in Japan: The Law Relating Thereto."[8] Foreigners took perpetual leases for an unspecified

Majesty's Envoy Extraordinary and Minister Plenipotentiary in Japan Osaka, 17 May 1867), Harold Williams Collection, National Library of Australia (henceforth HSW NLA), q1150/1716690, 212–14.

3 "The Japan Times and Land Ownership," *Japan Chronicle* (Kobe), 5 March 1902, 194.

4 Only the Treaty between Great Britain and Japan and its subsequent Notifications are being discussed. Treaties between the other powers and Japan were negotiated on a most favoured nation basis, so any new inclusions were assumed by all the treaties.

5 Treaties and Conventions 1854–1870, 212–14.

6 Treaties and Conventions 1854–1870, 212–13.

7 Treaties and Conventions 1854–1870, 213.

8 "Perpetual Leases. Correspondence between the British Legation and the Japanese Foreign Office," including "Foreign Settlements in Japan: The Law Relating Thereto," Summary written by Sir E. Satow, HBM Envoy, 26 April 1899. Allgemein Angelegenheiten Japans 1899–1904, vom

period over land they had bid for at auction, with the Japanese government as lessor. While foreigners could not own land outright, they could construct and own buildings on the land they leased. As long as the rent was paid, they were free to do with the land as they wished. They were not permitted to sub-let to Japanese or transfer the lease to a non-treaty subject. Any other matters such as "the transmission of the estate by will or inheritance, the mortgaging or subletting ... the settlement of the estate on marriage" were to "be dealt with ... according to the laws of their respective countries."[9]

Although it is not specifically stated in the notifications referred to above, foreigners also had the right to live outside the Foreign Settlement, in "the Native Town," renting from Japanese landlords. Upon the opening of the Port of Kobe in 1868, Francis Gerhard Myburg, the first British Consul for Hyogo and Osaka, reported that some thirty foreigners rented houses in the Native Town. While a number of those took short-term leases waiting for the construction of the Foreign Settlement, a number intended residing there for the longer term.[10] The conditions of foreigners' residency in the Native Town were very different to those in the Foreign Settlement.

Whereas the leases of those living in the Foreign Settlement were in perpetuity and under extraterritorial protections offering a measure of certainty, foreigners leasing in the Native Town from Japanese landlords had shorter-term leases and no such protections. As explained by the *Kobe Chronicle*, the Japanese landlords only offered leases for twenty to twenty-five years and could raise rentals or shorten leases arbitrarily.[11] Japanese landlords could also challenge improvements made at the foreign lessee's expense or confiscate any buildings constructed at the end of the lease and sell them for their own profit. As late as 1897, the *Kobe Chronicle* reported, in its usual dismissive tone, that renting from Japanese landlords was risky given that "the standard of commercial morality is very low in Japan."[12] As the landlord/tenant relationship was covered under Japanese law, disputes had to be adjudicated by the Japanese courts, which, as already seen throughout the previous chapters, foreigners considered inimical to their interests.[13]

1 Oktober 1899 bis 31 Maerz 1904, R18613, PA AA, 1–40 (hereafter "Perpetual Leases," Summary written by Sir E. Satow).

9 "Perpetual Leases," Summary written by Sir E. Satow, 1.

10 Peter Ennals, *Opening a Window to the West: The Foreign Concession at Kobe, Japan 1868–1899* (Toronto, Buffalo, London: University of Toronto Press, 2014) 25, 36.

11 Robert Young, "The Case of the Foreign Residents in Japan: 'Nineteenth Century' for August," *Kobe Chronicle*, 2 October 1897, 274.

12 Young, "The Case of the Foreign Residents in Japan," 274.

13 Ennals, *Opening a Window to the West*, 37.

Lingering Perception of Anti-Foreign Sentiment

With the revision of the treaties in 1899, while permission for foreigners to enter the interior of Japan was granted in exchange for giving up extraterritoriality, no such concessions were made by the Japanese with regards to granting foreigners' the right to own property. According to the *Japan Chronicle*, the Japanese government's initial draft proposal of the revision of the treaty with Britain of December 1888 did grant foreigners the right to own land. However, the government postponed allowing foreign land ownership, claiming "public opinion was not on their side" possibly due to a fear land prices would be pushed out of reach of the Japanese population. It decided that this matter should be dealt with outside the treaty.[14] The *Chronicle* expressed its view that the "illiberal and short-sighted law promulgated in 1874" prohibiting foreign land ownership should be removed.[15] Hoping that this restriction would be lifted in the nearer term, the *Japan Chronicle* expressed a separate view, arguing that "It is understood by foreigners that the opposition [of the Japanese government] is ... confined to a ... small body of conservatives, the surviving remnant of those who opposed foreign intercourse."[16]

The continuing Japanese ban on foreign land ownership limited the ability of foreign merchants to invest in and secure the future of their businesses. In the late 1800s the *Japan Chronicle* advocated for leases of at least fifty years for Japan to attract much needed foreign investment in manufacturing. It argued that "Capitalists will not be rash enough to erect factories on a mere twenty-year lease."[17] As the *Japan Chronicle* later inferred in its reportage in September 1901, this restriction was seen as a calculated strategy on the part of the Japanese government to limit not only foreign merchants' ability to secure their own business interests but also to restrict their ability to invest in Japan's growth.[18]

The refusal of the Japanese government to grant foreigners land ownership rights in the treaty ports was an on-going bone of contention for the foreign community. The revised treaties were supposed to ensure reciprocity of rights and Japanese residents in Britain, Europe and in parts of the United States had such rights.[19] Furthermore, the foreign community and the

14 "The Treaty Blue-Book and Land Ownership," *Japan Chronicle* (Kobe), 27 August 1902, 193.
15 "The Japan Times and Land Ownership," 194.
16 "The Japan Times and Land Ownership," 194.
17 "Japan as Field for Foreign Investment," *Kobe Chronicle*, 8 January 1898, 2.
18 "Right of Foreigners to Hold Land: A Japanese Merchant's View," *Kobe Chronicle*, 11 September 1901, 260.
19 "Landowning by Aliens in the United State," *Japan Chronicle* (Kobe), 4 December 1901, 535.

Japan Chronicle argued that Japan needed foreign investment capital to develop its industries and manufacturing, and that "so long as security is not forthcoming in the way of land ownership [for foreigners] so long must Japanese applications for foreign capital be refused."[20]

Foreigners' failure to secure land ownership rights led to some posturing on the morality and good behaviour of their Japanese counterparts, and additional questioning of Japan's ability to raise the much-needed foreign capital for its economic growth. On 5 March 1902, the *Japan Chronic*le used an article published a few days earlier by its Japanese-owned English language competitor, the *Japan Times*, to discuss the various issues at stake regarding foreign land ownership and its connection to foreign capital in Japan. The *Chronicle* quoted the *Japan Times* as saying that foreign capital

> will come to us [Japanese] freely only when capitalists abroad shall have become convinced that our borrowers have thoroughly awakened to the importance of manifesting the business integrity which they are at present unfortunately as a class supposed to lack.[21]

The equating of doing business with morality was a regular feature of the *Japan Chronicle*'s advocacy for foreign merchants' rights to do business on an equitable basis. The *Chronicle* reflected the beliefs of the foreign community that both the Japanese business community and the Japanese government regularly prejudiced the interests of foreign merchants through corrupt practices. Another example of the *Chronicle*'s posturing can be seen in its reporting on a case of alleged fraud involving the Hyogo Sōkō (warehouse) Kabushiki Kaisha and several Japanese banks. The *Chronicle* commenced its article saying, "Some extraordinary facts have come to light [which] serve to emphasize the charges … so frequently levelled against Japanese commercial morality."[22]

The *Chronicle* insisted that land ownership for foreigners would make them less vulnerable in a rapacious and immoral context, and regularly expressed the view that the foreign capital, upon which Japan depended to develop its industries, was reliant upon foreigners being able to own land. The *Japan Chronicle* thus agreed with the *Japan Times* in saying that "so long as Japan maintains her conservative attitude with regard to the ownership of land, it is clear such capital will not come into the country."[23]

20 "The Japan Times and Land Ownership," 194.

21 "The Japan Times and Land Ownership," 194.

22 "Japanese Commercial Morality," *Kobe Chronicle*, 9 July 1898, 19–20.

23 "The Japan Times and Land Ownership," 194.

Foreigners Leasing from Japanese Landlords

The revised treaties in 1899 stated that no changes would be made in foreigners' tenure of property in the Foreign Settlement, although there was an imposition of a house tax for those living in the Settlement to which the foreign community objected as they already paid a land tax to the Japanese government. For Nickel the revised treaties brought neither changes nor new burdens: he was already accustomed to leasing in the Native Town under Japanese law and to paying a house tax. He had however from the outset devised his own strategies to protect his land interests and ensure certainty over time for his investments. While the basis for leasing in the Native Town did not change, Nickel was able to take advantage of new methods being applied in the Foreign Settlement, opportunities that gave him greater control over his land investments.

By the time he settled in Kobe, Nickel already had extensive experience leasing land in Japan, starting with the period of his residence in Nagasaki. As seen in chapter 2, the local Nagasaki government's monthly House to House Checks recorded that while Carl Nickel rented from foreign leaseholders in the Ōura Foreign Settlement from at least 1862 to 1868, he became a leaseholder himself early in 1868.[24] In the April and July 1868 House to House Checks, he was listed as the leaseholder for 31 A/B Ōura, Sagarimatsu residing with his new wife, Eliza McLaren. Although no records remain of the specific lease arrangements, it appears Nickel established his hotel and bowling alley, the Falcon, at this location around 1870.[25]

In Kobe, from 1881 to the mid-1890s as the Kobe business directory listings show, Nickel moved his residence and business frequently. One single record of a pre-1899 lease arrangement with Nickel that has survived in the Japanese Foreign Ministry (*Gaimushō*) records shows that Nickel was already circumventing the Japanese government's ban on foreign land ownership as early as 1881. In November that year, Nickel rented a lot of 52.49 *tsubo* (one *tsubo* is three feet by six feet or one tatami mat size) for a house in Kitanagasa-dōri, 5-chome (identified in a 1910 map as No. 7-2). The owner was listed as Matsuura Tsunesaburō and the lease was for twenty-five years

24 Nagasaki Kyōryūchi Gaikokujin Meibō (Names and Populations of Foreign Residents in Nagasaki aka House to House Checks), October 1862 to March–May 1870, #14-12-7 compiled by the Nagasaki Bugyōsho (printed by Nagasaki Prefectural Library 2002), Nagasaki Museum of History and Culture (hereafter Nagasaki Kyōryūchi Gaikokujin Meibō).

25 Nagasaki Kyōryūchi Gaikokujin Meibō.

at the rate of ¥25 (¥121,270 or £635) per year.[26] As the details in the title deeds of another property show, Matsuura was a trusted employee of Nickel's and was one of Nickel and Holstein's front men for property purchases. This 1881 lease suggests that Nickel got around Japanese laws restricting foreigners' controlling land by purchasing the property in the name of his Japanese employee and leasing it back. Given the low equivalent value of ¥121,270 per annum rent for a house of this size in today's values, it was a favourable rate.

The few records that remain in public archives of leaseholds negotiated between foreigners and Japanese landlords under extraterritoriality reflect how informally they were recorded up until 1899, a process which proved problematic for some foreign lessees after 1899. Until 1899, leases taken out by foreigners in both the Foreign Settlement and the Native Town had to be registered with the relevant foreign consul, who then informed the Japanese Foreign Ministry (*Gaimushō*). The *Gaimushō* then issued the foreigner with a title deed and supposedly recorded that lease in its own records. Prior to 1899, no record of lease arrangements with foreigners was made on the official title deeds for the property held by the Japanese Land Registration Bureau. The Bureau only recorded the name of the Japanese owner or Japanese lessor of the property.[27] With the enactment of the revised treaties, some foreigners had problems trying to prove prior ownership of a leasehold or the property's boundaries. Copies of the lease arrangements and original title deeds may have been lost by the owners and details had not necessarily been recorded accurately by the *Gaimushō* or the foreign consulates.[28] From 1899, however, the process of recording foreign lease arrangements was formalized when the Japanese Land Registration Bureau commenced recording foreigner leases on the title deeds alongside the names of the Japanese owners.

Reinterpreting Perpetual Leases as Rights of Superficies

Despite assurances to the contrary, with the enactment of the revised treaties, the Japanese government changed perpetual leaseholds in the Foreign Settlement in a way that Nickel and his German colleagues accepted

26 Gaimushō Kiroku No. 223–23 held by the Kobe Public Archives (KPA); Yen conversions to 2019 values and others in this chapter are based on the website: https://yaruzou.net/hprice/hprice-calc.html. Conversion to British pounds was conducted on 14 April 2024.

27 "Perpetual Leases," Summary written by Sir E. Satow, 1–2.

28 "Perpetual Leases," Summary written by Sir E. Satow, 1–3.

but the British did not. First, as revealed in diplomatic correspondence, to the horror of the British, the Japanese government no longer recognized perpetual leases. So that foreign land-holders continued to have the certainty of perpetuity, the Japanese government and courts reinterpreted perpetual leases as a right of superficies over the land.[29] A right of superficies is "the right to use another person's land for the purpose of owning thereon structures or bamboos and trees" for the duration of a defined term.[30] Second, the Japanese government introduced a new tax called the house tax. The house tax was an impost on all Japanese building owners and was now payable by foreign landholders in the settlement, even though their normal rental payments already included a charge to cover a land tax. Foreign land-holders considered the reinterpretation of a perpetual lease as a right of superficies and the house tax to be infractions "of the Treaties and an invasion of their rights" outside the spirit of the original agreement around the perpetual leases.[31] Thus, in the wake of the revised treaties, British diplomats and the *Japan Chronicle* campaigned on behalf of the foreign community to have the original perpetual leases reinstated and to have foreigners in the Settlement exempted from house tax. These issues long remained a bone of contention.

A right of superficies as a substitute for land ownership was opposed strenuously by both the British Legation in Tokyo and the *Japan Chronicle* on behalf of the foreign community. In correspondence from 1899 to 1904 between Sir Ernest Satow the head of the British Legation (from 1895 to 1900), and the Japanese Foreign Minister, Viscount Aoki, Satow pointed out that "superficies is not and cannot be held to be, an equivalent of the term 'lease in perpetuity.'"[32] The *Japan Chronicle* also held a dim view of the merits of superficies as opposed to land ownership: in March 1902, the *Japan Chronicle* commented that the,

29 "Perpetual Leases," Correspondence from Sir E. Satow, HBM Envoy and Minister to Japan to Viscount Aoki, Japanese Minister of Foreign Affairs, 8 December 1899. Allgemein Angelegenheiten Japans 1899–1904, vom 1 Oktober 1899 bis 31 Maerz 1904, R18613, PA AA, 8–9 (hereafter "Perpetual Leases," From Sir E. Satow to Viscount Aoki, 8 December 1899), 8.

30 Hozumi, Nobushige, Masakasa Tomii and Kenjiro Ume, "Articles 265–269," *The Civil Code of Japan*. Translated by Dr L. Lönholm. (Yokohama, Shanghai, Hong Kong & Singapore: Kelly & Walsh Lim, 1898). 68–70; It was dedicated to 'His Lordship Marquis Hirobumi Itō, Minister President of State and President of the Committee for the Revision of the Codes.' A copy was held by C. Nickel & Co. Ltd. and remains in private hands.

31 "The House-Tax: The Construction of the Settlement and the Profit Made. (By an Old Resident)," *Japan Chronicle* (Kobe), 19 February 1902, 158; "The House-Tax & Foreign Residents," *Japan Chronicle* (Kobe), 5 March 1902, 193.

32 "Perpetual Leases," From Sir E. Satow to Viscount Aoki, 8 December 1899, 8.

> offer of superficies as set forth in the Civil Code ... has been set up by some as a good substitute for land ownership but without ... impressing foreign capitalists, [because] so long as security is not forthcoming in the way of land ownership, so long must Japanese applications [for investment capital from foreign sources] be refused[33]

However, Dr Ludwig Lönholm, a Professor of German Law at Tokyo University, took a different view. In an article published by the *Chronicle* in January 1898 Lönholm explained that, for foreigners, taking superficiary rights over a property was a legitimate way of getting around the Japanese law limiting leases to twenty to twenty-five years. He stated that while the "Japanese law ... limits leases to twenty years, [it] does not place any limit on the duration of a right of superficies." In his interpretation of Article 265 of the Japan Civil Code, a superficiary had "the right to use the land of another for the purpose of owning upon it buildings, trees or bamboo." The superficiary entered such an arrangement with the landowner "for an indefinite or a stated period." Dr Lönholm concluded that "rights may be acquired to the use of land for any term—fifty, a hundred or even a thousand and one years." He maintained that "leases" and "superficies" were very different legal concepts and that the rights of the lessee were not identical to those of a superficiary, implying the latter was more secure.[34]

While the *Japan Chronicle* published Dr Lönholm's thesis, it also outlined its objections to his claims, worrying that,

> this is a rather flimsy foundation upon which to build a superstructure of rights ... foreigners will still remain dubious about the practical working of the law of superficies in their favour.[35]

Somewhat missing Lönholm's point, the *Chronicle* refuted his claim that "no hindrance exists to the acquisition of a superficies ... say 50, a hundred ... years." The *Chronicle* cited the lack of fifty-year leases achieved in the previous ten years, reinforcing its view that Japanese landlords were opposed to extending leases beyond twenty to twenty-five years.[36] Furthermore, neither the *Chronicle* nor the British Legation was confident that the Japanese

33 "The Japan Times and Land Ownership," 194.

34 "Dr Lönholm on the Land Question," *Kobe Chronicle*, 8 January 1898, 1. Subsequent to this article, Dr Lönholm translated into English *The Civil Code of Japan* written by Hozumi, Masakasa and Kenjiro.

35 "Dr Lönholm on the Land Question," 1.

36 "Japan as Field for Foreign Investment," 2.

legal system would ensure that foreigners' rights would be protected in the event of a dispute or termination of those rights. Despite persistent representations by Satow and his successors to the Japanese government to secure the continued recognition of perpetual leases and elimination of the house tax, their efforts failed. And again, the *Japan Chronicle* took the opportunity to complain about the Japanese government's use of the rights of superficies and the courts likely unwillingness, in the *Chronicle's* view, to protect foreigners' interests in the case of disputes arising.

While the house tax did not impact Nickel's and Holstein's decisions, as they already paid this tax in the Native Town, they were persuaded by the merits of taking a right of superficies over a property. Given the time and difficulties involved in trying to persuade the Japanese authorities to allow foreign land ownership, Nickel was happy to disregard British concerns and follow Dr Lönholm's advice. From 1902 onwards, the company C. Nickel & Co. Ltd. and its successive managing directors, Nickel, and Holstein, purchased properties outright, placing them in the names of trusted Japanese employees and registering superficiary rights of 900 and 1,000 years over those properties. The Kobe Land Registration Bureau (*Kobe Chihō-Hōmukyoku*) recorded on the title deeds the name of the owner of the property, the name and company details of the lessee, the terms of the lease and any other details pertaining to the ownership and transfer arrangements of the property. While records are patchy, Nickel's strategy worked because Nickel owned his properties continuously until his death in 1906, and Holstein until 1919 and 1920, when all German private property was confiscated by the Japanese government as reparations for First World War, a subject that will be discussed in more detail in chapter 10. Documents listing the German properties confiscated by the Japanese government reveal that many other German property owners had also taken superficiary rights over some of their properties.[37] It is likely that Nickel and Holstein understood Dr Lönholm's interpretation of the Japan Civil Code and superficies as providing a way of securing their property investments through the exploitation of loopholes in the Japanese law. Nickel and Holstein may have supported the campaigns of the *Japan Chronicle* and the British Legation advocating for the Japanese government to allow foreign land ownership. However, at the same time, they demonstrated continuing nimbleness in

37 Control of Special Property. Hyogo Prefecture. Translation from the Official Gazette (of the Japanese government) 7 November 1919–19 January 1920. Akten betreffend Beschlagsnahme deutschen Eigentums in Japan anlässlich des Weltkrieges—lists of assets of German merchants resident in Tokyo, Yokohama, Kobe and Osaka, R265.002, PA AA.

getting on with the business of doing business by adopting the best possible solution available at the time.

Securing Control of Company and Private Properties

To provide a better understanding of the ways Nickel and Holstein used this device and to show how complicated it could be acquiring the properties they needed, the ways different properties were acquired are discussed. In 1902 Nickel first used superficiary rights to acquire a home, described by the *Japan Chronicle* in November 1902 as a "fine property at Suma."[38] The beachfront property was located on the boundary of Takatori and Suma west of Kobe near the present-day Suma Aquarium. The title deed held by the Kobe Land Registration Bureau in Suma shows that on 10 December 1902, Nickel registered a right of superficies of 1,000 years in his name for Lot 21, Wakamiya-chi-chome, Suma-ku, Kobe (also known as Rokken Estate).[39] The owner was Otojirō Taguchi of Yamamoto-dōri, 5-chome, Kobe. One year later, on 26 December 1903 Ishida Satoru was listed as the owner. Ishida was the employee we encountered first in chapter 5 as the named owner of a vessel involved in an accident. Otojirō and Ishida were both trusted employees of C. Nickel & Co. Ltd. and noted as such over the years in the *Japan Chronicle*.[40] In March 1907, eight months after the death of Carl Nickel, and presumably as part of the settlement of his estate, the ownership of the property was transferred to Ikezumi Hide, the Japanese wife of Charles Lange-Delacamp, another well-known German merchant in Kobe. Lange-Delacamp in turn registered a right of superficies for 1,000 years renting from his Japanese wife. The Rokken property was a prestigious holding: it was located next door but one to the grand Sumitomo House also on the beachfront in Suma and was a testament to Nickel's wealth at the time of his death. The grounds of the Sumitomo House, which was destroyed during Second World War, have been preserved as a public park. The former property of Nickel and Lange-Delacamp is now under the car park of the Suma Aquarium.

38 "New Motor-Car in Kobe," *Japan Chronicle* (Kobe), 5 November 1902, 469.

39 Kobe Chihō-Hōmukyoku (Kobe Land Registry Bureau—Suma Branch) 3-1-7, Naka-Ōchiai, Suma-ku, Kobe.

40 Kobe Chihō-Hōmukyoku (Kobe Land Registry Bureau) 1-1, Hatoba-chō, Chuo-ku, Kobe; "Claim for Compensation for Injuries: Anami Kumeo v. Messrs. Nickel & Co.," *Japan Chronicle* (Kobe), 10 November 1910, 840; "Arrest of a Japanese: Serious Charge," *Japan Chronicle* (Kobe), 4 February 1904, 124.

While in 1902 Nickel wasted no time registering a right of superficies of 1,000 years over his residential property in Suma, it was not until mid-1906 that a right of superficies was registered for the company property at 3 Kaigan-dōri.[41] Exactly when Nickel took out a lease on his company property is unknown. The business directory from 1895 suggests that Nickel first leased the property, originally known as 3 Native Bund, around 1894–95 presumably on a twenty to twenty-five-year lease. The title deed held in the Kobe Land Registration Bureau reveals that from 1890 to 1899, the property was owned by several generations of the Ōmichi family. Prior to 1899, the name of the lessee was not recorded. There is no extant evidence of any personal connection between Nickel and the Ōmichi family, but as Nickel held the lease for at least ten years from 1894 without apparent argument from the owner, it is possible there was a relationship. In 1906, under Holstein's management, the name of the Japanese owner of the property was changed to Nakamura Heisaburō, a company employee, and a right of superficies of 1,000 years was registered by the C. Nickel & Co. Ltd. Branch Office in Kobe. Perhaps the Ōmichi family name had died out and a new "friendly owner" needed to be found. It is also possible that Holstein only purchased the property outright in 1906, putting it in the name of a company employee, and taking a right of superficies over the property. Holstcin's action suggests that by 1906 adopting the practice of taking a right of superficies over a property had become well-honed. In 1911, Holstein, as the head of C. Nickel & Co. Ltd., which already owned the land, had the name of the "official" owner of the company premises changed to Matsuura Tsunesaburō. Matsuura, as mentioned earlier, was the owner and the lessor for Nickel's Kitanagasa property in 1881, indicating he had a relationship with Nickel and the company for over twenty-five years. In 1913, after C. Nickel & Co. Ltd. merged with J. Lyons & Co. to form Nickel & Lyons, the right of superficies for the property was transferred to the new entity. In 1916, two years after the German management had been dispossessed by the British board at the outbreak of First World War, the company moved location. The property at 3 Kaigan-dōri was sold and the superficiary rights abandoned.

To build its Shinzaike Shipyard east of Kobe, Nickel, through his company, commenced acquiring individual plots from the late 1800s, as shown by the title deeds for each of the ten pieces of land needed for the shipyard.[42] The ten adjoining blocks of land purchased were each placed at various stages in the names of trusted Japanese employees: Ishida Satoru, Otojirō

41 Kobe Chihō-Hōmukyoku, Chuo-ku, Kobe.
42 Kobe Chihō-Hōmukyoku, Chuo-ku, Kobe.

Taguchi, Nakayama Take, and Nakayama Tatsu to name a few.[43] In 1903 rights of superficies of 999 years were registered over these properties.[44] The ability to get around the Japanese ban on foreigners owning land by placing them in the names of trusted Japanese employees and taking superficiary rights of 1,000 years allowed Nickel and Holstein full control over their means of operation for the construction and repairs of vessels. The land increased significantly in value, thus representing a valuable investment for the company despite the ban on foreign companies owning land. Today, the shipyard has disappeared, and the area now supports two or three large *danchi* multi storey apartment buildings.

In a similar manner, from 1908 to 1912, title deeds show that Christian Holstein personally acquired three pieces of land to form his private estate in Suma in Hamayama 3-chome 3-ban, 4-ban and 5-ban. It was next door to Nickel's old property sold to Charles Lange-Delacamp's wife.[45] In 1912, Holstein placed the ownership of his three properties in the name of Ishida Satoru and registered rights of superficies of 1,000 years.[46] This property became a grand estate with an extensive beach front bounded by a high stone retaining wall, a palatial Japanese style two-storey timber house and an extensive Japanese garden with established pine trees, ponds, bridges and a European style gazebo. It was referred to in the Japanese press as his *bessō* or holiday house: his main residence was in Kobe in Kitano- chō.[47]

Risks of Nominating a Trusted Japanese Owner

For Holstein, placing a property of his in the name of a trusted Japanese employee was not entirely risk free. In addition to at least two other properties for which Otojiro Taguchi had been nominated as "owner," Holstein also nominated him as the "owner" of his home on "The Hill," his main house in Kitano-chō, a prestigious location in Kobe popular as a residential area amongst foreigners since the early days of the port. In February 1904, however, Holstein had Otojirō arrested on charges of trying to raise ¥2000

43 Evidence for these men being connected with C. Nickel & Co. have been found in articles written in the *Japan Chronicle* over the years.

44 Kobe Chihō-Hōmukyoku, Chuo-ku, Kobe.

45 Kobe Chihō-Hōmukyoku, Suma-ku, Kobe.

46 Kobe Chihō-Hōmukyoku, Suma-ku, Kobe.

47 "Matamata Daisōsaku Kaishi. Nidokushō Suma Bessō Sonota" (My Translation: Big Enquiry Commenced. Suma Holiday House of two German Merchants), *Kobe Yūshin Nippō*, 5 November 1914, KPA.

(¥7,746,658 or £40,572) by mortgaging this last house.[48] Otojirō was at that time aged thirty-one and had been employed in the company for ten years.

Just as it could be risky for a foreigner to nominate a Japanese as "owner" of a property, it could also be risky for those Japanese employees so designated. The *Kobe Yūshin Nippō* reported in November 1914 on the arrest and jailing for six weeks without charge of Holstein just after the outbreak of First World War, a story that will be recounted in chapter 10. The *Nippō* revealed that upon Holstein's arrest, one of his neighbours, a Mr Kusumoto, put in a claim to the Preliminary Court for unpaid monies. He stated he had provided the mortgage for Holstein to acquire the three Suma properties and was holding Holstein and Ishida Satoru, the legal owner of the property, responsible for the mortgage.[49] As the company, now known as Nickel & Lyons, was a public company with a British board which had terminated its German management at the outbreak of First World War, presumably there was no obligation for them to pay the mortgage on Ishida's behalf. There is no record of the outcome of the case, but Holstein continued to occupy this property until 1920, when it was confiscated by the Japanese government as war reparations and auctioned off to a certain Wadakyu Zaemon. In 1944, just before the end of Second World War, the land reverted to the Japanese government. Today only the view of the hills around Akashi, visible from the former property, remain; the luxury property and garden are also now under the Suma Aquarium and its carpark.

The extent to which members of the German community in general found ways around the Japanese prohibition on foreign land ownership can be seen in a number of sources. In 1920, the *Japan Chronicle*, protesting the Japanese government's decision to confiscate the assets of German merchants as reparations, published lists of properties owned by German residents in Kobe: its purpose in publishing such lists is explored in chapter 10. For this chapter, however, those lists are used to show the extent of Holstein's ability to acquire property. He was listed as owning land at Suehiro-cho in Moji, his *bessō* (holiday house) in Hamayama, Higashi-Suma, a house in Nakayamate-dōri, 7-chome, Kobe and a house on Mt. Rokko behind Kobe.[50] The German Foreign Ministry Archives also holds a file containing extensive

48 "Arrest of a Japanese: Serious Charge," 124.

49 "Sakukenjikyoku Holstein Shōkan Jyūdaijiken Hansekimeiryō" (My translation: Holstein Summoned to the Prosecutor's Office for an Important Criminal Act) *Kobe Yūshin Nippō*, 12 November 1914, KPA.

50 "Enemy Property in Japan: Security for Payment of Indemnity," *Japan Chronicle* (Kobe), 5 February 1920, 162; "Forced Sales of German Property: No Satisfactory Offers," 1 April 1920, 385; "German Property in Japan: Disposal Discussion," *Japan Chronicle* (Kobe), 27 May 1920, 611.

lists of German properties confiscated by the Japanese government.[51] The lists are taken from the Japanese government's lists of properties confiscated according to Imperial Ordinance No. 304 of 1919 and printed in the Japanese government's official gazettes of that year. Some of those properties, but not all, were acquired by Germans taking a right of superficies over the property. This suggests that the foreign community was not always in agreement on issues about which they lobbied for change with the Japanese government. While voices representing the British community protesting this device as a replacement for perpetual leases dominated the discussion, perhaps the German community were more willing to work within the confines of the Japanese legal system.

From the above analyses, we can see how German merchants willing to take a risk successfully secured control over the properties they acquired. While British merchants might have taken a right of superficies to acquire land outside the Settlement, the continued agitation by the British Legation and the *Japan Chronicle* on land ownership rights suggests that many foreigners in Japan were unable or unwilling to take the risks involved. These examples demonstrate that despite the objections of the British diplomats and the *Japan Chronicle*, it was possible for foreigners to circumvent the Japanese law banning foreigners from owning land by leasing for much longer than twenty to twenty-five years retaining control. Through their characteristic nimbleness, Nickel and Holstein took advantage of the loophole in the Japanese law with the complicity of their most trusted Japanese employees and succeeded in exercising control for a prolonged period.

Risks of Leasing Properties

Even so, the prohibition on foreigners owning land combined with poor Japanese government record keeping led to greater levels of risk and costly court cases. Two disputes reveal how the ban on foreign land ownership complicated the resolution of property disputes for C. Nickel & Co. Ltd. The first such dispute between the company and its neighbour and landlord, Akioka Kinu, began with a tit-for-tat series of claims from both parties about unpaid monies connected with a lease and which developed into a boundary dispute. From October 1907 to September 1910, the company leased a house with a small annex from Akioka in lot No. 24 Kaigan-dōri, 2-chome, Kobe

51 Control of Special Property. Hyogo Prefecture, 10 November 1919. Akten betreffend Beschlagsnahme deutschen Eigentums in Japan anlässlich des Weltkrieges, R265.002, PA AA.

next door to its own property at 3 Kaigan-dōri.[52] Akioka had agreed to the company pulling down the annex on the basis it be replaced at the end of the lease.[53] In March 1911, the *Chronicle* reported that C. Nickel & Co. Ltd. sued Akioka for the return of guarantee money they had paid when they leased the property.[54] Then in April 1911, Akioka countersued C. Nickel & Co. Ltd. for what she claimed was unpaid rent due after the property had been handed over.[55] The court decided in the first case that C. Nickel & Co. Ltd. had to forfeit the guarantee money as it had not paid the three months' rent due. In the second case the court ruled against Akioka stating that the company was not liable for the additional five months' rent Akioka claimed because the company had returned the property at the end of the lease.[56] While the court cases appeared to concern unpaid monies, the underlying cause was a boundary dispute. Akioka asserted, and C. Nickel & Co. Ltd. refuted, that during the lease, the company had "destroyed" a fence "made of boarding" by Akioka on the boundary and replaced it with a bamboo fence encroaching on her property by two feet.[57] In addition, it was also reported that the company had not replaced the annex as promised due to the boundary dispute.[58] While the court cases appeared to concern unpaid monies, the underlying cause was the boundary dispute. In October 1912, in a third case, Akioka sued C. Nickel & Co. Ltd. to have the bamboo fence removed.[59] When both Akioka and the company were asked to submit surveys of the land to the court, it appeared that either these surveys had not been appropriately recorded by the authorities or had been lost. It was also reported separately that Akioka had another property where she had built a brick wall encroaching on another part of C. Nickel & Co. Ltd.'s property.[60] There was no mention as to whether it was suing Akioka over this border dispute.

52 In Japan, buildings are either numbered in the order in which they were built or numbered clockwise around the block.

53 "Claim for Damages: Akioka Kinu v. C. Nickel & Co.," *Japan Chronicle* (Kobe), 13 April 1911, 636

54 "Claim for Recovery of Money Advanced: C. Nickel & Co. Ltd. v. Akioka Kinu," *Japan Chronicle* (Kobe), 23 March 1911, 502.

55 "Claim for Damages: Akioka Kinu v. C. Nickel & Co.," 636.

56 "Claim for Recovery of Money Advanced: Text of Judgement," *Japan Chronicle*, 27 April 1911, 731; "The Claim for Damages: Judgement," *Japan Chronicle*, 22 June 1911, 1180.

57 "Another Boundary Dispute: Akioka v. C. Nickel & Co.," *Japan Chronicle*, 19 October 1911, 706.

58 "Claim for Damages: Akioka vs C. Nickel & Co.," *Japan Chronicle*, 18 May 1911, 861.

59 "Another Boundary Dispute," 706.

60 "Claim for Recovery of Money Advanced: Conclusion of Hearing," *Japan Chronicle*, 13 April 1911, 631.

These court cases demonstrate how the ban on foreigners owning land created complex outcomes that were difficult to resolve. As a result, C. Nickel & Co. Ltd. took matters into its own hands by withholding paying rent and not restoring the annex, to pressure Akioka into accepting its assertion of its rightful boundary. With the poor recording of leases prior to 1899, it was presumably difficult for C. Nickel & Co. Ltd. to prove that the boundary of their premises, leased at least from 1894–95 if not earlier, had been changed. When their efforts to pressure Akioka failed, the company had to resort to the Japanese court. For the *Chronicle,* reporting on the boundary dispute, this was another opportunity to demonstrate its scepticism in the ability of the Japanese courts to deliver favourable outcomes for foreigners, especially given laws banning foreigners from owning property and the poor record keeping of lease arrangements.

Thus, while some German merchants ensured their property interests were protected through the device of superficies, they were still finding it difficult to establish rights comparable to those of bona-fide landowners. They complained that they were victims of poor record keeping by the Japanese authorities and as a result often chose to work outside the Japanese system. Even after 1899, the consequences of these choices could be costly and time consuming. The following story, involving three separate but related cases, is recounted to demonstrate the consequences for Christian Holstein of a complex web of leasing and sub-leasing arrangements and pre-existing contracts that had emerged informally, preventing him from asserting control over two investment rental properties. These tenancy disputes were closely followed by the *Japan Chronicle.*[61]

In November 1911, Christian Holstein sued a Mr J. Lundberg to force him to vacate a private furnished residence in Kitanagasa-dōri, 3-chome, Kobe northeast of Motomachi Station.[62] In a separate case, in January 1912, Holstein sued Lundberg for re-possession of the bakery next door to the house, with fixtures and fittings, and for damages and illegal occupation.[63] In both cases, Holstein claimed to be the holder of the most current lease.[64] The *Chronicle* reported that a previous lessor, a Mr Bonger, a Dutch national, had transferred the lease for the property to a Mr. Plate, also a Dutch national. Plate had in turn sub-let the house to a German, J. E. (Hans)

61 "Disputed Tenancy of a House: Holstein v. Lundberg. Judgement," *Japan Chronicle* (Kobe), 14 December 1911, 1059.

62 "Disputed Tenancy of a House," 1059.

63 "The Disputed Tenancy Case: C. Holstein v. J. Lundberg," *Japan Chronicle* (Kobe), 25 January 1912, 68.

64 "Disputed Tenancy of a House," 1059.

Schuh, who had in turn sub-let to J. Lundberg and two other unnamed Germans.[65] Christian Holstein had acquired Plate's right as lessor for the house and the bakery and claimed he had re-negotiated the sub-leases for both properties with Schuh.[66] Upon taking over the lease from Mr Plate, Holstein visited the premises to find that unbeknownst to him, Schuh had sub-let both the house and the bakery to a Mr Lundberg, a man Holstein considered to be of questionable character.[67] In the meantime, Schuh himself had left Kobe for Shanghai to evade a criminal charge for accepting stolen goods, and was not expected to return.[68] It was further revealed that Schuh had passed on the sub-lease to Lundberg on "very advantageous terms" no doubt due to his hasty departure from Kobe. According to the reportage, Holstein had tried to cancel Schuh's lease and evict Lundberg, but Lundberg refused to vacate either house or bakery, because he had acquired rights to occupy the building through his contract with Schuh.[69] Copies of lease documents and contracts were presented as evidence to the courts for both Holstein and Lundberg's claims to the property. The court decided in Lundberg's favour, on the basis Lundberg's contract for the sub-lease was with Schuh and not Holstein, and despite Holstein's counsel arguing that Schuh did not have Holstein's authority to sub-let the property to Lundberg.

During the second case, it was revealed that Holstein's name had not been registered on the property in the Kobe Land Registration Bureau records as it should have been. The *Japan Chronicle* reported that when he applied for an official certificate proving his lease arrangements Holstein only discovered "this mistake." While Holstein believed he had the right of possession from February 1907 for both house and bakery, he claimed that the bakery had been "incorrectly" registered "in the possession of another party [presumably either Bonger or Plate]."[70] It seems that at the time Holstein acquired the lease, his arrangement with Plate had been informal. Holstein's counsel then explained how the ownership had been "misrepresented until recently":

65 "The Disputed Tenancy Case: C. Holstein v. J. Lundberg," *Japan Chronicle* (Kobe), 8 February 1912, 257.

66 "Disputed Tenancy of a House," 1059.

67 "Disputed Tenancy of a House," 1059.

68 "Disputed Tenancy of a House," 1059.

69 "Disputed Tenancy of a House," 1059.

70 "The Disputed Tenancy Case: C. Holstein v. J. Lundberg," *Japan Chronicle* (Kobe), 22 February 1912, 350.

> Upon discovery of the mistake in the registry, the plaintiff [Holstein] proposed to correct it but as this was impracticable, he adopted the form of purchasing the property from the party to whose name it was registered ... Holstein's act in reality was merely registering as his own property what was already his own.[71]

The defence disputed the authenticity of Holstein's statement and claimed that "the story of alleged ownership of the building by plaintiff was made up on January 31 [1912] last just to patch up the case in his favour."[72] Regardless of these details, the court determined that with the handing over of the leases from Bonger, then to Plate (who sub-let to Schuh) there was precedent proving Schuh's right to sub-let to Lundberg.[73] Judgement was delivered in February 1912, again in favour of Lundberg, and Holstein's claims were dismissed with costs.[74] In a final court case relating to these properties, Holstein sued Schuh for unpaid rent and damages. Whether Schuh paid up or if Holstein finally succeeded in evicting Lundberg and regaining control of the two properties was not reported. Given that Schuh had absconded to Shanghai, it would have been difficult for Holstein to recover unpaid monies. Again, the *Japan Chronicle* implied that the difficulties faced by both Lundberg and Holstein could have been resolved had the Japanese authorities been more proficient in recording lease arrangements, or in making foreigners' lives easier by just allowing them to buy and sell properties outright.

Thus, foreigners whose leases were not registered formally with the Japan Land Registration Bureau and who were willing to sub-let to transient expatriates, suffered the consequences of difficulties in proving ownership of the leaseholds when trying to evict undesirable tenants. This speaks to the dangers of informal practices of registering lessors and their leasing of certain properties under extraterritoriality referred to earlier. Between records kept by the *Gaimushō*, the respective consular office and the individual lessor, there were bound to be inaccuracies or records could be lost over time. At the same time, Holstein's investment in these leases also reveals an appetite for risk and a tendency to administrative looseness since he appears not to have done his due diligence in checking the leases and subleases on these

71 "The Disputed Tenancy Case," 350.

72 "The Disputed Tenancy Case," 350.

73 "Disputed Tenancy of a House," 1059.

74 "The Disputed Tenancy Case: C. Holstein v J. Lundberg. Text of Judgement," *Japan Chronicle* (Kobe), 7 March 1912, 445.

properties along with any contracts involved. He was willing to act on his own initiative or take his chances with the Japanese courts to regain control of his properties.

Despite the Japanese prohibition on foreign ownership of land, and despite the reservations held by British diplomats on the Japanese permitting foreigners to take rights of superficies over properties as a substitute for land ownership, both Nickel and Holstein and many other German merchants succeeded in controlling their properties using this device. When it came to managing the risks of renting from a Japanese landlord or from holding a lease for a property with a provenance of ownership recorded loosely, when all other actions failed, Holstein resorted to the Japanese courts in a prolonged series of court cases challenging claims and counter claims on the basis that success might be achieved. In the next chapter several obstacles to doing business for foreign merchants collide in one case causing both challenges and opportunities for C. Nickel & Co. Ltd

8. The Case of the Dynamite Explosion and Its Long-Term Consequences

Abstract: The Dynamite Explosion Case in Kobe highlighted another restriction the Japanese government placed on foreign merchants. The government suddenly banned importers from storing foreign explosives in its purpose-built facilities, forcing them at great cost to redirect shipments to Nagasaki or Yokohama. With the agreement of the Kobe Harbour Authority, C. Nickel & Co. Ltd. elected to store explosives on retrofitted hulks in the harbour. Faced with a government seeking a monopoly of explosives, inadequate harbour regulations, problems managing an "unruly coolie" labour force and tensions between foreign and Japanese companies and Japanese authorities in general, C. Nickel & Co. Ltd. suffered devastating consequences resulting in its transformation into a new company Nickel & Lyons with consequences for its German management.

Keywords: explosives, *Chronicle*, courts, monopoly, "coolies," negligence

On 7 April 1910, at 6:30 a.m., a massive dynamite explosion occurred off Point Wada, just outside the limits of Kobe Harbour to the west. The damage and injury caused by the explosion was extensive and was heard "for miles around."[1] Shocks were felt as far west as Akashi and as far east as Osaka (sixty-three kilometres apart), while damage was sustained from Suma in the west to Nishinomiya in the east (twenty-five kilometres apart). Surprisingly, only the *sendō* (boat watchman) on the lighter in which the dynamite had been stored was killed, but many people throughout Kobe sustained injuries.[2] According to reports, the entire city of Kobe was "violently shaken, as though a severe earthquake had occurred, while the

1 "The Dynamite Explosion at Kobe: Enormous Damage. Full Details," *Japan Chronicle* (Kobe), 14 April 1910, 644.

2 "The Dynamite Explosion at Kobe: Enormous Damage," *Japan Chronicle* (Kobe), 14 April 1910, 644.

Holstein, Prue S. *The German Experience of Japan's Treaty Port System: A Case Study of C. Nickel & Co. Ltd., 1860–1923*. Taylor & Francis Group, 2025.
DOI: 10.4324/9781003706274-9

wrecked and damaged houses ... [giving] the impression that the city had been swept by a typhoon."[3] Houses and buildings near the explosion were completely destroyed and the force of the explosion broke windows and doors of many homes on "the Hill" in Kitano-chō and in the Foreign Settlement. The *Japan Chronicle* estimated that some 13,132 houses were damaged to the value of ¥165,000 (¥586,117,014 or £3,069,725) in total, roughly ¥13 (¥46,179 or £242) per house.[4] Given the numbers of small wooden traditional houses included in these figures, it is hard to equate 1910 values with today's equivalents which are built to withstand both earthquakes and typhoons. Hotels, hospitals and schools, and the Kobe Racquet and Athletic Club, also sustained damage. As the *Chronicle* described it, telephone lines were "torn down, heavy iron doors of godowns wrenched open" and tiles and walls damaged. "Here and there were men and women, swathed in bandages, none of whom were permitted to walk twenty yards before being stopped by sympathizing friends."[5] As a further measure of the force of the blast, "a heavy anchor ... five feet long ... belonging to the hulk which was blown up—was found high and dry west of Wakinohama Station on the Hanshin [railway] line."[6] Given the *Japan Chronicle*'s description of the shocking damage, it was a wonder there had not been massive loss of life, and had the explosion occurred later in the morning when more people were out and about, there may well have been.[7]

Investigations pointed to the cause of the explosion being a hulk belonging to C. Nickel & Co. Ltd. moored in the harbour, storing explosives. The company would be tied up in the Japanese courts for the next three years fighting for their existence. This chapter uses the Dynamite Explosion and its aftermath as a case study to examine the combined impact of all the elements that affected the business environment of C. Nickel & Co. Ltd. established in earlier chapters. The Dynamite Explosion Case represented all the issues that the foreign community had with the Japanese authorities which they considered inimical to foreign business interests so far: lack of storage for imported explosives; inadequate harbor regulations and poor oversight; reliance on the Japanese court system to arbitrate on disputes in lieu of proper regulation; labour management problems; and

3 "The Dynamite Explosion at Kobe: Enormous Damage," 644.

4 "The Dynamite Explosion at Kobe: Enormous Damage," 646; Yen conversions to 2019 values and others in this chapter are based on the website: https://yaruzou.net/hprice/hprice-calc.html. Conversion to British pound values was conducted on 14 April 2024.

5 "The Dynamite Explosion at Kobe: Enormous Damage," 644.

6 "The Dynamite Explosion at Kobe: Enormous Damage," 645.

7 "The Dynamite Explosion at Kobe: Enormous Damage," 646.

tensions in the relationships among foreign companies themselves and between those companies, Japanese companies and the Japanese authorities. The explosion and its aftermath also represented the culmination of the community's beliefs that Japanese authorities were intent on further undermining the position of foreign importers. It will also examine how the case resulted in a transformation of the company in the lead up to World War One.

Lawsuit Filed Against C. Nickel & Co. Ltd.

Immediately, the attention of the Japanese authorities and members of the foreign community turned to finding the party responsible for the explosion. The *Japan Chronicle* also began reporting on the mounting speculation over the cause of the explosion and the conflicting views about who was responsible. The *Chronicle* quoted the *Osaka Mainichi* newspaper reporting that the Japanese authorities had determined that the explosion was most likely due to "spontaneous combustion as a result of atmospheric change," as the dynamite had been stored for a long period of time.[8] On the other hand, the *Chronicle* also reported that Alfred Nobel & Co., a major Hamburg German manufacturer of some of the explosives in question, informed their importer in Kobe, C. Weinberger & Co., that "the cause of the explosion must have been due to carelessness as we have not experienced a similar case for forty years."[9]

Hulk No. 1069, on which the dynamite had been stored, belonged to C. Nickel & Co. Ltd., and so the Kobe Gas Co. sued it for damages, embroiling the two companies in a series of court cases from July 1910 until May 1913.[10] Kobe Gas Co.'s two recently installed gasometers, three quarters of a mile from the explosion, had been damaged—one blown over and one leaking, threatening Kobe's gas supply.[11] Immediately after the explosion, Kobe Gas Co. set up an enquiry to establish who was responsible.[12] In April 1910, the company filed a petition in the Kobe Local Court against C. Nickel & Co. Ltd. for the preservation of evidence. In July, it sued the company initially for ¥13,697.38 (¥48,654,817 or £254,824), but as the case proceeded through

8 "The Kobe Explosion: Report on Cause. The Control of Explosives. Attitude of Authorities," *Japan Chronicle* (Kobe), 21 April 1910, 686.

9 "The Dynamite Explosion at Kobe: Enormous Damage," 646.

10 "The Dynamite Explosion at Kobe: Enormous Damage," 647.

11 "Explosives and Explosions," *Japan Chronicle* (Kobe), 21 April 1910, 659.

12 "The Dynamite Explosion at Kobe: Enormous Damage," 645.

the courts to appeal, the cost of damages rose with Kobe Gas Co. increasing its claim to ¥15,688.99 (¥49,189,240 or £257,623) by April 1912.[13]

Kobe Gas Co. filed a writ holding C. Nickel & Co. Ltd. responsible for the explosion.[14] First, the writ claimed that the C. Nickel & Co. Ltd. hulk was moored "about three *chō* (327.27 metres) offshore at Mirume, instead of where it thought the hulk should have been at one mile or about fourteen *chō* (1,527.27 metres) off the coast."[15] Second, the writ claimed that the explosives had been incorrectly stored "packed in cases fastened with iron nails." Finally the writ claimed that the *sendō* in charge of the hulk—fifty-year old Ōkudokorō Harukichi who died in the explosion—was cooking his food on board the lighter and had been drunk.[16] The *Chronicle* reported that at the hearing which opened in December 1910, C. Nickel & Co. Ltd. denied responsibility for the explosion and their obligation to meet Kobe Gas Co.'s claim.[17]

The *Japan Chronicle* Speculates Anti-Foreign Policy Responsible.

Reflecting the interests of the foreign community in such a momentous explosion and keen to see how its ramifications would affect the community, the *Japan Chronicle* reported on its own investigation in the lead up to the court case.[18] It stated from the outset it suspected that the accident was a direct result of the Japanese authorities' plan to reduce the amount of imported explosives by restricting storage space available to foreign explosives importers. The *Chronicle* returned to this theme throughout its reportage until the commencement of the court case, continuing the trend noted in earlier chapters of focusing on issues of concern to the foreign

13 "The Recent Dynamite Explosion," *Japan Chronicle* (Kobe), 5 May 1910, 765; "The Dynamite Explosion of Kobe: Claim Against C. Nickel & Co.," *Japan Chronicle* (Kobe), 4 August 1910, 200; "The Kobe Dynamite Explosion Case: Further Hearing in Osaka," *Japan Chronicle* (Kobe), 25 April 1912, 725.

14 "The Dynamite Explosion at Kobe: Claim Against C. Nickel & Co.," 200.

15 "The Dynamite Explosion at Kobe: Claim Against C. Nickel & Co.," 200; "The Kobe Dynamite Explosion Case: Kobe Gas Company v. C. Nickel & Co.," *Japan Chronicle* (Kobe), 8 December 1910, 1009.

16 "The Dynamite Explosion at Kobe: Claim Against C. Nickel & Co.," 200; "The Kobe Dynamite Explosion Case: Kobe Gas Company v. C. Nickel & Co.," 1009.

17 "The Kobe Dynamite Explosion Case: Kobe Gas Company v. C. Nickel & Co.," 1009; "The Kobe Dynamite Explosion Case: Kobe Gas Company v. C. Nickel & Co.," *Japan Chronicle* (Kobe), 29 December 1910, 1146.

18 "The Dynamite Explosion Case: Judgement," *Japan Chronicle* (Kobe), 11 May 1911, 821.

business community broadly. As a result, the *Chronicle*'s version of events in this and in earlier cases favoured the members of the foreign community and aimed to hold to account the Japanese authorities and the Japanese courts.

The *Chronicle* was not wrong in pointing to the limited storage facilities for explosives in Kobe. Imported explosives were in high demand for use in the rapidly expanding coal mining and construction industries. About 20,000 cases a year were being imported into Kobe alone, more than half of the total imports of explosives into Japan. Imports were principally from Germany: three of the five main importers were German, and Alfred Nobel & Co. of Hamburg was the main supplier.[19] Alfred Nobel & Co. was founded in 1865 in Hamburg by the Swedish chemist and industrialist Alfred Nobel who also founded the Nobel Prizes. The rapid growth of imported explosives had led to the Japanese authorities becoming concerned about the storage of large amounts of dynamite onshore. The authorities commenced restricting storage space near ports, forcing merchants to find alternative storage in Nagasaki or Yokohama which was costly or to have dynamite stored on boats moored in the harbour.

The *Chronicle* noted that foreign diplomats had petitioned the Japanese government on behalf of foreign importers seeking new land-based magazine storage, to no avail.[20]

> For some time, there has been much friction between the Government authorities and the merchants who deal in explosives and the Government cannot be acquitted of a considerable share of responsibility for what has occurred.[21]

The *Chronicle* thus argued that "the present disaster is clearly due to the inattention paid [by the Japanese government] to the recommendations made [by the embassies]" for an increase in proper explosives storage facilities.[22] The *Chronicle* noted that in 1906, urged by the German government, the Japanese government had agreed to construct more explosives warehouses. Since then, the governments of Britain, Germany and the United States had demanded additional facilities; however, while the required expenditure was ¥1,000,000 (¥3,666,196,087 or £19,201,311), the Home Department settled

19 "The Dynamite Explosion at Kobe: Enormous Damage," 644–47; "Dynamite, Foreign and Home-Made: A Government Official on the Imported Article," *Japan Chronicle* (Kobe), 5 May 1910, 785.

20 "The Explosion and Responsibility," *Japan Chronicle* (Kobe), 14 April 1910, 614.

21 "The Explosion and Responsibility," 613.

22 "The Explosion and Responsibility," 614; "The Kobe Explosion: Report on Cause," 686.

on a budget of ¥250,000 (¥916,549,022 or £4,800,328) a quarter of the funds required for building proper storage.[23]

In the meantime, suggesting that local Kobe authorities were making efforts, the *Chronicle* reported that as a short-term measure, "the Kobe Harbour Office ordered explosives in Kobe to be kept on boats ... [on purpose fitted hulks on the harbour] in accordance with Article 9 of the Open Port Regulations."[24] C. Nickel & Co. Ltd. retrofitted a lighter to store explosives on behalf of two German companies, C. Weinberger & Co. and the China and Japan Trading Company, and one English firm, Drewell & Co. It stored in total, 110 tons of explosives including 3,094 cases of dynamite, fifty cases of detonators and 2,305 cases of gelignite.[25] A Japanese company, Nisshin Gumi, storing explosives on behalf of its client, the British importer Mollison & Co., had three lighters moored 720 yards from C. Nickel & Co. Ltd.'s lighter.[26] While after the explosion the dynamite on Nissin Gumi's lighters was reported as being "safe," "the craft were so badly damaged by the tremendous force ... they became waterlogged and were partially submerged."[27] Over 2,197 cases of explosives were later recovered from the sunken vessels or found floating in the harbour or washed up ashore.[28]

Kobe Harbour Poorly Regulated by the Authorities

The *Chronicle* returned regularly to the question of storage. The first point at issue was whether the lighter had been moored too close to shore and whether it had been appropriately retrofitted to store explosives. According to the *Chronicle*'s reportage, the Kobe Harbour Authority, responsible for overseeing the Harbour Regulations for Open Ports, "had examined and passed [the retrofitting of the hulk] before any explosives were stored." Together with the Kobe Water Police, the Harbour Authority had "chosen" the location and distance from shore where the hulk was moored, which "was continually inspected by them while all additions to the cargo [of explosives] or withdrawal therefrom had to be reported."[29]

23 "The Storing of Explosives: Accommodation to be Extended," *Japan Chronicle* (Kobe), 15 December 1910, 1045.

24 "The Kobe Explosion: Report on Cause," 686.

25 "The Dynamite Explosion at Kobe: Enormous Damage," 644.

26 "The Kobe Dynamite Explosion Case: Evidence in the Kobe Court," *Japan Chronicle* (Kobe), 26 October 1911, 745.

27 "The Dynamite Explosion at Kobe: Enormous Damage," 644.

28 "The Kobe Explosion: Report on Cause," 686.

29 "Stray Notes," *Japan Chronicle* (Kobe), 21 April 1910, 670.

In addition to Kobe Gas Co., several other parties also threatened legal action, claiming that C. Nickel & Co. Ltd. had not followed the Kobe Harbour regulations. The *Japan Chronicle* reported that, under the leadership of a sugar merchant named Nagahama Reizō, the residents of Point Wada blamed the company for damage to their houses. The residents disputed the Kobe Harbour Office's claim that the hulk lay within prescribed limits: arguing instead that the hulk had been lying two *chō* and twenty-six *ken* (218 to 327 metres) inside the harbour limit, too close to land.[30] Nagahama himself had been fishing near the hulk at the time of the explosion and was a key witness. According to him, some fishermen had measured the distance of the vessel from shore with a rope.[31]

The *Japan Chronicle* argued that the explosion was a direct outcome of the Japanese government's decision to reduce purpose-built storage on land for imported explosives. The *Chronicle* also tied this decision to its understanding that there was a Japanese government policy to restrict the quantity of imported explosives and considered the government was "not free from blame [for the explosion] in compelling importers to keep their explosives on a lighter instead of providing proper magazine accommodation ashore."[32] It noted also that over the past year there had been two or three explosions in the government magazine at Sakai, Osaka, of Japanese made explosives, with no investigation into the possible causes.[33] Instead of conducting an investigation, the *Chronicle* maintained that the Japanese in charge of the magazine ordered that "the amount of explosives stored there ... be reduced [from 20,000 cases imported] to 7,000 cases meaning some 13,000 cases had to be re-housed." The *Chronicle* then interpreted this decision as a way of reducing the imported explosives:

> The action of the authorities in refusing to provide proper accommodation for the imported article ... gives rise to the suspicion that it is desired to check the import ... by making the conditions [of storage] prohibitive.[34]

Homemade Explosives vs Imported Product

The *Chronicle*'s suspicions were confirmed when following the explosion, the local Kobe government introduced further restrictions, which it interpreted

30 "Stray Notes," 670.
31 "Stray Notes," 670.
32 "Stray Notes," 670.
33 "Dynamite, Foreign and Home-Made," 785.
34 "The Kobe Explosion: Report on the Cause," 686.

to mean that the Japanese intended to restrict imports of explosives. It reported breathlessly that the Governor of Kobe, the Superintendent of the Water Police, and other officials went straight to Point Wada to inspect the scene after the explosion. It also reported that Governor Hattori, Mr Fujii, Director of the Kobe Harbour Office, and Mr Gotō head of the Peace Preservation section of the Central Police of Hyogo Prefecture, announced that "future boats loaded with explosives shall not be allowed to remain either within ... the harbour or immediately outside, and that such boats shall proceed to Nagasaki or Osaka where proper storage for explosives is situated." According to the *Chronicle*, the Chief of the Kobe Police went further saying that in future the boats "are to be driven ... from Kobe waters." The *Chronicle* then noted that key explosives importers, Messrs Mollison & Co., Dodwell & Co., the China and Japan Trading Co. and Messrs Weinberger & Co. were informed that explosives could only be landed in Kobe under guarantee for immediate delivery to their clients. As there were only three explosives depots in Japan—Osaka, Yokohama and Nagasaki—these restrictions would be costly and onerous for importers of explosives.[35] To bolster its suspicion that the Japanese government wanted to eliminate foreign competition in favour of Japanese made explosives, the *Chronicle* noted that "the Government itself is a manufacturer of dynamite and ... is engaged in a competition with the imported article."[36]

Providing further proof that the Japanese government intentionally restricted imported explosives, the *Chronicle* reported that it was campaigning to denigrate foreign explosives. The government owned an explosives factory at Iwahana and, according to the *Chronicle*, was keen to secure the monopoly of the supply of explosives in Japan. The *Japan Chronicle* reported that the *Hokkai Times* had interviewed a Dr Ichimatsurō Matsuoka, who was on a visit to Hokkaido to test explosives in the Yubari and other mines. Dr Matsuoka was the chief of the Meguro and Iwahana Explosives Factories and a specialist in the manufacture of dynamite in Japan. He was also a member of the Explosive Investigation Committee in the Home Office of the Japanese government and had been decorated with the Fourth Order of Merit for his services, amongst other accolades. In his interview, he claimed that imported dynamite was "inferior in quality and also dangerous" and that "it is a pity that dynamite has not until recently been manufactured by [the Japanese military authorities.]" He then went on to extol the virtues of

35 "The Dynamite Explosion at Kobe: Enormous Damage," 647; "The Kobe Explosion: Report on Cause," 686.

36 "The Kobe Explosion: Report on Cause," 686.

the quality and cost effectiveness of Japanese explosives and its immunity to changes in climate conditions in comparison to what he considered to be inferior imported product. Moreover, he claimed that imported dynamite was manufactured by companies "to gain profit," as opposed to the Japanese manufacturers who were in his view not driven by the profit motive.[37]

Dr Matsuoka's comments provoked an outcry amongst the foreign community of explosive importers, and the *Japan Chronicle* published a letter to the editor protesting his comments signed by five major German importers, one British, and one American firm. They refuted Dr Matsuoka's claims that foreign dynamite was weakened due to the transportation times and was passed into "Japanese merchants' hands in a dangerous condition."[38] They accused Dr Matsuoka of denigrating their product, noting that the purpose "of his visit to Hokkaido was to oust, if possible, the imported article in favour of home-made." They reaffirmed the stability of imported explosives evidenced by no accidents in thirty years, citing the earlier explosions of Japanese-made explosives in Osaka mentioned earlier which had not been investigated.[39] They also pointed out that the explosives produced in Japan were all copies of foreign made products in any case.[40] Finally, the five foreign importers questioned Dr Matsuoka's impartiality given he was both chief of an explosives production facility as well as being a member of the government's Explosive Investigation Committee, concluding that "What Dr Matsuoka has to say about explosives manufactured under his own supervision would be … of a self-satisfied not to say, of a biased nature."[41]

Due to the explosion and possibly prompted by the foreign merchants' protests, by July 1910 the Japanese government did address the shortage of storage space when the Japanese Home Department included in its Budget for 1911 provision for "the erection of magazines to store explosives imported from foreign countries."[42]

Negligence May Have been the Cause

After four months reporting on the role of the Japanese government in limiting storage space, the *Japan Chronicle* now focused on how the

37 "Dynamite, Foreign and Home-Made," 785.
38 "The Kobe Explosion: Report on Cause," 686.
39 "Dynamite, Foreign and Home-Made," 785.
40 "Dynamite, Foreign and Home-Made," 785.
41 "Dynamite, Foreign and Home-Made," 785.
42 "Local and General," *Japan Chronicle* (Kobe), 7 June 1910, 9.

explosion might have been the result of negligence, and the safety issues resulting from what it considered "an unruly coolie" workforce. Evidence emerged that the *sendō*, Ōkudokorō Harukichi, the only fatality in the accident, had lit a fire on board, and had probably been responsible for the explosion:

> it is evident that a hulk where coolies are continually engaged in shifting the cargo ... trimming the vessel ... as the contents are removed, must involve ... an element of danger. It is surmised that fire was made on board for some reason or other ... but this is pure surmise.[43]

Evidence given in court revealed the extent to which it was known that the *sendō*, Ōkudokorō, was in the habit of flouting Kobe Harbour regulations. In December 1910, the court heard testimony from Sakakura Yoichirō, of Kobe, the landing and forwarding agent for the three lighters owned by Nisshin-Gumi on which Mollison & Co. had stored their explosives.[44] Sakakura said that the *sendō* on the Nisshin-Gumi lighters, Ōzaki Kametarō and Suimon Eikichi, had told him that the night before the explosion Ōkudokorō had visited "Ōzaki on the latter's lighter under the influence of drink, and asked him to partake of some sake ... Ōzaki refused ... as he was an abstainer." Ōkudokorō proceeded to drink the sake himself. To avoid Ōkudokorō, Ozaki moved to the other lighter manned by Suimon, and "Ōkudokorō, who was very drunk, stumbled and fell into the sea." The two *sendō* picked him up and took him to Ōzaki's lighter, gave him a dry kimono and let him sleep the night. The next morning, they returned him to his own lighter. Ōkudokorō told the two *sendō* he would light a fire to dry his wet kimono.[45] According to Sakakura's testimony, the two *sendō* warned Ōkudokorō "not to light a fire on the deck or he would be reprimanded by the police," so he said he would light the fire below the deck and the two *sendō* left. A half hour later "a volume of smoke was seen rising" and Ōkudokorō called out that some cases had ignited. Ōzaki and Suimon, then "terrified," headed towards shore in their sampans when the explosion occurred. Sakakura added he had been told that Ōkudokorō "was very fond of sake ... he became intoxicated after imbibing about four *go* (720 ml) of the liquor and was frequently forced to pass the night ashore."[46] Ōzaki and Suimon, the two other *sendō*, later

43 "The Explosion and Responsibility," 614.
44 "The Kobe Dynamite Explosion Case: Kobe Gas Company v. C. Nickel & Co.," 1146.
45 "The Kobe Dynamite Explosion Case: Kobe Gas Company v. C. Nickel & Co.," 1146.
46 "The Kobe Dynamite Explosion Case: Kobe Gas Company v. C. Nickel & Co.," 1146.

supported this testimony.[47] Another witness, Deta (*sic*, most likely Date) Kiyomatsu, a sake dealer of Fukiai, Kobe, said that Ōkudokorō used to call at his shop to drink sake. He "always spent [whatever money he had] on that drink." Deta said that on the day before the explosion Ōkudokorō came to his shop and became "very drunk on this occasion and could not walk properly."[48] Sakakura also said that he had been told that Ōkudokorō was also "in the habit of lighting a fire in a *konro* or small portable stove" on board the lighter to make tea.[49] Further witnesses attested to having seen fires on board Ōkudokorō's vessel.[50] The reportage of testimony, however, did not at that time address whether Ōkudokorō's employers, C. Nickel & Co. Ltd., had monitored the actions of their employee, or were even expected to do so.

The court hearing once more addressed the question of the distance of the hulk from the shore, revealing a laxity in the Harbour Authority's oversight of the regulations. In January 1911, Captain Fujii, Harbour-Master of Kobe, stated that when he had last inspected the lighter in July 1909, the hulk was moored one mile and two cables (equivalent to two kms) off the coast of Mirume. He had heard that the hulk had been seen once or twice moored at a spot slightly different to the position indicated, but he could not be certain and did not know the position of the vessel at the time of the explosion. Two successive witnesses testified that the vessel was moored 600 yards (548 metres) from the shore.[51]

Case against C. Nickel & Co. Ltd. Dismissed

Successive hearings indicated that while the way the explosives had been stored had not led to spontaneous combustion, C. Nickel & Co. Ltd. had not been rigorous in following regulations checking the condition of the explosives. Ōkubo Sen of the Uji gunpowder factory was brought in as an expert witness to confirm if spontaneous combustion had occurred. He confirmed that spontaneous combustion was unlikely but that a "fire kindled near the cases would cause them to explode." He added that it was

47 "The Kobe Dynamite Explosion Case: Kobe Gas Company v. C. Nickel & Co.," *Japan Chronicle* (Kobe), 26 January 1911, 144.

48 "The Kobe Dynamite Explosion Case: Kobe Gas Company v. C. Nickel & Co.," 1146.

49 "The Kobe Dynamite Explosion Case: Kobe Gas Company v. C. Nickel & Co.," 1146.

50 "The Dynamite Explosion Case: Kobe Gas Company v. C. Nickel," *Japan Chronicle* (Kobe), 2 March 1911, 365; "The Kobe Dynamite Explosion Case," 144.

51 "The Dynamite Explosion Case: Kobe Gas Company v. C. Nickel & Co.," 365; The Kobe Dynamite Explosion Case," 144.

"the duty of the owners ... to investigate the condition of the goods at least once a month and record the result in writing."[52] The *Chronicle* did not discuss whether C. Nickel & Co. Ltd. had adopted such measures checking the condition of the explosives.

Despite all the evidence from eyewitnesses suggesting the lighter was moored too close to shore and that the *sendō* had most likely lit a fire on board illegally, in May 1911, the court dismissed the Kobe Gas Co.'s claim against C. Nickel & Co. Ltd. for compensation for damages with costs.[53] The *Chronicle* reported that the court based its decision on the Kobe Gas Co.'s failure to produce evidence "sufficient to establish" that either Ōkudokorō had lit a fire or that C. Nickel & Co. Ltd. had violated the regulations on the storage of explosives. The company had obtained "the permission of the police" to refit the lighter for storing explosives, and that had been sufficient. Finally, no evidence had been provided by the Kobe Gas Co. to substantiate its claim that the lighter had been moored anywhere other than "on her original position."[54]

Not to be deterred, the Kobe Gas Co. lodged an appeal in the Osaka Appeal Court in September 1911, arguing that the explosion had been the result of carelessness on the part of C. Nickel & Co. Ltd. It repeated its claims that the *sendō* lit a fire on board the lighter illegally, did not store the explosives properly and moored the lighter too close to the shore. The counsel for C. Nickel & Co. Ltd. in turn "denied that the explosion was the result of carelessness" claiming "that the cause of the explosion was not accurately known ... as the lighter had been lost, together with its cargo and the watchman."[55] Because the Osaka Appeals Court could not arrive at a decision, it allowed C. Nickel & Co. Ltd. to "substantiate certain technical points."[56] The *Chronicle* detailed for its readers the explanations provided, but there was no new information. It then provided regular updates for its readers, not just because they might have been impacted by the explosion but also because many might have been interested in the debates around liability as the issues were worked out through the courts.

52 "The Dynamite Explosion Case: Kobe Gas Company v. C. Nickel & Co.," 365.

53 "The Dynamite Explosion Case: Judgement," 821.

54 "The Dynamite Explosion Case: Text of Judgement," *Japan Chronicle* (Kobe), 18 May 1911, 852.

55 "The Kobe Dynamite Explosion Case: Appeal in the Osaka Court," *Japan Chronicle* (Kobe), 5 October 1911, 598.

56 "The Kobe Dynamite Explosion Case: Osaka Proceedings to be Re-Opened," *Japan Chronicle* (Kobe), 25 January 1912, 174.

Kobe Gas Succeeds on Appeal

The evidence produced by the Kobe Gas Co. that finally proved to be C. Nickel & Co. Ltd.'s undoing was the report written by Mr Nakagawa, Director of the Kobe Meteorological Office, entitled "Report on the Dynamite Explosion in Kobe."[57] According to the Bureau's calculations of air and earth tremors and the condition of the sea at the time, "the point where the explosion occurred was within 4,500 feet [1,372m] off Wakinohama and not 6,600 feet or one mile and a quarter [1,800m], as stated in the evidence of the Kobe Harbour Master." The Kobe Gas Co. therefore alleged that C. Nickel & Co. Ltd. had been negligent in allowing their vessel to drift closer to shore.[58] After eight months, the Osaka Appeal Court delivered its judgement upholding Kobe Gas Co.'s right to claim compensation from C. Nickel & Co. Ltd.[59]

While the Court determined that the *sendō* had been "responsible for inexcusable negligence" and that the company was responsible for its employees, C. Nickel & Co. Ltd. continued to refute these claims stating that Ōkudokorō had been "faithful in his duties and zealous," that the company's management "had observed all precautions in engaging this sendō," and that it "did not neglect to superintend the conduct of the sendō."[60] Furthermore, evidence from a police examination indicated that C. Nickel & Co. Ltd.'s oversight of the *sendō*'s performance had amounted to

> two men ... calling occasionally at the lighter ... for the purpose of supervising the sendō ... that these men would return without getting on the lighter when the sendō replied to their inquiries that there was nothing unusual to report.[61]

C. Nickel and Co. Ltd. was found guilty of failure to manage the behaviour of the *sendō*, resulting in enormous damage to Kobe, which was punishable under the Japan Civil Code.[62] In addition, the Kobe Bureau of Meteorology's

57 "The Kobe Dynamite Explosion Case: The Kobe Gas Company v. C. Nickel & Co. Further Interesting Evidence," *Japan Chronicle* (Kobe), 7 March 1912, 435.

58 "The Kobe Dynamite Explosion Case," 435.

59 "Kobe Dynamite Explosion Case: Text of Judgement of Osaka Appeal Court," *Japan Chronicle* (Kobe), 4 July 1912, 22.

60 "Kobe Dynamite Explosion Case: Text of Judgement," 22.

61 "Kobe Dynamite Explosion Case: Text of Judgement," 22.

62 Hozumi, Nobushige, Masakasa Tomii and Kenjiro Ume. *The Civil Code of Japan.* Translated by Dr L. Lönholm. Kelly & Walsh Lim, Bremen, Yokohama, Shanghai, Hong Kong & Singapore, 1898. Article 709, upon which the Kobe Local Court relied, states that "a person who has intentionally or negligently violated the rights of another is bound to make compensation for any resulting

evidence that the lighter had been moored too close to shore was also damning, and although C. Nickel & Co. Ltd. appealed all the way to the Supreme Court, the right of Kobe Gas Co. to claim damages was upheld.[63]

Whereas the *Japan Chronicle* blamed the deficiencies in the Japanese authorities' management of the harbour, the Japanese court pinned the blame on C. Nickel & Co. Ltd. alone. The *Chronicle* presented the story as one of Japanese incompetence, in which C. Nickel & Co. Ltd. had had to navigate harbour regulations that were neither clear nor up to date and which involved the approval of more than one authority: the Kobe Harbour Office, the Kobe Water Police, and Kobe Customs all of which were responsible for elements of the storage of the explosives. Moreover, the oversight of those regulations was inconsistent, and the necessary checks and balances were not enforced by any of the authorities. Regulations around the oversight of *sendō* or watchmen on these vessels were also not clearly stated. Consistent with the assessment made by the *Chronicle*, the Japanese courts' judgement confirmed the foreign merchants' beliefs that the Japanese authorities' primary aim was to frustrate and impede their ability to do business, undermining their positions as importers.

Consequences of Losing the Case

While fighting this case must have been costly for C. Nickel & Co. Ltd. by the time the final decision was handed down, it seemed initially to be of little consequence to Christian Holstein. In addition to the Kobe Gas Co.'s lawsuit there were claims brought by several other parties including the Oriental Hotel which had all suffered considerable damage. As these cases were not reported on in detail, the final cost of this explosion is not known. The Eighth AGM of shareholders for C. Nickel & Co. Ltd. was held in January 1911, around the time the Supreme Court handed down its judgement for the Dynamite Explosion Case. While the Dynamite Explosion case was not mentioned in the *Chronicle*'s reporting on the AGM, it did report

consequence." Article 715 in the *Civil Code of Japan* further stated that "If a person has employed another for a certain business, and the latter causes damage to a third person in the course of the execution of such business, the employer is bound to make compensation, unless he has used due care in the selection of the person employed and in the control of the business, or unless the damage would have happened even though such care had been used."

63 "Kobe Dynamite Explosion Case: Text of Judgement," 22; "The Dynamite Explosion Case: Judgement in the Supreme Court. Messrs. Nickel's Appeal Rejected," *Japan Chronicle* (Kobe), 13 February 1913, 313.

that the directors proposed that the marine insurance fund be increased by ¥30,000 (¥99,199,647 or £519,548) to a total of ¥215,000 (¥710,930,801 or £3,723,424). They also transferred ¥1,628.93 (¥5,386,541 or £28,211) to the legal reserve fund to bring it to a total of ¥12,986.76 (¥42,943,527 or £224,912) to cover ongoing legal costs and claims. Furthermore, when representatives of the Kobe Gas Co. unexpectedly arrived at C. Nickel & Co. Ltd.'s offices to secure property against the final determination on damages, rather than have property confiscated the company handed over ¥17,000 (¥56,213,133 or £294,410) in negotiable paper.[64] Furthermore, at the same time as fighting the Dynamite Explosion Case, Holstein was expanding the company's business. The *Japan Chronicle* reported on an article appearing in the Japanese newspaper, the *Chūgai Shōgyō*, that

> Messrs Nickel & Co. Ltd ... [who] have established a branch office in Yokohama, appear to contemplate a large combination of railway transportation agents of Yokohama ... to secure the greatest interest in landing and transporting business as well as passing of goods through Customs.[65]

Some six months later, the *Chronicle* reported a deal whereby Holstein was taking over a company in Yokohama called Weston & Co.[66] The abovementioned activities suggest that the company was able to absorb the cost of the damages incurred.

While the financial consequences of C. Nickel & Co. Ltd.'s court loss to Kobe Gas Co. appear to have been contained, the most significant consequence of the Dynamite Explosion Case was a structural transformation of the company. In April 1913, the *Japan Chronicle* reported that the directors of C. Nickel & Co. Ltd. liquidated the company's assets and merged the company with a rival stevedoring company, J. Lyons & Co., to form Nickel & Lyons. The owner of J. Lyons & Co. was Jacob Lyons, the former British employee and junior partner of Carl Nickel's in the 1890s. In the absence of records or reportage, the exact reasons prompting the merger are unknown. The timing however suggests that it was connected to the loss to Kobe Gas Co., and the reason for the merger might have been to introduce a more conservative element in the management of the company. It might have

64 "The Kobe Dynamite Explosion Case: Remarkable Action by Gas Company," *Japan Chronicle* (Kobe), 1 August 1912, 205.

65 "Local and General," 9.

66 "Messrs C. Nickel & Company: Annual General Meeting," *Japan Chronicle* (Kobe), 26 January 1911, 151.

also been an opportunistic move by the board to further dilute the German control of the company by bringing back a former partner of Nickel's with experience of both the industry and of the company.

Nickel & Lyons is Formed

The formation of Nickel & Lyons resulted in a diminution of Carl Nickel's legacy: it distanced the company from its German origins and had personal consequences for Christian Holstein. In 1909 at the AGM, the British dominated board had expressed its continuing confidence in Holstein as managing director, renewing his contract for another four years until 1913.[67] However, while Holstein retained his position after the merger, he now had to share the role with co-managing director, a Captain Percy Watson, who had been managing director of J. Lyons & Co. Jacob Lyons was also invited on the board as director of the newly formed company further diluting German influence. Both Captain Watson and Jacob Lyons were much respected members of the British dominated foreign community and through this action, British control of the company was strengthened.

The reportage on the Dynamite Explosion Case in Kobe illustrates how this case resonated with the fears of the foreign community over the existing problems of a rapidly growing and poorly regulated port. The foreign community's concern with the lack of storage space for imported explosives, poor regulations and oversight of both shipping regulations and unruly "coolies," as well as its beliefs that the Japanese authorities were restricting the importation of foreign explosives, are all represented in this case. Foreign explosives importers believed the Japanese government had discriminated against them by arbitrarily limiting storage space in the government magazine in Osaka. As a result of the dynamite explosion in Kobe, the government initially introduced policies banning the entry of ships carrying imported explosives into Kobe Harbour. The importance of the role the *Japan Chronicle* played in representing the concerns of the foreign merchant community has also been made clear.

The Dynamite Explosion Case also illustrates the many challenges that Holstein, as the German managing director of C. Nickel & Co. Ltd., had to negotiate, together with his British dominated board, addressing the urgent needs of explosives importers for proper storage. With permission to retrofit

67 "C. Nickel & Co. Ltd.: Seventh Annual General Meeting," *Japan Chronicle* (Kobe), 30 December 1909, 1177.

lighters for storing explosives on the harbour, he had to negotiate with the Kobe Harbour Authority, the Kobe Water Police, and Kobe Customs to ensure the retrofitted lighter storing explosives met their requirements. He had also to take into consideration an unruly element in the company's casual labour workforce, and associated abuse of alcohol and disregard for Kobe Harbour laws against lighting fires on board the ship.

Throughout the Dynamite Explosion Case, Holstein continued to be the principal driver of the growth and expansion of C. Nickel & Co. Ltd., in partnership with his British dominated board, which was now compelled to act to ensure the long-term viability of the company. Following the Dynamite Explosion Case and the company merger forming Nickel & Lyons, Holstein's role as managing director was now shared with the British manager of J. Lyons & Co., Captain Percy Watson. A process of dilution of the German influence was commenced that the First World War hastened. As we will see in the next chapter, the outcome of the Dynamite Explosion in Kobe Case was to become a part of a process leading to the end of a decades-long and successful partnership between British and German merchants in the lead up to the First World War.

Part IV

World War One

9. World War One: The British Declare Economic War on German Merchants in Japan

Abstract: With the outbreak of war, the British government declared economic war on German merchants in Japan. In the decade, leading to war, Britain feared a rising German Empire threatened to overtake its commercial and naval supremacy. However, British and German companies had become closely entwined in Japan, and so the British government seeking to oust German merchants, capture their business and cripple German merchants well into the post-war period worked hard to sever those inextricable links. Not all links were severed and Japan, for its own national interests, was reluctant to comply with the wishes of its ally. In a convoluted court case, how the British government succeeded in ousting the German management from Nickel & Lyons and erasing the company's German legacy is revealed.

Keywords: war, partnerships, enemy, protection, Blacklist, courts

On 4 August 1914, the British government declared war on Germany two days after Germany invaded Belgium. Britain also declared economic war on Germany to damage Germany economically to end the war. During the wars of the eighteenth and nineteenth centuries, it was common practice for the British government to deploy the Royal Navy to blockade trade with enemy countries to capture markets and increase prosperity.[1] From the late 1800s, Britain feared that Germany's growing military and naval strength and its rapidly growing economy would eclipse Britain's world supremacy,

1 John McDermott, "'A Needless Sacrifice': British Businessmen and Business as Usual in the First World War," *Albion: A Quarterly Journal Concerned with British Studies* 21, no. 2 (Summer 1989): 268, https://doi.org/10.2307/4049929.

Holstein, Prue S. *The German Experience of Japan's Treaty Port System: A Case Study of C. Nickel & Co. Ltd., 1860–1923.* Taylor & Francis Group, 2025.
DOI: 10.4324/9781003706274-10

diminishing its prosperity.[2] Due to Germans migrating to Britain and its colonies particularly during the nineteenth century, by 1914, the German and British economies had become closely entwined. Germany had become Britain's largest European customer for exports and an important supplier of its imports.[3] By 1911 England was home to 53,324 German migrants. Claiming that German migrants "affected the economic position of Englishmen," "propagandists" contributed to a growing anti-German feeling which led to outbreaks of violence against German businesses and accusations of German workers being "spies in the service of the enemy."[4] At the outbreak of World War One, while conservatives were advocating economic war against Germany, moderates realized that banning trade with Germany completely would impact Britain's finances and its ability to prosecute war.[5]

The key question government ministries and departments faced in declaring economic war was how Britain, an export dependent country and a government and business community used to minimal government intervention (*laissez-faire*), could wage economic war against its "best customer without courting ruin."[6] 1914 was the year that the British government abandoned its *laissez-faire* approach to doing business, and introduced market intervention policies to achieve its aims.[7]

On 8 August 1914, the Trading with the Enemy Act was introduced banning business with German companies. As British and German merchants in Europe continued trading and exploiting loopholes in the Act, increasingly restrictive measures were introduced to close those loopholes. Because moderate and hardline British politicians and bureaucrats pressured by an anti-German media and public opinion could not agree on appropriate measures, and because the business community did not want to risk losing

2 Panikos Panayi, "German Business Interests in Britain During the First World War," *Business History* 32, no. 2 (1990): 245, https://doi.org/10.1080/00076799000000048.

3 John R. Davis, Margrit Schulte Beerbühl and Stefan Manz, "Introduction: Germans in the British Empire," in *Transnational Networks: German Migrants in the British Empire, 1670–1914*, eds. John R. Davis, Stefan Manz, Margrit Schulte Beerbühl (Leiden–Boston: Brill, 2012), 1–17; McDermott, "'A Needless Sacrifice,'" 263.

4 Panayi, "German Business Interests," 246. For a fuller account of the misperceptions on both the British and German sides in the lead up to war and the anti-German feeling within the British government, refer to Thomas G. Otte, *July Crisis: The World's Descent into War, Summer 1914* (Cambridge: Cambridge University Press, 2014).

5 McDermott, "'A Needless Sacrifice,'" 263.

6 John McDermott, "Total War and the Merchant State: Aspects of British Economic Warfare Against Germany, 1914–16," *Canadian Journal of History* 21, no. 1 (1986): 62, https://doi.org/10.3138/cjh.21.1.61.

7 McDermott, "'A Needless Sacrifice,'" 266.

business, such anti-trading with the enemy measures were ineffective until mid-1916. The government introduced the Statutory List penalizing any company dealing with German companies which quickly ended all trade with German companies.[8]

Initially, the moderate forces in the government, advocated for a policy of "business as usual" where trade only excluded goods for military purposes.[9] Moderates also urged British manufacturers to capture German business by copying and replacing German products, a policy that was impractical as the investment and expertise needed for new manufacturing facilities were unavailable in wartime.[10] Moreover, many British industry groups lobbied to protect their many partnerships with German companies fearing a loss of business to their American and other competitors.[11] From October 1915 onwards, as Britain's allies complained that British goods were getting through to Germany while their own goods were banned, the hardliners in the British government gained the ascendancy. Ignoring the consequences for British business, the hardliners expanded the list of contraband goods, made export licences more difficult to obtain and limited trade with neutral countries to prevent product reaching Germany.[12] In September 1915, such was the determination of the British government to damage the German economy, the head of the Board of Trade, Sir Arthur Thring was reported as saying the aim was not just to damage Germany economically, but also "to smash German firms and put British in their places."[13] The British Foreign Office by then having joined the hardliners, also argued "Germany must be hurt economically as well as militarily, not only during the war, but 'to destroy as far as possible the whole German financial and commercial recuperation ... after the war...'"[14]

In June 1915 Britain commenced targeting German business in countries where banning trade with "the enemy" had limited political fallout. For example, Britain did not want to upset the Americans, so took very little action.[15] Britain targeted countries still under British extraterritoriality such as

8 McDermott, "Total War and the Merchant State," 62–63; McDermott, "'A Needless Sacrifice,'" 263.

9 McDermott, "'A Needless Sacrifice,'" 265.

10 McDermott, "'A Needless Sacrifice,'" 266, 272.

11 McDermott, "'A Needless Sacrifice,'" 271.

12 McDermott, "'A Needless Sacrifice,'" 265, 274.

13 Foreign Office Cover Note referring to a statement made by Sir Arthur Thring, Board of Trade, 21 September 1915, FO 370/2388, The National Archives of the UK (henceforth TNA), 306.

14 McDermott, "Total War and the Merchant State," 72.

15 McDermott, "'A Needless Sacrifice,'" 264.

China and in neutral countries such as those in South America.[16] Even though extraterritoriality no longer existed in Japan, Britain still targeted German business. Under the terms of the Anglo-Japanese Alliance signed in 1902, the British government expected the Japanese government to work with it to stop German trade. However, as will be shown, tensions emerged between the British and the Japanese governments as Japan became torn between its role as Britain's ally and its desire to protect its own national interests.

This chapter draws on archival records held in the Ministry of the Blockade Files at the National Archives in London and reportage in the *Japan Chronicle* in Kobe. Because German and British business interests were so closely intertwined and enmities in Kobe's foreign community did not readily develop, this chapter first shows the lengths the British government had to go to implement its anti-trading with the enemy policies to provide context for what happened to Nickel & Lyons's German management.

Opportunities for Capturing British Business

As part of the British government's efforts to "smash German firms and put British in their places," in September 1914, the British Commercial Attaché in Tokyo, E. T. F. Crowe, reported on the relative strengths of German companies in Japan and where opportunities for British merchants to capture German business might lie. His report illustrated not just how competitive German companies were but also how dependent many British companies had become on their German partners. Crowe believed German companies' success was due primarily to them offering Japanese customers long-term credit in the form of promissory notes with the support of not just German but also British banks.[17] Long-term credit is offered to gain a competitive advantage and encourage customers to increase spending. Japanese merchants had been accustomed to long-term credit since the Tokugawa Era, using a system of *tegata* or promissory notes, a written promise to pay a stated sum to the bearer at a specified date, or on demand, still in use today.[18] In contrast, British merchants only offered three-month credit

16 McDermott, "Total War and the Merchant State," 71; Phillip Dehne, "'From 'Business as Usual' to a More Global War: The British Decision to Attack Germans in South America during the First World War," *The Journal of British Studies* 44, no. 3 (July 2005): 532, https://doi.org/10.1086/429709.
17 Memorandum by E. T. F. Crowe, 30 September 1914, Opportunities for capturing German business, TNA, FO 371/2020 (hereafter Memorandum by Crowe), 30 September 1914, FO 371/2020), TNA, 366.
18 A. F. Thomas & Soji Koyama, *Commercial History of Japan* (Tokyo: The Yūhodo Limited, 1936), 136–38; Memorandum by Crowe, 30 September 1914, FO 371/2020, TNA, 366.

to businessmen they considered a low credit risk. Ignoring the long-term Japanese custom of using promissory notes German merchants adapted to, Crowe opined,

> the system of long credits ... [offered by the Germans] has been received by the Japanese with great enthusiasm [whereas] the more conservative British traders have long looked askance [at the practice].[19]

Crowe also ignored the fact that while British traders might be reluctant to offer long-term credit, the Hong Kong Shanghai Banking Corporation (HSBC), a British bank was not. In China and Japan since the 1860s, HSBC had been financing German companies especially those representing British industry.[20] The Deutsche Asiatische Bank (DAB), in Japan since 1905, had been a late comer, but by 1914, both it and HSBC had substantial German trade finance businesses. Seeking to destroy relationships between German merchants and British banks in Japan, Crowe believed

> if the present war should ... cripple Germany's finances ... her businessmen will be unable to pursue these tactics, and if British and American firms can agree to restrict the credit system ... a great step forward will have been taken ... to check the advance of German trade.[21]

Crowe also acknowledged additional competitive strengths German merchants, and their companies offered—most notably a willingness to meet Japanese customers' market requirements and tight product specifications at cost structures requested, a flexibility that British manufacturers were unwilling or unable to offer. Crowe also recognized the value of German sponsorship of Japanese students in Germany in medicine, drugs, and pharmaceuticals guaranteeing that Japanese students developed certain product preferences.[22] With its own high regard for German expertise, the Japanese Meiji Government also fostered Japanese-German connections sponsoring German medical experts to educate Japanese students in Japan and sponsoring Japanese students to study in Germany.[23]

19 Memorandum by Crowe, 30 September 1914, FO 371/2020, TNA, 366,
20 Memorandum by Crowe, 30 September 1914, FO 371/2020, TNA, 366.
21 Memorandum by Crowe, 30 September 1914, FO 371/2020, TNA, 366.
22 Memorandum by Crowe, 30 September 1914, FO 371/2020, TNA, 371.
23 Hoi-eun Kim, *Doctors of Empire: Medical and Cultural Encounters Between Imperial Germany and Meiji Japan*. German & European Studies Series (Toronto: University of Toronto Press, 2014), 58–61.

Research conducted by Frank King into HSBC confirms much of Crowe's analysis of German merchants' business skills, while also showing how "unknown" forces in the British government seeking to destroy Germany sought to demonize German merchants. German merchants were criticized for "unfair trading practices ... in northeast Asia" and "for doing unspeakable things which were contrary to 'British methods'" inferring bribery and subsidies. British consular reports "warned that suspect German methods included a stricter attention to business, the learning of Chinese by German merchants ... and direct contact with Chinese merchants and officials'" hardly the stuff of "unfair trading practices."[24] German merchants' granting long-term credit was also considered to be an "unsound" business practice leading to "speculation" and "periodic trade depression."[25] Ironically, it must have been the "aggressive" business strategies and risk taking employed by the Germans Carl Nickel and Christian Holstein, not to mention abilities in speaking Japanese and building close relationships across transnational boundaries with stakeholders, that built a company attracting strong British investment, in 1902!

Enlisting Support to Prosecute Economic War in Japan

Under the Trading with the Enemy Act, it was now illegal for British merchants to work with German merchants in Japan and elsewhere. To destroy German business in Japan, first, the British government targeted British companies based in Britain with German partners/agents in Japan. Second, it targeted British owned companies based in Japan that worked with German owned Japan based companies which were all registered as Japanese companies under Japanese law. While the British government had authority over companies based in Britain, it had no authority over those based in Japan and had to seek the cooperation of its ally. As Japan also had to consider its own interests, British efforts to enlist the support of the Japanese government in closing down German businesses met with resistance. Third, the British government enlisted the support of British merchants identified as harbouring anti-German feelings, and who stood to benefit personally, complying with the British government's objectives as in the case of Nickel & Lyons.

24 Frank H. H. King, *The Hongkong Bank in the Period of Imperialism and War, 1895–1918; Wayfoong, the Focus of Wealth, Volume II of The History of Hongkong and Shanghai Banking Corporation* (Cambridge: Cambridge University Press, 1988), 531–32.

25 King, *The Hongkong Bank in the Period of Imperialism and War*, 530–32.

The British government encountered strong resistance from British companies in Britain; they did not want to terminate their German agents and partnerships in Japan.[26] The British Ambassador in Tokyo Sir William Conyngham Greene represented this concern: "German firms trading when British Banks, Shipping and Insurance Companies are permitted to help them, and German firms even continue to represent British Companies."[27] In the banking industry where the British HSBC had long partnered with German merchants in Japan, the pressure the British Foreign Office applied on HSBC to sever its German connections is clear. HSBC had built a strong business in trade finance amongst German merchants since the mid-late 1800s and had appointed four key German businessmen as directors to its board. From 1905, however, the bank was regularly criticized in London for "being mostly German" even though its ninety-one German shareholders at that time represented only 2.7 per cent of the total and Germans held only 5 per cent of its shares.[28] The Bank refuted such accusations, regarding them as "the stuff of political tracts" and of nationalistic "jingoists" and that such "rumours" were made "to disengage the British government from its long support of the bank" by "those who had long anticipated such a war and those who had done much to make war inevitable."[29] The strong anti-German feeling emerging in London flowed into foreign merchant communities in China and Japan as the German management of C. Nickel & Co. Ltd. (subsequently Nickel & Lyons) experienced from at least 1905 onwards a gradual process of disenfranchisement.[30]

Just as HSBC resisted pressure to sever its German connections, so British insurance companies resisted pressure to terminate their German partnerships. From the 1870s, many British companies had appointed German trading houses to represent British product lines and services in Japan. Two such German trading houses, C. Illies & Co. and H. Ahrens & Co., both having close relationships with Nickel & Lyons, held wide-ranging interests from infrastructure and arms to foodstuffs and textiles as well as shipping agencies. They also represented "a great many British goods, and ... British insurance

26 Telegram No. 259 from British Embassy Tokyo to Foreign Office, 14 December 1914, FO 371/2021, TNA (herein referred to as Telegram No. 259), 402.

27 Telegram No. 259, 402.

28 King, *The Hongkong Bank in the Period of Imperialism and War*, 527.

29 King, *The Hongkong Bank in the Period of Imperialism and War*, 529; King, *The Hongkong Bank in the Period of Imperialism and War*, 603.

30 "C. Nickel & Co. Ltd.: Third Annual Meeting," *Japan Chronicle* (Kobe), 25 January 1906, 116.

companies."[31] Insurance industry representatives in London appealed to the British Board of Trade in December 1914 pleading that while British insurance firms were solely insurance focused, for their German partners, "Insurance relates to the [German] Agent's ... business within his own personal control," business British firms could not otherwise access; "It is the German Agents who ... employ the [British] Companies." British companies claimed that severing their relationships with German companies "would not hurt the enemy," but would allow American and Japanese competitors to take over their business.[32] Reflecting confusion over the anti-trading policies and his role, in October 1914, the British Ambassador asked the Foreign Office if German firms were permitted to represent British companies as "several German firms here are agents for English Insurance companies, fire and marine and it is impossible to keep a check on them."[33] He was told that while the Act did not prohibit German firms acting as agents, "British companies should be encouraged to ... [start] replacing German agents."[34]

In July 1915, the Board of Trade instructed British insurance companies to terminate their agreements with their German agents due to national safety concerns.[35] That month the British Ambassador reported that C. Illies & Co., H. Ahrens & Co. and Otto Reimers had had their insurance agencies removed and given to British companies, and by November all such agencies had been terminated.[36] How the British government dealt with the insurance industry shows how willing it was to sacrifice in the short term British insurance companies' competitive position, for the sake of gains imagined in the longer term.[37] These gains were not realized, and British insurance companies became victims of the anti-trading with the enemy policy losing business to their American and Japanese competitors.

31 Memorandum by Crowe, 30 September 1914, FO 371/2020, TNA, 365–79; Letter British Embassy Tokyo to Foreign Office, 3 July 1915, FO 371/2385, TNA (hereafter Letter Embassy to FO 3 July 1915), 67. See also advertisements for British-German insurance partnerships appearing in the *Hiogo Daily News* throughout the 1880s and 1890s, Kobe Public Archives (hereafter KPA).

32 Letter on behalf of the British Insurance Companies to the Secretary of Board of Trade, 1 December 1914, FO 371/2019, TNA, 181–86; McDermott, "'A Needless Sacrifice,'" 276.

33 Telegram No. 191 from British Embassy Tokyo to Foreign Office, 20 October 1914, FO 371/2019, TNA, 160.

34 Telegram No. 169 from Foreign Office to British Embassy Tokyo, 21 October 1914, FO 371/2019, TNA, 161.

35 Memorandum by E. T. F. Crowe, German Representation of British Insurance Companies in Japan, 17 June 1915, FO 371/2385, TNA, 35–36.

36 Letter Embassy to FO 3 July 1915, 67; British Embassy Tokyo to Foreign Office, 6 November 1915, FO 371/2385, TNA, 70.

37 "Commercial Situation in Japan in 1913: Mr. Crowe on the "Good Old Days," *Japan Chronicle* (Kobe), 6 August 1914, 276–77.

Enlisting the Japanese Government's Support

In trying to enlist the Japanese government's support to enact its anti-trading policy the British government met resistance from the outset. Cracks in the British-Japanese relationship first appeared when Japan declared war on Germany on 23 August 1914, three weeks after the British. Whether Japan's declaration of war was consistent with the terms of the Anglo-Japanese Alliance remains debatable. Nevertheless, Japan's failure to seek Britain's full agreement on its entry into the war contributed to a growing distrust between the British government and its Japanese ally.[38]

Because the British Embassy had no authority over British or German merchants and companies registered in Japan, it had to rely upon the Japanese government to implement its anti-trading policies. In correspondence with the Foreign Office, the British Ambassador regularly expressed his frustration over having to request Japanese government ministers take action against Germans and their companies. Instead of deporting all German merchants as Greene expected, for example, the Japanese Minister for Home Affairs, Count Ōkuma Shigenobu, protected Germans:

> as long as they [the enemy] engage in peaceful and legitimate business their persons, lives, honour and property will be protected … and they will … be allowed to receive the redress of the Imperial Courts of Law.[39]

In Greene's view, this statement suggested the Japanese government had a sympathy towards German nationals that he did not expect from a British ally.

Furthermore, in Greene's view, securing support from the Japanese government was also made difficult because Japan had not introduced its own trading with the enemy proclamation due to concerns about infringing Japanese law.[40] So the British Ambassador had to urge and cajole the Japanese government into action. In December 1914, reporting to the Foreign Office with scepticism on the Japanese government's commitment to such efforts, he wrote,

38 Ian H. Nish, *Alliance in Decline: A Study in Anglo-Japanese Relations 1908–23* (London: The Athlone Press, 1972), 115–26.

39 Copy of Instruction of the Japanese Ministry of the Interior sent to The Foreign Office, 30 September 1915, FO 371/2390, TNA, 292–93.

40 Telegram No. 276 from British Embassy Tokyo to Foreign Office, 28 December 1914, FO 371/2021, TNA (hereafter Telegram No. 276), 410; Confidential No. 20 from British Embassy Tokyo to Foreign Office, 29 January 1915, FO 371/2385, TNA (hereafter Confidential No. 20), 242–46; Telegram No. 131 from British Embassy Tokyo to Foreign Office, 6 April 1915, FO 371/2385, TNA, 259.

> at present German Bank and German firms are allowed to carry on ... business as usual [in Japan] but ... after careful enquiry I cannot obtain proof that they are being encouraged [by the Japanese government][41]

The Foreign Office asked Greene to push the Japanese government harder to restrict German business. It proposed: "you should suggest [to the Japanese government] the desirability of prohibiting trading with the enemy, as has been done by France, Russia and Great Britain," adding "it is highly important not only to strangle German trade but also ... to prevent the entry of money into Germany."[42] Greene provided Baron Katō, the Japanese Minister for Foreign Affairs, with a "sketch of steps taken by His Majesty's Government to prohibit trading with the enemy."[43] The British Embassy regularly alerted the Ministry to "objectionable Germans" or suspicious transfers of funds for the Ministry to act against, often with disappointing results. Early in 1915, the British Ambassador reported to Head Office that after "repeatedly [calling] the attention of the Minister for Foreign Affairs to the risk of treating German population ... leniently" the Japanese Government had taken some action against "objectionable Germans."[44] The Japanese government had shut down two "pro-German newspapers," the *Deutsche Japan Post* and the *Japan Daily Herald*.[45] It had also deported four Germans including Martin Ostwald, "the objectionable editor of the *Deutsche Japan Post* [and also managing editor of the *Japan Daily Herald*] to whose activities ... the [attention of the] Japanese government were drawn [by the Embassy]." Also deported were K. Kuntze, aged 40, a staff member of the two newspapers, Georg Boden, aged 43, the Manager of the DAB and Erwin Eichelberg, aged 45, the Chief Brewer of the Kirin Brewery.[46]

How German nationals were deported, and the role played by the British Embassy is best illustrated in a bizarre case of the deportation of a British man, Mr Hugh Ball which undoubtedly served the Embassy's purpose as a

41 Telegram No. 259, 402.

42 Telegram No. 249 Foreign Office to British Embassy Tokyo, 24 December 1914, FO 371/2021, TNA, 408.

43 Telegram No. 276, 410.

44 Telegram No. 59 from British Embassy Tokyo to Foreign Office, 8 February 1915, FO 371/2386, TNA (hereafter Telegram No. 59), 170.

45 Letter from British Embassy Tokyo to Foreign Office, re: H. Ball, 27 February 1915, FO 371/2386, TNA (hereafter Letter from Embassy re: Ball), 194–96.

46 Letter from British Consul-General, Yokohama to the British Ambassador, 17 February 1915, FO 371/2386, TNA, 202; Instruction of the Minister of the Interior No. 134, Viscount Kanetaka Ōura, to Governor of Kanagawa Prefecture, 13 February 1915, FO 371/2386, TNA (hereafter Instruction of the Ministry of the Interior, No. 134), 203–5.

warning to those British who still had close German friends. In February 1915 Greene reported that the Japanese government had deported Ball for working for the *Deutsche Post* in Yokohama, allegedly helping it to "circulate seditious matter" and for "living in comfort on German money."[47] In fighting the deportation, Ball stated the Commercial Attaché had assured him he was not infringing the Trading with the Enemy Act.[48] In an interview with the British Consul, A. M. Chalmers Ball also stated, "I always had hopes of an understanding between England and Germany and to this end I worked until war broke out."[49] However, the covering note accompanying correspondence sent by the Embassy to the Foreign Office showed a lack of concern for Ball's situation:

> it is … difficult to make out exactly what Mr Ball has done, circulating seditious matter among Germans seems to be preaching to the converted, but perhaps what the MFA [Japanese Ministry of Foreign Affairs or *Gaimushō*] really means is that he has been associated with Germans in acts of sedition against Japan and Great Britain.[50]

Despite a lack of evidence, the British Embassy was keen to make Ball an example to those British still associating with Germans. The Ambassador stated that Ball's' deportation "would be an object lesson to the British community," confirming this assertion and the Embassy's conclusion that "in any case it seems a pity not to make an example of him if we possibly can," suggests an expediency behind Ball's deportation.[51] Britain did not have an extradition treaty with Japan so the Embassy could only advise the Japanese government on deportations and how to handle Ball.[52] When the *Gaimushō* asked Greene if he wanted Ball deported, Greene deferred to the Foreign Office, stating he had "no objection whatsoever."[53] Ball's Japanese wife, who was well connected, petitioned Count Okuma's Private Secretary,

47 Telegram No. 84 from British Embassy Tokyo to Foreign Office, 25 February 1915, FO 371/2386, TNA, 176; Letter from Embassy re: H. Ball, 195–96.

48 Letter from British Commercial Attaché to the British Ambassador, 17 February 1915, FO 371/2386, TNA, 229–30.

49 Letter from Hugh G. Ball to British Consul-General, Yokohama, 17 February 1915, FO 371/2386, TNA, 209–11.

50 Cover Note and correspondence "Expulsion of Mr Ball (British Subject)" From British Embassy, FO 371/2386, TNA, 8–9 February 1915 (hereafter Cover Note re: "Expulsion"), 168.

51 Cover Note re: "Expulsion," 168; Telegram No. 59, 170.

52 Cover Note re: "Expulsion," 168.

53 Telegram No. 40 British Embassy Tokyo to Foreign Office, 10 February 1915, FO 371/2386, TNA, 171.

Mr Yamazaki, to cancel the deportation.[54] In a strange twist of events, Mr Yamazaki told her that it was the British Ambassador and not the Japanese authorities, who insisted on Ball's deportation.[55] Still mystified as to why he was being deported, Ball, in a plea to the British Ambassador for help referred to "several British residents [who] still maintain their business relations with local German firms and nobody thinks any the worse of them."[56]

Whether the deportations represented the Japanese government's own initiative or its acquiescence to British wishes, or both, remains unclear. Greene reported to the Foreign Office in February 1915 that a further sixteen Germans had been deported: he indicated that "in most ... other cases, the deportation has been entirely the result of Japanese police enquiries." A review of the Japanese deportation papers for known deportees all state they were deported for being "subversive of the public peace and good order and [for actions] inconsistent with the interests of Japan." No other details were given.[57] Greene noted with apparent satisfaction that "an occasional case of deportation had ... [kept] the Germans more or less alarmed."[58] As evidence emerged that the British Embassy was working behind the scenes during the court case of Christian Holstein (see chapter 10), the above-mentioned details suggest the British Embassy went to great lengths to have Holstein deported and "crippled" economically well into the post-war future.

The British Ambassador could not understand why German business was allowed to continue in Japan. He and the British government failed to understand that the Japanese government had a history of protecting "enemy nationals" resident in Japan if they acted legally. Examples of this policy can be seen in that Chinese residents were allowed to remain in Japan during the Sino-Japanese war of 1894–95 as were the Russians during the Russo-Japanese War of 1904–5.[59] Crowe speculated that the Japanese government did not want to disrupt long-established business relationships with Germany which could be reactivated once the war had ended.[60]

54 Letter from British Consulate, Yokohama to the British Embassy, 27 February 1915, FO 371/2386, TNA (hereafter Letter from Yokohama to Embassy), 189.

55 Letter from Yokohama to Embassy, 189.

56 Letter from H. G. Ball to British Ambassador, 17 February 1915, FO 371/2386, TNA, 213–14.

57 Instruction of the Ministry of the Interior, No. 134, 203–5.

58 Japan Confidential, No. 300 Enclosure 2 in No. 1 Memorandum, British Embassy to Foreign Office, 29 September 1915, FO 371/2390, TNA, 286.

59 Memorandum from E. T. F. Crowe sent as an enclosure by British Embassy Tokyo, to Foreign Office, 30 September 1915, FO 371/2390, TNA (hereafter Memorandum as enclosure 30 September 1915), 294–97.

60 Memorandum as enclosure 30 September 1915, 294–97.

Furthermore, the British government failed to understand that German and British companies were registered in Japan and protected under Japanese law.[61] The Japanese government was therefore restricted in being able to act upon the British government's urgings.

The British Embassy also urged the Japanese government to prohibit the transfer of German funds overseas, encountering further problems unanticipated by its anti-trading with the enemy policies. In December 1914, Greene reported that while he had "induced" the Japanese government to prevent the transferal of funds to enemy countries, German funds still left Japan. The British Embassy drew Baron Katō's attention to three such cases, involving the Yokohama Species Bank, the Mitsubishi Bank and Sumitomo Bank. Baron Katō responded that either the bank in question had been unaware of the prohibition and that appropriate measures had been taken, or it had acquiesced to the needs of "long-standing" German customers.[62] Not legislating formally against the transfers of German funds allowed the Japanese government to be pragmatic recognizing long-standing relationships.

At the time the British Ambassador was exhorting the *Gaimushō* to stop German funds transfers, the Japanese government had already taken steps for its own reasons. At the commencement of World War One, Germany confiscated Japanese funds held in Germany. The British Ambassador reported to Head Office that as "the Japanese government could not get possession of their funds invested in Germany, they wished to keep control … of any German money which might be in Japan."[63] The Japanese confiscation of German funds however, presented unexpected problems for British companies, as transfers of German monies to pay for services rendered in Japan were also blocked. In December 1914, Crowe acknowledged that

> banking and especially foreign exchange banking, was a … complex business… [it was] not possible to lay down any hard and fast rules … without running the risk of thereby causing grave injury to British interests.[64]

61 "Nickel & Co. Limited: Statutory Meeting," *Japan Chronicle* (Kobe), 25 February 1903, 166. At the AGM, it was stated that although the newly formed Nickel & Lyons had been registered in Hong Kong, the board intended to register the Kobe Branch "as a juridical person under Japanese law so that although they were a British company, they would have the status in Japanese law."

62 Japan Confidential February 2. Section 2 Enclosure 1 in No. 1 Crowe to the Ambassador, 7 December 1914, FO 371/2385, TNA (hereafter Japan Confidential, Crowe, to Ambassador), 229; Letter from Baron Katō to British Ambassador, 17 February 1915, FO 371/2385, TNA, 257.

63 Confidential No. 20, 246.

64 Japan Confidential Crowe, to Ambassador, 229.

To protect British companies from losses, the Ambassador had to navigate a complex process assuring the Foreign Office on the one hand that British banks handling the transfers of funds from Japanese companies owned by Germans, protected under Japanese law, through Japanese banks were not in breach of the Trading with the Enemy Proclamation. The Ambassador then had to lobby the Japanese government to permit the funds to be transmitted. While the Trading with the Enemy Act could be enacted in theory, its application was hampered by the inextricable links of German, British and other firms working jointly on international business at that time.

In November 1914 Holstein was arrested by the Japanese military police and subsequently charged by the Japanese Preliminary Court with kidnapping a Japanese swineherd. He was not interrogated about the kidnapping, however. He was interrogated about the finances of C. Illies & Co., a company he was closely associated with. It seems the court failed to obtain any information from Holstein about C. Illies & Co.'s finances as it could only charge Holstein with the kidnapping (see chapter 10), suggesting the arrest had been at the British Embassy's behest to investigate a German company's finances.[65]

Because the anti-trading with the enemy policies failed to stop trade with German companies, in October 1916, the British government issued the Statutory Blacklist. Applying to seventy odd countries and continental groupings, it listed not just German companies but also companies as "intermediaries or fences behind whose names [German companies] shelter themselves."[66] Companies trading with an enemy firm were banned from trading "with any part of the British Empire" or shipping its goods on British steamers.[67] As a result, business dried up for German merchants.

Britain Questions Japan's Sincerity as an Ally

The British Embassy's increasing frustration with the Japanese government's failure to destroy German business led it to question its ally's sincerity based on self-interest. A memorandum written by the British Commercial Attaché in September 1915 is telling:

65 Report No. 432 and Encl. No. 1 written by Mr. George Guthrie, American Ambassador, 20 January 1916. R/901 23376, BArch.

66 "The Blacklist: Explanation by British Commercial Attaché," *Japan Chronicle* (Kobe), 12 October 1916, 576.

67 "The Blacklist," 576.

> the one and only step which the Japanese Authorities took against the Germans from a commercial point of view—and this was only half-hearted and semi-official step—was to prohibit enemies from remitting any funds abroad ... This was done because the Germans were said to be holding up large Japanese Government funds in Berlin.[68]

In Crowe's view, if the measure had been properly enforced it would have damaged German business, but "large remittances were made through neutral firms which the Japanese ought to have been able to detect if serious."[69] The British Embassy also assumed that Japanese employees in foreign companies were government spies and considered the failure to stop the transfer of funds was a deliberate ploy rather than a sin of omission. Crowe wrote:

> When any definite case has been submitted to the Japanese authorities, they have ... been prepared to investigate but with their supposedly efficient system of espionage and with Japanese servants and clerks in all German homes and offices, we cannot but feel if the Japanese were ... anxious to find what the Germans are planning, they could do so with ease.[70]

While the Japanese government's reluctance to stop transmission of German funds could be ascribed to difficulties ascertaining the true origin and destination of German funds, the British Embassy believed the delays and obfuscation were due to other reasons. It believed the Japanese government wanted to avoid upsetting "powerful commercial elements in the country ... Even where they do their best, the natural corruptibility of the Japanese official would ... leave many loopholes," suggesting a long-held perception by the foreign community that Japanese officials were beholden to business interests and inherently anti-foreign.[71] This perception has been shared by the *Japan Chronicle* and the foreign community in previous chapters.

The British Embassy also considered the Japanese government's reluctance to pursue "suspicious" Germans and disrupt German business was due to

68 Memorandum from Crowe as enclosure 30 September 1915, FO371/2390, TNA, 294–97.

69 Memorandum from Crowe as enclosure 30 September 1915, FO371/2390, TNA, 294–97; Letter from British Embassy Tokyo to Foreign Office, 30 September 1915, FO 371/2390, TNA (hereafter Letter from British Embassy Tokyo to Foreign Office), 287–91.

70 Memorandum from Crowe as enclosure 30 September 1915, FO371/2390, TNA, 294–97.

71 Covering note "Remittances of Enemy Funds by Banks in Japan," 15 September 1915, FO 371/2385, TNA, 390.

"pro-German sympathies discernible in various categories of [Japanese] Society" due to a long history of shared business ventures.[72] While maintaining the Japanese government was ill-disposed towards foreign business in general, the British government also assumed that German businessmen were held in comparatively high regard in Japan. In September 1915, the British Ambassador ascribed Japanese feelings of friendship towards Germans to long-standing, mutually profitable personal and business relationships and wrote that the Japanese government did not see why the

> European War ... to the man in the street a distant echo, should make a break in these pleasant relations ... there could be nothing gained in [the Japanese government] treating Germans harshly and much to lose by estranging German business.[73]

The Embassy's frustration with its Japanese allies reached a peak in the latter part of 1915:

> There is nothing [being done] to prevent the Germans from conducting business ... successfully [in Japan]. Thanks to the supineness of the Japanese authorities, [the Germans have been able to] retain part of their export trade ... The richer Germans still drive freely about in their motor cars—in the summer a great many took their holidays in the hills and there are always a great many of them to be found at the seaside.[74]

If the above statement revealed the resentment of some within the British community towards the wealth of some Germans in Yokohama in late 1915, there were also members of the British community whose sympathies lay with German merchants. The case of Hugh Ball reflected such close relations: Ball praised his German employers "who have been and are still very kind ... and who have offered to look after my wife and my house while I am absent."[75] He also referred to the British who still worked with Germans and who were not being penalized by the British Embassy. In a sense, the British Ambassador's stated view that Hugh Ball's deportation would be "an object lesson" to some British confirmed that several British

72 Letter from British Embassy Tokyo to Foreign Office, 287–88.

73 Letter from British Embassy Tokyo to Foreign Office, 288.

74 Memorandum from Crowe as enclosure 30 September 1915, FO371/2390, TNA, 294–97.

75 Enclosure No. 2 From H. G. Ball to British Consul-General, Yokohama, 17 February 1916, FO 371/2386, TNA, 206–7.

merchants shared with their Japanese counterparts' sympathies for their long-time German colleagues and friends.

Nickel & Lyons Oust German Management and Staff

Whereas the British Embassy had limited success in having the Japanese government destroy German business, it had more success enlisting the support of British business leaders with known anti-German sympathies who stood to gain from the seizure of German assets. At the end of 1914, the board of Nickel & Lyons set out to eliminate the remnants of its German antecedents, Christian Holstein and its five German employees, thereby erasing Carl Nickel's legacy. Given the company was registered under Japanese law, the board trod warily. The board reported at its Second Annual General Meeting (AGM) held in April 1915 that with the outbreak of World War One, a significant proportion of its German business had been lost.[76] The report also noted that the company was suffering from Japanese competition:

> much misrepresentation by unscrupulous [Japanese] competitors … desirous of [becoming] our heirs, executors and administrators, and these gentry have not hesitated to invent the most libelous statements … calculated to do this Company the most injury[77]

Rather than through the loss of its German business, the company thus couched its financial problems due to increased Japanese competition, and the latter's "underhanded" methods. The report also downplayed its German antecedents, emphasizing instead its British credentials. It acknowledged the company had previously had German directors and "important German business" connections prior to war, implying they had since been dispensed with. Holstein had by then been dismissed and was living in his residence in Suma defending himself in a lengthy court case against criminal charges explored in detail in chapter 10. The report also downplayed the amount of German capital held in the company, noting it was "less than one-third" of the total.[78] By 1915, the board now comprised three British, one Australian and one American director, all business leaders within the foreign community.

76 "Nickel & Lyons Limited: Second Annual General Meeting," *Japan Chronicle* (Kobe), 29 April 1915, 647.

77 "Nickel & Lyons Limited: Second Annual General Meeting," 647.

78 "Nickel & Lyons Limited: Second Annual General Meeting," 647.

The American, John Happer, was head of Standard Oil, a famed woodblock print collector and longtime friend of Christian Holstein.

In 1915, under the Trading with the Enemy Act, Nickel & Lyons dismissed its five German employees. This was not without consequences; as the company was registered in Japan, the five employees sued the company in the Japanese court for unfair dismissal. The cases commenced in the Kobe Local Court from November 1915 and finished in the Osaka Appeal Court around March 1917. They occupied much of the *Japan Chronicle*'s energies as it reported a rather convoluted story to the fascination of the foreign community. Nickel & Lyons' five German employees were technically dismissed at the end of 1914 for an end January 1915 departure, but remained employed, on reduced hours and wages finally being dismissed in August 1915 without the promised and customary payouts. In November 1915, H. Hoeper, J. H. Thomsen and P. Sillius sued Nickel & Lyons claiming while on contract, they had their salaries cut after the war commenced, and that in August 1915, were only sacked when they demanded unpaid monies from January to August. In March 1916, two additional employees, E. Krebs and T. Schmidt, also sued Nickel & Lyons, claiming that upon their dismissal they were told that "the firm could not pay their full salaries during the war, but when the war was over the balance due ... would be paid in lump sums." Krebs and Schmidt claimed that while they had understood they had been dismissed in August 1915, they had only recently been told by the company they had been dismissed in December 1914 and "that the money they had received ... [at that time] was out of consideration for their position" as enemy aliens.[79]

The board justified the dismissal and non-payment of monies owing to two key points. First it claimed the five employees had been terminated at the end of 1914 but kept on until the end of August 1915 "out of kindness."[80] The board justified the dismissal claiming that "being an English company [they] did not want Germans, whose services were of no value ... in the present circumstances."[81] However, a German shareholder, Mr Pietzecker, testified that the directors had told him that "although the firm was compelled to dismiss all the Germans in its employ, it would continue to use their services, the dismissal being only a matter of form."[82] It seems that the board still valued its German shareholders, suggesting that new investors may have

79 "German Claims for Salary: New Proceedings Against Kobe Firm," *Japan Chronicle* (Kobe), 16 March 1916, 437.

80 "Suits for Unlawful Dismissal," *Japan Chronicle* (Kobe), 25 November 1915, 893.

81 "Suits for Unlawful Dismissal," 893.

82 "German Claims for Wrongful Dismissal: The Suits Against Messrs. Nickel & Lyons," *Japan Chronicle* (Kobe), 17 February 1916, 264.

been difficult to find during wartime. The *Chronicle* subsequently reported Paul Hagen, the German Assistant Manager for Nickel & Lyons, saying that the managing director, Captain Percy Watson, had informed the German staff already in December 1914 that

> the war compelled the firm not to employ Germans ... as before [but] the Germans ... might work ... at home or in an upstairs room at the office. There was some work that they could do ... such as writing-up books, settling accounts, writing letters, etc.[83]

Hagen added that Watson reportedly told the five that the company did not intend to dismiss them, but that they would be paid at lower rates with the shortfall being made up in bonuses to be paid at the end of war. Employing the German staff on lower rates allowed the company to absorb some of the loss of German business while still having them perform needed tasks. The German staff were then terminated around August 1915 without the promised back pay or bonuses.

The second point the board raised was to deny the existence of contracts altogether. The chairman of the board, Alf Woolley, claimed that the board could dismiss the five with no back pay, bonuses or benefits as there were no contracts. Holstein, was brought in to testify stating the staff had been under contract with the former company C. Nickel & Co. Ltd. and that Nickel & Lyons had taken over those contracts.[84] As Hagen had not been under a contract to the former company, he could not sue for wrongful dismissal.[85]

To strengthen its case for dismissing the five, in February 1916, the board claimed that the British Consulate in Kobe had instructed them, as a British company to terminate its German staff. It produced a letter as evidence from the British Consul-General, "to show that no British firms ... could employ Germans ... official supervision over British firms concerning their employees being very strict [Nickel & Lyons] had no alternative but to dismiss their German employees."[86]

As the case progressed, in July 1916, Nickel & Lyons argued that the British Embassy had informed them that employing Germans increased the risk of espionage due to "a number of German plots ... discovered here and

83 "The Claims Against Messrs. Nickel & Lyons," *Japan Chronicle* (Kobe), 11 May 1916, 754.

84 "Law Reports: The Claim Against Messrs. Nickel and Lyons. Further Proceedings," *Japan Chronicle* (Kobe), 13 July 1916, 61.

85 "The Claims Against Messrs. Nickel and Lyons: Further Court Proceedings," *Japan Chronicle* (Kobe), 11 May 1916, 754.

86 "German Claims for Wrongful Dismissal," 264.

there … The defendant firm being shipping stevedores, the position of the firm could not be compared to that of other concerns," presumably those with fewer strategic implications.[87] The war was reason enough to sack its employees. As the *Japan Chronicle* reported, the counsel for the plaintiffs refuted these claims, stating "Even now there are some Germans [still employed] in certain British firms, the Court will easily understand that the so-called 'unavoidable cause' cannot be effective," suggesting the British Embassy had not succeeded in forcing all British companies to terminate their German employees.[88] Thus the extent to which the board of Nickel & Lyons could have legally ignored the British Embassy directives to terminate its German employees bears consideration. As the Kobe branch of Nickel & Lyons was registered as a Japanese juridical person, it was subject only to Japanese law, and Japan had not legislated against trading with the enemy.[89]

The dismissal of German employees revealed anti-German elements on the board. A desire to remove German influence had emerged amongst some shareholders at least as early as 1906. At the Third AGM held for C. Nickel & Co. Ltd., one of the shareholders "Mr Noel [employed by the British firm, Hunter & Co.] inquired about the number of "Europeans" employed in the office and their salaries."[90] The chairman [Alf Woolley] replied there were five "'Europeans' including the manager, Mr Holstein."[91] Even though the company employed British, German, Danish, Dutch and other European staff, both Noel and the chairman understood "European" to refer to the Germans in the company. Noel considered "possible retrenchment and reform" was necessary based on the reported decline in profit and on increased competition at that time. However, as seen in chapter 5, the decline in profit in 1906 had been due to continuing congestion of the port and "deficient Customs accommodation at the *Hatoba* … [and] demurrage [costs]" and not to increased competition. However, Noel persisted with his view that the company should have done better given "the past year had been a phenomenal one" and considered that it was "desirous of effecting some retrenchment in … expenses."[92] When the plaintiffs in the unfair dismissal case in 1916 argued that they had been sacked because of anti-German

87 "The Claim Against Nickel & Lyons: Further Court Proceedings," 754; "Law Reports: The Claims Against Messrs. Nickel & Lyons," 61.

88 "Law Reports: The Claims Against Messrs. Nickel & Lyons," 61.

89 "German Claims for Wrongful Dismissal," 264.

90 "C. Nickel & Co. Ltd.: Third Annual Meeting," 116; Meiji Portraits Website, http://meiji-portraits.de/, 2024.

91 "C. Nickel & Co. Ltd.: Third Annual Meeting," 116.

92 "C. Nickel & Co. Ltd.: Third Annual Meeting," 116.

sentiments on the board, their counsel noted in court that the chairman of the board, Alf Woolley, who defended the company's decision to terminate their employment, was "hostile to the Germans," and was well known for his anti-German sentiments.[93]

Only one of the five employees received a judgement in his favour, confirming the *Japan Chronicle*'s long-held view that the Japanese court system could not be trusted due to its susceptibility to vested interests. In the case of Krebs and Schmidt, the plaintiffs withdrew their claims for unknown reasons.[94] But in the case of Hoeper and Thomsen, and the separate case of Sillius, the courts used evidence from the same witness in different ways. The court dismissed the claims of Hoeper and Thomsen on the basis that "owing to the standing of [Holstein as] the witness" (Holstein was at the time appealing a criminal charge in the Osaka Appeals Court) his evidence that Hoeper and Thomsen had been under contract was deemed unreliable.[95] However, Paul Sillius, whose case had run concurrently with Hoeper and Thomsen's, succeeded in his claim because Holstein had proven that Sillius's contract had been taken over by Nickel & Lyons. The *Japan Chronicle* reported these outcomes without commenting on the contradiction, but it did suggest there had been a connection with Sillius's evidence in the criminal case against Holstein before the Osaka Appeals Court. As will be seen in the next chapter, there were indications that Sillius had been pressured by the Japanese judge to give damaging evidence against Holstein.[96]

Destroying German trade for the British in Japan was fraught. The British government had to deal with a close-knit foreign community with its close British-German partnerships which had developed over decades. British companies resisted pressure to break those partnerships for as long as they could. Nevertheless, the British government persisted with its anti-trading with the enemy policies believing it would make gains through capturing German assets and business. However, the only realistic way British companies could seize German trade was not through "restrictions against post-war Germans ... [but] to beat them on their grounds of efficiency."[97] Also unanticipated by the British was how the Japanese government sought

93 "Law Reports: The Claims Against Messrs. Nickel & Lyons," 61.

94 "Law Reports: The Claims Against Messrs. Nickel & Lyons," 61.

95 "Law Reports: Claims for Wrongful Dismissal," *Japan Chronicle* (Kobe), 28 September 1916, 498.

96 Letter No. 422 written by Mr. George Guthrie, American Embassy, enclosing his Report No. 432 and Encl. No. 2 with letter written by Mrs. C. Sillius (mother of Paul Sillius), 9 July 1915 (American Embassy translation). R/901 23376, BArch.

97 King, *The Hongkong Bank in the Period of Imperialism and War*, 605.

to protect German business interests with an eye to a post-war future. In the same way, the Japanese government resisted British diplomatic pressure to comply with the unequal treaties in the decades leading to war, the Japanese government only complied with those British requests that coincided with its interests. It was only when the Statutory Declaration was introduced in 1916 that German business ended.

Despite the mixed results of the British government's efforts, one British company did benefit from its aims of severing British-German partnerships. The British board of Nickel & Lyons, composed mainly of British community leaders, took advantage of the British government's proclamations to oust its German management and staff. The *Japan Chronicle*'s detailed reporting on these court cases reveals the interest the foreign community took in the fates of their colleagues, and in the inequities foreigners could still suffer at the hands of the Japanese courts. In its view foreigners were vulnerable to the influence of vested interests which in this case most likely included not just Japanese competition but also pressure from the British Embassy. While the five sacked German employees were lesser actors, they had nevertheless played a strong part in the success of Nickel & Lyons, into which the British shareholders had bought, reflecting the importance to the British merchants of partnering with their German counterparts.

These events marked the end of German-British partnerships in Japan. Furthermore, there is no evidence that the British captured German assets and business. The British insurance industry, for example, lost to their Japanese and American competitors. While German business was stopped in the short-term, it was revived as soon as the war ended. German merchants who had remained in Japan throughout the war commenced new businesses and a new generation of Germans relocated to the Port of Kobe.

10. World War One: The Swineherd Kidnapping Case

Abstract: Commissioned by C. Illies & Co. to supply the German Naval Squadron in Tsingtao with oil, coal, water and livestock prior to the First World War, Holstein found himself being pursued through the Japanese courts on charges of kidnapping a Japanese swineherd he had employed to look after some pigs just as Britain and then Japan declared war on Germany. Examining the Swineherd Kidnapping Case reveals not only how the close relationship between British and German merchants in Kobe was transformed with the war but also how one hitherto successful German merchant had the fight of his life and all he had worked for, as he became the focus of not only Japanese vested interests but also the British government's efforts of destroying German merchants well into the post war period.

Keywords: courts, "coolies", colonies, Chronicle, media, nationalism

Christian Holstein, the central figure in this chapter, so far remains unexplored. As few personal records remain from this period, discerning the man and his character has only been possible through third party reports in archival records and newspaper reportage. Through such records, we can see how he was perceived as the managing director of C. Nickel & Co. Ltd., as a senior member of the foreign community in Kobe and as a defendant in a long-running court case contrived against him that will be the subject of this chapter. Holstein was employed by C. Nickel & Co. Ltd. from 1897 as Carl Nickel's presumptive heir. He was elected to the company's board in 1905 and became its managing director from 1906–13 and then co-managing director until sometime in 1915. Ignoring the casual anti-German sentiment appearing amongst its British shareholders at least from 1906, the company's British-German board regularly acknowledged Holstein's risk-tolerant, entrepreneurial

Holstein, Prue S. *The German Experience of Japan's Treaty Port System: A Case Study of C. Nickel & Co. Ltd., 1860–1923*. Taylor & Francis Group, 2025.
DOI: 10.4324/9781003706274-11

initiatives that expanded and grew the company's business.[1] In 1909, the board renewed his contract "for another four years," and in 1913, he still retained his position albeit now sharing it as one of two managing directors of the company's successor, the newly formed Nickel & Lyons.[2] Unlike many of his British counterparts and critics, Holstein was not only fluent in English and German but was also proficient in Japanese and chose to work directly with his Japanese employees and customers rather than through intermediaries. From the way he handled disputes with his unskilled Japanese workforce (where disdain was often mutual) or lawsuits in the Japanese courts which were often subject to urgings from Japanese and later British vested interests, Holstein adopted the business focused, uncompromising, and authoritarian stance of his cousin and sponsor Carl Nickel. Also, like Nickel, Holstein engendered loyalty from his Japanese staff with whom he had long-term close relationships.

As a member of the foreign community that felt constantly under siege by the Japanese authorities, he was well respected for his long experience and connections amongst the British and German communities. His inclusion in and contribution made to committees of foreign merchants established to liaise with the Japanese authorities on such issues as the needed improvements of the Kobe Harbour reflected his standing. His support of charities associated with the maritime trade such as the Kobe Seamen's Institute reflected a generous person with a sense of social responsibility. Like many of his male contemporaries, he lived during this period from 1897 to 1923 as a single man working long hours and weekends, socializing through work with close male colleagues, accumulating wealth, and property. Although he visited Germany seldom, he retained close family ties with his siblings, Otto, and Christina. He only married in 1927 in his fifties. For the most part, he enjoyed close, long-standing, and loyal personal friendships with fellow professional and business colleagues in the foreign community, his staff, and with sea captains and others of his commercial constituency across British, German, American and Japanese communities. He was well integrated into the fabric of the Port of Kobe and remained so for the rest of his life. It was this support he would rely upon to survive in Japan through the First World War as he was pursued through the Japanese courts by vested interests over the Swineherd Kidnapping case from 1915 to 1921!

Having examined in chapter 9 how the British government's anti-trading with the enemy policies affected the German management of Nickel &

1 "C. Nickel & Co. Ltd.: Third Annual Meeting," *Japan Chronicle* (Kobe), 25 January 1906, 116.

2 "C. Nickel & Co. Ltd., Seventh Annual General Meeting," *Japan Chronicle* (Kobe), 30 December 1909, 1177.

Lyons, the focus now turns to how Christian Holstein was affected when he was charged with kidnapping a Japanese national. This chapter uses the Swineherd Kidnapping Case to further illustrate the complexities and contradictions of the relationships between the Japanese, British and German communities, as those relationships were transformed by war. It shows the impact of war on the Kobe mercantile community and how a successful German businessman's life and all he had worked for was nearly destroyed. Holstein, a senior member of the foreign community bridging the German and Anglophone divide, represented the kind of German merchant the British government had sought to "cripple" well into the post-war period. Important elements and events of this case have been reconstructed from reportage in the newspapers, the *Japan Chronicle*, the Japanese *Kobe Shimbun* and *Yūshin Nippō*, each demonstrating the different concerns and interests of their respective readerships. This allows us to understand more precisely how the foreign community in Kobe understood its position in Japan and provides an inkling of how Japanese readers might have come to form opinions about foreign merchants during the war. It also shows how the British government continued trying to influence the Japanese government not just as an ally, but also in the way it was accustomed to exercising informal power in China.

Emblematic of German-British-Japanese Collaboration until 1914

At the time he was accused of kidnapping a swineherd in 1914, Christian Holstein was a senior business leader in Kobe's foreign community. He was the thirty-nine-year-old co-managing director of Nickel & Lyons, a substantial international company he had played a major part in building. It was a company of over 2,000 employees, with a network of branch offices in Kobe, Osaka, Yokohama, Nagoya, Shimidzu, Yokkaichi, Shimonoseki and Moji, and a ship-building yard in Shinzaike.[3] In 1908, Holstein had also led a group of British and American investors in the construction of the luxury Tor Hotel (the present day site of the Kobe Club—the Tor Hotel survived until 1956 when it was destroyed by fire).[4] In addition, as seen in chapter 7, Holstein had amassed considerable personal property holdings in Kobe, Suma, Rokko and Moji.[5] By the end of 1914, however, Holstein

3 Front page advertisement for Nickel & Lyons, *Japan Chronicle* (Kobe), 7 January 1915.

4 "The Tor Hotel," *Japan Chronicle* (Kobe), 30 July 1908, 170.

5 A list of properties Holstein owned can be found in the following articles: "Enemy Property in Japan: Security for Payment of Indemnity," *Japan Chronicle* (Kobe), 5 February 1920, 162;

had become an "enemy alien," and his actions became the focal point of competing political, diplomatic and commercial interests engulfing him in an unfortunate confluence of forces. He was a German at the helm of a British company, accused of a crime committed against a Japanese, just as war had been declared by Britain and Japan against Germany, in an environment where his dominance of the stevedoring trade was resented by other companies both foreign and Japanese.

In August 1914, just after First World War broke out, the *Japan Chronicle* recounted an event that was possibly one of the last times the Japanese, British and German communities came together before the exigencies of war began to make enemies of the communities. In an article entitled "Departure of German Reservists: Scenes in Kobe" the *Chronicle* described the departure of fifty to sixty German residents of Yokohama and Kobe, undertaking military service in the German territory of Tsingtao.[6] The Kobe Station platform, ringing to the strains of the German national anthem, was described as

> crowded with foreigners, including many Englishmen and other non-Germans who had come to see their friends off to what may be described as the front. There was also a very large crowd of Japanese, and they gave the departing reservists a most enthusiastic ovation, flying German flags and shouting "banzai."[7]

It was also in the context of this long-time collaboration between the Japanese, British and German merchant communities, that a swineherd called Tsukamura Kanekichi entered Nickel & Lyon's employ and embarked on the German merchant steamer, the *Mark*, on the eve of the First World War. On 3 August 1914, at short notice, the *Mark* had pulled into Kobe Harbour.[8] Germany was already at war with Russia, and while it was not yet at war with Britain, to many war appeared inevitable.[9] The German government had commandeered the *Mark* to supply provisions for the German Far Eastern

"Forced Sales of German Property: No Satisfactory Offers," 1 April 1920, 385; "German Property in Japan: Disposal Discussed," 27 May 1920, 611.

6 "Departure of German Reservists: Scenes in Kobe," *Japan Chronicle* (Kobe), 6 August 1914, 265.

7 "Departure of German Reservists," 265.

8 "The Charge Against Mr Holstein: Opening of the Public Trial. Full Report of the Proceedings," *Japan Chronicle* (Kobe), 4 March 1915, 318.

9 "The Charge Against Mr Holstein: Speeches by Counsel for Defense," *Japan Chronicle* (Kobe), 25 March 1915, 438.

Naval Squadron based in Tsingtao (Qingdao), diverting it from its scheduled destination, Shanghai.[10] Tsingtao was in Shantung (Shandong Province), the German concession in China, a few days' sailing from Kobe. In Kobe the *Mark*'s regular cargo was unloaded, and a new cargo of oil, water, coal, and a herd of thirty-seven pigs was taken on board for the German Squadron.[11] The German government had recently appointed C. Illies & Co. to take over the provisioning of the government's ships from H. Ahrens & Co. In turn, C. Illies & Co. commissioned Nickel & Lyons to procure and load those provisions onto the *Mark*.[12] Already, as a letter subsequently made clear, over the preceding six months Nickel & Lyons had been commissioned to load several German government steamers, the *Prinz Adalbert, Ferdinand, C.F. Leist, Göttingen* and others, with provisions for the German Squadron in Tsingtao presumably with the board's approval.[13]

Events Leading to a Kidnapping Charge

As the Captain of the *Mark* was short-handed, Holstein together with Ishida Satoru, his long-time trusted employee, engaged Tsukamura as a swineherd to look after the pigs Holstein had acquired from another German named Bothe, who had been called to serve in Tsingtao.[14] It seemed Holstein had had a prior relationship with Tsukamura.[15] Tsukamura said Holstein told him that he would be going to Tsingtao and would be back in Kobe within eight days.[16] The ship reportedly departed hastily at 2:00 a.m. 5 August Japan time, within hours of Britain declaring war on Germany (4 August 1914).[17] According to the *Japan Chronicle*'s subsequent reportage, an hour before departure, the Assistant Naval Attaché Frigate Captain Fritz Blomeyer visited the *Mark*'s captain, Captain Ernst Loewe. He ordered Loewe to change his destination to the Marshall Islands, a German territory in the

10 "The Charge Against Mr Holstein: Opening of the Public Trial," 318.

11 "The Charge Against Mr Holstein: Opening of the Public Trial," 318–19.

12 "The Charge Against Mr Holstein: Opening of the Public Trial," 318.

13 Letter written 31 January 1918 by Christina Schwanck (sister of Christian Holstein) to Corvette Captain, v. Knorr, former Naval Attaché, German Embassy in Tokyo, Bundesarchiv Berlin (BArch), R/901 23376.

14 "Remarkable Claim for Damages: Sequel to a Charge Against a Foreigner," *Japan Chronicle* (Kobe), 4 February 1915, 174; "The Charge Against Mr Holstein: Opening of the Public Trial," 318–19.

15 "The Charge Against Mr Holstein: Opening of the Public Trial," 319.

16 "Remarkable Claim for Damages," 174.

17 "The Charge Against Mr Holstein: Opening of the Public Trial," 318.

Pacific where the German Squadron had been forced to hastily relocate. By the time the *Mark* arrived at the Marshall Islands, a voyage of some twenty days, Japan had also declared war on Germany on 23 August 1914. Tsukamura was now an enemy alien and so the captain of the *Mark* left him on Yaluit Island in the care of the German Governor. Tsukamura was incarcerated, allegedly in poor conditions, and was only discovered and released in September 1914, when the Japanese Navy arrived to destroy the German coaling station at the request of the British Navy.[18] Tsukamura then had to wait for a Japanese steamer to call by the islands before he could be returned to Japan, arriving in Kobe on 23 October, eighty days after his departure.[19]

The *Japan Chronicle*/Foreign Community's Perspective

According to the *Japan Chronicle*, it was only after the *Kobe Shimbun* published a vivid account of Tsukamura's alleged kidnapping that Holstein was arrested and subsequently tried in the Japanese courts. On 2 November 1914, Holstein was jailed for six weeks without charge until 11 January 1915, while the Preliminary Court conducted its investigation. After six weeks the Preliminary Court released Holstein, charging him with kidnapping the Japanese swineherd, thus beginning a long series of court cases from 1915 to 1921.[20] The *Chronicle* reported widely on evidence given in the Swineherd Kidnapping Case, reflecting the foreign community's interest in the fate of a well-known German merchant managing a well-known British company. From November 1914 until April 1921, the *Chronicle* recounted details of Holstein's six-week imprisonment, and the preliminary and public trials held in Kobe (1914–15), the appeals Holstein mounted in the Osaka Court and the Court of Cassation (1916–17), and finally the quashing of the original verdict and the re-trial held in the Hiroshima Court (1919–21). The *Chronicle* presented Holstein not as an "enemy alien," but as it would any respected member of the foreign community before the Japanese court, reflecting the importance it placed on the presumption of innocence and the cohesion of the foreign community.

18 Toneko Hirai, "MINAMI-E! Japan's Acquisition of Micronesia, 1914–1922" (PhD diss., University of Hawaii, 1994), 115–26; "The Charge Against Mr Holstein: Conflicting Points in Evidence," *Japan Chronicle* (Kobe), 4 March 1915, 362–63.

19 "The Charge Against Mr Holstein: Conflicting Points in Evidence," 362.

20 "Local and General," *Japan Chronicle* (Kobe), 19 November 1914, 918; "The Charge Against Mr Holstein: Result of Preliminary Examination," *Japan Chronicle* (Kobe), 14 January 1915, 59.

Despite the war-time context, the *Japan Chronicle* also presented the case as a *cause célèbre* to the foreign community, addressing the very bones of contention it had with how foreigners were handled in the Japanese courts since the revised treaties of 1899. The *Chronicle* criticized the "trial by media" conducted by what it considered a nationalistic Japanese press, leading to Holstein's arrest. It criticized Holstein's jailing without charge or bail in life-threatening conditions and later, it criticised the acceptance by the Japanese courts of questionable evidence from untrustworthy sources. The *Chronicle* also criticized what it considered to be the influence political and commercial vested interests exercised over the courts.[21] While the Japanese press alluded to the possibility of Holstein acting as an agent of the German government, at no time did the British owned *Japan Chronicle* suggest this.

The Japanese Press' Perspective

The *Kobe Shimbun* and the *Kobe Yushin Nippō* reported widely on the case in sensationalist language, displaying an unmistakable anti-foreign bias. The *Kobe Shimbun* reported on Tsukamura's story over some thirteen articles from Tsukamura's arrival back in Kobe early October until Holstein's arrest and incarceration, on 2 November 1914. Claiming a kind of victory, the *Kobe Shimbun* published an article on 4 November 1914 entitled, "Just Punishment from Heaven. Holstein Finally Jailed, A Victory for Kobe Citizens and our Company [the *Kobe Shimbun*]."[22] Accompanying the article was a photograph of Holstein alighting from his car outside the Nickel & Lyons building, with a black cross hand drawn across the photo. The *Kobe Shimbun* described in sensationalist terms how Tsukamura visited its office and over five hours recounted how he had been kidnapped, thrown into jail on Yaluit Island and handled "violently," claiming credit for bringing this case to the prosecutor's attention. In addition, the *Kobe Shimbun* insinuated there was more to the kidnapping incident than met the eye: it reported that upon interrogating Tsukamura, the prosecutor's office had discovered a "hidden incident."

21 "Notes and Comments," *Japan Chronicle* (Kobe), 19 November 1914, 918.

22 "Tenshū kudari kanzoku dokutan shōkai. Tsuhi ni kenkyo saru ... Shimin to wagasha daishōri" (Just Punishment from Heaven: [Holstein] Finally Jailed ... A Victory for Kobe Citizens and our Company [the Kobe Shimbun]), *Kobe Shimbun*, 4 November 1914, KPA, 6; "Matamata Daisōsaku Kaishi. Nidokushō Suma Bessō Sonota" (My translation: Big Enquiry Commenced. Suma Holiday House of two German Merchants), *Kobe Yūshin Nippō*, 5 November 1914, KPA; "Sakukenjikyoku Holstein Shōkan Jyuudaijiken Hansekimeiryō" (My translations; Holstein Summoned to the Prosecutor's Office for an Important Criminal Act) *Kobe Yūshin Nippō*, 12 November 1914, KPA.

While providing no details, it suggested this "incident" piqued the interest of the Japanese military police.[23]

The *Shimbun's* journalists also sensationalized the police interrogations of Holstein and Ishida Satoru from Nickel & Lyons, and of Robert Koops, Carl Friedrichsen and a man reported only as Fischer from C. Illies & Co. The newspaper referred to the long hours they spent under interrogation and their "pale drawn faces."[24] What the article lacked in detail and accuracy, it made up for in inflammatory statements, innuendo, and dramatic effect. The articles continued to refer to Nickel & Lyons by its former Japanese name, Nickel *Shōkai* (Company) and referred to Holstein as the managing director of a German company. The reporter was apparently unaware that the company had become British twelve years earlier and had been merged with another British stevedoring company in 1913 to form Nickel & Lyons. It possibly suited the Japanese newspaper's narrative and its commercial connections to have the company still identified as "the enemy" separate from Japan's British allies. From the tone of these articles, the *Kobe Shimbun* was marking its nationalist credentials by campaigning for the arrest and incarceration of an "evil" German merchant well before Holstein had been found guilty by the court.

Reflecting the British owned *Japan Chronicle*'s commitment to the cohesion of the foreign community, it criticized the *Kobe Shimbun*'s reportage, which it saw as inherently anti-foreign and as having more to do with harming foreign interests in Kobe than with the truth. The *Chronicle* decried the speculation and "trial by media" that the *Kobe Shimbun* indulged in. The *Chronicle* claimed that the Japanese media had "waylaid" Tsukamura upon his return to Kobe, had entertained him "lavishly" in *geisha* houses and subsequently published vivid accounts of Tsukamura's treatment in prison.[25] The dramatic wording of the titles and articles written by the *Kobe Shimbun* in the five months before the trial commenced, bear out this criticism. In the *Japan Chronicle*'s view, the "long series of wild and sensational stories about Mr Holstein and the foreign firms concerned [in the case]" was part of the Japanese press' campaign leading to Holstein's arrest and imprisonment.[26] Furthermore, the *Chronicle* stated:

23 "Just Punishment from Heaven: Holstein Finally Jailed," 6. (My translation).

24 "Just Punishment from Heaven: Holstein Finally Jailed," 6. (My translation).

25 "The Charge Against Mr Holstein: Opening of the Public Trial," 320; "Local and General," 918.

26 Between October 1914 and January 1915, the *Kobe Shimbun* wrote some twenty-seven articles on the experiences of the swineherd leading to the arrest of Christian Holstein.

> We regret to see … our vernacular contemporaries continue to publish violently worded articles relating to a foreign resident of Kobe … under arrest … with … the appearance of established facts … [which] are merely the tattlings of hangers-on … and the imaginings of people who … are not altogether disinterested observers.[27]

Influence of Vested Interests

Believing the Japanese courts to be under the influence of vested interests, the *Japan Chronicle* foreshadowed a miscarriage of justice. In its view, Holstein had been judged guilty before a proper trial and suggested that the *Kobe Shimbun* was acting on behalf of Japanese commercial interests keen to eliminate a major competitor, Nickel & Lyons. In 1921 it noted that "The real inspiration … [for the charge] was … commercial jealousy that has more recently inspired attacks on the stevedoring firm [Nickel & Lyons]."[28] When Holstein was finally acquitted, the *Japan Chronicle* editorialized:

> As soon as Japan came into the war, the organ of the Japanese stevedoring interests reproduced a photograph of the firm's office with a great black cross across it … a hint that the patriotic people of Kobe should obliterate it.[29]

The American Embassy believed that political motives were also behind Holstein's arrest. As the German Embassy closed at the outbreak of First World War, the interests of German residents in Japan were handled first by the American Embassy, until the Americans entered the war in 1917, and then by the Swiss Embassy. Diplomatic exchanges held in the *Bundesarchiv* (National Archives) files in Berlin confirm these foreign commentators' views that Holstein had been arrested for political reasons, and that in the absence of further proof, the Preliminary Court could only charge him with kidnapping a Japanese swineherd.[30] A key piece of evidence for this point emerged in 1916 when the American Ambassador, George Guthrie, reported to the Secretary of State in Washington, DC that Holstein had been arrested

27 "Notes and Comments," 918.

28 "A Bogus Kidnapping Case: An Old Wrong Righted," *Japan Chronicle* (Kobe), 21 April 1921, 550.

29 "A Bogus Kidnapping Case: An Old Wrong Righted," 550.

30 "The Charge Against Mr Holstein: Result of the Preliminary Examination," 59; Report No. 432 and Encl. No. 1 written by Mr. George Guthrie, American Ambassador, 20 January 1916. R/901 23376, BArch (hereafter Report No. 432 and Encl. No. 1, Guthrie, 20 January 1916).

by military police from Himeji (fifty kilometres west of Kobe) and not by the local police in Kobe. According to Guthrie's notes, Holstein advised him he had only briefly been questioned about the alleged kidnapping. He was questioned at length, however, about the German company C. Illies & Co., their business as agents of the German government, and about secret codes and monies belonging to the German government.[31] Guthrie suggested that the Japanese authorities had suspected Holstein of colluding with a potential enemy government, and the charge of kidnapping had been a pretext to interrogate him about this possible collusion.

As seen in chapter 9, the British Embassy was keen to direct the Japanese government's enquiries into persons of interest to restrict the transfer of German funds, so it is possible that the Embassy encouraged the Japanese government to investigate C. Illies & Co. and Holstein. In December 1914, the Embassy reported that at the outbreak of war, it was "not possible to state … how much German money" there was in Japan. It believed that the Deutsche Bank held a considerable amount on behalf of the German government. It believed also that monies were being collected by "an important German firm," C. Illies & Co., "agents for Krupp's, a major German arms manufacturer, which has large dealings with the Japanese Government in war and railway materials etc."[32] An opportunity to try to disrupt C. Illies & Co.'s operations and to discredit a prominent German merchant in the latter part of 1914 would have been welcomed by the British Embassy.

Despite the onset of war, Holstein still had important British friends: he retained the services of his close friend, Joseph Ernst de Becker, a highly respected British lawyer, and translator of Japanese legal codes. As Guthrie reported to Washington, D. C., de Becker had advised the American Embassy that Holstein had been arrested by the Japanese authorities "on a charge alleged not to have then been formulated" and that bail was denied while the "charge was being investigated." De Becker expressed the view the charge was "an entirely vamped up affair" and that Holstein's position and nationality, and the political atmosphere had all combined to bias the [Preliminary] Court against him.'[33]

Holstein may have been suspected of spying. As a German national and a prominent member of the German community, he had important

31 Report No. 432 and Encl. No. 1, Guthrie, 20 January 1916.

32 Japan Confidential February 2 Section 2. Enclosure 1 in No. 1. Crowe to British Ambassador, 7 December 1914, FO 371/2385, TNA, 229.

33 Letter No. 422, written by George Guthrie, American Ambassador to Secretary of State, Washington, DC, 20 January 1916. R/901 23376, BArch.

connections to members of the German diplomatic and military corps, which may have led the Japanese military authorities to view him with suspicion. At the outbreak of war, Holstein as a member of the German *Landsturm* or Military Reserve had been called by the German government to the service of the German Marine (East Asian Squadron) in Japan.[34] For helping to re-provision the German Squadron through his role managing Nickel & Lyons, Holstein was subsequently awarded an *Eisernes Kreuz 2. Klasse* (Second Class Iron Cross).[35] Through his service, Holstein formed a close association with the German Naval Attaché, Wolfram von Knorr, which lasted many years after the war. Von Knorr was based at the German Embassy in Tokyo coordinating the re-provisioning of the German Squadron in Tsingtao until the outbreak of war. According to British records, around the end of 1914, von Knorr, who they named a spy, moved to San Francisco where "he was instrumental in helping to victual and coal the German Pacific Squadron up to the battle of Coronel (1 November 1914)."[36] Despite the close connection with von Knorr, no evidence has been found that Holstein's relationship with him had involved espionage. When Holstein was interrogated by the military police, there was no evidence for the Preliminary Court to charge him with anything other than possibly kidnapping a Japanese national. It is likely that Holstein's role six months before war commenced was consistent with both the German government's interests in having the German Squadron re-provisioned and with his and his board members' interests in having Nickel & Lyons secure this lucrative business.

The *Japan Chronicle* Reported on the Court Cases

According to the *Japan Chronicle*, the Preliminary Court focused on its claims Holstein had misled the Japanese swineherd, intending to kidnap him. It claimed that despite Holstein telling the Swineherd he would be returning to Japan in eight days, Holstein had known all along that

> [the *Mark*] was to proceed … [to] the South Seas where the main forces of the German Asiatic Squadron were in hiding with the object of supplying

34 Die Polzeibehörde Hamburg. Antrage auf Verleihung des Ehrenkreuzes fur Frontkämpfer, Kriegsteilnehmer. 14 April 1936. In private hands.

35 Letter written to Christian Holstein by the German Ambassador, 12 October 1920, in private hands.

36 Letter from British Embassy Tokyo to Foreign Office, 27 February 1915, FO 317/2386, TNA, 194–96.

> war provisions … to German warships and … The accused, having shipped Tsukamura on the 'Mark' … had him transported to Bonham Island [the English name for Yaluit Island] a German possession, on the 31st of the same month.[37]

The Preliminary Court claimed that "the above indictment (on the charge of kidnapping) is supported by ample proof" and committed the case for public trial in the Kobe Local Court.[38]

At the public trial, the prosecution tried to prove that Holstein knew that the *Mark*'s destination had been changed from Tsingtao to the Marshall Islands, but the evidence reported by the *Chronicle* was murky and incomplete. Evidence was considered from at least seven German and three Japanese witnesses about the moment when the *Mark* was ordered to sail to the "South Seas" instead of Tsingtao, how those orders were given and by whom, and whether Holstein could have known of those orders. Witnesses' evidence conflicted not just with that given by Holstein, but also with evidence they had given at the earlier preliminary examination.[39] Witnesses either withdrew statements already made to the Preliminary Court, now claiming they had not had firsthand knowledge, or denied their previous evidence about the course of events.[40]

While the conflicting evidence could be ascribed to poor memory and the confusion of impending war, such evidence in hindsight reflected how Holstein's and his German colleagues' involvement in a commercial transaction, legal at the time, potentially had consequences for all of them with the outbreak of war. As seen in chapter 9, following Japan's declaration of war on Germany, an Imperial Rescript was issued on the 23 August 1914 guaranteeing German citizens the protections of Japanese courts of law.[41] Baron Katō, the Foreign Minister, and Mr Kashima, Mayor of Kobe, quickly followed with assurances Germans would be protected.[42] However, according to the *Chronicle*, such enjoinders on the Japanese community were not sufficient

37 "The Charge Against Mr Holstein: Text of Preliminary Judgement," *Japan Chronicle* (Kobe), 21 January 1915, 88.

38 "The Charge Against Mr Holstein: Text of Preliminary Judgement," 88.

39 "The Charge Against Mr Holstein: Opening of the Public Trial," 318–20.

40 "The Charge Against Mr Holstein: Conflicting Points in Evidence," 362–63.

41 "The Treatment of German Residents: The Home Minister's Injunction," *Japan Chronicle* (Kobe), 27 August 1914, 421; "The Treatment of German Residents: The Home Minister's Injunction," 421.

42 "German Residents in Japan: Official Assurances," *Japan Chronicle* (Kobe), 27 August 1914, 417; "Mayoral Proclamation in Kobe: The War and the German Community," *Japan Chronicle* (Kobe), 3 September 1914, 461.

to discourage the Japanese press from vilifying a German merchant, or dissuading Japanese business interests from trying to take over foreign business interests at the outbreak of war.[43]

At the opening of the public trial, the *Chronicle* reported that Holstein's lawyers believed the prosecutor's case against Holstein was based on evidence given by three people. Two were Japanese—Tsukamura, the allegedly kidnapped swineherd and Tamura Sokichi, a customs tallyman employed by Nickel & Lyons who had been on the *Mark* prior to its departure. The third was Paul Sillius, a German national and Assistant Manager of Nickel & Lyons, who appeared first in chapter 9 when he sued Nickel & Lyons for wrongful dismissal. The *Chronicle* reported that all three witnesses understood that the destination of the *Mark* was known to be the Marshall Islands. When asked by the court if he had heard "that the vessel was proceeding to the scene of war," Tsukamura reportedly replied, "Yes, one of the subordinate tallymen told me so, but as the *taishō* [big boss referring to Holstein] reassured me that I would be able to come back, I was at ease."[44] According to the *Chronicle*, Sillius testified that the *Mark* entered the Port of Kobe to receive orders from the German government. He said he understood the destination to have been altered from Tsingtao to the South Seas while the ship was being loaded with provisions.[45] Based on this evidence, the prosecutor concluded that Holstein had most likely known of the change of destination when he engaged Tsukamura.[46]

Reflecting the prejudice of both the foreign and Japanese elites against Japanese day labourers and low ranked Japanese officials, who they believed were susceptible to vested interests, the *Japan Chronicle* criticized the court's reliance on evidence from such unreliable and untrustworthy witnesses. The *Chronicle* reported that in examining "the swineherd Tsukamura as a witness [he was] not a man to be trusted," partly because he was entertained and coached by the *Kobe Shimbun*, which the *Chronicle* suspected of working with Japanese stevedoring interests.[47] The *Chronicle* also claimed that Tsukamura exaggerated his allegations of poor treatment whilst incarcerated on Yaluit Island; and the extent of the damages he claimed, which the *Chronicle* believed "would have set him and his heirs forever in a state of

43 "A Bogus Kidnapping Case: An Old Wrong Righted," 550.

44 "The Charge Against Mr Holstein: Resumed Hearing. Examination of Important Witnesses," *Japan Chronicle* (Kobe), 18 March 1915, 400.

45 "The Charge Against Mr Holstein: Conflicting Points in Evidence," 362.

46 "The Charge Against Mr Holstein: Resumed Hearing," 403.

47 "The Charge Against Mr Holstein: Opening of the Public Trial," 320.

luxury undreamed of."[48] In his evidence Lieutenant Hibino, the Japanese naval officer who rescued Tsukamura from jail on Yaluit Island, said that "though Tsukamura could not be said to have been treated well ... He seems to have been accorded such treatment as would become his station in life."[49] Furthermore, the *Chronicle* dismissed Tamura as "little more than a coolie," informing its readership that Tamura also had been convicted and jailed for manslaughter.

Finally, the *Japan Chronicle* addressed the damning nature of Sillius's evidence against Holstein, ascribing it to a confused mental state and judgement resulting from his arrest and interrogation by the Japanese police.[50] By the time Holstein appealed his conviction in the Osaka Appeals Court, he had a letter written by Sillius's mother, Carolina, dated 9 July 1915, claiming that "her son was mentally unbalanced." She had recently stayed in Kobe for a year with her son and recounted how he had been "taken prisoner by the Japanese authorities to be interrogated" and had been pressured by the Japanese military police to testify against Holstein.[51] Her son had apparently been subjected to "eleven hours cross examination" by the Japanese judges, without notes and without realizing the trial involved Holstein. As suggested in chapter 9, according to the American Ambassador, Holstein's interrogation had more to do with interest in C. Illies & Co.'s finances rather than with potentially kidnapping the swineherd. It is perhaps the case that the interrogation of Sillius may have been instigated by the British Embassy as a part of its campaign to halt transfers of German funds and to eliminate the influence of German firms and individual merchants such as Holstein.

Despite what the *Japan Chronicle* considered to be questionable evidence, it reported that Holstein's defence failed, and on 23 March 1915, the Kobe Lower Court convicted Holstein, sentencing him to three years penal servitude. The basis of the judgement was reportedly that although Holstein was uncertain about the *Mark*'s destination, he had told Tsukamura falsely it would proceed to Tsingtao, thereby committing the offence of kidnapping.[52] The *Chronicle* quoted the prosecutor as saying that the "Accused must have

48 "A Bogus Kidnapping Case: An Old Wrong Righted," 550.

49 "The Charge Against Mr Holstein: Conflicting Points in Evidence," 362–63.

50 "The Charge Against Mr Holstein: Speeches by Counsel for the Defense," 439.

51 "The Charge Against Mr Holstein: Opening of the Public Trial. Full Report of the Proceedings," 318–20; Letter No. 422 written by Mr. George Guthrie, American Embassy, enclosing his Report No. 432 and Encl. No. 2 with letter written by Mrs. C. Sillius (mother of Paul Sillius), 9 July 1915 (American Embassy translation). R/901 23376, BArch.

52 "Charge Against Mr Holstein: Full Text of Judgment," *Japan Chronicle* (Kobe), 15 April 1915, 554.

intended from the very beginning to sacrifice a Japanese … Anyone must have realized … the danger of a Japanese serving on board the *Mark* which proceeded to the South Sea in the wake of German warships."[53] Holstein challenged the prosecutor's claim saying, "Am I a person to know where … the warships of the German Government are? I … like the ordinary man in the street have no knowledge."[54]

Japan Chronicle's Campaign Against Japanese Jails

Apart from using the Swineherd Kidnapping Case to profile a foreigner facing the injustices of the Japanese courts as the *Japan Chronicle* saw it, the *Chronicle* also used the case to emphasize the dangers foreigners faced in a Japanese jail. For foreigners living in Japan, serving time in a jail was considered injurious to health. Prior to the end of extraterritoriality, the *Chronicle*, together with Joseph de Becker, had campaigned against the unsuitability of Japanese jails for convicted foreign prisoners and for those held without charge. The *Chronicle* reported its campaign resulted only in minor modifications to the diet provided to foreigners.[55] During Holstein's court case, the *Chronicle* criticized the unjustified and prolonged incarceration of Holstein without charge, for "such a simple issue."[56] The *Chronicle* described in detail the unsanitary conditions of the prison cell Holstein occupied. His cell was reported as being "two tatami mats in size" (each three feet by six feet), "unwarmed" and "draughty" with "an evil smelling convenience in one corner" and "holes in the floor from which rats ran over him at night."[57] The American Ambassador, choosing his words more diplomatically, reported the following from his interview with Holstein in January 1916. He stated that while the unsanitary conditions did have health implications for Holstein, the prison authorities showed compassion:

> Mr. Holstein has nothing but words of praise to give to the Governor and other officers of the prison … for their kindness and consideration. He states that the cell … was of the ordinary kind with a large bag of straw to sleep on with a blanket. The W.C. … was of the usual Japanese box

53 "The Charge Against Mr Holstein: Resumed Hearing," 403.

54 "The Charge Against Mr Holstein: Speeches by Counsel for the Defense," 440.

55 James E. Hoare, *Japan's Treaty Ports and Foreign Settlements: The Uninvited Guests 1858–1899* (Kent: Japan Library, Curzon Press, 1994), 104.

56 "The Charge Against Mr Holstein: Result of the Preliminary Examination," 59.

57 "Leader 'The Judgment in the Holstein Case,'" *Japan Chronicle* (Kobe), 15 April 1915, 538.

> character, the cell had observation holes ... so no privacy ... the flooring ... was of wood with wide spaces ... [allowing] the rats to enter and run over his body, face, and hands while he was asleep. When the cold ... set in ... he contracted rheumatism and haemorrhoids when by the kindness of the Governor and the doctors ... he was removed to the hospital where there was heat ... His food, clothes, and linen ... were furnished from his house.[58]

Holstein Finally Acquitted

In November 1916, Holstein's appeal to the Osaka Appeal Court revealed that one of Nickel & Lyons's board members was trying to help Holstein.[59] The American director, John Happer, a close friend of Holstein's, may have been behind this: Happer had reportedly accompanied Holstein to the opening of the public trial in March 1915.[60] As the *Chronicle* reported, during the 1916 appeal, evidence and exhibits already presented were reconsidered. It also reported that the defence applied for new witnesses with only one accepted, Ebisugi, a former Kobe policeman Nickel & Lyons had employed to investigate the matter. Ebisugi testified that the case was the "outcome of newspaper agitation" as the *Kobe Shimbun* had entertained Tsukamura.[61] According to the *Chronicle*, the Appeal Court ignored Ebisugi's evidence accepting the Kobe Lower Court's charge of kidnapping and restated the three-year prison sentence.[62]

In 1921 Christian Holstein was finally acquitted of the charges. He lodged a second appeal to the Court of Cassation in Tokyo. The judge quashed the verdict and sentence of the lower courts, referring the case to the Hiroshima Court for a retrial.[63] The *Chronicle* suggested that a retrial in the Hiroshima Court was advised because "a less commercial atmosphere prevails [there]."[64] In April 1921, more than six years after Holstein's initial arrest and two and

58 Report No. 432 and Encl. No. 1 written by Mr. George Guthrie, American Ambassador, American Embassy, 16 January 1916. R/901 23376 BArch.

59 "The Swineherd Kidnapping Case: Date of Appeal Proceedings," *Japan Chronicle* (Kobe), 26 October 1916, 667.

60 "The Charge Against Mr Holstein: Opening of the Public Trial," 318.

61 "Law Reports: Kidnapping a Swineherd. The Charge Against Mr Holstein," *Japan Chronicle* (Kobe), 7 December 1916, 897.

62 "The Alleged Kidnapping of a Swineherd," *Japan Chronicle* (Kobe), 26 July 1917, 147.

63 "The Alleged Kidnapping of a Swineherd," 147; "The Swineherd Case (Kobe)," *Japan Chronicle* (Kobe), 2 January 1919, 21.

64 "A Bogus Kidnapping Case: An Old Wrong Righted," 550.

a half years since the end of war, the Hiroshima court finally acquitted Holstein of the charges, stating there was no evidence Holstein knew about the change in the *Mark*'s destination or had any intention to kidnap the swineherd.[65] Passing judgement on the Japanese courts as a whole, the *Japan Chronicle* stated: "the charge ... was a preposterous one ... Happily the Courts are incorruptible, but they are less strong on law evidence and equity."[66]

While court cases in Japan could take several years, in this instance, the war and the complex diplomatic representation for German citizens in Japan increased the time taken. As the American Embassy initially represented German nationals until 1917, and then the Swiss Embassy, it took months for representations to the various government bodies to be made and replies received. For example, when Holstein's retrial commenced in Hiroshima, the Hiroshima Court demanded that the former captain of the *Mark*, Captain Ernst Loewe, and the former Assistant Naval Attaché, Frigate Captain Fritz Blomeyer, appear in court. Holstein wrote to the Swiss Ambassador on 21 August 1919 asking him to pass on the request to the relevant authorities in Berlin, which had to go via the Ambassador's ministry in Berne. As Loewe and Blomeyer were both retired living in Germany and were reluctant to return to Japan in case they faced retrospective charges, their request for immunity from prosecution had to be conveyed to the Japanese Ministry for Foreign Affairs (*Gaimushō*) via Berlin, Berne, and the embassy in Tokyo.[67] Some six months later, Viscount Yasuya Uchida, the Japanese Minister for Foreign Affairs, replied to the Swiss Chargé d'Affaires in Tokyo saying he could not guarantee them immunity due to the "impossibility of predicting the result of having these two witnesses before the court and how their depositions would be received."[68]

Records held in the *Bundesarchiv* also revealed that Holstein was convinced that the British Ambassador was behind the Japanese authorities' pursuit of him through the courts. On 31 January 1918, Holstein's sister, Christina Schwanck, wrote to the former Naval Attaché, Wolfram von Knorr, seeking his help to save her brother from imprisonment. Schwanck noted that when her brother lost his appeal, he was convinced that "the English Ambassador had been behind the whole court case" and that he believed the British Embassy was colluding with the Japanese government to

65 "Kidnapping a Swineherd: Retrial at Hiroshima. Tsukamura v. Holstein. Acquittal," *Japan Chronicle* (Kobe), 21 April 1921, 550.

66 "A Bogus Kidnapping Case: An Old Wrong Righted," 550.

67 Letter from Christian Holstein to the Swiss Ambassador, 21 August 1919. R/901 23376, BArch.

68 No. 38, Letter (in French) from Viscount Yasuya Uchida, Minister of Foreign Affairs to Dr John L. Gignoux, Charge d'Affaires, Swiss Embassy, 6 February 1920, R85991, PA AA.

"cripple" him commercially.[69] As detailed in chapter 9, the British Embassy campaigned to end British-German commercial partnerships and have Germans deported, so Holstein's belief may not have been outlandish. Schwank furthermore expressed the view that:

> This [Case] is without doubt about an intentional *Justizmord* [judicial murder]. Through the person of my brother, they [presumably the Japanese and British governments] want to punish the German government and cripple German shipping for the post-war period, something the English Ambassador had energetically worked for.[70]

Holstein's Fight Continues

For the *Japan Chronicle*, the Swineherd Case served an additional purpose: to stress to its readership that foreign merchants were not "fly-by-nighters" but were committed to Japan over the longer-term. First, Holstein spoke "proficient" Japanese.[71] Second, according to the *Japan Chronicle*, Holstein could have left Japan at any time had he so wished. The *Japan Chronicle* suggested:

> opportunities were almost thrust in [Holstein's] way of leaving the country which would have been highly satisfactory to the interest which had worked up the case. But he considered that he had been wronged and paid the Japanese Courts the compliment of believing that though it was a time of war, they would not endorse this wrong.[72]

Holstein's life was in Japan along with all he had worked for.[73] In a statement defending himself in the face of less than rigorous evidence, Holstein appealed to the court's sense of fair play saying:

69 Letter written by Christina Schwanck (sister of Christian Holstein) to Corvette Captain, v. Knorr, former Naval Attaché, German Embassy in Tokyo, 31 January 1918. R/901 23376, BArch (hereafter Letter written by Christina Schwanck to Corvette Captain, v. Knorr).

70 Letter written by Christina Schwanck to Corvette Captain, v. Knorr. *Justizmord* refers to the murder of an innocent person. In this case, a sentence of three years in the unsanitary conditions of a Japanese jail was considered by the foreign community to be a death sentence for foreigners.

71 "The Charge Against Mr Holstein. Opening of the Public Trial," 318.

72 "A Bogus Kidnapping Case: An Old Wrong Righted," 550.

73 "A Bogus Kidnapping Case: An Old Wrong Righted," 550.

> [I] am a permanent resident; I am not like a man who comes to the country temporarily ... to commit a breach of the law and then disappear. The firm ... employs 2000 men who earned their living through me ... Is it likely that I would jeopardise my standing, my position, and 20 years of strenuous work in such an absurd manner [as to kidnap a Japanese swineherd]?[74]

Holstein's impassioned speech serves to emphasize that the Swineherd Kidnapping Case represented for him the greatest challenge he had had to face in doing business in the wake of the Meiji Era and First World War. Caught up in a confluence of competing interests, he had to fight a Japanese judiciary potentially influenced not just by Japanese commercial interests but also by a British Embassy wanting to remove German commercial influence from Japan.

As Holstein was fighting for his acquittal in Hiroshima, he suffered two more blows. In addition to the health issues he developed in jail, he suffered a bad fall and broke his leg. The *Japan Chronicle*, demonstrating its ongoing sympathy for Holstein, noted that this accident occurred while Holstein had been fitting out ships for the repatriation of German prisoners of war taken at the fall of Tsingtao in November 1914, and other "former enemy subjects" wishing to return to their homelands.[75]

Another blow, and one that would once more tax Holstein's energies, was the confiscation of German properties by the Japanese government. In the midst of rumours that the Allied powers were preparing "to confiscate all German property, official and private as part payment of the indemnities Germany is called upon to pay," the *Japan Chronicle* reported that in June 1919 the Japanese government issued an Imperial Ordinance, the Enemy Property Control Act, confiscating German private property in Japan.[76] This decision ran counter to Count Okuma's assurances at the outset of war that German interests would be protected. With a sense of injustice, the *Japan Chronicle* stated:

> [Even though] Peace is supposed to have been restored between Germany and Japan ... and Germans ... informed that they were at liberty to start business again it has been decided [by the Japanese government] to sell

74 "The Charge Against Mr Holstein: Speeches by Counsel for Defense," 440.

75 "Local and General," *Japan Chronicle* (Kobe), 19 February 1920, 208.

76 "German Property in Japan: Rumoured Proposal for Confiscation," *Japan Chronicle* (Kobe), 5 June 1919, 863; "Enemy Property in Japan: Imperial Ordinance Issued," *Japan Chronicle* (Kobe), 3 July 1919, 15.

> them up. All lands and houses are to be sold … and the value is to be placed on credit of the new owners but without any power … to handle it. It is a part of a 'provisional confiscation' to become permanent in case of Germany's failure to fulfil the conditions of the Treaty.[77]

Trying to forestall the Japanese government auctioning off his and his compatriots' property, Holstein represented the Kobe German community's interests, becoming a source of frustration for the German Ambassador, Wilhelm Solf, as the latter recently arrived in Japan, negotiated terms with the Japanese government. A report written by Solf to the Foreign Ministry in Berlin referred to how, on the matter of liquidation of German properties, the German communities in Tokyo and Yokohama had left it to the judgement of the German Embassy in dealing with the Japanese government.[78] Working with the Kobe Committee, however, had been another matter. Solf had received the Kobe Committee's report and recommendations written up by Holstein from a meeting held on 22 November 1920.[79] The report accused Solf of accepting the Japanese government's Enemy Property Control Act as "*fait accompli*" instead of calling for the Act's repeal and for the honouring of Count Okuma's original decree protecting Germans during the First World War. Solf reported to Berlin, amongst several highly uncomplimentary references to Holstein, that Holstein's approach was like a "bull at a gate" and that Holstein claimed a "greater knowledge of jurisprudence and international law" than the civil servants of the German Embassy who, as Solf wrote, Holstein regarded as being "backward" and "incompetent." Solf had been sent to Japan to rebuild the German-Japan relationship. He may have prioritized this task over preventing the sale of German property, angering Holstein who had a greater sense of personal urgency, not to mention strong ideas about how his twenty-four years' experience in Japan had taught him to deal with Japanese officials.[80]

Adding to the frustration of the German community, the Japanese government not only sold the German properties but sold them at below market rates. A report from the Foreign Ministry in Berlin to the Asian-based

77 "Notes and Comments," *Japan Chronicle* (Kobe), 11 December 1919, 880.

78 Letter from Solf to the Foreign Ministry, Berlin, 30 November 1920. (My translation). Liquidationsmaβnahmen deutschen Eigentums, 1920–21, R266.948, PA AA (hereafter Letter from Solf to Foreign Ministry, 30 November 1920.)

79 Protokoll der Versammlung der Deutschen des Kobe-Distrikts, am Montag, den 22 November 1920, Abends 5 Uhr im Deutsches Konsulat Kobe. 25 November 1920. Liquidationsmaβnahmen deutschen Eigentums, 1920–21, R266.948, PA AA.

80 Letter from Solf to German Foreign Ministry, 30 November 1920. (My translation).

embassies referred to the German Foreign Minister Dr von Simons' announcement, via Reuters, that the British government had waived its rights to confiscate German private property, as had other powers including Japan.[81] The report also drew attention to the *Japan Chronicle*'s article in November 1920, which protested that properties had been sold while negotiations for the Allies including Japan had been taking place. The article also stated that the properties had been sold at below market values, and that "in some cases the victims of the sale of their property are still waiting for the half of the proceeds promised." Furthermore, the Japanese government had made "no announcement ... of any amelioration of the conditions" for German merchants.[82]

In the *Chronicle*'s view, the decision to sell German-held properties (a mix of properties held under perpetual lease, rights of superficies or leased from Japanese landlords) was anti-foreign on several counts. First, it set a precedent, "if this can be done in the case of German [held] property, it can be done and will be done ... to the property of other foreigners" including Japanese.[83] Second, in forcing the sale of German property, Japanese companies benefited from acquiring German property at below market value.[84] Third, when it became evident that the Japanese government would confiscate German-held property, the Japanese government denied British merchants the right to participate in the sale, stating that perpetual lease property, the bulk of property held by Germans in the former Foreign Settlement, "will not be sold to foreigners." As foreigners still did not have the right to purchase property outright in Japan, the Japanese government's action suggests that part of its motivation in confiscating German property was to recover more of the property acquired on a perpetual basis out of foreigners' hands.[85]

While Holstein lost his property holdings, he also lost is position as managing director, although it is not clear exactly when or how his employment with Nickel & Lyons was terminated. In a letter written in 1967 to Harold Williams, an Australian historian and long-time resident of Kobe, David Henry James recounted the role he played when sometime prior to

81 Cover letter from the German Embassy, Tokyo to the German Foreign Ministry, 19 February 1921, Liquidationsmaßnahmen deutschen Eigentums, 1920–21, R266.948, PA AA. (My translation).

82 "Notes of the Week," *Japan Chronicle* (Kobe), 11 November 1920, 649.

83 "The Confiscation of Private Property," *Japan Chronicle* (Kobe), 28 October 1920, 583.

84 "German Property in Japan. Rumoured Proposal for Confiscation," 863.

85 "Enemy Property in Japan: Security for Payment of Indemnity," *Japan Chronicle* (Kobe), 5 February 1920, 162.

November 1922, Christian Holstein claimed back pay and contract fees from Nickel & Lyons. The English born David James was a highly respected member of the British business community in Kobe and had come from the well-known James family which had been established in Kobe since 1883 by his father, a ship's captain who initially worked for Nippon Yusen Kaisha.[86] His brother, James Frederick James, joined Nickel & Lyons in 1913 and later became its managing director. While the nature of the termination of Holstein's employment is not clear, most likely he was terminated when he was initially found guilty of the kidnapping by the court in April 1915. As revealed in the lists of German property confiscated by the Japanese in 1920, Holstein had been allowed to retain his shareholding in Nickel & Lyons.[87] Nickel & Lyons agreed to arbitration, which appears to have been privately arranged, appointing David James as its representative. Holstein appointed Robert Young, the owner of the *Japan Chronicle* to act on his behalf. Young unexpectedly died in November that year, but according to David James, instead of appointing another representative Holstein deferred to James' judgement. James "ruled against Nickel & Lyons on legal and moral grounds," ordering them to pay Holstein ¥45,000 (¥73,454,898 or £384,712).[88] James wrote he had refused fees from either side, but, in an apparent gesture of post-war reconciliation had "asked Holstein to bring the German community back where it belonged and support the [International] hospital etc. which he did." James reflected in his letter to Harold Williams that he believed that the management of Nickel & Lyons had assumed that as he (James) had been severely wounded by the "Huns" during the war, he would "hate all Germans and see things from Nickel & Lyons patriotic point of view."[89] It was clear that an anti-German sentiment still lingered amongst some within Nickel & Lyons for some time after the war.

This chapter focused on a sequence of events and resulting court cases occurring over a seven-year period from October 1914 until April 1921,

86 Bernd Lepach, Meiji Portraits, http://meiji-portraits.de/meiji_portraits_j.html#20090527093346125_1_2_3_5_1, 2024.

87 "Leader: The Judgement in the Holstein Case," *Japan Chronicle* (Kobe), 15 April 1915, 538–39; Control of Special Properties. Translation from "Official [Japanese] Gazette," 11 November 1919. Liquidationsmaßnahmen deutschen Eigentums in Japan, March 1920–Oktober 1920, R265.002, PA AA, 4.

88 Yen conversions to 2019 values and others in this chapter are based on the website: https://yaruzou.net/hprice/hprice-calc.html. Conversion to British pounds was conducted on 14 April 2024.

89 Letter written by David Henry James, 16 August 1967, Papers of Harold Williams, Persons and Firms Series 3, folder 23, Harold Williams Collection, National Library of Australia (henceforth HWC NLA).

where Holstein fought charges of kidnapping a Japanese swineherd which threatened to destroy him, his right to remain in Japan and retain all he had worked for. Holstein demonstrated his commitment to remaining in Japan, going to great lengths fighting a Japanese court system potentially subject to vested interests relying on less than rigorous evidence.

Despite Holstein finally being acquitted, he endured further indignities in having his land confiscated and sold at below market prices. With his termination from Nickel & Lyons, his and his cousin's contribution to the company's success had been erased. Moreover, Nickel's desire to secure the protection of the British power base through the Anglo-Japanese Alliance ultimately worked against the interests of the company's German management and German interests. Examining Holstein's experiences has also shown how the British declaration of economic war against German merchants from the outset of the First World War and objectives of destroying German merchants well into the post-war period, erased the German contribution to the success of the Port of Kobe from historical records of the foreign community. However, the British government failed to eliminate German merchants entirely from Japan post-war in the way it intended as those who stayed during the war rebuilt their businesses once the war ended and a new generation of German merchants arrived in Kobe to establish new businesses.

While this work takes 1923 as its end point to cover the aftermath of World War One and its effect on Christian Holstein's life to that point, he went on to establish a new company as an import agent until his death in 1954, ensuring the family remained in Japan into the third generation for 140 years. Finally, this chapter shows that while pockets of anti-German sentiment persisted after the end of the war, there were members of the British community who worked to achieve a reconciliation between the British and German communities, echoing Robert Young's desire to see a cohesive foreign community continue to advocate for its interests with the Japanese authorities it believed still remained ambivalent to the presence of foreigners.

Conclusions

Examining the lives of German merchants, Carl Nickel and Christian Holstein and their company, C. Nickel & Co. Ltd., from 1860 until 1923 offers insights into how they as foreign merchants and as German merchants operated in treaty port Japan under extraterritorial privileges and then under Japanese jurisdiction. All foreign merchants contended with what they believed to be an obstructive Japanese government, unhappy with having the unequal treaties forced upon it. As German merchants, Nickel and Holstein faced additional challenges. They operated in a British dominated port where for forty years, German and British business became closely intertwined because British companies valued their German partners' entrepreneurial business skills and transnational networks. However, in the lead up to World War One as Britain feared losing its commercial and naval supremacy to a rising German Empire, an anti-German feeling grew amongst certain British people and with the onset of war, those German-British partnerships were forced to end. Histories have been written on treaty ports in Japan from 1858 until 1899 largely from a British perspective, providing a generalized diplomatic and cultural perspective rather than the day-to-day conduct of business from a merchant's point of view. Such histories have only cursorily mentioned merchants of non-British nationalities and the interdependencies between them. To understand how Nickel and Holstein dealt with the day-to-day commercial challenges over a sixty-three-year time span, the *Japan Chronicle*'s reportage becomes a valuable source. British and German diplomatic records plus third person accounts from Japanese, German, and British archival sources provide additional material. In the following I draw general conclusions around the presence of German merchants in China and Japan and the British influence in those treaty-ports and then draw specific conclusions around how Nickel and Holstein coped with the challenges of conducting business in Japan during this period working with their British partners.

Holstein, Prue S. *The German Experience of Japan's Treaty Port System: A Case Study of C. Nickel & Co. Ltd., 1860–1923*. Taylor & Francis Group, 2025.
DOI: 10.4324/9781003706274-12

A Time of Empire and the German Diaspora

Nickel and Holstein were a part of the German diaspora in northeast Asia. Commencing in the late 1600s, the movement of Germans overseas accelerated in the mid-nineteenth century around Britain's network of colonies and treaty ports in China.[1] From Japan's re-opening to the West in 1854 and the signing of the unequal treaties from 1858, Germans already on the China coast joined their British colleagues settling in the early treaty ports opened in Japan, Kanagawa, later becoming Yokohama and in Nagasaki.[2] While the foreign powers led by the British ruled over Chinese treaty ports informally for one hundred years, cooperating with or coercing the Chinese leadership, in Kobe they only governed the Foreign Settlement for forty years until 1899 when Japan regained judicial control over foreigners. Whereas the British had an informal imperial influence in China and business flourished, they had no such power in Japan. Despite regularly protesting breaches of the treaties at diplomatic levels, they failed to ensure an unfettered business environment for foreign merchants. While extraterritorial protections afforded foreign merchants some advantages operating outside Japanese jurisdiction until 1899, they had to deal with the many ways the Japanese found to obstruct and thwart their efforts even after extraterritoriality ended. The *Japan Chronicle*'s many campaigns protesting Japanese obstructionism over two decades attest to the British diplomats' failure under the unequal treaties and then under the revised treaties.

Arriving in Treaty Ports of Shanghai and Kobe

Nickel arrived in Shanghai China about 1859, illegally prior to the signing of the Prussia-China treaty in 1861. Indications are he was a ship's captain and was able to evade border controls. In Shanghai, he experienced what it meant to have extraterritorial privileges and a cooperative relationship between the British and the Chinese leadership. He then arrived in Japan

1 John R. Davis, Margrit Schulte Beerbühl and Stefan Manz, "Introduction: Germans in the British Empire," in *Transnational Networks: German Migrants in the British Empire, 1670–1914*, eds. John R. Davis, Stefan Manz, Margrit Schulte Beerbühl (Leiden–Boston: Brill, 2012), 1–17.

2 Jürgen Osterhammel, "British Business in China, 1860s–1950s," in *British Business in Asia Since 1860*, eds. Richard P. T. Davenport-Hines and Geoffrey Jones (Cambridge: Cambridge University Press, 1989), 191.
James E. Hoare, *Japan's Treaty Ports and Foreign Settlements: The Uninvited Guests 1858–1899* (Kent: Japan Library, Curzon Press, 1994), 56.

in 1860 also illegally. He falsely claimed American protection until he could claim Prussian citizenship when the Prussia-Japan treaty was ratified in 1863. Utilizing his transnational connections—German, American, British and Japanese—he built a waterfront empire in Kobe from 1880 in the stevedore and cargo handling business taking advantage of extraterritoriality as well as deploying entrepreneurial and transnational skills. Based on his Shanghai experience, he most likely expected that the British would protect the rights of foreign merchants in Japan.

Treaty ports in China and Japan varied significantly in size and make-up of the foreign community. Shanghai and Kobe had a close relationship, both were considered model treaty ports and both had significant German populations. There were significant differences in the levels of British influence over the respective host governments however. In Shanghai, the British dominated the management of the International Concession, based not on its numbers—the Chinese living in the Concession outnumbered the British—but based on its wealth.[3] Moreover, the British forged a cooperative and arguably coercive relationship with the Chinese leadership best seen in the establishment of the Imperial Maritime Customs Service, a joint British Chinese initiative staffed by foreigners which provided ideal conditions for foreign merchants conducting business, collecting customs duties, and managing the harbour.[4] In contrast, in Kobe, while the British dominated the Foreign Settlement in numbers (there were no Japanese living in the Settlement), management of the Settlement was shared between the foreign powers including the Germans, the second most numerous, the French, Americans, Dutch and others, and German influence was strong. Outside the management of the Foreign Settlement, the British in Kobe had little to no influence over the Japanese government or the management of authorities such as the Kobe Harbour Authority or the Japanese Customs House which were both Japanese controlled.

The twenty-two-year-old Christian Holstein arrived in Kobe in 1897 to become Nickel's successor. He arrived just as the port was transitioning from consular jurisdiction and extraterritoriality to foreigners having to submit to the Japanese courts. This was a time of confusion over jurisdiction, with Japanese officials' oversight of Japanese laws ranging from lax to over-zealous

3 Isabella Jackson, "Who Ran the Treaty Ports? A Study of the Shanghai Municipal Council," in *Treaty Ports in Modern China: Law, Land and Power*, eds. Robert A. Bickers and Isabella Jackson (Milton Park, Abingdon, Oxon; Routledge, 2016), 43–47.

4 Jürgen Osterhammel, "Britain and China, 1942–1914," in *The Oxford History of the British Empire, Volume III: The Nineteenth Century*, eds. Andrew Porter and William Roger Louis (Oxford: Oxford University Press, 1999), 156–57.

and foreign merchants taking advantage of the many gaps and loopholes emerging in the Japanese legal processes.

British-German Collaborations

The growing intertwinement of the British and German economies occurring in Europe over decades was also reflected in the close intertwinement of German and British business interests in treaty port China and the British colony of Hong Kong and extended to treaty port Japan until 1914.[5] While little is known about the nature of German-British collaborations in Shanghai, the German presence was significant.[6] Such collaborations in Hong Kong have been documented and in Kobe, from the opening of the port in 1868, records show many British companies partnered with their German counterparts. British merchants valued German business skills, entrepreneurialism, risk-taking and transnational networks, not to mention generous lines of credit and a willingness to adapt to Japanese market needs. Such a close intertwinement continued successfully in Kobe from 1858–1914 when war broke out.

Extraterritoriality vs Entrepreneurialism and Transnational Connections

Findings and conclusions of this section are grouped into the following key areas. First, this work confirms that while extraterritorial privileges from 1858 to 1899 gave Nickel and Holstein advantages over their Japanese competition, their entrepreneurialism, innovativeness, risk-taking and transnational networks were key to their success. Taking advantage of extraterritorial privileges, Nickel ignored Japanese authorities' directives that constrained his Japanese competitors and exploited his unskilled Japanese labour while they had no right of recourse through the Japanese courts. However, Nickel's innovativeness, entrepreneurialism and transnational connections also proved significant. He consolidated a fragmented

5 Davis, Schulte Beerbühl and Manz, "Introduction: Germans in the British Empire," 1–17; John McDermott, "'A Needless Sacrifice': British Businessmen and Business as Usual in the First World War," *Albion: A Quarterly Journal Concerned with British Studies* 21, no. 2 (Summer 1989): 263, https://doi.org/10.2307/4049929.

6 Stefan Manz, *Constructing a German Diaspora: The "Greater German Empire," 1871–1914* (New York, London: Routledge, 2017), 39, 40–41.

cargo carrying industry, establishing a company that offered a full-line service including cargo loading and unloading, freight forwarding, customs clearance and delivery to the customer, a ship's towing service, and ship's chandlery. He employed a multinational workforce leveraging their linkages with potential clients. He also employed at short notice up to 2,000 to 3,000 unskilled Japanese and Chinese day labourers as stevedores a day on low rates of pay. He capitalized on the congestion of the Kobe Harbour and its lack of infrastructure by entering the salvaging and ship's repair businesses. Holstein continued Nickel's legacy building C. Nickel & Co. Ltd. (becoming Nickel & Lyons in 1913), into a company of over 2,000 regular employees, a large fleet of vessels and with branch offices from Moji in the west to Yokohama in the east. Having regained its sovereignty in 1899, the Japanese required that foreigners submit to the Japanese courts. Nickel and Holstein embraced the Japanese courts, litigating commercial disputes against foreign and Japanese alike. They exploited loopholes and gaps in Japanese legal processes and the court system through adopting a wide range of tactics of denial of prior knowledge and of liability, changing ownership of vessels or property, or prolonging cases at great cost to their litigants but not always with successful outcomes. In short, from 1880–1914, Nickel and Holstein's success was not just due to extraterritorial privileges, but also due to their entrepreneurial skills, transnational connections and risk tolerance taking advantage of emerging business opportunities and their ability to exploit loopholes in the Japanese court system.

Second, Nickel and Holstein sought to manage the various Japanese authorities and the opaque laws and regulations and lax oversights, not to mention a perceived anti-foreign sentiment, by ignoring, avoiding, evading, or subverting the restrictions presented by those authorities in their conduct of business. Such authorities included the Japanese government and the various ministries and local gubernatorial authorities, the Kobe Harbour and Kobe Customs authorities, the various port authorities along the Inland Sea and the Japanese courts, amongst no doubt others. Until the end of the Shimonoseki Campaign, all foreigners relied upon British diplomats and the British navy to protect the foreign community against anti-foreign samurai. Once peace reigned from 1868 until 1899, Nickel dealt with the authorities himself setting his own policies. He falsely claimed American protection to remain in Japan. He ignored Japanese officials' directives in the Kobe Harbour and subverted the Japanese ban on foreigners owning property. After 1899 and the loss of extraterritoriality, Japanese authorities developed laws circumventing the revised treaties further restricting foreigners in their business operations. While foreigners could now enter the interior to deal directly with Japanese suppliers, the Japanese government enacted the Shipping Law banning foreign companies from coastal trading. Based on lax oversight of the Japanese authorities, Nickel continued operating his tugboats outside the harbour until the Japanese tightened oversight two years later and he suffered the consequences. While foreigners were still banned from owning land in Japan, a ban that was only lifted in 1926/1927, Nickel and Holstein acquired large portfolios of commercial and private property, adopting a practice the British frowned upon, taking a right of superficies over the property leasing it back for 900 to 1,000 years. When the Japanese government restricted the storage of foreign explosives in Osaka, Holstein secured an agreement from the Kobe Harbour Authority on retrofitting a hulk to store those explosives on the Kobe Harbour and on the distance, it was moored from shore. However, due to administrative looseness on the company's part, the company suffered devastating consequences from a massive explosion that occurred. Nickel and Holstein both learnt they could sometimes get away with ignoring, subverting or circumventing such restrictions and sometimes not. And, knowing that the Japanese court system was full of deficiencies and loopholes, they took their chances litigating their rights exploiting those loopholes often regardless of cost.

Third, this work shows that a significant part of the success of C. Nickel & Co. Ltd was due to Nickel and Holstein leveraging their multinational connections as members of an influential German community collaborating with their British colleagues. The size, wealth and influence of the German community from the opening of the Port of Kobe was substantial and German-British business interests became closely intertwined. Nickel demonstrated his transnational abilities. His close friends and contacts—the German born American colleague in Nagasaki, Gustav Wilckens; the American David Tillson, both of whom he met in Nagasaki but who relocated to Kobe; his German colleague, Julius Helm, whom he had met in Yokohama; and his one-time employee becoming a junior partner, the British Jew, Jacob Lyons—were all a part of his valuable transnational networks. In the early 1900s, Nickel then acquired two competitor Hong Kong Chinese stevedoring companies. The staffing of his company included German, British, Danish, Dutch, Dutch Burgher, Japanese and Chinese amongst no doubt other nationalities. In 1902, Nickel took advantage of the Anglo-Japanese Alliance by taking his company public and registering it in Hong Kong as a British company. He appointed to his board British, German, an Australian and an American—all business leaders and men of influence in Kobe, guaranteeing not only the capital required but also access to informal British power structures to replace extraterritorial protections forfeited in 1899.

Holstein had an equally extensive network of British, American, German and Japanese connections who not only helped him further his company's ambitions but also helped him build his new business after World War One.

World War One

With the arrival in 1897 of his relative and successor, Christian Holstein, Nickel hoped the company's continuing German legacy would be assured. As soon as war was declared on Germany, the British government waged economic war on German merchants in Japan. Having no jurisdiction in Japan, it could only urge its Japanese allies to deport Germans and confiscate their assets. It had not realized that Japan had a history of protecting residents of belligerent nations unless they broke the law. While the British government had jurisdiction over British companies in Britain and could force them to end their German partnerships, it had no jurisdiction over British companies in Japan which were registered as Japanese companies. Many of those companies valued their German connections and ignored British directives. It was only when the British government published the Statutory List also known as the Blacklist in 1916, banning any company from business dealings in Britain if they were caught dealing with a German company, that it succeeded in ending German business. The British government did successfully enlist the support of some British business leaders in Japan with anti-German sentiments, some members of the Nickel & Lyons Board included. Despite being registered as a Japanese entity and having no legal obligation to do so, it complied with the British Embassy's wishes terminating the employment of its German management, thus ending the company's German legacy. The German staff took the directors to court, but due to what appeared to be undue influence over the Japanese court from vested interests, all failed in their quest for compensation except one former employee, Sillius, who won compensation in what seemed to be a behind-the-scenes arrangement of quid pro quo.

The fate of Christian Holstein was also tied to the Board's desire to eliminate the company's German legacy. Caught up amidst competing interests, Holstein was charged and tried for kidnapping a Japanese swineherd in a case lasting six years until 1921. Evidence suggested charges were fomented by either or both Japanese business interests and the British embassy colluding with the British dominated board of Nickel & Lyons, but this is not altogether clear. Tying this German businessman in endless court cases for six years led to the end of Holstein's ties to Nickel & Lyons. Holstein's persistence in proving his innocence and ultimately being acquitted demonstrated his long-term commitment to Japan and his right to remain and retain all he had worked for. This was not the end of his troubles. Despite assurances the Japanese government would protect Germans, it confiscated all German property (contrary to the actions of the Allies) including Holstein's ostensibly as a guarantee against Germany not fulfilling its reparations obligations at the end of the First World War. It was more likely a ruse for regaining land leased in perpetuity by foreigners, in this case Germans either as a perpetual leasehold or under a right of superficies, an objective long held by the Japanese government. While many but not all German merchants left Japan after the First World War, Holstein remained in Japan. Some years after the War, Holstein enlisted the support of one of his many British connections, David James, to secure reparations from Nickel & Lyons, and in a gesture of reconciliation, Holstein brought the German community back as members of the foreign community in the financial support of such institutions as the International Hospital. From the early 1920s onwards in a post-war environment, the German community gradually re-joined the wider foreign community in support of mutual interests advocating for the community's interests with the Japanese government.

In that sense, this study traced the rise of two German merchants in Japan, and the company they built, over the decades of Japan's modernization and then the fall of German influence in the company as war broke out. In the absence of company archives, this story has been recreated from a variety of sources, not least the reportage of the British owned *Japan Chronicle*. The *Chronicle* aimed to show its foreign merchant readership where their interests were not being well served by the Japanese authorities through reporting on the many court cases and other incidents in which Nickel and Holstein and their company were involved. It also sought to influence its elite Japanese readership in the hope of effecting improvements in the Japanese court system for foreigners. Harold Williams opined that while the *Chronicle* "served the foreign community faithfully," its editor, Robert Young, could engender the ire of its Japanese readership for his "constant criticism of the Japanese."[7] Nevertheless, despite the *Chronicle*'s bias, it has helped in the reconstruction of a story for which only disparate traces remain in archives.

This research first reinscribes in the history of the treaty ports in Japan the role played by some German merchants in the development of international

7 Harold S. Williams, "Foreign Owned English Newspapers in Kobe: Shades of the Past," *Mainichi Daily News*, 21 February 1981. Extract found in file on Kobe Newspapers & Journals, Folder 80, HWC NLA.

trade in Kobe otherwise lost when many German merchants left Japan after World War One. It also provides an indication of the many long-standing German-British partnerships and collaborations that existed prior to the First World War, which remain undocumented by either the British or the German consular authorities. Through being forced by the British government to dissolve their partnerships, such British companies lost their business to Japanese and American competitors.

Second, this research coincides with and contributes to a resurgence of interest in German-Japan relations and the respect Japanese elites and authorities developed for German institutions and its national character. The desire for Japanese to emulate German success over the decades was due to the influence of the many German experts or *yatoi*, employed by the Japanese government and German professors employed by the university sector, to build systems and institutions across the military, law, education Japanese Constitutional Monarchy and even court practices.[8] German merchants such as Carl Nickel and Christian Holstein, through the companies they built, their innovativeness and risk-taking, the wealth they created and the extent to which they worked directly with their Japanese employees, clients and colleagues, also influenced the Japanese elites favourably towards German culture and institutions. After Japan's defeat in 1945, the American Occupation Forces regarding Germany as the birthplace of militarism and fascism, sought to eliminate what they saw as the Prussian influences in Japan's military, legal systems and government.[9] The German legacy is however now being viewed in broader terms as a significant contribution to Japan's modernization through scientific, medical, pharmaceutical, educational, philosophical, musical and other fields of academia.

Third, this study contributes to the growing field of the study of German colonialism both formal and informal, and how the German colonial period contributed to globalization through transnational and intercultural processes. As an example, *German Colonialism Revisited: African, Asian and Oceanic Experiences* brings together works from a range of military and art historians, literary scholars, cultural theorists and linguists to examine the

8 Bernd Martin and Peter Wetzler, "The German Role in the Modernization of Japan: The Pitfall of Blind Acculturation," *Oriens Extremus* 33, no. 1 (1990): 77–88; Hoi-eun Kim, "Made in Meiji Japan: German Expatriates, German-Educated Japanese Elites and the Construction of Germanness," Special issue, Rethinking Germans Abroad, *Geschichte und Gesellschaft* 41, no. 2 (April–June 2015): 288–320, https://doi.org/10.13109/gege.2015.41.2.288.

9 Miyake Masaki, "Japan's Encounter with Germany, 1860–1914: An Assessment of the German Legacy in Japan," *The European Legacy: Towards New Paradigms* 1 no. 1 (June 2008): 245–49, https://doi.org/10.1080/10848779608579402.

extent German colonialism was a shared experience in which both colonizers and colonized were changed.[10] Moreover, how Germans and Chinese perceived one another under Germany's colonization of colonial Tsingtao (Qingdao) on the Shantung Peninsula has become a focus. Despite Chinese expressions of indignation at the "national disgrace" of being colonized, a generally positive image amongst the Chinese of the legacy of German colonialism and its contribution to China's modernization has emerged.[11] While the presence in Japan of Germans, and British for that matter, could only be referred to as an informal and not a colonial presence, Japanese exposure to Germans in Japan contributed to a perception of many Japanese of a cultural compatibility, leading to Japan's adoption and adaptation of a range of German systems across military, legal, educational and other spheres.

This research also contributes to the study of German colonialism in northeast Asia. It shows how Nickel and Holstein leveraged their transnational relationships with British, German, other European and Japanese clients and employees in Japan. They also leveraged their networks across formal German colonies in the South Pacific and Tsingtao and the then British colony of Hong Kong as well as the informal "colonies" of the Chinese treaty ports of Shanghai amongst others, to build a company dominating the market for cargo handling. The role played by C. Nickel & Co. Ltd. and its successor Nickel & Lyons as the market leader led to aggressive activity of their Japanese and British colleagues in seeking to grab control of the company and in the British case oust the Germans.

During this research, questions were asked around the importance of investigating the topic of German merchants in Japan when foreign merchants, perceived as a generalized mass, had already been written about albeit from a limited perspective in Anglophone scholarship. Apart from the fact that no one has written about how foreign merchants did business day-to-day in Japan, there is a belief that the experiences of British merchants can teach us as much as we need to know about doing business in Japan in the Meiji period. Sensitivities were also raised about the roles played by Germans in Japan during both the First and the Second World Wars, as well as the roles they potentially played in those wars. This research

10 Nina Berman, Klaus Mühlhahn and Patrice Nganang, eds., *German Colonialism Revisited: African, Asian and Oceanic Experiences* (Ann Arbor: University of Michigan Press, 2014).

11 Yixu Lu, "Germany's War in China: Media Coverage and Political Myth," *German Life and Letters* 61, no. 2 (2008): 202–14, https://doi.org/10.1111/j.1468-0483.2008.00419.x; Yixu Lu, "Colonial Quingdao through Chinese Eyes," in *The Cultural Legacy of German Colonial Rule*, ed. Klaus Mühlhahn (Berlin: de Gruyter Oldenbourg, 2017), 127–42.

proves, however, that German merchants held the same goals that their Anglophile colleagues adhered to, namely, to make their fortunes rather than play a part in their country's national ambitions. German merchants became caught up inadvertently in political events that extended beyond their original purpose of being in Japan. How German merchants survived during the First World War teaches much about what can happen when a segment of the foreign community moved from being regarded as valued colleagues to suddenly becoming "enemy aliens" for a range of reasons. However, the ability of German merchants to readily accommodate Japanese market needs and build close transnational relationships, combined with their distance from the theatres of war and their desire to continue making money, ensured that not only their Japanese hosts protected them and their interests for the sake of future business but also so did many of their British friends.

The story of these two German merchants, pieced together from an array of fragments, shows the importance of considering continuities across time periods of great and complex change. Japan's modernization and entry into the international sphere is often presented as a series of discrete and momentous periods, dominated by diplomatic and political elites. Nickel, who was connected to but not a member of the establishment, and Holstein, who was a member of the establishment, lived through these periods, making day-to-day decisions against the broader sweep of major world events. Their lives and efforts also remind us to consider the treaty ports of Japan, and perhaps those elsewhere, in all their complexity, with different actors of different nationalities all managing challenges according to their own imperatives. Such an understanding of treaty port history provides a better sense of their colourful and complex nature. Finally, the history of these two merchants reminds us to consider more carefully these often-ignored individual actors. While merchants were certainly committed to making their fortunes, their ability to weather many obstacles in those turbulent times provides us with a richer understanding of history.

Finally, from the early 1920s onwards in a post-war environment, the German community gradually re-joined the wider foreign community in support of mutual interests. As Christian Holstein built his new business, his and his company's names appeared on the lists of funders and volunteers of Kanto Earthquake Relief Committee following the Kanto Earthquake in 1923 when the two communities came together to support the many foreigners based in Yokohama who relocated to Kobe.[12] Holstein's name also appeared as a key funder of the International Hospital.[13] And, reflecting the on-going bones of contention the *Japan Chronicle* and the foreign community had with the Japanese authorities even in 1926, he was invited to join a protest against the Japanese government's proposed Luxury Tariff Bill. The Luxury Tax was being placed on imported items such as soaps, clocks, tea and other products the community considered by the foreign community to be anything but luxury goods. A committee was appointed and Holstein, along with his British friend, the respected Dr J. E. de Becker, was asked to join as two of three "grey eminences" to help lobby the Japanese government.[14] Holstein's willingness to be included in such initiatives signalled not just his own rapid return to a measure of wealth, but also a resumption of collaborations between British and German merchants where the interests of the foreign community and its perceived need to continue representing its interests with the Japanese authorities was paramount.

12 "Relief Fund: Further Subscriptions," *Japan Chronicle* (Kobe), 20 September 1923, 420; "Earthquake Relief Committee (Foreign): Kobe, Japan," *Japan Chronicle* (Kobe), 4 December 1924, 764.

13 "International Hospital: Subscription List," *Japan Chronicle* (Kobe), 9 December 1926, 699.

14 "Foreign Community of Kobe: Public Meeting. Protest Against Tariff Proposals," *Japan Chronicle* (Kobe), 17 July 1924, 82; "Luxury Tariff: International Committee's Report," *Japan Chronicle* (Kobe), 23 October 1924, 568.

Bibliography

Records from Archives, Libraries and Museums

Australia

The National Library of Australia, Canberra.
Harold S. Williams Collection, HWC NLA

1083. HWC NLA: Despatches No. 13, 27 February 1861, January–June 1861, 87.
1083. HWC NLA: Despatches No. 16, 1 February 1860, January–June 1860, 43.
1083. HWC NLA: Despatches No. 19, 2 March 1861, January–June 1861, 89.
1083. HWC NLA: Despatches No. 5, 14 April 1863, January–July 1863, 144–45.
1083. HWC NLA: Despatches No. 5, 16 August 1859, June–December 1859, 11.
1083. HWC NLA: Despatches No. 5, 5 January 1861, January–June 1861, 82.
1083. HWC NLA: Despatches of HBM Consulate Nagasaki to Sir Rutherford Alcock, British Consul-General, Japan, June 1859–December 1863.

q1150/1716690. HWC NLA: *Treaties and Conventions Concluded between Japan and Foreign Nations: Together with Notifications and Regulations Made from Time to Time, 1854–1870: Notification: Arrangements for the Establishment of Foreign Settlements at the Port of Hiogo and of Osaka* (published by Sir Harry S. Parkes, Her Britannic Majesty's Envoy Extraordinary and Minister Plenipotentiary in Japan Osaka, 17 May 1867), 212–14.

HWC NLA: China Directory for 1862. Japan/Nagasaki, Hong Kong: Shortrede & Co. Germans are listed according to the country from which protection was obtained.

HWC NLA: The Chronicle and Directory for China, Japan, and the Philippines for 1865, *Japan Chronicle* (Kobe).

HWC NLA: The Chronicle & Directory for China, Japan & the Philippines 1872, The Hiogo (Kobe) Directory and The Nagasaki Directory. Kobe: Hong Kong Daily Press.

HWC NLA: Treaty between Great Britain and Japan. Signed at Yedo, 26 August 1858. Treaties and Conventions, Concluded between Japan and Foreign Nations 1854–1870, Yokohama: Daily Japan Herald Office 1871, 57–61.

Persons and Firms Series 3, folder 23. HWC NLA: Letter written by David Henry James, 16 August 1967, Papers of Harold Williams.

Subject Files Series 1 Folder 47. HWC NLA: German Community: Extract from *Geschichte des Club Concordia Festschrift zum 50 Jährigen Stiftungfest* 1879–1929, Papers of Harold Williams.

Germany

Bundesarchiv (National Archives of Germany) Lichterfelde,
Berlin (BArch)

R/901 23376 BArch. Letter No. 422 written by George Guthrie, American Ambassador to Secretary of State, Washington, DC, 20 January 1916.

R/901 23376 BArch. Report No. 432 and Encl. No. 1 written by Mr. George Guthrie, American Ambassador, American Embassy, 16 January 1916.

R/901 23376 BArch. Report No. 432 and Encl. No. 1 written by Mr. George Guthrie, American Ambassador, 20 January 1916.

R/901 23376, BArch. Letter from Christian Holstein to the Swiss Ambassador, 21 August 1919.

R/901 23376, BArch. Letter No. 422 written by Mr. George Guthrie, American Embassy, enclosing his Report No. 432 and Encl. No. 2 with letter written by Mrs C. Sillius (mother of Paul Sillius), 9 July 1915 (American Embassy translation).

R/901 23376, BArch. Letter written by Christina Schwanck (sister of Christian Holstein) to Corvette Captain, v. Knorr, former Naval Attaché, German Embassy in Tokyo, 31 January 1918.

Geheimes Staatsarchiv Preuβsicher Kulturbesitz (Prussian Secret State Archives)
Berlin

A review of Prussian, British and American diplomatic correspondence held in the *Geheimes Staatsarchiv Preuβsicher Kulturbesitz* (Prussian Secret State Archives) revealed no mention of Carl Nickel, suggesting he was outside the purview of the Prussian Consulate in Nagasaki.

Politischen Archiv des Auswärtigen Amts (German Foreign Ministry Archives), Berlin (PA AA)

R18613, PA AA. Allgemein Angelegenheiten Japans 1899–1904, vom 1 Oktober 1899 bis 31 Maerz 1904. "Perpetual Leases. Correspondence between the British Legation and the Japanese Foreign Office," including "Foreign Settlements in Japan: The Law Relating Thereto." Summary written by Sir E. Satow, HBM Envoy, 26 April 1899, 1–40.

R18613 PA AA. Allgemein Angelegenheiten Japans 1899–1904, vom 1 Oktober 1899 bis 31 Maerz 1904. "Perpetual Leases." Correspondence from Sir E. Satow, HBM Envoy and Minister to Japan to Viscount Aoki, Japanese Minister of Foreign Affairs, 8 December 1899, 8–9.

R85991, PA AA. Letter No. 38 (in French) from Viscount Yasuya Uchida, Minister of Foreign Affairs to Dr John L. Gignoux, Charge d'Affaires, Swiss Embassy, 6 February 1920.

R265.002, PA AA. Control of Special Property. Hyogo Prefecture. Translation from the Official Gazette (of the Japanese government), 7 November 1919–19 January 1920. Akten betreffend Beschlagsnahme deutschen Eigentums in Japan anlässlich des Weltkrieges—lists of assets of German merchants resident in Tokyo, Yokohama, Kobe and Osaka.

R265.002, PA AA. Akten betreffend Beschlagsnahme deutschen Eigentums in Japan anlässlich des Weltkrieges, Control of Special Property. Hyogo Prefecture, 10 November 1919.

R265.002, PA AA. Liquidationsmaβnahmen deutschen Eigentums in Japan, March 1920–Oktober 1920, Control of Special Properties.Translation from "Official [Japanese] Gazette, 11 November 1919, 4.

R266.948 PA AA. Liquidationsmaβnahmen deutschen Eigentums (Measures to Liquidate German Property) 1920–21. Cover letter from the German Embassy, Tokyo to the German Foreign Ministry, 19 February 1921.

R266.948, PA AA. Liquidationsmaβnahmen deutschen Eigentums, 1920–21. Letter from Solf to the Foreign Ministry, Berlin, 30 November 1920.

R266.948, PA AA. Liquidationsmaβnahmen deutschen Eigentums, 1920–21. Protokoll der Versammlung der Deutschen des Kobe-Distrikts, am Montag, den 22 November 1920, Abends 5 Uhr im Deutsches Konsulat Kobe, 25 November 1920.

Staatsarchiv Hamburg
Hamburg

BN 332-5, SA 8008 399 Staatsarchiv Stadt Hamburg. Death certificate Kate Emily Nickel died Hamburg 5 May 1911 (born: Law, widowed: Smith).

Staatsarchiv Stadt Hamburg. Address Book is accessed through the website of the at http://agora.sub.uni-hamburg.de/subhh-adress/digbib/view?did=c1:39310&sdid=c1:39349&hit=2. Updated 2021.

Niedersächsisches Landesarchiv,
Stade

Sig.: Rep.84 Nr. 97, Niedersachsen Landesarchiv Staatsarchiv, Stade. Birth Registration: Hinrich Holstein 1 October 1725.

Sig.: Rep.84 Nr. 98 Bl. 198 V, Niedersachsen Landesarchiv Staatsarchiv, Stade. Marriage Registration: Johann Christian Holstein 17 August 1792.

Film Number: 1189000, *Niedersächsisches Landesarchiv*, Stade. Marriage certificate for Johann Christian (II), 360.

Sig.: Rep.84 Nr. 99 Bl. 101 V, Niedersachsen Landesarchiv Staatsarchiv, Stade. Death Registration: Johann Christian Holstein 6 February 1811.

Japan

Kobe Public Archives (KPA)

Gaimu-sho Kiroku No. 223-23, KPA.

Business Directories from 1861, 1863–1900 are kept by the Kobe Public Archives, the ones referred to are as follows:

E206-1 KPA. The Japan Herald Directory & Hong List for Yokohama, 1870. Yokohama: *Japan Herald*, 1870.

E206–1 KPA. Hong List and Directory 1872, Yokohama: *Japan Gazette*, 1872.

E206–1 KPA. The China Directory 1874. Hong Kong: *China Mail* Office, 1874.

E206-1 KPA. Hong List and Directory 1875. Yokohama: *Japan Gazette*, 1875.

E206-2 KPA. Hong List and Directory 1878. Yokohama: *Japan Gazette*, 1878.

E206-3, KPA. The Japan Directory, 1879. Yokohama: *Japan Gazette*, 1879.

E206-3 KPA. Japan Directory, 1880. Yokohama: *Japan Gazette*, January 1880.

E206-4 KPA. Japan Directory 1881. no publishing details survived.

E206-4 KPA. Japan Directory 1882. Yokohama: *Japan Gazette*, 1882.

E206-12 KPA. Japan Directory, Hyogo 1890. Yokohama: *Japan Gazette*, 1890.

E206-16 KPA. Japan Directory 1894, Kobe Directory.

E206-20 KPA. Japan Directory 1898. Zainichi Gaikokujin Kikan Meikan, Dai 20 ban 1898, Kobe Directory.

E206-21, KPA. Japan Directory. 1899. Zainichi Gaikokujin Kikan Meikan, Dai 21 ban 1899, Kobe Directory.

KPA. *The Nagasaki Shipping List*. 6 January 1869.

Yokohama Public Archives (YPA)

YPA. *The Japan Weekly Mail*, 2 June 1883, 1.

YPA. Japan Directory 1916. Yokohama: Japan Gazette, 1916.

Nagasaki Museum of History and Culture

Nagasaki Museum of History and Culture. Nagasaki Kyōryūchi Gaikokujin Meibō (Names and Populations of Foreign Residents in Nagasaki, aka House to House Checks) October 1862 to March–May 1870, #14-12-7 compiled by the Nagasaki Bugyosho (printed by Nagasaki Prefectural Library 2002).

United Kingdom

The National Archives of the UK (TNA)

FO 370/2388, TNA. Foreign Office Cover Note referring to a statement made by Sir Arthur Thring, Board of Trade, 21 September 1915, 306.

FO 371/2019, TNA. Letter on behalf of the British Insurance Companies to the Secretary of Board of Trade, 1 December 1914, 181–86.

FO 371/2019, TNA. Telegram No. 169 from Foreign Office to British Embassy Tokyo, 21 October 1914, 161.

FO 371/2019, TNA. Telegram No. 191 from British Embassy Tokyo to Foreign Office, 20 October 1914, 160.

FO 371/2020, TNA. Memorandum from E. T. F. Crowe, Opportunities for capturing German business, 30 September 1914. 365–79.

FO 371/2021, TNA. Telegram No. 249 Foreign Office to British Embassy Tokyo, 24 December 1914, 408.

FO 371/2021, TNA. Telegram No. 259 British Embassy Tokyo to Foreign Office, 14 December 1914, 402.

FO 371/2021, TNA. Telegram No. 276 Foreign Office to British Embassy Tokyo, 28 December 1914, 410.

FO 371/2385, Confidential No. 20 from British Embassy Tokyo to Foreign Office 29 January 1915, 242–46.

FO 371/2385, TNA. British Embassy Tokyo to Foreign Office, 6 November 1915, 70.

FO 371/2385, TNA. Covering note "Remittances of Enemy Funds by Banks in Japan," 15 September 1915, 390.

FO 371/2385, TNA. Japan Confidential February 2. Section 2 Enclosure 1 in No. 1 Crowe to the Ambassador, 7 December 1914, 229.

FO 371/2385, TNA. Letter from Baron Katō to British Ambassador, 17 February 1915, 257.

FO 371/2385, TNA. Letter from British Embassy Tokyo to Foreign Office, 3 July 1915, 67.

FO 371/2385, TNA. Memorandum by E. T. F. Crowe, German Representation of British Insurance Companies in Japan. 17 June 1915, 35–36 and 39.

FO 371/2385, TNA. Telegram No. 131 from British Embassy Tokyo to Foreign Office, 6 April 1915, 259.

FO 371/2386, TNA. 6, Letter from British Consul-General, Yokohama to the British Ambassador, 17 February 1915, 202.

FO 371/2386, TNA. Cover Note and correspondence "Expulsion of Mr. Ball (British Subject)" from British Embassy Tokyo, 8–9 February 1915, 168.

FO 371/2386, TNA. Enclosure No. 2 from H. G. Ball to British Consul-General, Yokohama, 17 February 1916, 206–7.

FO 371/2386, TNA. Instruction of the Minister of the Interior No. 134, Viscount Kanetaka Ōura to Governor of Kanagawa Prefecture, 13 February 1915, 203–5.

FO 371/2386, TNA. Letter from British Commercial Attaché to British Ambassador, 17 February 1915, 229–30.

FO 371/2386, TNA. Letter from British Consulate-General Yokohama to British Embassy, 27 February 1915, 189.

FO 371/2386, TNA. Letter from British Embassy Tokyo to Foreign Office, regarding H. Ball, 27 February 1915, 194–96.

FO 371/2386, TNA. Letter from H. G. Ball to British Ambassador, 17 February 1915, 213–14.

FO 371/2386, TNA. Letter from Hugh G. Ball to British Consul-General Yokohama, 17 February 1915, 209–11.

FO 371/2386, TNA. Telegram No. 40 British Embassy Tokyo to Foreign Office, 10 February 1915, 171.

FO 371/2386, TNA. Telegram No. 59 from British Embassy Tokyo to Foreign Office, 8 February 1915, 170.

FO 371/2386, TNA. Telegram No. 84 from British Embassy Tokyo to Foreign Office, 25 February 1915, 176.

FO 371/2390, TNA. Copy of Instruction of the Japanese Ministry of the Interior sent to The Foreign Office, 30 September 1915, 292–93.

FO 371/2390, TNA. Japan Confidential, No. 300 Enclosure 2 in No. 1 Memorandum, British Embassy Tokyo to Foreign Office, 29 September 1915, 286.

FO 371/2390, TNA. Letter from British Embassy Tokyo to Foreign Office, 30 September 1915, 287–91.
FO 371/2390. TNA. Memorandum from E. T. F. Crowe as an enclosure to Foreign Office, 30 September 1915, 294–97.
Public Record Office, FGO 83/21–2. Lists of Aliens arriving at English ports.

Probate and Wills Office, London, UK

England & Wales National Probate Calendar Index of Wills and Administration 1861–1941, London, UK. Last will and testament of Carl Nickel, 23 July 1906. Found through Ancestry.com and obtained through the Probate and Wills Office, London, UK.

Journal Articles

Aaslestad, Katherine. "Paying for War: Experiences of Napoleonic Rule in the Hanseatic Cities." *Central European History* 39, no. 4 (December 2006): 641–75. https// 10.1017/S0008938906000215.
Bytheway, Simon James and Martha Chaiklin. "Reconsidering the Yokohama 'Gold Rush' of 1859." *Journal of World History* 27, no. 2 (June 2016): 281–301.
Crawcour, E. S., Kozo Yamamura. "The Tokugawa Monetary System: 1787–1868." *Economic Development and Cultural Change* 18, no. 4, part 1 (July 1970): 489–518.
Dehne, Phillip. "From 'Business as Usual' to a More Global War: The British Decision to Attack Germans in South America during the First World War." *Journal of British Studies* 44, no. 3 (July 2005): 516–35. https://doi.org/10.1086/429709.
Kakegawa, Tomiko. "The Japan Chronicle and Its Editors: Reflecting Japan to the Press and the People, 1891–1940." *Japan Forum* 13, no. 1 (2001): 27–40. https://doi.org/10.1080/09555800020027647.
Kim, Hoi-eun. "Made in Meiji Japan: German Expatriates, German-Educated Japanese Elites and the Construction of Germanness." Special issue, "Rethinking Germans Abroad (April–June 2015)." *Geschichte und Gesellschaft* 41, no. 2 (August 2015): 288–320. https://doi.org/10.13109/gege.2015.41.2.288.
Lu, Yixu. "Germany's War in China: Media Coverage and Political Myth." *German Life and Letters* 61, no. 2 (2008): 202–14. https://doi.org/10.1111/j.1468-0483.2008.00419.x
Martin, Bernd and Peter Wetzler. "The German Role in the Modernization of Japan: The Pitfall of Blind Acculturation." *Oriens Extremus* 33, no. 1 (1990): 77–88.
Marzagalli, Silvia. "Port Cities in the French Wars. The Responses of Merchants in Bordeaux, Hamburg and Livorno to Napoleon's Continental Blockade, 1806–1813." *The Northern Mariner/Le Marin du Nord* VI, no. 4 (October 1996): 65–73.
Masaki, Miyake. "Japan's Encounter with Germany, 1860–1914: An Assessment of the German Legacy in Japan." *The European Legacy: Towards New Paradigms* 1, no. 1 (June 2008): 245–49. https://doi.org/10.1080/10848779608579402.
McDermott, John. "'A Needless Sacrifice': British Businessmen and Business as Usual in the First World War." *Albion: A Quarterly Journal Concerned with British Studies* 21, no. 2 (Summer 1989): 263–82. https://doi.org/10.2307/4049929.
McDermott, John. "Total War and the Merchant State: Aspects of British Economic Warfare Against Germany, 1914–16." *Canadian Journal of History* 21, no. 1 (1986): 61–76. https://doi.org/10.3138/cjh.21.1.61.
Panikos Panayi. "German Business Interests in Britain During the First World War." *Business History* 32, no. 2 (1990): 244–58. https://doi.org/10.1080/00076799000000048.

Stahncke, Holmer. *Friedrich August Lühdorfs Handelsexpedition nach Japan*. Deutsche Gesellschaft für Natur- und Völkerkunde Ostasiens, no. 39. Tokyo: OAG aktuell, 1988.
Swanson, Darren Lee. "Them and Us: Perceptions of the Japanese Amongst the Foreign Community: Race Theory and Race Relations in Post-Extraterritorial Japan." *Electronic Journal of Contemporary Japanese Studies* 12, no. 1: 1–23.
Taylor Atkins, E. "Jammin' on the Jazz Frontier: The Japanese Jazz Community in Interwar Shanghai." *Japanese Studies* 19, no. 1, (1999): 5–16.
Treat, Payson J. Review of *Great Britain and the Opening of Japan, 1834–58* by William Gerald Beasley. *The American Historical Review* 58, no. 1 (Oct. 1952): 120–21.
Zielke, Erich. "Konsul Louis Kniffler: Der Pionier des Deutschen Japanhandels." *Journal of Business History* 25, no. 1 (1980): 1–11. https://doi.org/10.1515/zug-1980-0101.

Monographs

Pre-1920

Alcock, Sir Rutherford. *Capital of the Tycoon: A Narrative of a Three Year's Residence in Japan Vols. I & II.* First Edition. London: Longman, Roberts & Green, 1863.
[Berg, Albert]. *Die Preußische Expedition nach Ost-Asien. Erster Band.* Berlin: Verlag der Königlichen Geheimen Oberhofbuchdruckerei, 1864. http://www.deutschestextarchiv.de/book/show/berg_ostasien01_1864.
Chamberlain, Basil Hall. *Things Japanese*. Sixth Edition. London: Kegan Paul, Trench, Trubner & Co. Ltd. Kobe: Japan Chronicle Press, 1939.
Colquhoun, Archibald Ross. *The Mastery of the Pacific*. New York: The MacMillan Company, 1902.
Greenbie, Sydney. *Japan, Real and Imaginary*. New York: Harper & Brothers, 1920.
Hozumi, Nobushige, Masakasa Tomii and Kenjiro Ume. *The Civil Code of Japan*. Translated by Dr Ludwig Lönholm. Yokohama, Shanghai, Hong Kong & Singapore: Kelly & Walsh Lim, 1898.
Montalto de Jesus, Carlos Augusto. *Historic Shanghai*. Shanghai: The Shanghai Mercury Limited, 1909.
Murata Seiji. *Kobe Kaikō Sanjūnen-shi*. Kobe: Kaikō Sanjūnen Kinenkai, Volume 1, 6 May 1898 and Volume 2, 25 October 1898. Digitized copy at NLA: http://www.dl.ndl.go.jp/info:ndljp/pid/805190.

Post-1921

Alpers, Else. *Kehdingen Bilderbogen: Land an der Niederelbe gestern und heute*. Stade: Friedrich Schaumburg, 1972.
The Australian Pocket Oxford Dictionary. Fifth Edition. Melbourne: Melbourne University Press.
Bähr, Johannes Jörg Lesczenski and Katja Schmidtpott. *Handel ist Wandel: 150 Jahre C. Illies & Co.* München: Piper Verlag GMBH, September 2009.
Beasley, William Gerald. *Great Britain and the Opening of Japan*. London: Luzac, 1951.
Becker, Bert. *France and Germany in the South China Seas, c. 1840–1930: Maritime Competition and Imperial Power.* Cambridge: Palgrave Macmillan, 2021.
Berman, Nina, Klaus Mühlhahn and Patrice Nganang, eds. *German Colonialism Revisited: African, Asian and Oceanic Experiences*. Ann Arbor: University of Michigan Press, 2014.
Bickers, Robert, and Isabella Jackson. "Introduction: Law, Land and Power: Treaty Ports and Concessions in Modern China." In *Treaty Ports in Modern China: Law, Land and Power*, edited by Robert A. Bickers and Isabella Jackson, 1–19. Milton Park, Abingdon, Oxon; Routledge, 2016.

Burke-Gaffney, Brian. *Holme, Ringer & Company: The Rise and Fall of a British Enterprise in Japan 1868–1940*. Leiden: Global Oriental, 2013.

Chapman, David, and Karl Jakob Krogness, eds. *Japan's Household Registration System and Citizenship: Koseki, Identification and Documentation*. London and New York: Routledge, 2014.

Clark, Christopher. *Iron Kingdom: The Rise and Fall of Prussia, 1600–1947*. London: Penguin Books, 2007.

Cortazzi, Hugh. "Part I: The Revision of Japan's Early Commercial Treaties." In *Culture, Power & Politics in Treaty Port Japan, 1854–1899: Key Papers, Press and Contemporary Writings, Volume 1*, edited by James E. Hoare, 243–70. Folkestone, Kent: Renaissance Books, 2018.

Darwin, John. *Unlocking the World: Port Cities and Globalization in the Age of Steam, 1830–1930*. London: Penguin, May 2022.

Davenport-Hines, Richard P. T. and Geoffrey Jones. "British Business in Japan since 1868." In *British Business in Asia Since 1860*, edited by Richard P. T. Davenport-Hines and Geoffrey Jones, 217–43. Cambridge: Cambridge University Press, 1989.

Davis, John, Margrit Schulte Beerbühl and Stefan Manz. "Introduction: Germans in the British Empire." In *Transnational Networks: German Migrants in the British Empire, 1670–1914*, edited by John R. Davis, Stefan Manz, Margrit Schulte Beerbühl, 2–17. Leiden–Boston: Brill, 2012.

De Goey, Ferry. "Western Entrepreneurs and the Opening of Japanese Ports." In *Culture Power and Politics in Treaty-Port Japan, 1854–1899: Key Papers, Press and Contemporary Writings, Volume 1*, edited by James E. Hoare, 140–66. Kent: Renaissance Books, 2018.

Eberstein, Bernd. *Hamburg China: Geschichte einer Partnerschaft*. Hamburg: Christians, 1988.

Eberstein, Bernd. *Preußen und China: Eine Geschichte schwieriger Beziehungen*. Berlin: Duncker & Humblot, 2007.

Ennals, Peter. *Opening a Window to the West: The Foreign Concession at Kobe, Japan, 1868–1899*. Toronto, Buffalo, London: University of Toronto Press, 2014.

Fairbank, John K., Edwin O. Reischauer and Albert M. Craig. *East Asia: The Modern Transformation: Volume 2*. London: George Allen & Unwin Ltd., 1965.

Fukuoka, Mariko. "German Merchants in the Indian Ocean World: From Early Modern Paralysis to Modern Animation." In *Early Global Interconnectivity Across the Indian Ocean World, Volume 1*, edited by Angela Schottenhammer. 259–92. Cham, Switzerland: Palgrave, 2019.

Fukuoka, Mariko. "Prussia or North German? The Image of 'Germany' during the Prusso-Japanese Treaty Negotiations in 1860–1861." In *Mutual Perceptions and Images in Japanese-German Relations, 1860–2010*, edited by Sven Saaler, Kudō Akira and Tajima Nobuo, 67–88. Leiden, Netherlands: Brill, 2017.

Fukuoka, Mariko. *Puroisen Higashi Asia Ensei to Bakumatsu Gaikō* (The Prussian East-Asian Expedition and the Japanese Diplomacy in the Late Edo Era). Tokyo: Tokyo University Press, 2013.

Halbwachs, Maurice. *On Collective Memory*. Translated by Lewis A. Coser. Chicago and London: The University of Chicago Press, 1992.

Helm, Leslie. *Yokohama Yankees: My Family's Five Generations as Outsiders in Japan*. Seattle: Chin Music Press, 2013.

Hoare, James E. *Japan's Treaty Ports and Foreign Settlements: The Uninvited Guests 1858–1899*. Kent: Japan Library, Curzon Press Ltd. 1994.

Hoare, James E. "Japan's Treaty Ports and Treaty Revision: Delusions of Grandeur?" In *Culture, Power & Politics in Treaty Port Japan, 1854–1899: Key Papers, Press and Contemporary Writings, Volume 1*, edited by James E. Hoare, 252–60. Kent: Renaissance Books, 2018,

Howland, Douglas. *International Law and Japanese Sovereignty: The Emerging Global Order in the 19th Century*. Basingstoke: Palgrave MacMillan, 2016.

Jackson, Isabella. "Who Ran the Treaty Ports? A Study of the Shanghai Municipal Council." In *Treaty Ports in Modern China: Law, Land and Power*, edited by Robert A. Bickers and Isabella Jackson, 43–60. Milton Park, Abingdon, Oxon; Routledge, 2016.

Jones, Hazel J. *Live Machines: Hired Foreigners and Meiji Japan*. Vancouver: University of British Columbia Press, 1980.

Kim, Hoi-eun. *Doctors of Empire: Medical and Cultural Encounters Between Imperial Germany and Meiji Japan*. German & European Studies Series. Toronto: University of Toronto Press, 2014.

King, Frank H. H. *The Hongkong Bank in Late Imperial China, 1864–1902: On an Even Keel: Volume 1 of The History of the Hongkong and Shanghai Banking Corporation*. Cambridge: Cambridge University Press, 1987.

King, Frank H. H. *The Hongkong Bank in the Period of Imperialism and War, 1895–1918; Wayfoong, the Focus of Wealth: Volume II of The History of Hongkong and Shanghai Banking Corporation*. Cambridge: Cambridge University Press, 1988.

Lloyd, Terence H. *England and the German Hanse, 1157–1611: A Study of Their Trade and Commercial Diplomacy*. Cambridge: Cambridge University Press, 1991. https://doi.org/10.1017/CBO9780511560279.007

Lu, Yixu. "Colonial Quingdao through Chinese Eyes." In *The Cultural Legacy of German Colonial Rule*, edited by Klaus Mühlhahn, 127–42. Berlin: de Gruyter Oldenbourg, 2017.

Manthorpe, Victoria ed. *The Japan Diaries of Richard Gordon Smith*. London: Viking/Rainbird, 1986.

Manz, Stefan. *Constructing a German Diaspora: The "Greater German Empire," 1871–1914*. New York, London: Routledge, 2017.

McCabe, Patricia. *Yokohama, Japan: Gaijin Bochi, the Foreigners' Cemetery*. London: British Association for Cemeteries in South Asia, 1994.

McKay, Alexander. *Scottish Samurai: Thomas Blake Glover, 1838–1911*. Edinburgh: Canongate Press, 2012.

Meissner, Kurt. *Deutsche in Japan, 1639–1960*. Tokyo: Deutsche Gesellschaft für Natur-und Völkerkunde Ostasiens, 1961. https://oag.jp/img/1961/01/oag-mitteilung-sup-Bd-26-deutsche-in-japan-komplett-1639-1960.pdf.

Moazzin, Ghassan. *Foreign Banks and Global Finance in Modern China: Banking on the Chinese Frontier, 1870–1919*. Cambridge; New York: Cambridge University Press, June 2022.

Murphy, Kevin C. *The American Merchant Experience in Nineteenth Century Japan*. London, New York: Routledge/Curzon 2003.

Nish, Ian H. *The Anglo-Japanese Alliance: The Diplomacy of Two Island Empires*. London: The Athlone Press, 1966.

Nish, Ian H. *Alliance in Decline: A Study in Anglo-Japanese Relations 1908–23*. London: The Athlone Press, 1972.

Nish, Ian H. "Japan Reverses the Unequal Treaties: The Anglo-Japanese Commercial Treaty of 1894." In *Culture, Power & Politics in Treaty Port Japan, 1854–1899: Key Papers, Press and Contemporary Writings, Volume I*, edited by James E. Hoare, 348–60. Kent: Renaissance Books, 2018.

O'Connor, Peter. "The Japan Chronicle and Its Three Editors, Robert Young, Morgan Young and Edwin Allington Kennard, 1891–1940." In *Britain and Japan Biographical Portraits, Volume 4*, edited by Hugh Cortazzi, 334–47. London: Taylor Francis Group 2003.

Osterhammel, Jürgen. "Britain and China, 1842–1914." In *The Oxford History of the British Empire, Volume III: The Nineteenth Century*, edited by Andrew Porter and William Roger Louis, 148–69. Oxford: Oxford University Press,1999.

Osterhammel, Jürgen. "British Business in China, 1860s–1950s" In *British Business in Asia Since 1860*, edited by Richard P. T. Davenport-Hines and Geoffrey Jones, 190–216. Cambridge: Cambridge University Press 1989.

Otte, Thomas G. *The China Question: Great Power Rivalry and British Isolation, 1894–1905*. Oxford: Oxford University Press May 2007.

Otte, Thomas G. *July Crisis: The World's Descent into War, Summer 1914*. Cambridge: Cambridge University Press 2014.

Paske-Smith, Montague. "Supplement No. 3: Reproduction of List of Foreign Hongs and Residents and Plan of the Foreign Concessions in Nagasaki, 1867." In *Western Barbarians in Japan and Formosa in Tokugawa Days, 1603–1868*. Kobe: J. L. Thompson & Co. Ltd. 1930.

Phipps, Catherine L. *Empires of the Waterfront: Japan's Ports and Power, 1858–1899*. Harvard East Asian Monographs, no. 373. Cambridge, MA and London: Harvard University Press, 2015.

Refardt, Otto. *Die Deutschen in Kobe* (*Alt Kobe*). Tokyo: Deutsche Gesellschaft für Natur- und Völkerkunde Ostasiens, Tokyo: OAG, 1956.

Reimers, Carolin. *Zeit ist Geld: Der Kaufmann Hinrich Ahrens und die Anfänge des deutschen Handels mit Japan*. Münster: Monsenstein und Vannerdat, 2010.

Reinhardt, Anne. "Treaty Ports as Shipping Infrastructure." In *Treaty Ports in Modern China: Law, Land and Power*, edited by Robert Bickers and Isabella Jackson, 101–19. Milton Park, Abingdon, Oxon; Routledge, 2016.

Rössler, Hörst. "Sugarbakers, Farmers, Goldminers: From Hanover via London to New Zealand." In *Transnational Networks: German Migrants in the British Empire, 1670–1914*, edited by John R. Davis, Stefan Manz and Margrit Schulte Beerbühl, 101–15. Leiden–Boston: Brill, 2012.

Saaler, Sven. "150 Jahre japanisch-deutsche Beziehungen." In *Unter den Augen ders Preußen-Adlers: Lithographien, Zeichnungen und Photographien der Teilnehmer der Eulenberg-Expedition in Japan, 1860–61*, edited by Sebastian Dobson and Sven Saaler, 37–45. Munich: Iudicium, 2011.

Sano, Mayuko. "Disturbed Reciprocity: Rutherford Alcock's Diplomacy and Merchant Communities in China and Japan." In *Chronicling Westerners in Nineteenth-Century East Asia*, edited by Robert S. G. Fletcher and Robert Hellyer, 21–42. London: Bloomsbury Publishing, 2022.

Saya, Makito. *The Sino-Japanese War and the Birth of Japanese Nationalism*. Tokyo: Kodansha, 2009.

Schrecker, John E. *Imperialism and Chinese Nationalism: Germany in Shantung*. Cambridge, MA: Harvard University Press, 2013.

Skabelund, Aaron Herald. *Empire of Dogs: Canines, Japan and the Making of the Modern Imperial World*. Ithaca & London: Cornell University Press, 2011.

Stahncke, Holmer. *Die diplomatischen Beziehung zwischen Deutschland und Japan 1854–1868*. Wiesbaden: Franz Steiner Verlag, 1987.

Thomas, Alsen F. and Soji Koyama. *Commercial History of Japan*. Tokyo: The Yūhodo Limited, 1936.

Thorpey, John. *Invention of the Passport: Surveillance, Citizenship, and the State*. Cambridge, New York: Cambridge University Press, 2000.

Tong, Te-kong. *United States Diplomacy in China, 1844–1860*. Seattle: University of Washington Press, 1964.

Varma, Nitin. "Contractors, Contracts, Coolies." *Coolies of Capitalism Book: Assam Tea and the Making of Coolie Labour*. Berlin, Boston: De Gruyter, 2017.

von Volborth, Carl-Alexander. *Heraldry: Customs, Rules and Styles*. Poole, Dorset: Blandford Press, 1981.

Williams, Harold S. *Foreigners in Mikadoland*. Tokyo: Charles E. Tuttle Company, 1963.

Williams, Harold S. *The Story of Holme Ringer & Co., Ltd. in Western Japan 1868–1968*. Tokyo: Charles E. Tuttle Company, 1968.

Williams, Harold S. *Tales of The Foreign Settlements in Japan*. Tokyo: Charles E. Tuttle Company, 1958.

Newspaper Articles

Hyogo/Hiogo News (Kobe)

Hiogo News, 18 May 1870, Kobe land sales, 158.

Hiogo News, 26 January 1870, Establishment of D. H. Tillson & Co., 31.

Hiogo News, 26 January 1870, notice of winding up of the business, KPA, 31.

Hiogo News, 26 January 1870, notice of winding up of the business, 31.

Hiogo News, 3 June 1869, Kobe land sales, 381.

Hiogo News, No. 1. 23 April 1868, KPA, 4.

Hiogo News, No. 1. 23 April 1868, notice of winding up of the Warren & Tillson Co.

Hiogo News, No. 1. 23 April 1868.

Hyogo News, 3 July 1888, KPA, 1.

Japan Gazette

Japan Gazette, "Kobe Land Sales." September 1868, 6.

The Japan Weekly Mail, "Eliza Nickel's Obituary." 2 June 1883, 1.

Kobe Chronicle Weekly 1897–1901

Kobe Chronicle Online 1900–1940. Leiden and Boston: Brill, 2013. http://primarysources.brillonline.com.rp.nla.gov.au/browse/japan-chronicle.

Kobe Chronicle. "An Alleged Breach of Contract: Nickel v. Lynn." 26 April 1899, 321–24.

Kobe Chronicle. "Alleged Infraction of the Customs Law: A Foreigner Summoned." 27 March 1901, 272.

Kobe Chronicle. "Alleged Infraction of the Customs Law: Second Hearing. Judgement." 3 April 1901, 293.

Kobe Chronicle. "Alleged Violation of the Customs Law: Acquittal on Appeal." 1 May 1901, 394.

Kobe Chronicle. "Application to Attach a Steam-Launch: Nickel & Co. vs Jack Yong & Co." 21 March 1900, 234.

Kobe Chronicle. "Attachment of a Russian Steam Launch." 16 May 1900, 419.

Kobe Chronicle. "Charges of Embezzlement: Messrs Nickel Proceed Against an Employee." 25 September 1898, 247–48.

Kobe Chronicle. "Claim for Damage Done in Discharging Cotton: A Re-Hearing." 22 May 1901, 468.

Kobe Chronicle. "Claim for Damage Done in Discharging Cotton: Action in the *Kobe Chiho Saibansho*." 24 April 1901, 372.

Kobe Chronicle. "Claim for Damaged Cargo: Interesting Question." 16 October 1897, 317–23.

Kobe Chronicle. "Commercial Firms Under the New Treaties." 30 July 1898, 69.

Kobe Chronicle. "Coolie Question." 12 February 1898, 108–9.

Kobe Chronicle. "Custom House Scandal." 18 December 1897, 502.

Kobe Chronicle. "Customs-House Frauds: Heavy Sentences." 30 July 1898, 74.

Kobe Chronicle. "Dinner to Mr. Ōhmori: Presentation of an Address." 14 November 1900, 416.

Kobe Chronicle. "Dr Lönholm on the Land Question." 8 January 1898, 1.

Kobe Chronicle. "Hamburg Case: Hearing of the Appeal." 11 December 1901, 563.

Kobe Chronicle. "Harbour Regulations for Open Ports: Imperial Ordinance No. 139." 17 September 1898, 234.

Kobe Chronicle. "Infringement of the Shipping Law." 6 November 1901, 452.

Kobe Chronicle. "Japan as Field for Foreign Investment." 8 January 1898, 2.

Kobe Chronicle. "Japanese Commercial Morality." 9 July 1898, 19–20.

Kobe Chronicle. "Japanese Coolies for China." 8 August 1900, 123.

Kobe Chronicle. "Japanese Steamers Again." 13 February 1898.
Kobe Chronicle. "Kobe Customs House Frauds: Findings of the Preliminary Judge." 26 March 1898, 263.
Kobe Chronicle. "Kobe Customs Scandal." 8 January 1898, 28.
Kobe Chronicle. "Kobe's Curious Customs." 7 April 1898, 300.
Kobe Chronicle. "Landing Facilities at Kobe." 22 October 1898, 334.
Kobe Chronicle. "Landowning by Aliens in the United States." 4 December 1901, 535.
Kobe Chronicle. "Late Mr. Charles Sutton: A Will Case at Yokohama." 30 May 1900, 460.
Kobe Chronicle. "Local and General." 5 September 1900, 207.
Kobe Chronicle. "Military Coolies." 5 September 1900, 205–6.
Kobe Chronicle. "New Harbour Office: Banquet at the Tokiwa Kwadan." 5 April 1899, 257.
Kobe Chronicle. "Relief Fund Second List." 13 December 1899, 507.
Kobe Chronicle. "Right of Foreigners to Hold Land: A Japanese Merchant's View." 11 September 1901, 260.
Kobe Chronicle. "Scandal in the Kobe Customs." 4 December 1897, 472.
Kobe Chronicle. "Squeezes and Commissions." 9 October 1897, 286.
Kobe Chronicle. "Trial Trip of a New Launch." 8 January 1898, 52.
Young, Robert. "The Case of the Foreign Residents in Japan: 'Nineteenth Century' for August," *Kobe Chronicle*, 2 October 1897, 272–75.

Japan Chronicle Weekly 1902–41 (Kobe)

Japan Chronicle Online, 1900–1940. Leiden and Boston: Brill, 2013. http://primarysources.brillonline.com.rp.nla.gov.au/browse/japan-chronicle.
Japan Chronicle. "Another Boundary Dispute: Akioka v. C. Nickel & Co." 19 October 1911, 706.
Japan Chronicle. "Alleged Kidnapping of a Swineherd." 26 July 1917, 147.
Japan Chronicle. "Armed Attack on a Stevedore's Office: Extraordinary Incident." 26 December 1907, 822.
Japan Chronicle. "Arrest of a Foreigner in Kobe Harbour." 17 September 1902, 273.
Japan Chronicle. "Blacklist: Explanation by British Commercial Attaché." 12 October 1916, 576.
Japan Chronicle. "Bogus Kidnapping Case: An Old Wrong Righted." 21 April 1921, 550.
Japan Chronicle. "Burning of the Ship R. D. Rice: Inquiry at the American Consulate. The Vessel Scuttled." 8 May 1901, 416.
Japan Chronicle. "C. Nickel & Co. Limited: Annual Meeting." 4 February 1904, 137.
Japan Chronicle. "C. Nickel & Co. Ltd.: Annual General Meeting." 2 January 1908, 15.
Japan Chronicle. "C. Nickel & Co. Ltd.: Seventh Annual General Meeting." 30 December 1909, 1177.
Japan Chronicle. "C. Nickel & Co. Ltd.: Third Annual Meeting." 25 January 1906, 116.
Japan Chronicle. "C. Nickel & Company Limited: Meeting of Shareholders." 2 February 1905, 130.
Japan Chronicle. "C. Nickel and Company Ltd.: Annual Meeting." 27 December 1906, 816.
Japan Chronicle. "Charge Against Mr. Holstein: Conflicting Points in Evidence." 4 March 1915, 362–63.
Japan Chronicle. "Charge Against Mr. Holstein: Full Text of Judgment." 15 April 1915, 554, 556.
Japan Chronicle. "Charge Against Mr. Holstein: Opening of the Public Trial. Full Report of the Proceedings." 4 March 1915, 318–20.
Japan Chronicle. "Charge Against Mr. Holstein: Result of the Preliminary Examination." 14 January 1915, 59.
Japan Chronicle. "Charge Against Mr. Holstein: Resumed Hearing. Examination of Important Witnesses." 18 March 1915, 400–403.
Japan Chronicle. "Charge Against Mr. Holstein: Speeches by the Counsel for the Defense." 25 March 1915, 438–41.

Japan Chronicle. "Charge Against Mr. Holstein: Text of Preliminary Judgement." 21 January 1915, 88.
Japan Chronicle. "Charge of Assault Against a Foreigner." 7 May 1902, 426.
Japan Chronicle. "Charge of Assault Against a Foreigner: Appeal to the Osaka Court." 20 May 1903, 445.
Japan Chronicle. "Charge of Assault: A Foreigner Sent to Prison for Fifteen Days." 2 April 1902, 278.
Japan Chronicle. "Claim Against the Tonkin." 16 September 1903, 267–68.
Japan Chronicle. "Claim for Compensation for Injuries: Anami Kumeo v. Messrs. Nickel & Co." 22 September 1910, 531.
Japan Chronicle. "Claim for Compensation for Injuries: Anami Kumeo v. Messrs. Nickel & Co." 10 November 1910, 840.
Japan Chronicle. "Claim for Compensation for Injuries: Sequel to a Collision in Kobe Harbour." 25 May 1911, 904.
Japan Chronicle. "Claim for Compensation for Personal Injury: Sequel to an Accident in Kobe Harbour. Judgement." 18 April 1912, 689.
Japan Chronicle. "Claim for Damages: Akioka Kinu v. C. Nickel & Co." 13 April 1911, 636.
Japan Chronicle. "Claim for Damages: Akioka vs C. Nickel & Co." *Japan Chronicle*, 18 May 1911, 861.
Japan Chronicle. "Claim for Recovery of Money Advanced: C. Nickel & Co. Ltd. v. Akioka Kinu." 23 March 1911, 502.
Japan Chronicle. "Claim for Recovery of Money Advanced: Conclusion of Hearing." 13 April 1911, 631.
Japan Chronicle. "Claim for Recovery of Money Advanced: Text of Judgement." 27 April 1911, 731.
Japan Chronicle. "The Claim for Damages: Judgement." 22 June 1911, 1180.
Japan Chronicle. "Claim for Salary by a Japanese: Nickel v. Tajima. The Appeal." 17 September 1902, 270.
Japan Chronicle. "Claim for Salary." 4 June 1902, 518.
Japan Chronicle. "Claim for Wages: Plaintiff and Judge's Advice." 16 June 1904, 742.
Japan Chronicle. "Claims Against Messrs Nickel and Lyons: Further Court Proceedings." 11 May 1916, 754.
Japan Chronicle. "Collision in Kobe Harbour." 13 January 1904, 47.
Japan Chronicle. "Commercial Situation in Japan in 1913: Mr. Crowe on the 'Good Old Days.'" 6 August 1914, 276.
Japan Chronicle. "Confiscation of Private Property." 28 October 1920, 583.
Japan Chronicle. "Coolie Affray at Kobe: Foreigner Assaulted. Sentence on Coolies." 8 April 1909, 562.
Japan Chronicle. "Customs Facilities in Kobe." 31 August 1905, 257.
Japan Chronicle. "Death and Funeral of Mr. Aug. Evers: Interesting Career of Old Resident. Touching Tribute at the Graveside by Mr. Krien (German Consul General in 1904)." 9 June 1904, 709–10.
Japan Chronicle. "Death of Mr. C. Braess." 9 February 1911, 225.
Japan Chronicle. "Death of Mr. C. Braess: Funeral Service at Kasugano." 9 February 1911, 225.
Japan Chronicle. "Death of Mr. C. T. M. Nickel." 16 August 1906, 213.
Japan Chronicle. "Death of Mr. Herman Trotzig: A Sixty Years' Resident of Japan." 24 July 1919, 144.
Japan Chronicle. "Death of Mr. J. Lyons: A Thirty-Year's Resident." 4 May 1916, 721.
Japan Chronicle. "Departure of German Reservists: Scenes in Kobe." 6 August 1914, 265.
Japan Chronicle. "Disappearance of a Foreigner." 30 April 1902, 400.
Japan Chronicle, "Disputed Tenancy Case: C. Holstein v. J. Lundberg." *Japan Chronicle*, 8 February 1912, 257.
Japan Chronicle. "Disputed Tenancy Case: C. Holstein v J. Lundberg. Text of Judgement." 7 March 1912, 445.
Japan Chronicle. "Disputed Tenancy Case: C. Holstein v. J. Lundberg." *Japan Chronicle*, 22 February 1912, 350.

Japan Chronicle. "Disputed Tenancy Case: C. Holstein v. J. Lundberg." 25 January 1912, 68.
Japan Chronicle. "Disputed Tenancy of a House: Holstein v. Lundberg. Judgement." 14 December 1911, 1059.
Japan Chronicle. "Domiciliary Searches in Kobe: Charges Not Yet Stated. Mr Holstein Arrested." 12 November 1914, 891.
Japan Chronicle. "Dynamite Explosion at Kobe: Enormous Damage. Full Details." 14 April 1910, 644–47.
Japan Chronicle. "Dynamite Explosion Case: Judgement in the Supreme Court. Messrs. Nickel's Appeal Rejected." 13 February 1913, 313.
Japan Chronicle. "Dynamite Explosion Case: Judgement." 11 May 1911, 821.
Japan Chronicle. "Dynamite Explosion Case: Kobe Gas Company v. C. Nickel." 2 March 1911, 365.
Japan Chronicle. "Dynamite Explosion Case: Text of Judgement." 18 May 1911, 852.
Japan Chronicle. "Dynamite Explosion of Kobe: Claim Against C. Nickel & Co." 4 August 1910, 200.
Japan Chronicle. "Dynamite, Foreign and Home-Made: A Government Official on the Imported Article." 5 May 1910, 785.
Japan Chronicle. "Earthquake Relief Committee (Foreign): Kobe, Japan." 4 December 1924, 764.
Japan Chronicle. "Enemy Property in Japan: Imperial Ordinance Issued." 3 July 1919, 15.
Japan Chronicle. "Enemy Property in Japan: Security for Payment of Indemnity." 5 February 1920, 162.
Japan Chronicle. "Exemption from Court Expenses: Action Against Messrs Nickel & Co." 28 April 1910, 725.
Japan Chronicle. "Explosion and Responsibility." 14 April 1910, 613–14.
Japan Chronicle. "Explosives and Explosions." 21 April 1910, 659.
Japan Chronicle. "Fire in Kobe Harbour." 3 August 1905, 136.
Japan Chronicle. "Fires in Kobe." 19 March 1908, 351.
Japan Chronicle. "Forced Sales of German Property: No Satisfactory Offers." 1 April 1920, 385.
Japan Chronicle. "Foreign Community of Kobe: Public Meeting. Protest Against Tariff Proposals." 17 July 1924, 82.
Japan Chronicle. "Foreigner Charged with Assault." 19 March 1902, 263.
Japan Chronicle. "Foreigner Charged with Assault." 29 January 1902, 80.
Japan Chronicle. "Foreigner Charged with Assault: Sentenced to 15 Months Imprisonment." 18 March 1903, 247.
Japan Chronicle. "Foreigners and the Revised Treaties: A Japanese Legal Comment." *Japan Chronicle*, 27 August 1902, 209.
Japan Chronicle. "German Claims for Salary: New Proceedings Against Kobe Firm." 16 March 1916, 437.
Japan Chronicle. "German Claims for Wrongful Dismissal: The Suits Against Messrs Nickel & Lyons." 17 February 1916, 264.
Japan Chronicle. "German Property in Japan: Disposal Discussion." 27 May 1920, 611.
Japan Chronicle. "German Property in Japan: Rumoured Proposal for Confiscation." 5 June 1919, 863.
Japan Chronicle. "German Residents in Japan: Official Assurances." 27 August 1914, 417.
Japan Chronicle. "Glut at the Customs: An All-Round View." 14 September 1905, 340.
Japan Chronicle. "Glut at the Customs: Another Point of View." 7 September 1905, 318.
Japan Chronicle. "Glut at the Customs: Views of a Cotton Expert. Views of Landing Agents." 24 August 1905, 241–42.
Japan Chronicle. "'Gorotsuki' in Kobe: A Growing Danger." 13 February 1908, 197.
Japan Chronicle. "Hamburg Appeal: Claim the Appeal is Illegal." 1 October 1902, 317.

Japan Chronicle. "Hamburg Case." 18 March 1903, 233–34.
Japan Chronicle. "Hamburg Case: Another Adjournment. Value of Expert Evidence. Judgement." 30 July 1902, 105–6.
Japan Chronicle. "Hamburg Case: Judgement of the Supreme Court. Conviction Confirmed." 18 March 1903, 247–48.
Japan Chronicle. "Hamburg Case: New Trial." 25 June 1902, 584.
Japan Chronicle. "Hamburg Case: Procurator Recommends Acquittal." 19 February 1902, 156.
Japan Chronicle. "Hamburg Case: Text of Judgement." 6 August 1902, 130.
Japan Chronicle. "Harbours and Ports." 21 December 1905, 798.
Japan Chronicle. "Hiogo & Osaka Chamber of Commerce: Annual General Meeting." 2 March 1905, 255–56.
Japan Chronicle. "House-Tax & Foreign Residents." 5 March 1902, 193.
Japan Chronicle. "House-Tax: The Construction of the Settlement and the Profit Made. (By an Old Resident)." 19 February 1902, 158.
Japan Chronicle. "Hyogo and Osaka General Chamber of Commerce: Annual Meeting." 11 February 1903, 123–24.
Japan Chronicle. "International Hospital: Subscription List." 9 December 1926, 699.
Japan Chronicle. "Japan Times and Land Ownership." 5 March 1902, 194.
Japan Chronicle. "Japanese Law Courts: Their Constitution and Procedure." 3 September 1902, 226.
Japan Chronicle. "Kidnapping a Swineherd: Retrial at Hiroshima. Tsukamura v. Holstein. Acquittal." 21 April 1921, 550.
Japan Chronicle. "Kobe Customs: New Regulations." 31 August 1905, 258.
Japan Chronicle. "Kobe Dynamite Explosion Case: Appeal in the Osaka Court." 5 October 1911, 598.
Japan Chronicle. "Kobe Dynamite Explosion Case: Evidence in the Kobe Court." 26 October 1911, 745.
Japan Chronicle. "Kobe Dynamite Explosion Case: Further Hearing in Osaka." 25 April 1912, 725.
Japan Chronicle. "Kobe Dynamite Explosion Case: Kobe Gas Company v. C. Nickel & Co." 8 December 1910, 1009.
Japan Chronicle. "Kobe Dynamite Explosion Case: Kobe Gas Company v. C. Nickel & Co." 29 December 1910, 1146.
Japan Chronicle. "Kobe Dynamite Explosion Case: Kobe Gas Company v. C. Nickel & Co." 26 January 1911, 144.
Japan Chronicle. "Kobe Dynamite Explosion Case: Osaka Proceedings to be Re-Opened." 25 January 1912, 174.
Japan Chronicle. "Kobe Dynamite Explosion Case: Remarkable Action by Gas Company." 1 August 1912, 205.
Japan Chronicle. "Kobe Dynamite Explosion Case: Text of Judgement of Osaka Appeal Court." 4 July 1912, 22.
Japan Chronicle. "Kobe Dynamite Explosion Case: The Kobe Gas Company v. C. Nickel & Co. Further Interesting Evidence." 7 March 1912, 435.
Japan Chronicle. "Kobe Explosion. Report on Cause: The Control of Explosives. Attitude of Authorities." 21 April 1910, 686.
Japan Chronicle. "Kobe Foreign Board of Trade: Extraordinary General Meeting." 15 June 1905, 721.
Japan Chronicle. "'Kobe Harbour Works' A Remarkable Situation: Some Official Correspondence. Wednesday, October 23." 31 October 1907, 68–70.
Japan Chronicle. "Kobe Seamen's Institute: Annual Meeting." 5 May 1910, 774–75.
Japan Chronicle. "Kobe Youth's Temptation." 9 March 1905, 286.
Japan Chronicle. "Law Reports: Claims for Wrongful Dismissal." 28 September 1916, 498.

Japan Chronicle. "Law Reports: Kidnapping a Swineherd. The Charge Against Mr. Holstein." 7 December 1916, 896–97.
Japan Chronicle. "Law Reports: The Claim Against Messrs. Nickel and Lyons. Further Proceedings." 13 July 1916, 61.
Japan Chronicle. "Leader 'The Judgment in the Holstein Case.'" 15 April 1915, 537–38.
Japan Chronicle. "Local and General." 8 May 1901, 411.
Japan Chronicle. "Local and General." 18 June 1902, 564.
Japan Chronicle. "Local & General." 19 November 1902, 509.
Japan Chronicle. "Local and General." 24 May 1906, 629.
Japan Chronicle. "Local and General." 7 June 1910, 9.
Japan Chronicle. "Local and General." 19 November 1914, 918.
Japan Chronicle. "Local and General." 19 February 1920, 208.
Japan Chronicle. "Luxury Tariff: International Committee's Report." 23 October 1924, 568.
Japan Chronicle. "Mayoral Proclamation in Kobe: The War and the German Community." 3 September 1914, 461.
Japan Chronicle. "Messrs. C. Nickel & Company: Annual General Meeting." 26 January 1911, 151.
Japan Chronicle. "Murder of a Coolie in Kobe: Further Particulars." 23 September 1903, 297.
Japan Chronicle. "Negligence of Employes: An Important Point." 9 April 1908, 459.
Japan Chronicle. "New Motor-Car in Kobe." 5 November 1902, 469.
Japan Chronicle. "Nickel & Co. Limited: Statutory Meeting." 25 February 1903, 166.
Japan Chronicle. "Nickel & Lyons Limited: Second Annual General Meeting." 29 April 1915, 647.
Japan Chronicle. "Nickel and Lyons Limited: First Annual Meeting." 16 April 1914, 642.
Japan Chronicle. "Notes and Comments." 11 December 1919, 880.
Japan Chronicle. "Notes and Comments." 19 November 1914, 918.
Japan Chronicle. "Notes of the Week." 11 November 1920, 649.
Japan Chronicle. "Obituary: Mr. Alf Woolley." 30 December 1920, 906.
Japan Chronicle. "Oil Ship Destroyed by Fire: Burnt to Water's Edge." 1 May 1901, 400.
Japan Chronicle. "Peaceable Persuasion." 19 March 1908, 343.
Japan Chronicle. "Penalty of Entering an Unopen Port." 30 July 1902, 98.
Japan Chronicle. "Recent Armed Attack in Kobe: Prisoners at Large." 20 February 1908, 229.
Japan Chronicle. "Recent Armed Attack in Kobe: Trial of Accused. Judgement." 12 March 1908, 317.
Japan Chronicle. "Recent Dynamite Explosion." 5 May 1910, 765
Japan Chronicle. "Regulations Respecting Tugboats." 25 June 1902, 592.
Japan Chronicle. "Relief Fund: Further Subscriptions." 20 September 1923, 420
Japan Chronicle. "Remarkable Claim for Damages: Sequel to a Charge Against a Foreigner." 4 February 1915, 174.
Japan Chronicle. "Reminiscences of Kobe, the Port's Beginnings." 9 January 1901, 25.
Japan Chronicle. "Robert Young: A Memoir: Thursday, 9 November 1922." 16 November 1922, 632–34.
Japan Chronicle. "Sanguinary Affray at a Boarding House: Stevedore Coolies Again." 30 July 1908, 169.
Japan Chronicle. "Seizure of a Foreign Launch near Yokohama." 7 May 1903, 414.
Japan Chronicle. "Steam Launch Collision in the Harbour: Two Men Drowned. Four Men Reported Missing." 15 October 1902, 387.
Japan Chronicle. "Storing of Explosives: Accommodation to be Extended." 15 December 1910, 1045.
Japan Chronicle. "Stranded NDL Launch." 20 August 1902, 174.
Japan Chronicle. "Stray Notes." 21 April 1910, 670.
Japan Chronicle. "Stray Notes." 29 April 1909, 652.
Japan Chronicle. "Suits for Unlawful Dismissal." 25 November 1915, 893.

Japan Chronicle. "Swineherd Case." 2 January 1919, 21.

Japan Chronicle. "Swineherd Kidnapping Case: Date of Appeal Proceedings." 26 October 1916, 667.

Japan Chronicle. "Tor Hotel." 30 July 1908, 170.

Japan Chronicle. "Trade and Commerce: Shares and Companies in Japan." 2 November 1905, 577.

Japan Chronicle. "Treatment of German Residents: The Home Minister's Injunction." 27 August 1914, 421.

Japan Chronicle. "Treaty Blue-Book and Land Ownership." 27 August 1902, 193–94.

Japan Chronicle. "Typhoon: Steam Launch Stranded at Kawasaki." 13 August 1902, 151.

Japan Chronicle. Front page advertisement for Nickel & Lyons, 7 January 1915.

Young, Robert. "History of Kobe," and Miss Gertrude Cozad, "Romance of Kobe." In *The Japan Chronicle Jubilee Number 1868–1918*. Kobe: *Japan Chronicle*, 1918.

Kobe Shimbun (Kobe Newspaper)

Kobe Shimbun. "Tenshū kudari kanzoku dokutan shōkai. Tsuhi ni kenkyo saru [...] Shimin to wagasha daishōri." (My Translation: "Just Punishment from Heaven: [Holstein] Finally Jailed [...] A Victory for Kobe Citizens and our Company [the Kobe Shimbun]"). 4 November 1914, 6.

Kobe Yūshin Nippō

Kobe Yūshin Nippō. "Matamata Daisōsaku Kaishi. Nidokushō Suma Bessō Sonota." (My translation: "Big Enquiry Commenced. Suma Holiday House of two German Merchants"). 12 November 1914, KPA.

Kobe Yūshin Nippō. "Sakukenjikyoku Holstein Shōkan Jyūdaijiken Hansekimeiryō." (My translation: "Holstein Summoned to the Prosecutor's Office for an Important Criminal Act"). 12 November 1914, KPA.

Mainichi Daily News

Mainichi Daily News. Williams, Harold S. "Foreign Owned English Newspapers in Kobe: Shades of the Past." 21 February 1981. Extract found in file on Kobe Newspapers & Journals, Folder 80, Harold S. Williams Collection, NLA.

Nagasaki Newspapers

The Nagasaki Express. "Mrs. Nickel shoots Japanese boy in an accident." 28 January 1871, 218

Nagasaki Times. "Nickel departed for Hiogo (Kobe) on the Feloong." 15 August 1868, 30.

Nagasaki Times. "Nickel departed for Shanghai on the *Costa Rica*." 7 November 1868, 78.

Nagasaki Times. "Nickel returned from Shanghai to Nagasaki on the *Orissa*." 21 November 1868, 86.

Nagasaki Times. "Mr. and Mrs. Nickel returned from Shanghai to Nagasaki on the *Feloong*." 5 December 1868, 94.

Rising Sun & Nagasaki Express. "Death Notice {David Holmes Tillson}." 4 February 1882, 3.

Rising Sun and Nagasaki Express. "Sale of Falcon Hotel." 11 August 1877, 2.

North China Herald and South China & China Gazette (Shanghai)

The N.C. Herald and S.C. & C. Gazette. "Award to Nickel of Testimonial." 10 January 1896, 34.

The N. C. Herald and S. C. & C. Gazette. "Nickel breaking a strike in 1892." 2 December 1892, 821.

North China Herald. "Latest Shipping Intelligence, Passengers." 5 April 1862, 54.

The North China Herald. "Man of War Boat Race." 27 February 1873, 186.

The North China Herald. "Nickel's horse racing in the Kaiser Cup at the Shanghai Paper Hunt Club Races came last." 23 March 1887, 326.

The Japan Weekly Mail (Yokohama)
The Japan Weekly Mail. 2 June 1883. Yokohama Public Archives (YPA)

Sydney Morning Herald
Sydney Morning Herald. "Trade with the Enemy. Royal Proclamation." 8 August 1914, 14.

Personal Records

Die Polzeibehörde Hamburg. Antrage auf Verleihung des Ehrenkreuzes fur Frontkämpfer, Kriegsteilnehmer. 14 April 1936.
Email from Rick Taniguchi, aka Ryōhei Taniguchi member of the Kobe Gaikokujin Kyoryūchi Kenkyūkai (Kobe Foreign Settlement Research Society). 1 May 2017
Email to author from Lane Earns, the Nagasaki Foreign Settlement Website, 26 August 2014.
Email to author from Christine Heitmann, *Staatsarchiv Hamburg*, 1 August 2017.
Holstein Family *Ahnenpaß*, a record of Aryan ancestry required by the Nazi Party prepared in 1940. Each entry was researched and verified by the Registry in Idar Oberstein.
Letter from the German Heraldic Society to Otto Holstein, 11 August 1940.
Letter from Otto Holstein to Christian Holstein, 20 August 1940.
Letter from Otto Holstein, Idar-Oberstein, Germany to Christian Holstein, Kobe, Japan, 22 September 1940.
Letter written to Christian Holstein by the German Ambassador, Wilhelm Solf, 12 October 1920.
Unpublished notes by Gerd Bahr, historian and writer in Plattdeutsch, https://de.wikipedia.org/wiki/Gerd_Bahr, "Über die Entwicklung der Kehdinger Kuesten und Fluschiffahrt," May 2013.

Theses

Rauck, Michael. "Die Beziehungun zwischen Japan und Deutschland, 1859–1914." PhD diss., Friedrich-Alexander-Universität Erlangen-Nürnberg 1988.
Swanson, Darren Lee. "Treaty Port Society and the Club in Meiji Japan: Clubbism, Athleticism and the Public Sphere." PhD diss., University of Sydney, 2016. http://hdl.handle.net/2123/16921.
Toneko Hirai, "MINAMI-E! Japan's Acquisition of Micronesia, 1914–1922." PhD diss., University of Hawaii, 1994.

Website References

Burke-Gaffney, Brian. Nagasaki Institute of Applied Science and Lane Earns, University of Wisconsin–Oshkosh, USA: Nagasaki Foreign Settlement Website, http://www.nfs.nias.ac.jp/. Updated 19 June 2017, but this website has since been taken down to be rehoused in the future.
Eberstein, Bernd. "Kaufleute, Konsuln, Kapitäne: Frühe deutsche Wirtschaftsinteressen in China." Catalogue for an exhibition held on Tsingtau at the German Historical Museum, 1998. http://www.dhm.de/archiv/ausstellungen/tsingtau/katalog/auf1_1.htm. Last accessed 2021.

The Hongkong Directory: With List of Foreign Residents in China, 1859. Hong Kong: Armenian Press, 1859. https://archive.org/details/hongkongdirectoooounkngoog/page/n8/mode/2up 2024.

Japan. Correspondence Inclosure 3 in No. 57, Protest of the Master of the United States ship "Monitor," Yokohama, 23 August 1864, Correspondence with H. M. Envoy and Minister Plenipotentiary in Japan, 1865. 19th Century House of Commons Sessional Papers. https://parlipapers-proquest-com.rp.nla.gov.au/parlipapers/docview/t70.d75.1860-036818?accountid=12694, 69–70.

Japan. Correspondence No. 37. Mr. Alcock to Lord J. Russell, Yedo, 10 November 1859, Japan, Correspondence with H. M. Envoy and Minister Plenipotentiary in Japan, 1860. 19th Century House of Commons Sessional Papers. https://parlipapers-proquest-com.rp.nla.gov.au/parlipapers/docview/t70.d75.1860–036818?accountid=12694, 78–79.

Japan. Correspondence No. 41. Alcock to Lord J. Russell, 6 December 1859, Japan, Correspondence with H. M. Envoy and Minister Plenipotentiary in Japan, 1860. 19th Century House of Commons Sessional Papers. https://parlipapers-proquest-com.rp.nla.gov.au/parlipapers/docview/t70.d75.1860-036818?accountid=12694, February 2021, 89

Japan. Correspondence with H. M. Envoy and Minister Plenipotentiary in Japan, 1858–68. 19th Century House of Commons Sessional Papers. https://parlipapers-proquest com.rp.nla.gov.au/parlipapers/docview/t70.d75.1860- 036818?accountid=12694.

Japan Centre for Asian Historical Records, Imperial Ordinance No.77, Expansion of Vessels Mooring Area in Kobe Port, Original script signed by the emperor, 1892. https://www.jacar.archives.go.jp/aj/meta/MetSearch.cgi?SUM_KIND=MetaSummary&SUM_NUMBER=20&IS_KIND=SimpleSummary&IS_SCH=META&IS_STYLE=eng&DB_ID=G0000101EXTERNAL&GRP_ID=G0000101&IS_START=1&IS_EXTSCH=&DEF_XSL=defaulten&IS_SORT_KND=ASC&IS_SORT_FLD=&IS_TAG_S1=InfoSDU&IS_KEY_S1=A03020128700&IS_NUMBER=20&ON_LYD=on, 2021.

Kobe Ports and Harbors' Office: https://www.pa.kkr.mlit.go.jp/kobeport/en/outline.html.

Kobe Ports and Harbors' Office: https://www.pa.kkr.mlit.go.jp/kobeport/en/pdf/thedevelopmentofkobeport.pdf, 2025.

Kobe Trade Information Office: https://cityofkobe.org/about-kobe/history/, 2025.

Lepach, Bernd. Meiji Portraits Website. http://www.meiji-portraits.de/. Leipzig, Germany. Updated 19 December 2020.

Nippon Yūsen Kaisha. History of Nippon Yusen Kaisha. https://www.nyk.com/english/profile/history/.

Sugar Refiners & Sugarbakers Database compiled by Bryan Mawer, http://www.mawer.clara.net/sugarbbio.html, 2000.

Index

For Product Safety Concerns and Information please contact our EU representative GPSR@taylorandfrancis.com Taylor & Francis Verlag GmbH, Kaufingerstraße 24, 80331 München, Germany